THE NEW CALIFORNIA WINE

THE
NEW
CALIFORNIA
WINE

A GUIDE TO THE PRODUCERS AND
WINES BEHIND A REVOLUTION IN TASTE

JON BONNÉ
PHOTOGRAPHY BY ERIK CASTRO

TEN SPEED PRESS
Berkeley

The people who are experimenting are not generally found among the large growers, but are more likely discovered among the hills and retired nooks in the counties nearest the bay. I find that they have worked cautiously. Most of them are men of small property and limited means, and do the greater part of the work themselves. I think that the finest wines of the State will eventually be found to have been made by this class of viticulturists. They have time and they use it properly; they have ambition and they follow it. They do not reckon their time at so many dollars an hour. Very likely it will require some length of time before their products are appreciated, but the time will come either in their lives or in those of their children following. I know several people, the exact counterpart of those above described, and believe them the fore-runners of a new era of wine making in our State.

—Arpad Haraszthy, 1891

Contents

Introduction

"I hear you hate California wine."

The spokeswoman for one of the state's most powerful wine personalities was on the phone. I wasn't in the mood.

"If I hated California wine," I replied, "would I be doing what I do?"

I knew, when I moved to California in 2006, that I was facing long odds. I had come to a place that believed, above all, in the superiority of its wines. Anyone who didn't embrace that belief was viewed as a threat. And in the past I had dared to voice my dissatisfaction with a California wine culture that I saw as often self-satisfied and underwhelming. Worse, I was from the East Coast, an outsider. My years spent in New York, where I learned from my father about European wines from Vouvray to Valpolicella, were a liability instead of an asset.

Six years earlier I had moved to Seattle, and while there I came to love West Coast wines—in particular the pioneering wines of Washington State. I began my wine-writing career there. Clearly,

I was no foe of American winemaking. But none of that mattered the moment I landed at the Oakland airport.

I had come to the Bay Area to run the wine section of the *San Francisco Chronicle*, six to ten pages of some of the country's most influential wine journalism. The California wine industry was not pleased: their work was about to be judged by someone whose palate was honed not on hefty Cabernet and Zinfandel but on nuanced Old World wines.

I approached my work earnestly. But from the moment I arrived, I had to confront my own deep skepticism about California's winemaking reality. Again and again I was disappointed by what I found to be the shortfalls of California wine: a ubiquity of oaky, uninspired bottles and a presumption that bigger was indeed better.

The truth was, I had come to California to be convinced. I was looking for signs that skeptics like me were wrong, and that what had long been a near-magical land for wine could still achieve greatness.

Whatever I might have thought about California wines at that point, I had started from a place of love. In February 1985, when I was twelve, my father took our family to California. At the time I was far more interested in the Apple factory tour in Cupertino, but Dad had always brought us up around wine. He gave me my first glass at age five, and soon enough I was having a bit with dinner most nights. When he took us to Napa Valley, it was clear we were somewhere special. We visited the Robert Mondavi Winery, with its campanile and familiar arch, the brick-and-mortar icon from the labels I had often seen around the house. Even then I knew we had arrived at the cradle of American wine. California wines at the time were vibrant, the industry invigorated by its speedy rise to rival Europe in quality.

Why, then, had California wine fallen into such a stupor years later? That was the question I set out to answer. I wanted to reconcile these two Californias—the one I remembered that was so full of promise and life, and the one that was stuck in a self-satisfied funk.

. . .

My first couple of years in California were tough. I hunted desperately for local wines worth praising while I featured lots of imports in the newspaper's wine section, arguing that the Bay Area in fact had a critical mass of great importers (like Berkeley's Kermit Lynch). This argument did not sit well among partisans of California's wines, but I couldn't overlook the sad fact that Napa had become a bombastic shell of its earlier, humbler self. Its top names—Beaulieu and Beringer and even Mondavi—had grown into big corporate entities, while its smaller labels were locked in an arms race, each trying to create bigger, riper, and more outrageous wines.

Still, I had come prepared with good leads. Just two weeks into the job I had to choose our winemaker of the year, and quickly enough I selected Paul Draper of Ridge Vineyards. Draper's work was beyond reproach: for nearly forty years he had been at the helm at Ridge, where he made not only the state's benchmark Zinfandel-focused wines, Geyserville and Lytton Springs, but also one of the finest Cabernet-based wines in the world, Monte Bello.

My choice of Draper came with a subtler message. In the midst of an industry that had blindly embraced technology and by-the-numbers winemaking, he was an outspoken traditionalist. He rejected commercial yeasts and fancy flavor-enhancing techniques and was a vocal critic of the science-minded efforts of the University of California at Davis, one of the top winemaking schools in the world.

More than that, he believed that the making of wine was sacrosanct, a true expression of the land. Wine "was traditionally the central symbol for transformation, because the grape transforms itself simply by being broken by man, because it transforms itself with nothing else," he told me at the time.

By choosing Draper, I had set a theme for my work. I quietly kept searching for wines that I felt reflected what I knew California could offer. The following year, my winemaker of the year was Josh Jensen of Calera. Known as Mr. Limestone, Jensen in the 1970s had pioneered the quest for great Pinot Noir grown on calcareous soils that

approximated those of Burgundy—and paid a critical price over the years for stubbornly refusing to give in to the whims of fashion.

Slowly, I encountered other winemakers with similar beliefs. I found people who remained committed to restrained, compelling wines that spoke clearly of their origins—and who shared my frustration with California's modern style.

Some, like Draper and Jensen, had been toiling for decades; others were upstarts with the same energy and ambition as the pioneers from previous generations. Eventually, the brushstrokes began to turn into something recognizable: the seeds of a new movement, a new California wine in the making.

This was more than just a blip. Wines from emerging producers like Lioco, Broc Cellars, and Matthiasson, which just a few years earlier would have been decidedly fringe for California, had by 2010 amassed a loyal audience. They were being sought out by the disillusioned fans of an earlier California generation who believed that modern winemaking had forsaken them. They also attracted sommeliers and wine buyers who had previously all but written off California as well as those who had shunned domestic wine in favor of imported until finally finding bottles that spoke their aesthetic language. That year, I wrote a piece for *Saveur* magazine making a case for the New California wine—and by that time, talk of a grand revival no longer seemed unrealistic.

…

New California's winemakers share similar sensibilities: an enthusiasm for lessons learned from the Old World, but not the desire to replicate its wines; a mandate to seek out new grape varieties and regions; and, perhaps most important, an ardent the belief that place matters. They are true believers in terroir. This is crucial because California's future ultimately depends upon wines that show nuance, restraint, and a deep evocation of place.

But California is also somewhat obsessed with size. Although there are hundreds of small family wineries throughout the state, the industry is dominated by its Big Three: Gallo, Constellation Wines, and the Wine Group. In 2011, according to industry investor David Freed, the Big Three were

The New California Wine

responsible for more than 64 percent of the state's wine shipments; they made two of every three bottles of California wine. If you don't recognize their names (though certainly Gallo is ubiquitous), you know their brands. Gallo's empire covers everything from Barefoot to Louis Martini to Apothic and Turning Leaf. After a blitzkrieg buying spree over the past decade, Constellation now owns Robert Mondavi, Ravenswood, Clos du Bois, and nearly two dozen other labels. And the Wine Group controls much of the rest of the supermarket shelves, including brands like Franzia, Cupcake, Glen Ellen, and Concannon.

That doesn't even factor in the massive influence of Fred Franzia's Bronco Wine Company, maker of twenty million cases worth of Charles Shaw wines (better known as Two Buck Chuck) and dozens of other labels. It is estimated that Bronco and the four next largest labels—Trinchero (Sutter Home, Ménage à Trois), Kendall-Jackson, Delicato (Gnarly Head, Irony), and Treasury Wine Estates (a former division of Australian brewer Foster's that encompasses Beringer, Meridian, and more)—account for another 20 percent of the California wine industry. In other words, sea change in the overall market for California wine only happens when the Fred Franzias of the world get involved.

Yet California's state of the art has typically been judged on an elite roster of producers. When the state's wine style shifted in the 1990s, it happened not among makers of table wine but among a small set of mostly Cabernet specialists.

That's why, when I sought signs of change in California winemaking, I knew I needed to hunt among the little guys. Change always comes first at a small scale—in part because, as vineyard owner David Hirsch might put it, you have to apply yourself to a specific place in order to begin to understand the thousand tiny things that allow you to make great wine.

. . .

The winemakers you'll find in the following pages aren't meant to represent all of the state's ambitions. Rather, they are pioneers, setting the agenda for the New California wine.

Not every young winery appears. Some are too wedded to the aesthetics of the previous generation; others may be too new. In this book you'll also find some older wineries like Calera and Ridge, with reputations that stretch back for decades. They appear here because they have stayed the course through darker times.

The book is divided into three sections. The first part, "Searching for the New California," aims to take you along on my journey to discover the many changes taking place and meet the people behind them. The second part, "The New Terroir," is a road trip through some of the regions that are helping to redefine California winemaking. The third, "Wines of the New California," lays out essential producers and their wines and discusses the changes in winemaking and wine styles in recent years.

Each section addresses an aspect of what I've come to believe: this is the best time in a generation to drink California wine. More than that, today marks the arrival of a mature American wine culture, where producers are confident enough *not* to mimic the Old World or obscure the nuances of terroir with clever cellar work, but rather seek greatness in a uniquely American context.

That is the wonderful reality of the New California.

1

SEARCHING FOR THE NEW CALIFORNIA

The New Winemakers

It's late on an unseasonably warm February afternoon in Steve Matthiasson's backyard, on the sort of luminescent winter day that reminds you why you live in California. "Backyard" isn't really fair: we are behind a trailer park on the northwestern outskirts of Napa, the final stretch of land as flat fields open into vineyards and reach to the base of Mount Veeder. Matthiasson's five acres mark the last of an old Italian farm; his barn is filled with a century's worth of detritus, including old fruit-picking boxes and seeders with corn in them that have been rusticating since the 1960s. Nearby is his vintage 1905 Victorian farmhouse, refurbished to a cheery shade of yellow.

By day Matthiasson is one of Napa's top vineyard consultants, offering advice to some of its famed wineries, including Stag's Leap Wine Cellars and Araujo. When he's not doing that, Matthiasson can be found here, tending his few acres of vines, or perhaps checking on a nearby Chardonnay vineyard he leases. Although his house sits at the edge of the

Napa district known as Oak Knoll, at the south of the valley, Matthiasson forsook the Merlot and Cabernet popular there to plant several obscure Italian grapes like Refosco and Schioppettino. Under his Matthiasson Wines label he bottles not only these but a handful of savory reds as well as a Napa Valley white blend that combines the grapes and traditions of both Bordeaux and Italy's Friuli region—mixing Sauvignon Blanc, Sémillon, Tocai Friulano, and Ribolla Gialla. It has quickly become one of California's most compelling white wines.

A small posse of New California partisans has gathered. In addition to Matthiasson, there's Tegan Passalacqua, winemaker for Turley Wine Cellars, arguably California's most famous Zinfandel house; Dan Petroski, who by day makes Cabernet at Larkmead Vineyards up in Calistoga but also owns his own label, Massican, which, like Matthiasson's, pays tribute to the regional wines of Friuli; Angela Osborne, a young New Zealander who has worked several gigs as assistant winemaker while building her own small label, A Tribute to Grace, under which she makes a deep and soulful Grenache; and Jasmine Hirsch, whose family owns one of the state's key Pinot Noir vineyards, high above the remote Sonoma Coast.

We're sitting around a weathered wooden table, eating salami that Matthiasson cured himself and tasting Petroski's new 2011 wines, whites barely finished with fermentation. It has been a cold vintage, one that thrilled those around the table, even as it frayed the nerves of winemakers more dependent on California's ability to exploit ripeness. None of that here. Petroski's wines are lean and jumpy. "I'm not sure this one will clear 12 percent alcohol," he says, recapping a bottle.

Our impromptu tasting wraps up. Matthiasson invites us for a stroll—past his chicken coop and avocado tree, through his rows of vines—to look at his new saplings of Ribolla Gialla, a native Friulian grape rarely found in the New World, now growing atop old Merlot stumps. It is still February, of course. A chill sweeps in from the nearby San Pablo Bay, and as the sun dips toward the western horizon, we gaze out at the silhouette of Mount Veeder, which has been home to wine grapes since at least the 1860s, and talk of Ribolla Gialla and Schioppettino, grapes that could barely have been imagined in Napa even a decade earlier.

This is not the California I expected.

TEGAN PASSALACQUA

Tegan Passalacqua is driving me through Coombsville, just east of the city of Napa. Approved by the federal government in 2011, this is Napa Valley's newest subappellation—a crescent-shaped swath of mostly volcanic soils that sits in the shadow of Mount George, which rises above the city of Napa, veined by fire trails and dotted by scrub.

A trip through Coombsville is a visit through Passalacqua's past and his emotional landscape. The vacant field near a car lot, he recalls, used to be old Zinfandel vines. A Cabernet vineyard used to be a dairy. (Unsurprisingly, "they have a huge nitrogen problem" with their soil, he notes.) His parents still live a quarter mile from the quiet side street where he lives with his wife, Olivia: "I grew up out here, and I used to ride my bike all through here."

Vineyards aren't quite in Passalacqua's blood (his father drove a cement truck for three decades) but Napa certainly is: his family has lived here for three generations. It's not entirely surprising that he has become one of California's notable viticulturists.

Passalacqua manages Turley's far-flung plantings, from Napa's Howell Mountain all the way to Paso Robles, and makes the wines. But he has become the wine equivalent of what Malcolm Gladwell would call a connector: he hunts great sites, often in underappreciated regions, and then links them either to his day job or to a roster of winemaking friends, including consultant Mark Herold; Abe Schoener of the Scholium Project; and Morgan Twain-Peterson of Bedrock Wine, himself an estimable vineyard sleuth. Scratch the backstory of many truly interesting California wines, and Passalacqua's name appears.

Perhaps because he remembers Napa as a blue-collar town, more auto shops than ascots, he views this matchmaking as a counterbalance to wine country's outrageous real estate values. This fact comes up when I ask him whether Napa can return to a more restrained style of wine.

"In a way, we're out of the conversation," he says, "because we can't afford to get into the debate." Indeed, it's hard for any winemaker to buy in, seeing as land now often tops $250,000 an acre in the area. "It's a very hard thing for me, having grown up in Napa. How do I own my own vineyard?"

NATHAN LEE ROBERTS AND DUNCAN ARNOT MEYERS

Several mornings a week, Nathan Roberts roasts his own coffee, which explains why he often is seen toting a plastic bag full of freshly roasted beans. When he offers me an espresso as we taste a set of wines made by Roberts and his longtime friend and business partner, Duncan Arnot Meyers, it's a welcome pause to appreciate his work with a different beverage.

We're standing in their tidy warehouse in Healdsburg, northern Sonoma's answer to the up-valley Napa refinements of St. Helena. The two are suiting up in clip shoes and spandex for a long bike ride with their New York distributor, Doug Polaner, and their friend and fellow vintner Pax Mahle, who owns a label called Wind Gap. (The two wineries shared space in an old apple plant in nearby Forestville for several years.) But before the ride, we taste.

First, a Chardonnay made from a recently revived vineyard a few miles east of Santa Cruz. Then a rosé made from the Portuguese grape Touriga Nacional, found in an old Port-wine vineyard in Lake County, the very rural enclave northeast of Napa. Next, a Gamay Noir—the grape of Beaujolais—grown above three thousand feet in the foothills of the Sierra Nevada. Back to the Santa Cruz Mountains for a Pinot Noir grown in the Peter Martin Ray Vineyard, owned by the son of legendary 1950s-era vintner Martin Ray. Then to Sonoma for a white field blend made from a smattering of random grape varieties in the old Compagni Portis Vineyard, one of the last to maintain this sort of patchwork of white grapes. And on it goes.

Roberts and Meyers both grew up in Napa, went to school together, and were in the same Boy Scout troop. Roberts had the deeper ties in wine. His grandmother is Margrit Biever Mondavi, Robert Mondavi's widow; she helped design the Arnot-Roberts label. His mother, Annie Roberts, was executive chef at Robert Mondavi Winery, and his father, Keith, is a master cooper—a skill that Nathan acquired. When he and Duncan need a new barrel (which is rarely, as neither is keen on the taste of oak in wine), he crafts it himself.

"We are California kids. We love Northern California. Our intent is to express the potential of Northern California," Meyers tells me.

While Roberts remained in Napa, Meyers went to college in Colorado and worked at becoming a professional cyclist. But he ended up as a wandering cellar rat. By 2001 they were rooming together and making their first wine together, a field blend from Sonoma's Dry Creek Valley. They soon founded Arnot-Roberts, though Meyers later interned for influential winemaker John Kongsgaard and was assistant winemaker at Pax Wine Cellars, Mahle's original label.

It's clear that they're most informed by what they fill their glasses with each night—forthright bottles from the Old World: good Chablis, Trousseau from Jura producers like Jacques Puffeney, Blaufränkisch from the Austrian producer Moric, in the hills outside Vienna.

"It's more that inspiration comes from those wines," Meyers continues, "and that's what we love. But we believe California can deliver wines that have similar characteristics while having all of what California can offer."

So they spend most of their time hunting for new vineyards—frequently during long bike rides through the Sonoma hills. That led them to perhaps their most challenging vineyard—and the one that helped to make them spokesmen for California's subtler ways.

Clary Ranch is located in the Middle Two Rock area outside Petaluma, in the heart of Sonoma dairy country. The vineyard, planted in 2000, is subject to constant weather from the nearby Pacific Ocean, which is sucked inland from Bodega Bay through a sort of funnel known as the Petaluma Wind Gap. The persistent wind and fog make for precipitously long ripening seasons. Rare is the year that Meyers and Roberts harvest Syrah before mid-November.

"What seemed to inspire us most is that we love wines that are grown at the edge," Meyers explains. Hence their Clary Ranch Syrah—just above 12 percent alcohol in a ripe year, barely above 11 percent in a cooler one, and sometimes not ripe enough to make at all. The austere but heady 2008 was a particular bit of sommelier catnip, with its more-Rhône-than-Rhône intensity—a wine that forced critics to rethink California. Just like the Cabernet mavericks a generation before them, two Napa boys had managed to lap the French. "We're unabashedly aware," Roberts says, "that we're working backwards from what we like to drink."

TED LEMON

It's a soggy December day, and Ted Lemon meets me at his winery in Sebastopol. We hop in his car, and after a quick stop for coffee to ward off the damp chill, he drives further west through the tiny Sonoma hamlet of Occidental. We turn onto a small paved road, weaving through one-time timberland, to his Haven Vineyard, located on the northernmost of three ridges west of town. He walks down a row, his boots squishing in the mud, and then stops suddenly, bends down, and yanks out a yellowish flower, a spotted cat's ear. This one plant is an intruder in his meticulously chosen cover crop.

In 2001 Lemon and his wife Heidi finally scraped together the money to buy these ten acres for their winery, Littorai. Below the ground is a mix of shale, sandstone, and serpentine known as the Hugo-Josephine complex, found primarily in west Sonoma County and once considered ideal for timber. Above it sit rows of mostly Pinot Noir interspersed with a carpet of clover, legumes, and bunchgrass—and the occasional errant wildflower.

Almost no one in California has managed to bridge the traditions of Europe and California as Lemon has. In 1982, fresh out of winemaking school in France, he became the first American ever to run a domaine in Burgundy, Domaine Guy Roulot. When patriarch Guy Roulot died, his family, one of the most prestigious in the commune of Meursault, needed a winemaker. The young American, just twenty-four at the time, came with good references.

Fast-forward thirty years, and Littorai has become perhaps the best curator of the tiny parcels of California coast that can yield Pinot Noir as extraordinarily complex as those produced in Burgundy. But if some California winemakers fall over themselves to wrap themselves in a Burgundian mantle, don't mention this to Lemon.

"Being a slave to Europe is as much a mistake as saying that superripe California is a great expression," he tells me. "Both ends of the expression miss the important center of the argument, which is to take European notions and see how they're best expressed in California. You'll never hear what the land is saying if you just say, 'In Europe, they do this.'"

Though Lemon could have stayed in Burgundy, California called. He took a string of winemaking jobs, but he didn't want to make "big, flamboyant wines," and he recalled the path to success followed

Anderson Valley for having established one of its first, and longest-running, contracts for fruit by the acre from grower Richard Savoy. But Lemon didn't simply want to make outstanding wines; he wanted to truly understand the endless tiny details of the sites he had chosen.

The next step, inevitably, was to begin farming for himself. In 2001, however, that was a rare undertaking for most California winemakers thanks to the spiraling cost of land. Lemon was fortunate to be so entranced by the coast; it was about the only place left to purchase property. He wanted virgin soil so he wouldn't have to undo someone else's mistakes, and he quickly opted to farm using biodynamic principles, a rigorous (and slightly mystical) set of standards that mesh organic farming with homeopathic vineyard treatments and consideration of lunar phases.

The goal wasn't merely to make great wine—although that was important—but also to use that wine as a barometer to better understand the potential of specific places and how best to farm them. It wasn't so much about harvesting grapes as plumbing the deeper mysteries that made wine culturally significant. This upended set of priorities cast Lemon in the role of a lonely warrior. "That's when you break this awful barrier of the language of 'fruit,'" he tells me. "That's an awful phrase, when you talk about 'great fruit.'"

ABE SCHOENER

"I hope it's not too many," says Abe Schoener as he begins uncorking nearly three dozen wines on his back porch as the Napa River floats lazily by.

We may be in Napa, but Schoener's house is down a narrow road that straddles the Napa

by many Burgundy domaines after World War II: rather than sell their wine to local brokers, they began selling directly to top sommeliers in Paris. In this way, they built their reputations at the restaurant table and controlled their own business. With $10,000 in seed money, Ted and Heidi decided to do the same.

Lemon has long been a diviner of top vineyards. He was one of the first winemakers to designate on his label the name of the Hirsch Vineyard, a remote ridgetop planting north of the mouth of the Russian River that, in no small part thanks to Littorai, is now one of California's defining spots for Pinot Noir. He remains a kingmaker in Mendocino's marina, a working-class corner of town that speaks to the town's past as a bedroom community for the nearby naval shipyards on Mare Island. The back of his rented bungalow, which is perched on pilings over the last stretch of river before the water begins to empty into San Pablo Bay, is site of the occasional bacchanal.

Schoener is the creator of the Scholium Project, one of California's most deliberately unconventional wineries. This mostly one-man operation (he finally signed up an assistant winemaker a couple years ago, amending his routine use of New York sommeliers as harvest staff) has captivated the imagination of the wine avant-garde across the country. In 2012, a bottle of Scholium left in a room full of sommeliers—I actually tried this experiment—was drained within ten minutes. Schoener had quickly become the Pied Piper of wine's trendy set.

Why? He combines the outré—twin Verdelhos made in wildly different styles, skin-fermented Sauvignon Blanc made in tribute to a reclusive Italian prince, a copper-hued rosé made from 130-year-old Cinsault grown in the Central Valley town of Lodi—with his charisma as a former assistant dean of St. John's College in Maryland. Observing him at times feels like watching an entire Aristophanes play—a collision of philosophy, parody, and omniscient chorus in a single, bespectacled personage.

The Scholium wines entered the scene in the mid-2000s, at a time when California was otherwise in the depths of what Ted Lemon would call its "exuberant" phase. The wines, with their hipster chic credibility, tweaked the state's generally ossified wine industry. In a business where aesthetic clichés are ubiquitous—the vineyard photo at sunset, the hardworking vintner examining his glass—Schoener's harvest photos resembled outtakes

from a Brooklyn art project that went on a bender and woke up in a barrel room.

All this was more surprising because, by his own admission, Schoener's wines often fail. Sometimes they require years in the barrel to resolve their faults; sometimes they are simply dumped down the drain. These failures are reflected in the name, Scholium, essentially an annotation to a manuscript, and the winery's larger mission, which Schoener describes as "a commentary, an essay, a study." It is his grand experiment in the culture of wine, enacted in real time.

How does an academic with a background in the liberal arts wind up crushing grapes? Certainly it has happened before—as with Warren Winiarski, who went from teaching at the University of Chicago to making the Cabernet from Stag's Leap Wine Cellars that would win the 1976 Judgment of Paris tasting, the moment that proved California wines could be as good as French.

In fact, it was Stag's Leap where Schoener landed after arriving in California, where he worked for a fellow St. John's alum (Winiarski) and ultimately befriended John Kongsgaard, whose kids were interested in the college. Kongsgaard, the influential former winemaker for Newton Vineyards, had by that time become a magnet for innovative white winemaking in Napa.

Kongsgaard agreed to let Schoener intern at Luna Vineyards the following year, and Schoener became Kongsgaard's student. That dynamic lingered for years, with Schoener addressing his benefactor as *il dottore*. I happened to witness Kongsgaard's first visit to Schoener's winery in the suburban city of Fairfield, in Solano County, east of Napa. The cellar room was filled with Kongsgaard's cast-off barrels, which Kongsgaard clambered over, smelling them and noting more than a few technical faults. "Abe just jumped in without having been plagued by that conservatism, and he's friends with enough of us to keep from sliding off that cliff," Kongsgaard told me after that visit.

Which brings us back to Schoener's porch, down by the river. "I wanted to look at everything that I've made from the delta," he says, still pulling corks.

What Schoener is referring to is the Lost Slough Vineyard. It lies outside the town of Rio Vista, below sea level in the midst of the Sacramento River delta, partway to the Central Valley, a sort of no-man's-land for wine. Something about Lost Slough has a strong psychic grip on Schoener, and it has become the source for many of his white wines. There were those twin Verdelhos—crisp and clean Naucratis, named for one of the ancient Egyptian delta cities, and rich, barrel-fermented Gemella, its name Latin for "twin." There's also Riquewihr, a hard-hitting Gewürztraminer named for a key town in Alsace, and the Wisdom of Theuth, named for an Egyptian god invoked by Socrates. (You may have noticed a high-minded classicism in the Scholium names. It's Schoener's way of referencing his old

career and, I suspect, adding an academic sheen to the wines.)

We taste a half dozen of these before moving through a blitz of Schoener's other wines: the Lodi rosé, named Rhododactylos (my favorite of his names, borrowed from Homer and meaning "rosy fingered"); the Prince in His Caves, a Sauvignon Blanc from Sonoma fermented on its skins, like a red wine; and even his wines from another project in the Maury area of southern France. (Schoener also makes wine for Brooklyn's Red Hook Winery, applying his sensibilities to Long Island fruit.)

What's left unsaid is that the wines, while compelling, have at times been difficult to drink, in no small part because Schoener often asserts that California's defining quality is sugar-filled grapes, and thus high alcohol. ("It's not so much that I love them," he told me by way of explanation. "It's that it's the wines they make.") His wines have become curious cultural devices—catalysts for conversation about the current state of California's art. No matter. His charisma has done more to advance the state's new mode of wine than ten marketing departments ever could.

The porch table is littered with bottles and glasses as the autumn harvest sun radiates off the water. As a finale, we try Schoener's two Cabernets, both from the Sonoma slope of the Mayacamas Mountains, on the other side of which is Napa Valley. These are somewhat removed from the Scholium story, as they're both relatively conventional Cabernets—no crazy notions or cellar legerdemain. I imagine it doesn't help Schoener much that I usually find these to be his best efforts. "There really was a model for those wines," he says, "and it was Napa Cabernet from the 1970s."

This doesn't entirely hold—the alcohol levels are a good two percentage points beyond Napa's

1970s fare—but the oak presence is modest and the aromas of tobacco and dried sage are pronounced. Made by anyone else, they would hold their own as classically styled Cabs. Under Schoener's hand, they are evidence of a counterreformation.

Finally it occurs to me: Schoener's radicalism—really, the radicalism of all the winemakers trying to change the story line in California—isn't so different from the beliefs that brought modern California wine its fame in the first place. The spirit of curiosity is very much the same—and a complete reversal from the sense of entitlement that pervaded the industry for years.

A GENERATION STANDS

Lemon's lonely warrior stance, Schoener's esoterica, and Matthiasson's rethinking of the Napa way, are just a few flashes of the irreverence that has appeared of late. There have always been holdouts for a classic style—people like Calera's Josh Jensen, or the Cabernet maker Cathy Corison (who gained notoriety for spurning Napa's high-octane tendencies)—but they had become antithetical to modern mainstream California winemaking.

By 2011, however, it was clear that a generational shift had taken place. Wines that were once considered only interesting footnotes were moving into the mainstream. A decade earlier, it was hard to drum up interest in California wines among many top wine buyers—notably in New York, the nation's largest wine market. Even in San Francisco, many sommeliers were hesitant in the mid-2000s to buy much in the way of California wine.

California wines had become saddled with a reputation for being too simplistic and heavy-handed, too overwhelming for sommeliers to pair with food—and, frankly, too expensive. During his time as wine director at San Francisco's restaurant Quince, David Lynch recalled, the fancy Cabernets on the list "were the bane of my existence."

Suddenly, California wines had found a new relevance. After being pariahs in Manhattan's top restaurants, they were again being discussed with reverence. Chambers Street Wines, New York's retail haven for traditionally made European bottles, appointed a dedicated buyer for American wine and stocked its front shelves with producers like Dashe Cellars and La Clarine Farm. "We want wines to taste like where they come from," explains John Rankin, the store's domestic buyer. "I think for a long time California did a lot of things to obscure that, and now people are trying to take the makeup off."

At Dovetail on Manhattan's Upper West Side, wine director Amanda Reade Sturgeon not only sought out current releases like Lioco Chardonnay but also, for a spell, old bottles like the 1975 Chappellet Chenin Blanc, providing a window for diners to understand the continuity between California's older wines and recent vintages. At spots like Jean-Georges, wines like Dan Petroski's tiny Massican label shared space with Chablis. The goal of serving such wines wasn't to emulate Old World nuance, but to highlight American bounty.

"These are California wines at the end of the day," says John Ragan, wine director of restaurateur Danny Meyer's Union Square Hospitality Group. "I think people want to taste that sunshine and that richness a little bit."

The shift came full circle to San Francisco, where restaurants that had been resistant to including homegrown wines on their lists began to embrace California again. Locavore spots like the restaurant Nopa prided themselves on it. At Charles Phan's

Out the Door, wines like Scholium Project's Midan al-Tahrir white and Broc Cellars' Carignane were served from taps.

These changes weren't limited to the coasts. Not only in the small wine boutiques of Brooklyn, but also in Charleston, South Carolina, Omaha, Nebraska, and Miami, the California avant-garde had built a following. In part this was thanks to a new millennial generation of drinkers who came to wine without the insecurities and programmatic ways of their parents' generation, and with a keen radar for inauthenticity.

If the baby boomers were hidebound by their familiarity with big-ticket varieties like Cabernet and Chardonnay—after all, their thirst had spurred California winemakers to dump cheap jug blends in favor of single varietals—their kids wanted little to do with their parents' wines. And with projections from the Wine Market Council that this generation would total seventy million potential wine drinkers, there was a big market for the New California.

As often as not, these wine lovers were born after the 1976 Judgment of Paris (see page 25). They grew up with wine on the dinner table. They were omnivorous, and they wanted wines that told them an honest story. At last, they had a bounty from California to drink.

Winemaker Nick de Luca in the Area 51 Vineyard

The Rise and Fall

"We were a big, young country," Robert Mondavi wrote in 1998, "oriented toward mass production and scientific research, and in our wine making we emphasized crop yields, sugar levels, and profit margins. The great European wineries, with centuries of tradition and craft behind them, put their emphasis on less tangible qualities such as style, character and bouquet. To my mind, the contrast was stark: we were treating wine as a business, the great European chateaus were treating wine as high art."

That was his conclusion after his first trip to Europe in 1962. Mondavi returned to his family's winery, Charles Krug, determined to elevate California. He spent years trying to redirect Krug toward fine wine, but he always lost the argument, his family convinced he was becoming ever more the snob. Things exploded after he punched his brother Peter—in a scuffle over a mink coat for Robert's wife, Marge—and was essentially barred from the family's winery. By 1966 Robert was courting investors to pursue his own dream for California.

Even in the 1960s Mondavi was targeting the chasm between the art of wine and the technocratic winemaking that had flourished in the postwar era, the treatment of wine as just another industrial product. To this day, it is California wine's great shortfall. What the state lacks in historical legacy it has typically tried to make up for with a combination of brashness and rigid science. Indeed, the tension between the two—winemaking as cultural expression and winemaking as commercial endeavor—has defined California's struggle.

THE SCAR OF PROHIBITION

What had created this split, and what would define California wine for the better part of the twentieth century, was Prohibition. The Drys did not spare wine in their crusade against alcohol, and the enactment of the Volstead Act in 1919 was effectively a death sentence for California's wine industry.

It is hard to overemphasize the impact of Prohibition. Wineries were forced to shutter their doors unless they made sacramental wine or could find other loopholes. Growers either struggled along by selling robust grapes like Alicante Bouschet, which could be shipped east for home use, or by producing grape concentrate (often with labels "warning" consumers not to add yeast or leave unattended, lest the juice ferment into wine). In the first years after the passage of Volstead, it seemed like fruit sales might become a booming business. But a brief boom gave way to a collapse of the grape market in 1925—and a persistent grape surplus that didn't subside until 1971.

But the real damage wasn't economic; it was cultural. Decades' worth of winemaking knowledge was lost. Prohibition was repealed in 1933, but the industry's rebirth didn't begin in earnest until after World War II, during a postwar industrial boom that sought efficiency in all things. Table wine from California was a sideline; American consumers' real thirst was for brandy and fortified wines. "A whole generation of maturing Americans, grown accustomed to bathtub gin and moonshine, were ignorant of wine," wrote Leon Adams, one of California wine's great promoters and cofounder of the Wine Institute. Rebirth came with a thirst not for finer products but for simpler, more potent concoctions. There was little economic motive to grow better, more expensive grapes, and little demand for the wine that could be made from them. Napa had fewer acres planted with wine grapes in 1963 than in 1917.

The work of reviving California's winemaking tradition was crucially aided by the University of California, whose wine studies department survived Prohibition by focusing on work that didn't involve fermentation. Professor Frederic Bioletti, who had aided researcher E. W. Hilgard in his great late-1800s cataloging of California's grape bounty, ran the viticultural department starting in 1912 and kept it going through Prohibition. But its work flagged until after the war, when two researchers, A. J. Winkler and Maynard Amerine, resumed their study of the crucial questions of California wine: what to grow, where to grow it, and how to make a marketable wine. Their publications, beginning with Amerine and M. A. Joslyn's *Commercial Production of Table Wines* in 1940, and the development of the Winkler scale of climate regions shortly after, would become a road map for California wine's rebirth.

Ultimately, the University of California at Davis became California's great academic engine for wine. But the industry's focus also left Davis with a mandate, in Winkler's words, "to cut costs, improve quality and assist the industry."

Admittedly, Europe's wine regions had faced their own share of hardship, including the devastation of two world wars, but at least they had a continuity of tradition and knowledge. In America, a robust nineteenth-century wine industry had been wiped away. Few people knew how to make great wine in California, and not many more across the country had a thirst for it.

SIGNS OF REVIVAL

Yet there was a desire in California to make great wine again. In the midcentury period following World War II, the industry's true believers insisted that rebirth had to come not by pursuing simple wines but by attempting to make great ones, a belief they shared with Robert Mondavi. This group included John Daniel Jr. of Inglenook and André Tchelistcheff of Beaulieu Vineyard, who crafted the era's greatest Cabernets, and renegades like Martin Ray in the hills above Saratoga, who strived to rival Burgundy with his Pinot Noir and Chardonnay.

Consider this the beginning of California wine's modern era: when the Mission-style arch of the Robert Mondavi Winery appeared along Napa's Highway 29 in 1966. Designed by architect Cliff May, whose work on ranch houses and *Sunset* magazine's headquarters reflected the essence of California postwar design, it was a revelation, evoking the best of both California's Spanish history and midcentury present, a stark contrast to the rustic barns and chunky industrial buildings that dotted

the valley, or even the occasional Victorian remnant of nineteenth-century greatness, like Beringer's Rhine House in St. Helena.

The creation of the Mondavi winery, of May's timeless arch framing the Oakville benchland, was meant to serve as a visual cue for Mondavi's evangelism. Very quickly, the early Robert Mondavi wines became benchmarks for a more refined chapter in California, wines like the inaugural 1966 Cabernet Sauvignon, or the 1968 Fumé Blanc, a Sauvignon Blanc that Mondavi renamed with a French moniker, which hinted at both its oak aging and the grandeur of Pouilly Fumé, one of the world's great Sauvignon Blanc–based wines.

Mondavi's wasn't the only big dream. The Chappellet family had established itself on Pritchard Hill, building a pyramid of a winery overlooking the valley. In 1972 a Frenchman named Bernard Portet cofounded a new winery in Napa's Stags Leap District, Clos du Val, with businessman John Goelet. That year brought a raft of new wineries, including Caymus and Warren Winiarski's Stag's Leap Wine Cellars. Around the same time, a lawyer named Jim Barrett partnered on the old Chateau Montelena property in Calistoga. Farther south, young Paul Draper had taken the helm of tiny Ridge Vineyards in the mountains above the town of Cupertino. In the Central Coast's remote Gavilan Mountains, a Burgundy lover named Richard Graff tapped into calcium-rich soils, hoping to make Pinot Noir and Chardonnay to rival those of the Old World.

THE JUDGMENT OF PARIS

As the 1970s arrived, California wine was surging. The postwar industry had focused on competent and clean winemaking, and it had already paced Europe on that front. "Inexpensive California jug wines are of much higher quality than the vin ordinaire consumed prodigiously by working-class Frenchmen," crowed *Time* magazine in 1972. "The great Château wines of France outshine the New World's best, but the grape gap is closing."

Pioneers like Mondavi and Winiarski were determined to close that gap, and their hopes would be affirmed when, in May 1976, wine merchant Steven Spurrier arranged for a tasting in Paris of ten red and ten white wines, California Cabernet and Chardonnay against red Bordeaux and white Burgundy. When results came from the mostly French judges, including Aubert de Villaine of Domaine de la Romanée-Conti and Odette Kahn, editor of *La revue du vin de France*, the Americans were clearly triumphant. The 1973 Stag's Leap Cabernet and 1973 Montelena Chardonnay both took the top spots. (Mondavi's wines weren't in the lineup, although two of his alumni—Winiarski and Mike Grgich, Barrett's winemaker at Montelena—were behind the winning wines.)

A bunch of American upstarts had beaten the French at their own game. Practically overnight, the world embraced the possibility of California wines.

BRAND CALIFORNIA

By the late 1970s, the state was flush with the spoils of Paris. Wine lists across the country added California fare, just as California cuisine was redefining modern American cooking. Ambitious young winemakers like Ric Forman were pioneering advances like barrel fermentation for Chardonnay. A passel of winemakers trained at UC Davis were quietly taking over cellars, people like John Kongsgaard, whose family had been in Napa for

several generations, and Cathy Corison, who along with Zelma Long was among the first female winemakers in modern California.

Most of the attention was on wines with the pedigree of the California coast, but in fact the state's great grape engine had long been found in hotter inland vineyards—perhaps from the Lodi area, east of San Francisco Bay, and more often from the Central Valley, the stronghold of California's midcentury industry, in cities like Stockton, Fresno, and of course Modesto, whence came E&J Gallo, the state's largest wine company.

These were the seeds of Brand California: a somewhat hazy belief in the quality of the California appellation, one that didn't make geographic judgments. Even as the best of California wine was becoming more refined in the 1970s, Brand California was largely being built on the cheap wine that had ruled the market since Prohibition's end, although the packaging was getting fancier.

As Brand California grew, the chemistry-based curriculum at the University of California at Davis, intended as a teaching tool to help students understand the basics of winemaking, was quickly coming to dominate cellar practices. The program emphasized sanitary practices over creativity; it insisted on commercial cultured yeasts to ensure uniform fermentation, even though for centuries wine had been fermented using indigenous yeasts found in vineyards and cellars; it advocated routine acidification, in which acid is added to wine to balance its chemistry. On the vineyard side, for many years the Davis curriculum taught that, aside from variations in water retention, the different composition of various types of soil didn't particularly matter.

All these ideas were based on sound academic principles, resulting in a curriculum that would suit everyday industrial work. But the program also spread the belief that winemaking could be done according to a formula. While the Europeans had their own issues—particularly when it came to microbiological problems that left some wines tasting unclean—Californians increasingly believed that wine could be engineered to be delicious. As Ridge's Paul Draper put it, "Basically Davis rejected traditional winemaking as old wives' tales that made bad wine."

Even on the matter of California's most famous wines, let's not romanticize the past. The era's winemaking had its shortfalls; Joe Heitz and many other top vintners would frequently make acid adjustments, often on moderately ripe wines that didn't need the chemistry tweak, in order to approximate the chemistry of European wines.

Research conducted during and after World War II tried to sort out where specific types of grapes should be grown, in essence dividing hot California from cool California. But according to that model, climate was everything. "The whole idea of soil versus climate in California was decided in favor of climate many years ago by professors Amerine and Winkler," Richard Graff, one of the early hunters of limestone soils, said in 1977, "for the simple reason that the factor of climate produces differences in grapes which are measurable in the laboratory. The differences in grapes which are the result of soil are *not* measurable in the laboratory."

Nor was 1970s farming necessarily a point of pride. The era's less efficient practices in the field—high yields, wide spaces between rows, sprawling trellises, inefficient irrigation—might have held California's ripeness in check. But with it came an obsession with high yields, which meant that farming practices were dictated less by biological balance than by balance sheets.

Most wineries in the 1970s were utterly focused on growth. So-called small operations, for example Mondavi and Beringer, had an expansion boom, producing hundreds of thousands of cases. By the time wine scientist Richard Peterson showed up at an ambitious new project, the Monterey Vineyard, it already had ten thousand acres of vineyards sprawled across the Salinas Valley, the heart of Steinbeck country.

Soon the Davis graduates of the 1970s would be the new rock stars. A handful, like Kongsgaard and Corison, put their chemistry-heavy learning at a distance, eager to mirror the practices of old European hands who had resettled in Napa, like André Tchelistcheff and Philip Togni, a student of famed Bordeaux enologist Émile Peynaud. But more often, the Old World equation—in which the vintner toiled in both field and cellar—was replaced by winemaking as a self-contained job. Here was California's other great chasm. Winemakers were winemakers; growers were growers. Unless you were a maverick like Winiarski, farming was just a field hand's job.

FIGHTING VARIETALS

By the time the 1980s arrived, California wine was booming—and feeling more than a bit self-satisfied. A grape glut in the late '70s plus ambitious growth projections (in 1970, the Bank of America predicted Americans would drink four hundred million gallons of wine annually by 1980) had given rise to an ever-increasing raft of inexpensive wine. While the table wines of the past were typically blends from low-grade grapes—like Gallo's Hearty Burgundy and Almaden's Mountain Chablis—the turn of the decade brought a novel concept: selling cheap wine by varietal name.

The notion of varietal wines had been championed since writer and merchant Frank Schoonmaker crusaded for it before World War II, hoping to emulate Europe's finer practices, but the boom in plantings had given rise to a belief that Americans would in fact drink more wine if they could better understand it, especially if it was packaged in a proper 750 ml bottle with a cork rather than a jug or box. The so-called fighting varietals entered the scene in the early 1980s. Brands like Glen Ellen and Mondavi's Woodbridge soon soared.

No one was entirely sure which varietal wines would stick, and the spirit of exploration was still strong; Johannisberg Riesling, Chenin Blanc, and Napa Gamay, for example, all fought in the varietal wars. But the Paris tasting had crowned a king and queen. Nothing could match the dominance of Cabernet and Chardonnay. The latter, a one-time asterisk in the book of California winemaking, was of particular interest after a San Francisco lawyer named Jess Jackson produced one in 1982 under his Kendall-Jackson label. Its slight touch of remaining sugar found favor with drinkers, especially women. Soon Chardonnay was virtually synonymous with white wine. America had found its beloved beverage.

There were speed bumps in California's progress, of course. As the Reagan era unfolded, a backlash—fueled, in part, by the French—arose, as some considered California wines too big, too robust. In response, some vintners grew occupied with the prospect of creating "food wines." Picked earlier and often doctored with acid, they were, by turns, either vibrant or screechingly tart. To believers in the 1970s boom, these moves seemed foolishly reactionary. The wines were soon savaged by

a new breed of wine critic, including an upstart publication, the *Wine Spectator,* and an ambitious young reviewer from Maryland, Robert Parker, who was shifting his focus from Bordeaux to the West Coast.

THE LONG BOOM

Right on schedule, the predictions of the early 1970s were coming true: America was finally becoming a nation of wine drinkers, and California wanted to capture every last dollar.

But there was one other fly in the ointment. Throughout the 1980s, evidence kept mounting that the AxR1 rootstock on which many of California's vineyards were planted had a fatal flaw: susceptibility to a new biotype of the vine louse phylloxera. Only in 1989 did Davis finally issue a decree to stop using AxR1, but by that point the damage was done. As phylloxera devastated vineyards, growers were forced to tear out their relatively young plantings and start again. Thousands of acres would have to be replanted, at an eventual estimated cost of more than a billion dollars. The runaway success of the California wine industry finally faced a hurdle it couldn't muscle past.

As the 1990s began, California launched another planting boom, though not a wholly voluntary one, given phylloxera's toll. This new wave of vineyards corresponded with a massive influx of money, particularly into Napa Valley. Previously, the model for success had been at large scale, but a few wineries had deliberately stayed small, charging top dollar and selling scarce wines in small amounts, often via mailing lists, to justify those high prices. Hints of this cultlike status had emerged in the late 1970s, notably with Al Brounstein's Diamond

Creek, which became the first Cabernet to top $100 with its 1978 vintage.

But the first winery created with the sole purpose of becoming a cult hit was arguably Harlan Estate. Bill Harlan, who had founded the real estate firm Pacific Union, bought property west of Oakville in 1985. Having spent years in Napa Valley, as cofounder of St. Helena's posh Meadowood resort and part owner of the Merryvale winery, he had a sense for the financial workings of wine. So he decided to create a project with a remarkable focus; he produced fewer than two thousand cases each year, sold either through restaurants or a nearly impregnable mailing list.

Harlan wasn't alone. New money was surging into California. Napa had long hosted its share of escapees from elsewhere; early modern pioneers, like the Chappellets and the Davies family, which bought Schramsberg, had come from Los Angeles and even farther. But the Napa they settled into was pastoral and quiet. Now serious cash was flooding the valley. By the time Harlan's first commercial vintage was released in 1996, he had a raft of competition—names like Colgin, Bryant Family, Dalla Valle, Araujo, and, most notably, Screaming Eagle. Some had arrived earlier than others (Dalla Valle in 1982), and a few acquired long-standing properties, as when Bart and Daphne Araujo purchased the legendary Eisele Vineyard in 1990, a site responsible for some of the great 1970s Cabernets.

The cults, born out of the industry struggles and the vineyard devastation of the 1980s, quickly came to represent the pinnacle of California winemaking, an industry built around big money and meticulously tended, usually young, vineyards. Grow big? No, the new game was to blossom small. This new goal was encapsulated by Jean Phillips of Screaming Eagle, who in 1986 acquired

a fifty-seven-acre vineyard. It was mostly planted in white grapes, but she soon decided to replant it and make her own wine. The 1992 debut vintage of Screaming Eagle hit the wine industry like a neutron bomb. At less than two hundred cases, and with a 99-point rave from the increasingly influential Robert Parker ("one of the greatest young Cabernets I have ever tasted"), Screaming Eagle set the standard for unattainability.

Napa was becoming addicted to prestige and was quickly turning into the Hamptons West. The annual Napa wine auction, which had once been a relatively quiet community affair, spiked from collecting $447,000 for charity in 1988 to a dazzling $9.5 million in 1999. (It would be eclipsed again in 2005, on the far side of the dot-com boom.) Public Napa kept churning along, with its winery tours and bustling traffic along Highway 29. But the real action now was in private Napa. Wineries were built far from the public eye, shrouded in mystery; for many years Screaming Eagle, hoping to discourage looky-loos, managed to keep its address a secret. Here was a way for California, or at least an elite set of newcomers, to redefine the terms of engagement with the Old World.

"EYE OF THE HURRICANE"

And what of the wines? They were getting flashier, with deep extraction of flavors and lots more new French oak, the typical signals of attempted self-importance. Restrained, traditional winemaking began to seem quaint, its practitioners stuck in the previous decade.

A handful of talents for hire emerged, each with a knack for crafting wines that made the desired impact. While Harlan relied on his longtime winemaker Bob Levy, Dalla Valle and Screaming Eagle turned to Heidi Peterson Barrett, daughter of wine scientist Richard Peterson and wife of Chateau Montelena's Bo Barrett, and she soon became synonymous with a stylish and successful style of wine. But one person more than any other set California on a path toward the style that would define it for the next fifteen years. "Certainly," James Laube, the senior editor for California at the *Wine Spectator,* told me one day over lunch, "Helen Turley is in the eye of the hurricane."

A Georgia native raised by teetotaling Baptist parents, Turley made her name as winemaker for two Sonoma wineries, B.R. Cohn and Peter Michael, but by the early 1990s she had become a winemaking gun for hire, acquiring a roster of top clients, including Bryant Family and Colgin, plus others like Martinelli in Russian River Valley. She also worked with her brother Larry Turley, making the wine for his Zinfandel-focused Turley Wine Cellars when he launched it in 1993. Entranced by the possibility of producing Pinot Noir out on the Sonoma Coast, Helen Turley and her husband, John Wetlaufer, in 1985 hatched their own tiny label, Marcassin, which would extend the cult model to both Pinot and Chardonnay. If California had been seeking a style of wine that would set it apart, Turley was the master of the pursuit of maximum impact.

But the formula for stratospheric success was becoming more broadly evident. Vineyards needed to be fastidiously planted, densely spaced on the vertical trellises that had been northern Europe's great viticultural innovation. These young vines were farmed for dramatically low yields—often two tons per acre or less, perhaps half the standard in European vineyards—with underdeveloped grape bunches cut away weeks before harvest. All this propelled the remaining grapes to dramatic ripeness levels.

With this meticulous work came a huge spike in farming costs, although prices for the top wines enjoyed a far bigger spike. The master of the form was viticulturist David Abreu, a longtime Napan who had learned farming at Caymus and Inglenook before building his own consultancy, where he employed many techniques popular in Bordeaux. Clients like Colgin, Bryant, and Grace Family gravitated to Abreu's precise, manicured, and expensive farming methods. Globe-trotting consultant Michel Rolland soon arrived from Bordeaux to offer his own talents. His early work for Harlan caught the attention of others hoping to advance on the cult battlefield. Rolland's long friendship with Robert Parker was, at least tangentially, also a draw; his projects had an uncanny ability to find favor with Parker's publication, the *Wine Advocate.*

Indeed, a symbiotic relationship was emerging between top critics and the top wines. A decade earlier, California wine had been benchmarked mostly by wine competitions like the California State Fair and a handful of regional writers. But as production exploded—after barely budging the previous decade, the state's grape crush figures ballooned nearly 60 percent between 1990 and 2000—critics, especially Parker, saw an opportunity to become kingmakers, to create a new quality hierarchy. The *Wine Spectator* shifted from tasting wines as a panel and gave individual critics—in California's case, Laube—full responsibility for evaluating wines.

Critics increasingly swore by blind tastings during which they sampled large flights of wines sent for evaluation. This setup absolved them, theoretically, from making judgments about the source of the wines, but there were still opportunities to game the system. Some of the new elite leveraged the power of their early high scores. Properties such as Harlan and Screaming Eagle, for example, soon earned enough clout that they could give writers an ultimatum: either they could visit the winery and taste in a setting advantageous to the vintner or they wouldn't taste at all. Parker actually seemed to prefer tasting this way, and it soon became a standard practice.

Lessons about the success of these new practices reverberated through the California wine industry. The Screaming Eagles of the world defined a pinnacle of style. Long growing seasons producing ripe grapes, like 1994, found particular favor, as did wines with softer tannins that were ready to drink upon release. "The thing is that people used to make their wine and hold it for five years," Laube says. "They couldn't do that anymore. The economics dictated that they needed to get their wines out, sold, drunk, and reordered."

LESSONS OF '97

The year 1997 was one that grape farmers dream of: a warm spring and early bud break, then a warm and constant summer. Harvest began remarkably early, with Napa's sparkling-wine grapes delivered in July. The years of post-AxR1 replanting were past, the new vines had begun to mature, and the perfect weather delivered a highly productive bumper crop unthreatened by fall rains. Not only could the brave leave their grapes on the vine, further bumping up ripeness, but in some cases they had no other choice, as cellars ran out of room to process additional fruit.

Praise came big, too. Parker doled out four perfect 100-point scores—to Harlan Estate, Screaming Eagle, Bryant Family, and Abreu's Madrona

Ranch—while Laube didn't mince words, ultimately proclaiming that it was "the vintage of the century for California Cabernet Sauvignon."

Finally, here was a signal that affirmed the past decade's work to erase the struggles of the 1980s—proof that crafting wines in the bigger, more dramatic style was not just possible but essential. It was after 1997 that many of California's most successful wines crept north of 14 percent alcohol—and stayed there. Exuberance was everything. Extreme ripeness was soon seen as being the essence of California sunshine.

This exuberance would last precisely one year. The weather in 1998 was everything '97 wasn't: cold, wet, and dismal. It could not offer the ripe and almost raisiny flavors, unctuous textures, or high alcohols of the prior year. The pure id of the '97s was gone. The 1998 wines were mostly panned.

The following year, 1999, was a more classically styled vintage: the wines were more taut, tannic, and fresh than those of 1997, but they were certainly riper than the grim '98s. They got a cautiously upbeat reception, but by that point the standard was clear. Bigger was going to be better. Believe otherwise and you would be punished.

Few were punished worse than Tim Mondavi. By then in charge of winemaking for the Robert Mondavi Winery, which had grown into a powerhouse of a public company, Mondavi was still faithful to the style of wine he had learned not only through the 1970s, but also through his travel to Bordeaux to work on Opus One, Mondavi's partnership with Philippe de Rothschild. Though the winery was at a corporate scale, Mondavi's wines—in particular the 1994 Reserve Cabernet, which, Parker said in 1996, "may turn out to be the greatest Mondavi has yet made"—were still standard-bearers.

Four years later Parker released his annual California report. He heaped praise on the usual suspects, including Helen Turley's Marcassin, Martinelli, Bryant Family, and Harlan (although even he was wary of it becoming "increasingly expensive"). But when it came to Mondavi, Parker's tone was one of dismay. He chastised Tim Mondavi for "an almost obsessive mission" to make lighter-styled efforts that, to Parker's taste, were "indifferent, innocuous wines that err on the side of intellectual vapidness over the pursuit of wines of heart, soul, and pleasure." ("I was a poster child for staid old ways," Tim recalls, "and tacked on a board.")

Parker continued, "I believe he is going against what Mother Nature has given California, the ability to produce wines of exceptional ripeness and gorgeously pure, intense flavors." Parker found his nearly four-hour tasting at Mondavi to be "almost agonizing," as he sampled wines with "intricate aromas that were too subtle and restrained," and that were "collectively superficial, with tart, almost stripped-out personalities."

This would be your fate for loyalty to a classic style. California's new mandate was Big Flavor: opulent fruit and the resultant high alcohol. You could hope to be rewarded for compliance. You diverged at your own peril.

THE REIGN OF BIG FLAVOR

It had been a momentous run for California since the late 1980s. Vineyard plantings were booming; Napa's had more than doubled in a decade to forty thousand acres, Sonoma's to fifty-two thousand. No one had to make a case for California wines anymore; they dominated shelves and wine lists from coast to coast. The hopes for a boom that began in the early 1970s, amplified by the Judgment of Paris and reinforced by a big infusion of cash in the 1990s, had all been realized, proof positive that American wine had finally shaken off the yoke of Prohibition.

Parker, as much as anyone, was ready to celebrate. "At the conclusion of what is undoubtedly the most extraordinary decade California wine has ever experienced," he wrote in the same December 2000 issue of the *Wine Advocate* in which he excoriated Mondavi, "it is no exaggeration to say that California wine has come of age and can now rival or surpass the world's finest wines."

Not everyone had enjoyed the benefits of the boom. Tim Mondavi's drubbing would soon be moot; the Robert Mondavi Winery was sold in 2004 to Constellation Brands, the world's biggest wine company. Veterans like Warren Winiarski of Stag's Leap Wine Cellars were ever more disenchanted with the high-impact style. It was, he told me just after selling his own winery in 2008, part of a "new parochialism" that had guided California winemakers to train their palates almost entirely on their own concentrated wines, willfully disregarding other styles practiced elsewhere in the world. "This is a moment," he said, "whose time has to come to an end."

Big Wine began to consolidate its efforts, dominating both the high and low ends of the business. Rarified labels like Etude found themselves in the same corporate family as Beringer white Zinfandel. Even as so-called boutique wines were being priced well above $50, no matter their provenance, Bronco Wine Company's Fred Franzia threw a massive wrench into pricing models in 2002 when he revived an old Napa label, Charles Shaw, under which he would sell a low-end wine at the grocery store Trader Joe's. Charles Shaw wines, better

At the heart of Big Flavor lies a quest for ripeness. Achieving it has always been a key goal in winemaking, but California is one of the few places in the world where a ripe vintage—depending on your definition—has become a default expectation every year.

That was a marked change from the 1970s, when ripeness levels were still a concern, in part due to a mix of high yields and less-efficient farming methods. The measure of ripeness used in California is degrees Brix, which reflects the amount of sugar in an aqueous solution (1 degree Brix equals one gram of sugar in one hundred grams of liquid). In the 1970s, Cabernet picked at 22 or 23 Brix would have been considered successfully ripe. Indeed, in 1943 researcher Maynard Amerine cautioned that red-wine grapes shouldn't exceed 23 or 24 Brix—levels that would have brought scorn in the 1990s and early 2000s.

What had happened to rewrite the rules about when grapes were ripe? Was it a case of the frog in ever-warmer water? One year you're at 24 Brix, you're at 24.4 the next, and suddenly 28 Brix seems not only possible but necessary, as you add water to reinvigorate the virtual raisins you've harvested.

In California's case, the quest for an extra-long ripening season and absurdly robust flavors was born out of the concept of physiological ripeness—the point at which the grape has matured so its flavors hit a peak, its seeds are brown enough that they won't release unripe flavors, and the skin is just a bit soft, but before the grape's acidity starts to drop too far and its chemistry falls out of balance. But what is the optimal point of ripeness? Defining it has created a schism between the proponents of Big Flavor and pioneers in a post–Big Flavor world, those participating in wine's equivalent of a culture war.

When winemakers insist they pick for flavor, as many do, what does that mean? Does it mean that the flavor of the ripe, mature grapes will be reflected in the wine? One of the great misconceptions of winemaking is that grapes will taste in wine as they do in the vineyard—as though the transformative process in the cellar simply passes flavor through unimpeded. Among the simplest changes: malic acid in the grape is often transformed into softer lactic acid, shifting the sugar-acid balance of flavor. Grapes typically taste tarter than the wine they will become. As winemaker Ted Lemon puts it, "You want a tart apple for that pie, because when you bake it, then, damn, that's good apple."

Particularly in modern Napa, the love of ripeness necessitates sugar numbers that have little in common with viticultural traditions elsewhere. This isn't the difference between 23 and 24 Brix, but between 23 and 28 Brix, sometimes even higher. Achieving these numbers requires either allowing the grapes to shrivel on the vine as the grape's water content evaporates or, in the case of irrigation-happy California, propping up fully ripe grapes with enough water to keep them maturing late into the season.

Flavors can then be balanced out in the winery with water, the addition of acid, and the removal of alcohol. At that point, the resulting wine is not so much the artistry of the winemaker as the ministrations of a technocrat. It's not winemaking, really. It's the extraction of maximal flavor.

known as Two Buck Chuck, were the flip side of cultdom.

Drowned out by the roar of Big Flavor, and by the rise of the Big Wine companies, was any real discussion of California terroir. There had been a twenty-year boom in the creation of federally regulated wine appellations, or American Viticultural Areas, but the more that Big Flavor winemakers talked a good game about a sense of place, the harder it was to locate in the glass. It wasn't simply that the wines increasingly tasted all the same, although that was my conclusion when I arrived in 2006. It was that the industry had convinced itself en masse that their wines *did* manifest California terroir. Or perhaps they simply didn't care.

Which was worse? The notion that California winemakers were apathetic about terroir, or that they believed in a sort of macro-terroir—California as defined by a blend of ripeness and hubris?

SCIENCE IN THE CELLAR

Leo McCloskey, one of Paul Draper's early understudies at Ridge, grew along with the wine industry over the years, joining the ranks of Helen Turley, Michel Rolland, and others in perfecting a Big Flavor formula. But in a way he was more populist than the others, offering his services to clients who perhaps couldn't afford superconsultants like Turley. He famously claimed that his consultancy, Enologix, could use a series of scientific markers, mostly from analyzing wine samples with a liquid chromatograph, to tailor flavors that brought raves from both Laube and Parker. All of this allowed the modern winemaker to overcome the strictures of terroir. "If you're in Sonoma and your benchmark is Napa or Bordeaux," McCloskey would tell clients,

according to David Darlington's book *An Ideal Wine,* "you have to rearrange Mother Nature."

One of McCloskey's more straightforward tricks was "draining down sweet," or removing a wine, particularly Cabernet, from the grape skins before it finished fermentation. This process, which Europeans also used, lowered the amount of tannins and other compounds extracted from the skins, yielding a softer and plusher wine.

It was but one of a long list of techniques that had become commonplace by the early 2000s. Rolland's specialty was micro-oxygenation, in which tiny amounts of air are filtered through a wine to soften its texture. Micro-ox was a huge hit in California, not only for fancy wines but for cheap ones, which also utilized a growing range of oak products—chips, blocks, staves, powder—as low-cost methods to mimic barrel aging.

The longtime practice of quietly adding water to a wine to reduce its total alcohol level and freshen it up had given way to a new set of technologies. As ripe flavors became nearly mandatory, alcohol adjustment grew to be a crucial part of the industry, with an estimated 45 to 60 percent of California wine being treated.

In one method, the spinning cone, a portion of wine was passed through a conical column where it was distilled using a vacuum rather than heat—once to remove aroma components, another time to remove alcohol—and then recombined. This method, however, was expensive, and thus primarily used by large concerns like Gallo, for whom producing wines with higher alcohol involved serious costs (wines with 14 percent alcohol or higher are no longer considered "table wine" by the federal government and are taxed at higher rates).

Smaller wineries wanted in, and in 1992 a wine scientist named Clark Smith founded a company

the same options as the big guys for tweaking alcohol levels until, as Smith would demonstrate, they found a flavor "sweet spot." At its peak, Vinovation was processing two million gallons of wine annually for about a thousand wineries.

Little of this work was ever discussed, as evidenced by the name of the firm that purchased Smith's business in 2008: Winesecrets. One reason for this, Smith argues, is that what had once been a culture of openness had evolved into a world of trade secrets and nondisclosure agreements, especially after a lengthy lawsuit between Chardonnay mogul Jess Jackson and his winemaker, Jed Steele. "The wine industry has done very little to educate anybody about what's going on now," Smith says. "We're perfectly comfortable if they think we stomp grapes with our feet."

Alcohol adjustment was just one part of a growing arsenal of methods for manipulating wine. The acidification of wine, which had been accepted in the mid-twentieth century, also evolved as Big Flavor came to dominate the industry. Wines might be acidulated before fermentation to help prevent microbes that caused spoilage, then deacidified before bottling to punch up robust flavors and remove the tartness that could lead to critical disapproval. This one-two punch had the benefit of allowing a vintner to claim that a wine was unfiltered, which Parker and other critics took as a particular sign of quality. Since wine criticism hinged on a simple barometer of deliciousness, what was the harm?

A starker option was the use of dimethyl dicarbonate, known commercially as Velcorin. Introduced in 1988, Velcorin was pitched as a solution to rid not only wine but also sports drinks and bottled tea of bacterial taint—again, without using filtration. It was particularly appealing to some vintners

called Vinovation to capitalize on a patent he had obtained for using the reverse osmosis process on wine. In reverse osmosis, wine is forcibly passed through a semipermeable membrane; larger molecules are held back. The permeate, which passes through, is a combination of water, alcohol, acetic acid, and other compounds. The permeate can then be processed to remove some of the alcohol or potential flaws like ethyl acetate (which causes instability and a smell reminiscent of nail polish remover), then recombined. Initially, wineries were drawn to Vinovation by the possibility of fixing flaws, such as those caused by the yeast *Brettanomyces*, but soon they saw that they could have for its ability to reduce the amount of sulfur dioxide used in the cellar. Grape must or wine could be biologically neutralized, allowing commercial yeast and enzymes to work uninhibited.

Once a product was dosed, Velcorin would break down over several hours into trace amounts of carbon dioxide and methanol. But the compound itself is extremely toxic, enough to require a trained technician in the equivalent of a hazmat suit. For evident reasons, its use was controversial, and thus little discussed. A few vintners dubbed it "the Death Star," not only for its potentially toxic nature but also for the more philosophical reason that it created a biological blank slate, eliminating not only microbes that could cause spoilage but also those, like vineyard yeasts, that helped to give certain wines their individual character. Velcorin was, in true California style, an efficient solution to one of those pesky biological problems—unless you happened to believe that microbial activity gave wine its distinction. Otherwise, winemaking could be as tidy as crafting a sports drink.

The belief that indigenous yeasts from the vineyard could be beneficial was not only becoming rarer, it was increasingly considered a liability, thanks in part to the strictures of winemaking-school textbooks. The alternative? Using commercial yeast (which might have been a necessity if you were working with lower-grade grapes) in combination with high levels of sulfur dioxide to kill off native microflora. Cultured wine yeasts had been in use for decades, but if in the 1970s winemakers were stuck with a few simple selections, the commercial yeast industry blossomed in the 1990s and 2000s. It offered isolates that could tolerate alcohol levels of 16 percent or more, encouraging the use of superripe grapes, even though these yeasts required an array of added nutrients and enzymes

to keep chugging along. You could easily neutralize grape must and then engineer your preferred means of fermentation, picking yeasts to punch up favored qualities. You might order, say, Lalvin BA11 if you wanted a white wine with more texture and "fresh fruit aromas of orange blossom, pineapple, and apricot." And if your wine's color was a bit wan or you wanted just a touch of phantom sweetness, you could obtain some of the grape concentrate known as Mega Purple, which became a widely used additive not only for inexpensive wines, but also for spendy ones (see page 97).

If twenty years earlier the California wine industry was happy just to be part of the global conversation, it had quickly become addicted to being on top. There was a sense of self-satisfaction at having come to dominate the conversation, leaving France in particular to rue its fallen ways. Technological manipulation had become pervasive not only for cheap table wines but also for expensive ones. And there was little doubt that this was the right path forward.

By the time I arrived in California, a sense of entitlement pervaded the industry. Question California's path? Question the hard-fought victories of Big Flavor? Blasphemy.

A VISIT TO MONTE BELLO

It is a precipitous trip to see Paul Draper at Ridge Vineyards' facility atop Monte Bello. You wind five miles up a mountain from the Silicon Valley town of Cupertino until you reach a crest and gaze upon the entire Santa Clara Valley below. As you descend into Ridge's cellar, an old timber building built into the limestone-rich earth by San Francisco physician Osea Perrone in the 1890s, you wonder how

anyone would have ventured to this windswept ridge more than a century ago, much less select it as the place to replicate the glories of Bordeaux.

But they did. Hence Monte Bello has always been a place I could return to and brush away my residual cynicism about California.

I walk down the cellar steps one September morning and find Draper in his office, in an alcove just off the fermentation room. His staff is setting out plastic cups with twenty-eight samples from different portions of the Geyserville Vineyard. I taste one; it's succulently sweet but vibrant. Draper briefly steps away for a call. His daughter Caitlin has just gone into labor. It's going to be a busy day

I follow him up to the spacious barrel room where the next release of Monte Bello, the 2011, is aging in long, single-stacked rows of barrels. Grown atop this mountain and always aged in oblong American oak barrels—each time I visit, Draper points out that until the turn of the twentieth century, American and Baltic oak were more revered than French—Monte Bello is an iconoclastic wine for California. And yet it is a pinnacle of American Cabernet.

When I first interviewed Draper in 2006, he was as frustrated as I was by the state of California wine. He bristled at a generation of winemakers that seemed to pay lip service to terroir. Four years later I visited him on the occasion of his fortieth anniversary at Ridge and found him in much the same funk. This time he seems brighter. He asks me to name a few younger winemakers who are doing good work.

"It seems to me a lot of the small new people you are talking about are seeing that possibility, and are turning that corner," he tells me as we sit down to taste. "But fine producers from the '90s, let's say?

The majority of them, I don't hear they're turning that corner. I think they're committed."

Ridge has always tilted at California's winemaking norms. From its founding days, when a group of Stanford Research Institute scientists assembled the property and made the first wines, it has always been serious-minded, almost a meditative endeavor. And when Draper showed up in 1969, having schooled himself in original nineteenth-century Bordeaux winemaking texts, it was just the place to write an alternate story line for California.

With Draper in charge of the cellar, Ridge began to expand—growing to forty-three thousand cases in the next decade—courting primarily an East Coast clientele that saw the parallels between Ridge's wines and those of Bordeaux. While Napa was booming, Ridge enjoyed a more serene exploration of California's possibility. When California Zinfandel went on its own detour to ripeness, driving connoisseurs away from the grape, Ridge was courting fans of a cultivated version of California taste.

Ridge's geographic isolation in the Santa Cruz Mountains also allowed it to avoid the stylistic arms race. As California wines bulked up in the 1990s, Monte Bello rarely topped the mid-13s in alcohol. This fate wasn't solely Ridge's. Other mavericks, like Josh Jensen at Calera, also went their own way, and Jensen, like Draper, went for years at a time without his wines being reviewed by major critics.

The Big Flavor era only put Ridge's wines in starker relief. A wine like Monte Bello seemed too quiet, and Draper became another poster child for recalcitrance, for an unwillingness to embrace the bounty of the West Coast sun. "I guess it bothers me as a Californian," Draper tells me over lunch, duck breast with a summer bean salad. "It's hard for me to admit that, but people would come up and say, 'This is the only California wine I buy.' And we'd say, 'Oh, God, that's really a shame.'"

Soon a handful of local collectors join us. They've secured a few bottles of the 1971 Monte Bello, one of the five American Cabernets from the 1976 Judgment of Paris. Draper wants to taste it blind, so we sit around the table with two glasses, one holding the '71 and the other holding a mystery wine. Both are astonishing in their vitality.

The other, it turns out, is another Ridge legend, the 1971 from Eisele Vineyard in Calistoga—an early Draper experiment. Ridge made Eisele for one year only, picked it at a ripe 25 Brix and intended it as a one-off chance to work with fruit from Napa, where heat was easier to come by than in the Santa Cruz Mountains. The 1971 Monte Bello in my glass is heady, full of aged bouillon aromas but showing perk. But the Eisele hums seamlessly with bright red fruit, scents of mint tea, and an underbrushy complexity. It is one of the best Cabernets I have ever had. More than that, it is a reminder that there have always been true believers like Draper—those who didn't get swept up in the triumph of Paris, who didn't succumb to Big Flavor's temptations. Rather they continued a most crucial task: their devout meditation on California's potential for greatness.

While we're taken with the two wines, an assistant quietly comes back into the room and whispers to Draper. With a glass of the 1971, his third vintage on the mountain, the master of Monte Bello toasts his fortune. He has just become a grandfather.

The New Farming

California's revival inevitably had to begin in the field. This would be the major change from the Big Flavor era, ruled as it was by the philosophy of the cellar. The sum of Big Flavor's viticultural progress? Grow grapes as ripe as anyone wanted—the sustainability of that model be damned—and tweak them for the desired result.

To change course, California had to invert the belief that winemakers, not farmers, would guide its progress. Better yet, the same person had to embrace both roles.

That was a lesson Ted Lemon had learned in Burgundy and applied all through his years exploring California's possibilities. For nearly two decades Lemon hoped to secure land for what would become his home vineyard and winery. When he finally did, in 2003, he was going to farm it according to his own beliefs—which meant discarding most of the tenets of Californian viticulture.

His "model farm," as he calls it, is two miles west of the town of Sebastopol. The floor-to-ceiling windows of his winery office provide an unimpeded view from his desk of the field beyond. In the gentle hills of west Sonoma, where they undulate toward the coast, the Pivot Vineyard is a postage stamp—just three acres set on a thirty-acre parcel—planted with Pinot Noir. Deliberately small, the vineyard is nonetheless precisely the right size to be Lemon's laboratory for his beliefs about farming, views honed over thirty years. It is no surprise that he sometimes refers to himself as "the ego of the farm."

Lemon farms the Pivot, and most of his vineyards, biodynamically, employing a mode of farming that combines organic techniques with more holistic and spiritual practices. But his methods are far more nuanced than the guidelines followed by many biodynamic farms. Lemon is as likely to quote UC Berkeley agro-ecologist Miguel Altieri, whose work focuses on agriculture that's both environmentally and culturally sustainable, as he is to reference Rudolf Steiner, the founder of biodynamics. Many current biodynamic precepts, Lemon argues, "deny the farm its potential to individuate." And of course he refuses to get official certification. To give up his own farming decisions to a third-party certifier, as he puts it, "would be to shirk my duty and diminish the path we are on."

On the day I visit, Lemon is in a philosophical mood, as he often is when he is considering farming. ("It's fascinating to me that we've abandoned Goethe's observational approach to nature," he tells me at one point, which, it should be noted, is not the easiest sentence to jot down during a bumpy ride through western Sonoma.) His work in the field is, of course, to make wine. But more broadly, it's an exercise in farming as a path to decoding the mysteries of the soil.

To understand how the son of a New York magazine editor would find himself making compost teas and picking weeds, it helps to remember that Lemon was handed the reins of Domaine Guy Roulot at the age of twenty-four. That gave him the chance to absorb Burgundian notions, notably that winemaking is simply a coda to the crucial work that takes place in the vineyard. But at the time, the state of farming in Burgundy was relatively grim, as dependent on chemicals as anywhere else. The soils were essentially dead, so much so that agronomist Claude Bourguignon would quip that the Sahara's sands had more life than Burgundian earth. As much as France revered the concept of terroir, Lemon realized that many of its greatest vineyards were created not out of reverence for the sanctity of place, but rather because of their proximity to transportation, or politics, or the will of powerful men. "That was the great revelation to me when I was twenty-something," Lemon says. "It was that great terroir didn't come down on a moonbeam from God."

Lemon returned from France in the mid-1980s with a lot on his mind. California was perhaps the perfect place for him as he puzzled through the importance of site. He took a job in Napa, but he soon found that "terroir wasn't a very Napa Valley kind of thing." Plantings were big and often installed with little regard for the particulars of the ground below—although there were the seeds of interest in techniques like the use of permanent cover crops to improve soil health.

Perhaps more troublingly for a young man thinking about the bigger questions of agriculture, there was little interest in farming beyond the current crop—doing more than watering vines, adding fertilizer, anything to ensure a solid harvest. Decisions were made with little concern for their long-term impacts. "What was out there to learn from as models?" he says. "Not much. That's why I blew it up."

By the time Lemon landed in Napa, Big Wine was dominant. The state's old institutional farming memory had been wiped out. Viticultural research was focused primarily on the arid Central Valley, with the goal of achieving abundant yields for making table wine. Soils were viewed primarily in terms of their water retention, and there was virtually no interest, as there was in Europe, in how soil content might change a wine's character. Even water was merely another input to be managed.

If once California's immigrants farmed with natural rainfall and tended their low, head-trained

vines like a bush, the advice of the postwar era advocated widely spaced vines on high trellises, with minimal pruning to ensure big yields. Irrigation water flowed through furrows during the dry season. Chemical fertilizer was still a miracle drug to most farmers, especially with the midcentury co-ops and big wineries interested primarily in low-dollar tonnage. It wasn't that UC Davis didn't have an interest in fine wine, but its viticulture and enology program after the war had been crafted to help rebuild the basics of an industry demolished by Prohibition.

If, in the 1960s and '70s, the primary goal of winemakers was maximum production, making wines from commodity fruit sold by the ton, how could terroir even enter the discussion? How could California start to ask more essential questions about farming the land?

EGO OF THE FARM

It took a decade after the founding of Littorai in 1993 before Lemon and his wife, Heidi, could purchase their thirty-acre farm outside Sebastopol, another four before a harvest. In the interim, Lemon had been goading his growers—including David Hirsch on the Sonoma Coast and Rich Savoy in Anderson Valley—to improve their methods. Lemon's was the only vineyard block at Hirsch to be organically farmed. But organic wasn't enough. Even biodynamics only took him so far. What he really wanted were answers to the same questions he had asked in France. What makes a great vineyard? What innate qualities in the field can transcend the many bad decisions of humans?

If he could start farming from scratch, Lemon figured, perhaps he could edge closer to answers.

BIODYNAMICS AND BEYOND

The organic farming of grapes came up in California at the same time as organics for other crops, in the late 1970s and early 1980s, at which point the back-to-the-landers had begun to question to what extent chemical farming was responsible for the state's bounty. Some old farmers had always farmed organically, but amid the 1970s coastal vineyard boom, there was little incentive to do so. But in 1979 California passed a legal definition of organic practices (even if it wasn't enforced), and soon early efforts at organic farming could be found in vineyards like Frog's Leap, which Larry Turley and John Williams founded in 1981. By 2012, at least 11,513 acres of vineyard were certified organic. But a federal bureaucratic muddle made it virtually impossible to qualify wine as "organic" unless, among other things, it completely avoided the use of the preservative sulfur dioxide. After a raft of flawed wines were produced in the 1970s and '80s, most wineries distanced themselves from the term, instead labeling their wines "made from organic grapes."

At the same time, biodynamic farming had taken hold in Europe, particularly in Austria and the Loire Valley. Eventually California took notice, and growers like Jim Fetzer of Mendocino's Fetzer family, who were pioneers in organics, implemented biodynamic practices by the late 1990s. Based on the teachings of Austrian philosopher Rudolf Steiner, biodynamics was often described as "beyond organic." But it was more a holistic system based upon two controversial precepts: the use of homeopathic preparations, like Preparation 501, which involves stuffing crushed quartz into a cow horn, burying it, and retrieving it months later to spray in a dilute solution; and a near-spiritual planning of farming activities around lunar phases, which is meant to maximize cosmic forces. Days are divided into four categories: root, leaf, flower, and fruit. You might pick on a fruit day, till the soil on a root day. These notions drew both praise and derision. The buried cow horn became skeptics' rallying symbol.

Organic grape farming was firmly in the mainstream by the mid-2000s, thanks to long-time vineyardists like Phil Coturri and consultants like "Amigo Bob" Cantisano. If once wineries avoided the organic label, large brands—notably Fetzer's Bonterra—found a growing market in organically grown wine, even amid worries in the larger farming world that organics had become industrialized, usurped by big business.

California's blank-slate nature offered promise, especially when compared to the overfarmed soils of Burgundy: "We have this opportunity to redefine what wine farming will be for the future. Those opportunities are gone for the great wine regions of Europe."

He knew he first needed to create "world-class compost." He not only wanted to fertilize the vines, but he wanted to do it with material that was unique to the site itself. This is why nearly half the Pivot's acreage is open fields, a rotational replanting of grasses and legumes ultimately designed for animals to forage. Manure is still trucked in—the Pivot is still a work in progress—but Lemon spends countless hours working it into compost, which is a nice way of saying that one of California's most honored winemakers occupies his days with cow shit.

Spend time with these notions for a while and Lemon's true mission comes into focus. Most grape growers would tell you they tend vines, a crop as reliant on human symbiosis as the apples

Biodynamics got major boosts when Fetzer and Sonoma's Benziger family, which had built the huge Glen Ellen brand, embraced its precepts on a wide scale. So did Bonny Doon's Randall Grahm, who even put his wines' "sensitive crystallizations" on labels, something that looked halfway between a kaleidoscope image and a rolled condom.

Steiner's original ideas had some rust on them, and not just because of their occasionally woo-woo nature, but also because Steiner himself, with his often mystical notions, had become as flawed a symbol as the cow horn. By the late 2000s there was tension over the role of Demeter, biodynamics' official US arbiter. In addition to establishing rigid standards for farming, Demeter, based in Philomath, Oregon, also tried to police the use of the word "biodynamics," sometimes sending missives to winemakers who used the term without being certified as adhering to their guidelines. And it charged a royalty fee for members to use the Demeter logo.

This created an opening for a growing number of uncertified biodynamicists. Demeter was unhappy, but their disgruntlement hardly detracted prominent growers like David Hirsch or Ted Lemon, who pursued "applied biodynamics," a path advocated in both Europe and the United States, notably by consultant Andrew Lorand. Lorand's approach focused on tailoring farming decisions to each site rather than adopting some of biodynamics' more rigid practices, particularly the use of the lunar calendar to govern vineyard work, a practice that Lemon finds too "mechanistic." Lorand's work also inspired a movement among a group of several of Austria's top vintners, Respekt, that meshed biodynamic principles with organic certification. Respekt's model has attracted increasing interest in California.

So has the research of UC Berkeley agronomist Miguel Altieri, who focused on holistic farming methods based on increasing biodiversity in the vineyard. Planting French prunes or wild blackberries, for instance, could attract a parasitic wasp that attacks grape leafhoppers. Similarly, a handful of Californian growers have been drawn to the work of Masanobu Fukuoka, the Japanese farmer-philosopher whose beliefs were often summed up as "do-nothing" farming but were in fact a light-touch approach, promoting permanent cover crops and less plowing of soil.

or marijuana that Michael Pollan described in *The Botany of Desire*. Much as Lemon loves his vines, he concluded that the plants are only a temporary part of good farming. Great and sustainable farming is ultimately learning to love the dirt below. "The dissociation with the love of the plants from the love of the dirt is what gets us in trouble," he says.

Lemon wanted to pursue the notion at the crux of biodynamics: the self-sustaining farm. Lemon grows most of the requisite herbs—nettles, chamomile, and so on—that are needed to make compost teas and preparations used for soil and plant health. Walk into his barn and you'll find them drying from the rafters. But he takes issue with the one-size-fits-all calendars and guidelines set out by Demeter, biodynamics' official certifying authority (see Biodynamics and Beyond, above), which has meant turning his back on officialdom in order to pursue a more customized path.

Although he irrigated early on to help the vines get established, the Pivot—like most of Lemon's vineyards—is now dry-farmed, without adding

Prudy Foxx at Lester Family Vineyard

water. This isn't simply stubbornness, although a stubborn stance toward water usage is probably a smart idea in California. Instead it's based in the belief that irrigation obscures the ability to understand the potential of the land. Because so few winemakers have a chance to farm for themselves, they often have little say in such things. "When you divorce the hand that controls the irrigation valve from the hand that makes the wine," Lemon tells me, "you've got a problem."

"YOU CAN DRINK THAT STUFF"

Lemon's is a privileged position. Few winemakers can afford to purchase and farm their own land. Instead, most find themselves in a subtle negotiation with landowners to get the farming they desire. Cover crops? Yeah, right. Organics? Get real.

The haggling is understandable given that growers have come to fear, more than anything, having their crops rejected—which is why they grew comfortable in the 1990s with requests for routine irrigation and ever-riper grapes and all the trappings of Big Flavor. Having become dependent on modern fail-safes, many are skittish about requests from the New Californians, upstarts who ask for less water on the crop, less sugar in the grapes, less fertilizer on the soils.

This becomes evident one day as I ride up the twists of Eureka Canyon Road in the forested hills near Corralitos, due east of Santa Cruz. Somewhere up here are two acres of Pinot Noir and another of Chardonnay, rediscovered by Prudy Foxx, Santa Cruz's eminent viticultural advisor. For about a decade the site, Legan, provided fruit to a winery in San Martin, which, I was told, farmed it hard and then walked away. Foxx thinks this parcel would be a good match for Duncan Meyers of Arnot-Roberts, who has come to take a look.

We hoof up the hill. The south-facing slope is steep, and Monterey Bay shimmers in the distance. But the vineyard is a bit of a patch job. One ten-foot cordon, or vine arm, thick as a wrestler's bicep, extends far down a row, taking up the space where another vine died—a casualty from years of farming for maximum yield. But Meyers is taken by the bay's moderating influence and the mix of native plants at the woods' edge, a hint at the complexity of the soils below. "This is going to be so exciting in five years."

Before long, however, things grow complicated. Antonio, a local vineyard manager, joins us. Immediately he asks Meyers what tonnage price he'll pay. (It's a bit early for such things, seeing as not one piece of fruit has been seen, not one wine from the vineyard tasted.) Perhaps $3,500? Meyers doesn't blink—it's a reasonable price—but he's more interested in how the vineyard will be farmed.

"We need to go in with the heavy artillery," Antonio says, a typical cocktail of herbicides like Roundup and antifungal sprays. Meyers winces. "If it's going to be full conventional," Meyers replies, "I probably don't want the fruit. I just want that on the table."

It turns out that bad weather had created serious mildew problems at Legan. Antonio's fruit was rejected; he has grown gun-shy. They discuss some less intrusive possibilities, perhaps a product like Surround, a bentonite clay–based product used to shield grapes from mildew. But Roundup, the great undiscussed factor in California, keeps lingering in the conversation. "You can drink that stuff," Antonio says.

"Well," Meyers replies, "that's what the Monsanto folks want you to think."

WATER WARS

In the 1970s California borrowed from Israeli water engineers a new system for irrigation. Drip emitters doled out water close to the vine roots, along tubes that allowed for far stingier water use than the old methods. Previously, if you wanted to water your vines, you needed either overhead sprinklers or ground furrows, neither particularly efficient at trapping moisture in the soil through California's dry summers.

Even in 1973, wine researcher A. J. Winkler acknowledged that many of the best vineyard sites near the coast, with soils deep enough to trap winter rainfall, could function without additional water. And irrigation was a relatively rare practice across the North Coast, at least in part because extra water was scarce.

"When we planted our vineyard in 1974, drip was just coming in—no one in Sonoma County carried drip hose yet," recalled onetime Sonoma grower Terry Harrison in a 2011 presentation. "Prior to that, practically all wine grapes in the North Coast were dry-farmed. The main reason for irrigating, as I remember it, was to get better yields. That is great for the Central Valley, which is hotter and drier, but is not what we want here."

With the advent of drip irrigation, more growers began to irrigate their vineyards simply because they could (drip required far less water per acre). Soon enough, especially as vineyards were replanted, California's coastal vineyards began to be veined by a seemingly endless supply of irrigation hoses.

In the late 1980s, growers realized that they could manipulate the ripeness of their fruit through deficit irrigation. By starting out stingy and watering later, between the coloring of grapes known as veraison and harvest, they could boost ripening during a final stretch. In other words, by parching the vine early, it would grow more efficiently at the season's end.

Even in the mid-twentieth century, it was known that grapevines were deep-rooted plants, able to explore the soil to a depth of thirty feet or more. But irrigation was a matter of managing the first few feet. "Where good irrigation water is available and carefully managed, grapes are being grown successfully on soils less than 2 feet deep," Winkler wrote in 1973.

Because drip is applied at the surface directly above the root, it tends to draw the root environment closer to the surface. This has the effect of making the vines, which otherwise might drive their roots deep into the subsoil in search of more water and nutrients, largely dependent on the first few feet. In turn, this makes them more reactive to sudden changes in temperature, or to drought.

Tegan Passalacqua has been on a crusade against unnecessary irrigation for years. One day he takes me up to the Mead Ranch Vineyard, in the hills above Napa near Atlas Peak. Its Zinfandel vines were dry-farmed for a century by the Meads, until they opted to install irrigation, as many landowners were counseled to do in the 1980s. That rapidly led to soil degradation and problems with nematodes, tiny worms that can strangle a vine by feeding on its roots. By the time Turley Wine

Cellars began using Mead in 2001 for its Old Vines Zinfandel, nematodes were drawn to the water and were devastating the shallow-rooted vines.

It was a relatively easy fix. Damaged vines got replanted while others were deprived of their constant drink. The vines were watered by hand twice in the first year—just like giving a dry garden its long drink—and not again.

"Irrigation, I think, is the biggest issue in California," Passalacqua says. But that's a tough message to spread. When Passalacqua suggested dry farming at a meeting of vineyardists from the Carneros region, which straddles Napa and Sonoma Counties and gets twenty-three inches of rainfall annually, "these growers were looking at me like I was some asshole."

California's biggest worry on this front is that its growing season is typically bone-dry, with rainfall all but halting by June. But grapevines have adapted to some of the driest places on earth. In an extreme, there's the Greek island of Santorini, where Assyrtiko vines subsist on just a few inches of water annually. But there are also the chalky coastal stretches of Spain's Andalusia, where sherry has been made for centuries on just over twenty inches of rain per year. Sunny stretches of southern France subsist on about twenty-four inches of rain annually—a good analogue for many parts of California. And they have a tradition of farming without irrigation (seeing as it's illegal in many French appellations).

Which explains Passalacqua's crusade. In his view, irrigation is a lazy solution, even in many mountain vineyards whose owners swear by it. It's a bit like a stage mom, rushing vines along and depriving them of the extended adolescence they need to mature for a decades-long life. If vines in most Turley vineyards need a drink, Passalacqua and his workers water by bucket. And he has repeated this practice over and over again throughout the state, from Lodi to Paso Robles to the Sierras. "To me," he says, "irrigation was just a way to increase yields."

Certainly dry farming is feasible where water is abundant, in places like the remote Precious Mountain Vineyard on the Sonoma Coast, which can receive up to eighty inches of rain annually. But it is also practiced in Paso Robles, on sites like the Benito Dusi Vineyard, which has existed without irrigation since 1925. Farther south, in arid Riverside County, old vines grow without irrigation in Rancho Cucamonga, with just eight inches of annual rainfall.

At Dominus Estate in Yountville, Christian Moueix has long been on a campaign against irrigation. This dates back to his first efforts at adapting Napanook, the historic vineyard site on which grapevines were first planted in Napa by George Yount in 1836. "My first sentence was, 'I will need twenty years to make a good wine,'" Moueix recalls. "My second sentence was, 'I will make a wine without irrigation or acidification, or I won't make my wine.' For us it's just common sense."

No small statement coming from Moueix, whose family also happens to control Château Pétrus, home to the world's most expensive Bordeaux. Because Napanook sits on a relatively deep and fertile fan of alluvial soils, Moueix and his technical director, Tod Mostero, decided they not only didn't need more water, but in fact needed to drain away excess winter moisture to slow vine growth.

"I have seen in this valley irrigation while they were picking," Moueix says. "What do you expect then? It brings a green character. They think it compensates for alcohol, it lowers the alcohol. Not at all. The problem of irrigation is that the roots in a plant tend to remain superficial. When the roots are superficial, you don't get terroir. It's nice, it's pleasant, it's sugary maybe. But you don't get depth. It's not a terroir wine. It could be done in a nursery almost."

Moueix retained a company called Fruition Sciences, run by two young Frenchmen, Thibaut Scholasch and Sebastien Payen, that reconceived the sort of data-based water management first seen in the early 1980s. The two weren't insistent on dry farming, but they deduced not only that too much water is used in California, but also that poor water management both adds cost to winemaking and can diminish quality. Dilution in grapes can create weaker aromas, while the high sugars demanded for a ripe style of wine require both an unhealthily low vine yield and extra water to try and resuscitate a plant that has essentially signaled it is done ripening, to say nothing of more water and acid added in the winery to correct the wine's chemistry.

Scholasch and his partner measure the flow of sap in vines using a heated sleeve, much like a blood pressure cuff, and combine it with other soil and weather data to create a baseline for water use. Their discovery? Even many water-stingy farmers were still overwatering. To start the season with a long drink, or to maintain regular irrigation, has "the vine behaving like a junkie," as Scholasch puts it.

So Scholasch revised downward old assumptions about water needs. He posits that in much of California, eight to sixteen inches of annual rainfall should suffice, even with a typical dry summer. In some cases Fruition reduced wineries' water usage by 80 percent or more—150 swimming pools worth at one thirty-acre vineyard alone. These are important changes, not just for California generally, but specifically for some areas like the Coombsville area east of Napa, where failing wells have led to drastic water restrictions.

The practicalities of limiting water use notwithstanding, there is a philosophical reason for weaning a vineyard away from irrigation. One reason that Europeans limit the use of water is their belief that it can obscure a site's true signature. If you rely on routine watering, David Hirsch suggests, you're not truly expressing terroir. Rather, "you're just gardening."

FARMING AGAINST THE SUN

Sun is California's backbone, its defining trait. So the most important battle in farming California wine grapes is determining how to manage the sun, how to use it to the best advantage. Achieving moderate ripeness levels is rarely an issue, except in colder years like 2011, when the challenge was to shift farming practices to the more European goal of absorbing every bit of sunlight. But in most years the smart money is on trying to protect vines from an overabundance of photosynthesis.

California has been grappling with this issue for decades, well before Australian vineyard researcher Richard Smart began spreading the gospel of canopy management in the early 1990s. What's the trick? Mostly to stop thinking about farming as though you're in northern Europe. Cover crops must be employed not just for soil health but to create competition with the vine; irrigation typically must be drastically reduced; roots need extra annual growth cycles to drive farther down.

These things raise the hackles of those who adhere to more standard industry beliefs—like the notion that a vineyard should be ready to produce commercial-quality grapes after three years. (Most

plantings in Europe aren't used in top wines until about fifteen years of age, and for good reason.) Elsewhere in the world such haste might be considered disrespectful of the terroir; in California, the rush to establish is a point of pride, an ecological extension of manifest destiny.

It has become a frequent pastime to draw comparisons between California's climates and those of northern Europe, even though California's latitudes—and thus the overhead sun—are more similar to those of Barcelona and Casablanca. Of course, the influence of the nearby Pacific complicates such comparisons, and some spots within a few miles of the Pacific coast do parallel the relative chill of Europe's finer growing areas. Parts of the Sonoma Coast and Santa Cruz Mountains, for instance, struggle to reach the same 2,200 degree-days Fahrenheit of heat found in Burgundy's Côte d'Or. But it's hard to use Europe as a benchmark, not only because of difference in latitude, but also because of different rain patterns, peak harvest temperatures, and particularly the extended late-season summer that California enjoys well into October. "We have an extra month," as Kevin Harvey of Rhys Vineyards, one of California's most astute students of climate comparison, puts it. "We have two Septembers."

There is a need, then, to modulate the sun as much as harness it. It might not be as dire as winemaker Ehren Jordan put it to me a few years ago—"California," he said, "is more like Tunisia"—but the sun can be as much enemy as friend. Indeed, when Winkler and his fellow UC Davis researcher Maynard Amerine laid out climate regions in 1943, they were not optimistic about areas that they categorized as Region III on Winkler's scale, a designation that now encompasses much of Napa and Sonoma. "It is a mistake to hope to produce dry wines of the

Rhys viticulturalist Javier Meza

finest quality every year in this region," they wrote, "even on the less fertile soils, since the summation of heat is usually too great."

A bit harsh, perhaps. It may have been the case that they were preoccupied with the fine wines of northern Europe, like the German-native white varieties popular in Napa for much of the twentieth century. But perhaps, as Ted Lemon suggests, "they should have been going to the southern half of Italy or Spain."

The state had its own effective system of vine training decades ago, one first affectionately and then pejoratively called "California sprawl." A vine's long canes would run along a trellis and then flop over, the fruit dangling below in dappled shade. But midcentury vineyard experts wanted something more orderly than sprawl. Their inspiration? Northern Europe, of course. It didn't take long before the Guyot system of vine training, in which vertically grown canes sprout up from a horizontally laid vine cordon, became as common in California as it was in Bordeaux and Burgundy.

Not only did the Guyot system and its variations offer the grapes far more sun exposure, but they also created a vertical wall of leaves that could be worked, often by machine—a setup with distinct appeal to California's efficiency-minded industry. Besides, this approach made fine wines in France, and France was still the pinnacle of refinement. So why wouldn't it be right for California?

This system, which would be fine-tuned into a method called vertical shoot positioning, soon became a widespread practice in the state's better vineyards, especially after it became clear how easily drip irrigation lines could be run along their tidy rows.

But the harvest cycle today is different than it was midcentury. The growing season has lengthened by several weeks. Forty years ago bud break was typically in April; now it's in March. The threat of early October frosts has diminished; fall rains often arrive a few weeks later. Combine these changes with the views on farming that became prevalent by the '70s—aggressively handling young vines with methods conceived for sun-deprived France—and it becomes evident that the Big Flavor school of viticulture was hinged as much on flawed beliefs about California's climate as it was on a deliberate hunt for ripeness.

"People say, no, it has everything to do with the winemaker and the styles of wine and the raters," Gregory Jones, a professor and climate researcher at Southern Oregon University, and one of the most prominent voices to discuss climate change in wine, tells me. "What they don't understand is that in the 1960s and '70s the climates weren't conducive to the kind of hang times that they have today. You couldn't have hung fruit in California fifty years ago for as long as they do today."

Jones not only redid the climate-region work of Winkler and Amerine—finding, for instance, that Russian River Valley is the warmest region on earth producing fine Pinot Noir—but also famously sounded a warning that climate shifts could imperil some of the world's best growing regions. (The Napa Valley Vintners organization, not pleased with those findings, commissioned their own climate study, one that found a small warming trend, primarily at night, but concluded there was no dramatic rise.) Jones also looked at long-term data and concluded that, among other things, the average climate in California wine's formative years was far more moderate than it has become; Napa Valley, for instance, had gained 605 degree-days Fahrenheit in the growing season between 1930 and 2002.

Jones discovered one other crucial fact: the climates of the western United States, at least as pertain to wine, bear almost no resemblance to those anywhere else on earth. (The closest analogue might be Chile.) With Bordeaux viticulturist Kees van Leeuwen, Jones conceived models of climate suitability for wine grapes that seemed to work everywhere but the West Coast. Their conclusion? Many of Davis's climate suppositions, and the viticulture lessons adopted from Europe, simply didn't apply. Diurnal temperature swings in California, for instance, are far greater than those in most of the Old World. California has not only sun but also intense daytime heat that propels ripening (and can, with less intensive farming, make a place like Napa almost magical for grapes).

"Get off a plane in Bordeaux and you sweat, and get off a plane in Napa and you don't," Jones continues. "We can ripen varieties to similar quality characteristics, but they're different. Bordeaux does what it does in a shorter growing season, with higher nighttime temperatures and lower daytime temperatures, and rain during the growing season. Napa has these high daytime temperatures and low nighttime temperatures, and growth goes to almost nothing at night. Everything grows during the day."

How to compensate for the different growing conditions? The easiest way might be to grow a bigger or more sprawling vine than you would in a colder place, spreading photosynthesis across more surface area to slow down or divert growth and ripening. That might entail a bushier leaf canopy, which is then hedged as grape clusters begin the coloring process, known as veraison, a move that retards sugar production and prolongs the ripening process. It could be as simple as growing an extra cane, or kicker cane, on the vine, which diverts carbohydrates and growth from other parts of the plant before being cut off as the fruit completes its ripening. (I once witnessed a version of this in a sprawling San Joaquin Valley vineyard, where monster canes, often eight or ten feet long, are used to absorb sunlight before being cut as the fruit reaches maturity.)

In some ways this is little more than a tidy reinterpretation of California sprawl. Wider trellis crossarms—which spread out leaf canopies and create longer, arched canes—are creating more uniform growth and higher yields, even on high-yield grapes grown industrially in Lodi or the Sacramento River delta. "I'm thinking that is turning into the trellis of choice for a lot of us," says Ernie Dosio, a major farmer of San Joaquin grapes.

Modern tools can also temper the sun's impact. Stephy Terrizzi of Paso Robles's Luna Matta Vineyard, for instance, applies Surround, the kaolin clay powder more typically used for mildew, to prevent sunburn, using it as a sort of grape sunscreen.

Further south, in Santa Barbara County, Mike Roth of Martian Ranch grows white grapes like Albariño and Grenache Blanc at soaring yields, up to nine tons per acre, before cutting away perhaps half the fruit in the last couple of weeks before harvest. This counters prevailing wisdom: it's thought that thinning grapes after their seeds harden is a waste, and that you'd need to sacrifice three-quarters of your fruit to get any sugar bump. But what if your goal is the opposite, to avoid too much sugar?

FROM THEORY TO PRACTICE

"All these little things seem small and yet cumulatively are really powerful," says Bart Araujo as we traverse a block of Cabernet in his Eisele Vineyard. Along with us are his wife, Daphne, their vineyard manager, Caleb Mosley (a Monte Bello veteran), and Steve Matthiasson, who consults on the vineyard.

In 1990 the Araujos bought the Eisele Vineyard, but this spot in the northern Napa town of Calistoga had first been planted in 1886, and in recent decades proved itself as a source for excellent Cabernet. Calistoga isn't exactly a cool place, with up to 3,600 degree-days Fahrenheit during the growing season, making it a Region IV on Winkler's scale (although Winkler, in more temperate times, designated it Region III). While sun here is abundant, Eisele sits at the confluence of two watersheds that help modulate the ripeness of the grapes. It thrives on a complex intermingling of soils, an agglomeration of cobbles, loam, and coarse sand. Every year it yields a profound, dark-fruited Cabernet with particularly fine tannins.

The Araujos knew they had acquired a historic place. At a time when the obvious Napa play was to farm for dramatic ripeness, they chose a more radical option. Realizing that top estates, like Burgundy's Domaine de la Romanée-Conti, insisted on organic and biodynamic practices, the couple converted to biodynamics, rejecting the vague brushstrokes of sustainable farming that are associated with so much of California. Theirs may be the only winery to hire both superconsultant Michel Rolland and to have once joined Renaissance des Appellations, a vintners' group founded by the high prelate of biodynamics, Loire vintner Nicolas Joly.

"One day I woke up and said, 'Wait, that's such a cop-out,'" Bart explained. "What does sustainable mean? It means I get to farm as close to organic as possible, but if I get scared, I can nuke anything I want."

Eisele tends to have slightly more abundant yields per acre than many of its counterparts— "three point eight tons," Mosley reads off a sheet as we stand in a block of Merlot. Mosley and Matthiasson laid extra canes over adjacent vines to create partial afternoon shade. They also widened the trellis crossarms, creating a bushier, more exposed canopy that allows more indirect sunlight through the middle of the vine. And they typically leave fourteen leaves per shoot—low for Napa—to slow photosynthesis. (Even so, at times, Araujo still finds itself flirting with Big Flavor ripeness.)

They planted more cover crops between vines to increase competition for soil nutrients. Given the estate's meticulous ways, this entailed the use of thirteen different blends of plants, each chosen for a mixture of soil health and the ability to attract beneficial insects. Umbelliferous flowers, or those with umbrella-like blooms—plants like yarrow, wild carrot, and Queen Anne's lace—draw tiny predatory wasps, for instance. They also sought out native species like California buckwheat over invasive ones like wild fennel.

This work to increase vineyard biodiversity is increasingly crucial as California slowly accepts that its wine country is too often a patchwork of monocultures. Recent findings, including work by UC Davis researcher John Williams, show distinct benefits for vineyards that incorporate native vegetation, including better water quality and better carbon sequestration.

"I honestly don't know how many people are crazy enough to go to the lengths that we are," Matthiasson told me. "But we're producing a luxury good. And we can control about 50 percent of the inputs. So I think we have to be maniacal about controlling what we can."

THE QUIET RADICAL

Over the years Matthiasson has become the thinking man's viticulturalist. In 2006 he was hired by one of Napa's most thoughtful types, Warren Winiarski of Stag's Leap Wine Cellars, not for his hard-and-fast answers but for his willingness to avoid them. "The people I work with," Matthiasson tells me, "like gray areas."

To get to his house I drive through a nondescript part of the city filled with tour-bus parking and ball fields, the plumbing of the real Napa. An open gate sits between two houses in a subdivision. I turn in and drive down a tree-lined gravel driveway, which leads to the farmhouse where Matthiasson lives with his wife, Jill Klein Matthiasson.

Here the Matthiassons enjoy a back-to-land existence. They produce much of their own food, tending nectarine and avocado trees as well as a flock of chickens that are constantly trying to escape. Come to dinner and you're likely to be served an elk chop that Steve either hunted or bartered for, as well as grilled peaches from Jill's orchards. (She sells fruit at the Napa farmers' market and makes jam for loyal customers.)

They may be settled in Napa, but there's something innately midwestern about the Matthiassons' pace of life, which makes sense given that Steve was born in Winnipeg and regularly visited his family's farms in Manitoba and North Dakota. After a punk-rock phase, he studied philosophy at Whittier College and then migrated to San Francisco. He

worked as a bike messenger, rode in the first Critical Mass ride in 1992 to protest for cyclists' rights, and spent his free time skateboarding and volunteering at community gardens before studying agricultural development at UC Davis. That led to an internship in Merced, California, where he monitored insects and earthworms as part of a sustainable orchard program. There, in 1994, he met Jill, who was an organizer for a community alliance that connected small farms to urban markets. A month after they started dating they made their first wine together in a garage.

Steve launched his own consulting firm and was soon hired by the Lodi-Woodbridge Winegrape Commission to help develop their sustainable farming program. The result, Lodi Rules, became the model for similar efforts statewide (see Sustainability, page 58). But both Steve and Jill longed to be closer to the coast, and in 2002 they set up shop in Napa. Quickly Steve collected a roster of blue-chip clients, including not only Winiarski but also Spottswoode, David Arthur, and Saintsbury. His serene demeanor—North Dakota?—allows the sandy-haired Matthiasson to get away with a sort of subtle daring in his advice. I suspect that some of this dates back to San Francisco, where the quietude of volunteer gardening tempered his punk days.

In 2005 Steve joined wine veteran George Vare on a trip to Friuli (see Finding Friuli, page 242), a trip that cemented Matthiasson's belief that

In place of specific organic or biodynamic standards, a growing number of California grape growers in the mid-2000s began to adopt guidelines for "sustainability," efforts meant to reward those who found a full conversion too costly or impractical.

In principle, these efforts—not unlike France's *lutte raisonée* movement—advocated farming improvements such as less use of chemicals in the field, the improvement of soil health, and the use of more natural fertilizers. Many were born out of the integrated pest management program implemented by UC Davis, which sought less intrusive means of pest control. The Lodi area was early to the game with its Lodi Rules program, first implemented in 2005, which included the state's first third-party viticultural audits. A similar effort from the Central Coast Vineyard Team, SIP Certified, was built around point-based self-evaluations.

Such programs, which bore consumer-friendly names like Napa Green, were often pitched as broader in scope than organics. Fair enough: they often included standards for the treatment of vineyard workers, biodiversity, and energy usage, topics not addressed in organic standards. But some also adhered to stubborn beliefs about the best choices for wine quality and vineyard health (points might be deducted if you regrafted your own uncertified heritage vines, for instance) and often skirted key issues like overall vineyard size. No matter how impeccable the farming, how sustainable could one thousand contiguous vineyard acres be?

The most profound loophole, however, remained the use of synthetic chemicals, particularly the weed killer glyphosate, better known by its brand name, Roundup. California growers had a seemingly bottomless addiction to the stuff. Banishing its use was a nonstarter for most sustainability programs.

The biggest sustainability muddle came from the California Association of Winegrape Growers and the Wine Institute, whose guidelines were unveiled with great fanfare in 2010. The program's initial standards set a remarkably low bar, as they allowed the use of soil fumigants and widespread use of herbicides. This was an attempt at a big-tent approach that would allow many to participate in the program, but it also provided a cloak of sustainability for the industrial practices of many growers.

Loopholes in many sustainability programs led to talk of "greenwashing." But the larger problem was that their criteria often seemed out-of-date, half measures designed to preserve the status quo. Even as some of the world's finest wine estates embraced biodynamics, big farming could hardly be convinced to reform its use of chemical fertilizers or strip-sprayed herbicides.

physical ripeness could be achieved in California grapes without dramatic sugar levels. Picking could occur far earlier. Now his Cabernet- and Merlot-based reds are typically aging in barrel by the time his neighbors are harvesting. As he rarely appears anywhere without a set of pruning shears, his advice is certainly informed by time in the field.

But that doesn't mean his fellow Napans listen. The fall of 2012 brought a picture-perfect harvest after two cold years, with the promise of wines with ripe flavors at 13 percent alcohol. Yet vintners kept telling Matthiasson they needed to wait, crossing their fingers for a year of 15 percent wonders. "You can't believe it, but the winemaker mantra this year is that sugars aren't high enough to pick," he wrote me. "It's sort of like they got knocked off the horse two years in a row, and they are desperate to climb back on and reaffirm their place as the makers of the best overdone wines in the world."

"It's like a mass hypnosis," he continued, "insane. This year has the potential to be once in a decade— dry spring, long season, no heat spikes or rain, a heavy crop that's moderating sugars—and it's getting screwed up by winemakers trying to make it into something that it's not."

"A DEFEAT OF MY PHILOSOPHY"

Still, Matthiasson has powerful allies. At Dominus, Christian Moueix is on a crusade to keep vines from irrational exuberance. His vineyards yield about four tons per acre, slightly higher than at Château Pétrus. But in Bordeaux he has, on average, twice as many vines planted per acre. Each vine in California grows more than twice as much fruit as its French counterpart—an effective, and profitable, means of governing ripeness.

Like Matthiasson, Moueix is a critic of another frequent tactic to maximize sunlight: removing extra leaves as fruit matures. This can prevent disease and mildew, but it also can expose fruit to direct sun and spike sugar levels. The threat of disease in humid Europe makes leafing common. But midseason leafing in California can be disastrous, as it was in 2010, when growers worried about a lagging vintage pulled leaves in midsummer, just in time for their delicate grapes to be walloped by a brutal heat wave. "You don't deleaf on July 15," Moueix says. "It's like . . . the British going on the French Riviera and getting sunburned."

There are alternatives. Trimming away the leaves early, just as grape berries are developing, can protect them by creating tougher skin, like building a tan. Napa's John Kongsgaard typically does this for his Chardonnay. But higher yields, as Moueix has deduced, might be the most potent tool for managing the California sun—an approach not much different from that used in the 1970s (although with better farming).

Lest you think Moueix's idea is new, vineyard manager Rafael Rodriguez, who oversaw farming at Inglenook in the 1950s and '60s, recalls routinely harvesting Cabernet around 22 Brix in late September. Vines were pruned and trellised in a less effective manner than they are today, of course, trimmed early in the season for a moderate crop. The lack of efficiency in that era was certainly less deliberate than Moueix's modern approach, but it had a similar effect—as a natural damper on ripeness.

By the 1990s the winemakers at what had become the Niebaum-Coppola Winery had adopted a very different philosophy. Rodriguez recalls being appalled when he witnessed the farming of that era: growing a heavy crop early in the season, then cutting at least half the grapes away to "put the vine in shock"—thus spurring a final burst of Big Flavor ripeness.

"To me," Rodriguez continues, "it was a defeat of my philosophy personally. It made me cry when I saw those fields loaded with grapes . . . and just a few little bunches left. I said, 'What the hell? You are throwing money away to the ground.'"

The Secret Life of Grapes

What grows best in a land of plenty? It's an uncomfortable question in California, a state that has invested heavily in Cabernet Sauvignon and Chardonnay, and thus has convinced itself of those grapes' widespread viability. It's particularly uncomfortable if you're standing in the Library Vineyard, which wraps around St. Helena's public library.

A rangy patch of old head-trained vines, Library is exactly what its name connotes: a collection of historically significant, and increasingly rare, grape specimens. The Library is typically considered to contain Petite Sirah, but an ampelography (vine identification) project headed by Carlisle Winery's Mike Officer used DNA testing to uncover a wide array of different grape varieties on which the pre-Prohibition California wine industry was built. The vineyard includes Syrah, Alicante Bouschet, and Trousseau, but also archaic grapes like Aramon and Peloursin, whites like Chasselas and Monbadon, and even some mystery grapes. Originally owned by the Jackse family, which helped found

Napa's original wine co-op after Prohibition, it now belongs to the city of St. Helena, and since 2001 it has been leased and organically farmed by Turley Wine Cellars. However, it functions something like a city park; locals often walk their dogs right through on the way to the nearby Napa River. To ensure the vineyard's genetics are preserved, Turley planted a two-acre replica of the Library's mix of vines on its property just north of town.

Tegan Passalacqua is showing me around. He leads me over to a stunted vine with a few lingering clusters of bright green grapes. We pick a few. It's one of the last remaining vines in Napa Valley, and probably anywhere in California, of Green Hungarian, a grape of eastern European provenance that had a brief jag of popularity as a midcentury table wine, made by popular labels like Souverain and Wente.

"Is that the first time you've tasted Green Hungarian?" he asks.

Well, of course. Though well past its peak ripeness, it's still tart, like a slightly underripe Asian pear.

Farther east, toward the river, there's an old abandoned white-grape vineyard tucked behind a line of walnut trees. The vines have been ignored, yet branches with dessicated clusters crawl along the ground. We drive to the other side of the parcel and find the same—only this time there are black grapes, most unidentifiable but clearly belonging to an old bushy planting. Vines being vines, they have woven themselves amid the scrubby trees so that clusters seem to hang from tree branches. What are they? God only knows.

We hop back in the car and drive down the narrow lane toward Highway 29. A police cruiser passes us, stops, and wheels around to follow at a snail's pace. Passalacqua quickly flips on his headlights in the coming dusk.

"How funny would it be," he asks, glancing in the rearview mirror, "if we got booked for performing ampelography?"

WHAT TO PLANT

Farming wine grapes in California has long been complicated by one particular factor: *Vitis vinifera*, the species of grape used to make most fine wine, is in no way native to North America. This means that wine grapes grown here are inherently alien, although they have adapted well enough. That immigrant status would ultimately be of great benefit, since the grafting of European *V. vinifera* vines to native American rootstock helped to beat back the scourge of phylloxera, which devastated vines around the world in the nineteenth century. But from the moment that the first Spanish missionaries brought with them the Mission grape, planting it up and down their mission trail, Californians have been struggling to answer the question of which vines truly belong here.

The nineteenth-century scramble to answer that question reached a high point with the work of E. W. Hilgard in the late 1880s and early 1890s. Hilgard, in charge of the state's agricultural experiment stations, along with a team that included Frederic Bioletti, his trusty foreman and later an influential professor of viticulture, coordinated the planting of a wide range of European grapes across the state, everything from Italian Refosco to French Cabernet Franc. What followed was a burst of extraordinary experimentation, the results of which were published in a series of reports that detailed precisely how various wine grapes grew, both in farmers' fields and in seven experimental vineyards spread through the state. One of those plantings, near the town of Jackson, in Amador County southeast of Sacramento, would become a motherlode of genetic material for everything from Cabernet Sauvignon to Trousseau.

Hilgard's work provides an encyclopedic look at what is and what might have been. If you wondered how the Piemontese grape Freisa fared in Cupertino ("agreeable and vinous flavor, and clean taste") or Grenache managed in Fresno ("quality poor for dry wine"), Hilgard knew. Perhaps more importantly, he and his fellow researchers began to assess which grapes might be appropriate for California's wine industry. Merlot, for instance, was "a very uncertain bearer, and its use is advisable only in locations protected from hot winds and under commercial conditions that promise adequate reward for high quality."

Even then, Hilgard and his counterparts knew that what lay in the fields often wasn't what it seemed. Until the advent of DNA testing, ampelography, or the classification of grapevines, was an inexact science (see Hunting a Vine's Identity, at right). He was, for instance, confounded by the puzzling range of grapes bundled under the term "Burgundy," which included Crabb's Black Burgundy (actually the Italian grape Refosco) and Chauché Noir (likely some form of Trousseau).

Which is not to say that California's winemakers were awaiting clarity to forge ahead. In 1896, as Hilgard was publishing his work, the French expatriate Paul Masson was busy planting cuttings of Pinot Noir and Chardonnay imported from France on his hilltop vineyard in the Santa Cruz Mountains. Hilgard's would-be rival, Charles Wetmore, head of the state's viticultural commission, was busy planting his own vineyard, Cresta Blanca, in Livermore, using cuttings from lauded French origins, including Sauvignon Blanc from

HUNTING A VINE'S IDENTITY

Recent DNA testing has helped to confirm the lineages of many wine grapes that, until recent years, were otherwise simply conjecture or tales passed from farmer to farmer. The most famous grape whose mysterious identity was solved is California's beloved Zinfandel. Its origin myths proliferated for the better part of a century, but it most likely arrived on the East Coast in the early 1800s and, like so many thirsty fortune seekers, made its way west with the Gold Rush.

Only in 2002 did geneticist Carole Meredith finally identify it as a Croatian cultivar, Crljenak Kaštelanski, identical to Italian Primitivo, which in turn was ultimately matched to the ancient grape Tribidrag (see Zin's Mystery, page 258).

In recent years, and mostly thanks to Meredith's development of a DNA database of grapes at UC Davis, clear links between California and the Old World have finally begun to be untangled. "If you have a mystery grape here in California," she explains, "and you want to know what it is, you're limited to how many grapes you can compare it to." By the time she left Davis, the database encompassed about six hundred varieties, and it has since expanded. But mysteries remain, in part because grapes can occasionally mutate in the wild.

Château d'Yquem and Cabernet from Château Margaux.

Just thirty years earlier, the prospect of trading out Mission vines for finer European varieties had been novel. But after pioneers like Agoston Haraszthy carried grape specimens back from abroad to help spark California's wine industry, the late nineteenth century witnessed a diversity of European *V. vinifera* flourishing and spreading through California. In a sort of viticultural mashup, some—such as Zinfandel, Carignane, Alicante Bouschet, and the like—were often thrown together in a single vineyard to create the field blends preferred by the Italian settlers of the time. German immigrants sought out not just Riesling but also Gewürztraminer, Sylvaner, and less noble fare like Palomino and Burger to make wines reminiscent of those from their homeland.

So when Trousseau, Grüner Veltliner, or Verdelho are described today as radical new additions to California, remember that all of them were part of Hilgard's catalog of vineyard bounty before essentially being forgotten through the long years of Prohibition. After Prohibition, the state's growers viewed their vineyards through a stark prism of productivity. Amid a hunt to find better—or at least more productive—versions of Cabernet and Chardonnay, the diversity of the field rapidly faded. This lead to what vine researcher Carole Meredith calls "a genetic bottleneck," with a wide proliferation of just a handful of cultivars.

Yet even as UC Davis was making value judgments in the 1960s about what California wine should consist of—for example, Grüner Veltliner, "only fair in quality," wasn't endorsed for planting, while more obscure Roter Veltliner was—it was clear that many grapes from the nineteenth century had quietly survived in the fields. It is worth wondering what might have been if not for the trauma of America's failed noble experiment.

THE CLONE WARS

It is heartening, then, to see just how murky the history of California's vines has been, with case after case of mistaken genetic identity. Hilgard confronted this even in the 1800s—surmising, for instance, that Pinot St. Georges (probably Negrette) was distinct from Pinot Jura, which in fact was likely Pinot Meunier. Even when a grape's identity has been confirmed, its origins on these shores are rarely easy to trace. How did a particular variety get here? How did it spread across the state? The more that vintners insist they've found the answers, the more elusive those answers prove to be.

Consider the convoluted history of Chardonnay, a grape propagated by Masson in the 1890s, and by Charles Wetmore, who was planting cuttings from Meursault, in Burgundy, on his Livermore Valley property in the 1880s, and then by the Wente family of Livermore, who first brought over their own cuttings from France in 1912. They later would tout the prevalence of the so-called Wente clone throughout California, though in fact the evolution of the vine had created not one but many Wente clones. And most of those had taken winding paths through the state—replanted from vineyard to vineyard, their growing habits adapting and changing over the years. When a farmer today talks of "Wente clone Chardonnay," it covers a wide range of plant material with very different characteristics in the fruit.

Davis did attempt to bring some order to the process. In the late 1960s, it released two popular Chardonnay clones, known as 4 and 5, both of which were based on a Wente selection taken from Louis Martini's Stanly Ranch Vineyard in 1964 by Davis grape breeder Harold Olmo. Occasionally they made very good wine, although in 1990 Gerald Asher wrote, "Winemakers have sometimes been leery of these Davis clones, believing that their healthy yield capacity is at cross-purposes with quality."

One crucial trait had been isolated: these clones were hardy and vigorous, perfect choices for a state

that was falling in love with this particular grape. In the 1960s, Chardonnay was still a side note—as late as 1968, its acreage didn't even warrant a line in the state's grape reports—but forty years later, with more than ninety thousand acres planted, it would be California's most prolific grape.

Pinot Noir's situation was even more tangled. Much of California's early Pinot material was sneaked in from France. Then, in the 1950s a clone from a viticultural station in Wädenswil, Switzerland, became prevalent on the West Coast. Later, cuttings taken from the vineyards of such pioneers as Joseph Swan, David Bruce, and Louis Martini made their way around California.

In 1987 and 1988, Oregon winegrowers and their counterparts at Oregon State University persuaded Raymond Bernard, a scientist at the Office National Interprofessionnel des Vins in Dijon, to share genetic material he had isolated in Burgundy. Nicknamed the Dijon clones by university staff, they soon made their way into California. Bernard had worked for years to isolate the most productive and hardy plant material in the Côte d'Or, disease-free vines that would ripen evenly and quickly, ensuring safety from late-season weather.

The Dijon clones quickly revolutionized the industry. Known by their original French numbers, such as 115, 667, 777, and 828, these offered just what California had been seeking in Pinot Noir: disease-free vines that ripened with regularity. Indeed, they became so pervasive by the 2000s that in 2008 Pinot expert Allen Meadows complained

The New California Wine

of "excessively narrow clonal selections." Noting that Pinot Noir is the most mutable of grapes (some geneticists might prefer the word "adaptable"), Meadows continued, "The bad news is that the average US pinot plantation is not 10 years old and even those that are have not yet reached full maturity, which the Burgundian experience would have us believe is a minimum of between 25 and 35 years of age. So, while time may be slowly solving the problem of excessive similarity between wines, in the meantime the fruit produced by these clones is not transparently revealing the true characters of your sites where they are planted."

In other words, the great historic purpose of Pinot Noir—to reveal the qualities of the place in which it was grown—was being obscured by a narrow genetic selection. But the problem with the Dijon clones wasn't their use; it was their overuse. Their ubiquity in new plantings through the 1990s, especially in richer soils in places like Russian River Valley, indeed created the sort of monotony that Meadows described.

TOO PERFECT?

Mostly, the Dijon clones were one of those too-perfect solutions. The promise of disease-free Pinot material was irresistible to California's official vine repository, UC Davis's Foundation Plant Services. FPS, as it is known, had little tolerance for the sort of passing around of vine material that was common in the 1970s and 1980s. Its staff viewed viruses as anathema to good farming, and it was their job to isolate vines, clean them up, and then distribute presumably disease-free material.

Like other research institutions, FPS could clean up a vine either by heat-treating a small sample to essentially cook out the disease, or else taking a shoot-tip culture, in which a tiny tip of the vine is cut and grown on sterile media, then propagated into a full specimen in the belief that viruses won't express themselves in just the tip. While the resulting material is presumably free of disease—"presumably" being the key word—many vintners remain unconvinced that these cleaned-up clones provide the same quality as plants reproduced in the field.

The result is an unofficial vine trade. In part, that involves importing so-called suitcase clones, vine cuttings smuggled in from abroad, typically from Europe. (Burgundy in particular is the target for such things, although Italy has become a source for those wanting obscure varieties like Ribolla Gialla without putting them through a three-year quarantine.) But there also is a steady unofficial traffic in heritage vine material. A vintner might obtain field cuttings of, say, Pinot that can be traced back to the old vines originally planted in California at places like Calera or Mount Eden Vineyards.

This practice stems from a reasonable logic: why not use vines that are suited to California, either through adaptation or human selection over the decades? Certainly Pinot Noir has existed in California more for than a century. Vineyard practices in Europe have begun to favor the process of *massale*, or mass selection, in which a diverse set of the best-performing vines from a vineyard are sampled and replicated in order to propagate the best collection of vine genetics in a specific site. The belief is that this genetic selection from the field will ultimately create a healthier vineyard, and more complex wine, than a narrow selection of nursery cuttings with an identical genetic makeup.

Yet the prevailing institutional wisdom, vigorously espoused by FPS director Deborah Golino and her staff, has been that plantings—and especially replantings—should always be done with certified vines, essentially hitting a genetic reset button. Propagate your own plants from the field? No way. "Using field selections can result in severely diseased vines and even the death of vines," she told one industry publication.

Of course, Golino is charged specifically with keeping California vines free of disease. So she dismisses the belief held by many winemakers that a disease like leaf roll virus, even if it serves to limit yields, can help vines resist water stress and potentially result in higher-quality wine. (Indeed, Golino and other Davis researchers planted a test vineyard to try to provide scientific evidence that virus-infected vines make inferior wine, although it was unclear how they would measure the subjective matter of wine quality.)

Needless to say, the stance of FPS tweaks more than a few growers. Davis's recommendations—get allegedly virus-free material and then replant, replant, replant—make sense if you're Big Wine, but such a cookie-cutter approach is often dismissed by top winemakers, who see the value in mass selection, of gathering the best vine cuttings, and then replicating them to preserve individual vineyards' genetic fingerprints, rather than have everyone use the same genetic material.

"Go to a talk by Deborah Golino or the USDA, or any of these virologists, and you're going to be afraid that if you walk down the streets of Sebastopol you're going to get AIDS. It's in the fucking air," says Ted Lemon, referring to the Sonoma County town where his own estate is situated. "You can't tell me that if we've been collecting wood in our vineyards for fifteen years that we're not in good shape in terms of virus. It's not going to express itself."

SIDING WITH HISTORY

Nowhere has this clonal revolt thrived more than in the Santa Cruz Mountains. Take the work at Rhys Vineyards, where owner Kevin Harvey is a true believer in heritage vine material. Even in his tiny quarter-acre Home Vineyard, a handful of Dijon picks are mixed with ten unofficial selections, at least some carried from Burgundy with the usual mysterious provenance. His dense Skyline Vineyard, on the ridgeline west of Los Gatos, is planted entirely from *massale* material.

Those vines thrive not far from Mount Eden Vineyards itself, in Saratoga, home to the Martin Ray plantings that have a direct lineage back to some of California's earliest importations of Chardonnay and Pinot Noir. It's no surprise that proprietor Jeffrey Patterson calls this a "mother vineyard," the source of the so-called Mount Eden clone of Pinot Noir, which itself traces back to Paul Masson's nearby historic winery.

The mountains are similarly a source for Cabernet heritage. Mount Eden's old Cabernet plantings have a lineage back to La Questa, the historic vineyard founded by San Francisco doctor Emmet Rixford in the 1880s. Rixford's vines in turn traced their history to the Bordeaux commune of Margaux.

There are several Cabernet selections with a similarly long lineage, like clone 6, rescued from the old Jackson station, or those replicated from the old Concannon plantings in Livermore. But the draw of La Questa has proved irresistible. When replanting the historic Monte Bello site, one of California's defining places for Cabernet, Ridge Vineyards eschewed the standard industry-blessed clones, instead focusing on historic selections like those from La Questa. Indeed, when Ridge acquired the site in 1959, the existing Cabernet vines planted in the late 1940s had come from the old Fountaingrove winery, founded in Sonoma in the 1880s.

At least four of those early specimens are now being cleaned up "to try to save a little bit more of the genetics," says David Gates, Ridge's vice president of viticulture. Ridge recently replanted portions of Monte Bello using, among other things, a version of La Questa treated to eradicate virus. There's also clone 2, a sort of ur-vine for California. Harold Olmo selected it through fieldwork in Oakville and Calistoga, as well as the Kunde property in Sonoma, but its lineage ultimately traces back to Châteaux Margaux and Lafite Rothschild in the nineteenth century.

In Calistoga, Bart and Daphne Araujo have a preference for unsanctioned *massale* propagations of the Cabernet vines indigenous to their Eisele Vineyard, a selection now dubbed the Eisele clone. That Cabernet, growing on the property at least since Milt and Barbara Eisele bought the property in 1969, has its own mysterious origins—you might be sensing a theme here—and it helped to make some of Napa's most memorable wines, both Ridge's legendary 1971 and many vintages from Joseph Phelps. "Joe Phelps called it 'the gold,'" Daphne recalls.

LIVING WITH VIRUS

And what of this trembling fear of virus in the field?

For sure, there are diseases that can be fatal not only to individual vineyards but also to entire wine regions. Eutypa dieback, which can hamper vine growth and ultimately kill off a vine, is a pervasive problem. But it is a fungal disease, spread by dead wood not only in vines but also in several tree species. Then there's Pierce's disease, which virtually wiped out the wine industry in the Temecula area outside Los Angeles and remains the industry's great terror. But it is carried by insects, the blue-green and the glassy-winged sharpshooter, and prevented by removing vegetation around vineyards and monitoring the shipment of grapes and nursery-grown vines.

Leaf roll virus—particularly two resilient new strains, v3 and v5—is California's other pervasive problem. The bright crimson color that sometimes appears across the state's vineyards might look picturesque, but in fact it's typically a sign of the virus being spread by both grape mealybugs and exotic vine mealybugs.

For all the fear of devastation, what is leaf roll's primary symptom? A gradual drop in vine productivity. It can be a kind of governor in young vines; older vineyards, which frequently manifest signs of leaf roll, often keep producing excellent fruit. "I have a lot of 125-year-old vines that have leaf roll in them that are doing great," says Ridge's David Gates.

Viruses like leaf roll are the primary reason that viticulturists are admonished to go to vine nurseries for clean genetic material. However, the presumably clean cuttings from nurseries often end up having virus as well. Vineyard consultant James Stamp is routinely hired by clients to check nursery increase blocks—planted to replicate certified vines—for the presence of viruses before they ever leave the nursery. In a sampling of nursery vines across the state, Stamp found virus in eighteen of sixty-eight increase blocks.

"This industry is full of disasters that occur on a regular basis, going back to phylloxera in 1989," he tells me. "I think it has to do with the fact that it's a monoculture. Things get planted rapidly without a lot of research and development."

Stamp is hardly a believer in living with virus, especially with the rise of new concerns like red leaf associated virus; he even advocates genetic modification to help eradicate vine diseases. But he also notes that grapevine breeding is less controlled, and more disease prone, than with some other crops, like potatoes, whose pristine seeds are replicated in laboratories. The proximity of so many vineyards in areas like Napa can hasten the spread of vine disease, as can vineyards' proximity to certain crops like citrus. And many European clones once thought to be virus-free, Stamp points out, like the 337 clone of Cabernet Sauvignon, manifest their share of virus. So does some mother-clone material.

Is this just the generally unclean reality of vine biology having its laugh? Scientists like Stamp assert that viruses hurt wine quality—and some certainly do. At the same time, however, it's hardly folklore that many winemakers find that what winds up in the bottle from virus-impacted vines can often show far more character than the rubber-stamp wines made from rubber-stamp clones. Like a number of vintners, Cathy Corison, whose Kronos vineyard was planted in 1971, views the ailments mostly as a way to naturally limit the plants' vigor. This isn't the most economically advantageous choice. When yields on these vines slip to about a ton per acre or less, it is hard for them to be profitable. But the intensity and balance in the fruit certainly surpasses that of much of the produce from large, uniformly planted vineyards that were designed for efficiency rather than distinct expression.

None of this is to dismiss the value of the work done by Davis or vine nurseries to provide growers with clean, productive genetic material. But the mandate for virus-free vineyards has had one major side effect on the California wine industry: a flat-out assault on the state's historic vines.

IN WITH THE OLD

It is now a common assumption that in areas like Napa Valley, replanting will have to occur every twenty years or so, largely because of diminishing productivity from the eventual presence of vine viruses, but just as often because of phylloxera. California's last major replantings occurred in the 1990s, and before that in the late 1970s, a time when, based on UC Davis recommendations, many growers in California flocked to the AxR1 rootstock, a cross of the *V. vinifera* grape Aramon and the native American *V. rupestris* species.

One small problem: An alternate form of the phylloxera louse, biotype B, was more than able to attack AxR1. Soon enough California found itself in the midst of another phylloxera epidemic.

Actually, there were several problems. While researchers offered up using the AxR1 rootstock as a defense against the pest, they actually knew that the rootstock had been susceptible to phylloxera in the early twentieth century, though they surmised California wouldn't be vulnerable to an infestation. And they offered AxR1 as a clear solution. "For California conditions it would seem to be the nearest approach to an all-purpose rootstock in the coastal counties," wrote researcher A. J. Winkler in the 1973 edition of his book *General Viticulture*. "This is the case where the choice of a stock cannot be based entirely on its resistance to phylloxera."

By the time researchers finally confirmed the vulnerability to biotype B in the late 1980s, it was too late; pressure from wineries had forced scientists into a flawed choice, one that ultimately would cost the wine industry more than a billion dollars in replanting costs.

Ironically, a solution had been there all along, in the discarded choices of the past. One rootstock that had fought off phylloxera was St. George, an old selection based on an American native grape species (*V. rupestris*) that had been popular in California through much of the twentieth century. While St. George had fallen from favor for occasionally excessive vigor and its vulnerability to worms known as nematodes, it also had produced some of the heartiest and most durable vines in California. Most of the state's remaining century-old vines are planted on St. George.

In the Old World, the long-held belief has been that wine quality improves with vine age—that mature vines are required to make the greatest wines. But if you believe the opposite, that young vines make great wine, forced replanting isn't necessarily a bad thing—aside from the economics, since it might cost $50,000 per acre to replant in Napa, with a decade before a grower sees a profit.

In the 1990s, as successive waves of big reds were grown from young vines, it became evident that California was the one spot where vine age no longer corresponded to quality, or at least to success. The 1994 Colgin Herb Lamb Vineyard Cabernet, which earned 96 points from critic Robert Parker, came from a vineyard only in its fifth commercial harvest. The catalyst for this belief: a surge of new money arriving in Napa, with newcomers wanting to plant their own vineyards to make their mark. Add up the cost of farming for several seasons in Napa, plus the cost of land, permits, and fancy winemaking facilities, and you can see why Napa quickly filled with a lot of expensive young-vine Cabernet.

Of course, young vines weren't a bad choice for that purpose. One of their defining traits is robust sugar production. As the style of California Cabernet ratcheted up through the 1990s, winemakers wanted more fruit flavor and more sugar, which adolescent vines were glad to produce. (More difficult to achieve was physiological ripeness, in which the grapes' seeds and skins mature on pace with sugar. The wait for maturity in young vines often necessitated high sugar levels.) Some viewed these young-vine qualities as a big plus. Chuck Wagner of Caymus Vineyards famously prided himself on dismissing the virtue of old vines. (He similarly shrugged at the notion of terroir.) As Wagner would repeat on more than one occasion, "I've never been a believer that old vines make better wines."

But older vines have history on their side—none more so than Zinfandel and a handful of related grapes like Petite Sirah and Carignane, together the core of pre-Prohibition field blends. While more fashionable varieties boomed and busted, these old vineyards slogged along, surviving Prohibition and later being repurposed for making white Zinfandel and cheap table wines. Ultimately, in the case of vineyards like the Bedrock site in Sonoma Valley, endurance paid off when winemakers circled back, seeking the concentration and depth that old-vine fruit can offer.

"With these vineyards we're looking at a one-hundred-year life cycle," says winemaker Morgan Twain-Peterson as we depart the Casa Santinamaria Vineyard in the Sonoma crossroads known as Boyes Hot Springs. Planted in 1905 and showing bald patches and shrubby new rootstock where ancient vines finally died, Casa Santinamaria is a curious survivor, ten acres of Zinfandel and Petite Sirah but also a patchwork of white grapes (including Muscadelle, Sémillon, Chasselas, and more) that have often been labeled simply as "Sémillon."

Another day we go to look at Bedrock. This is Twain-Peterson's prize, one of California's oldest remaining vineyards, planted on the alluvial rundown from the Monte Rosso area, high above on Mount Veeder. It is now owned by Twain-Peterson and his father, Joel Peterson, founder of the Ravenswood label. Peterson provides a cultural touchstone; he is Dr. Zinfandel, perhaps the grape's most loyal proponent. And Bedrock's roots are firmly wrapped around the history of California wine. They wind back to 1854, when two famed generals, William Tecumseh Sherman and "Fighting" Joe Hooker, planted what then was the Madrone Ranch.

Of some 119 acres, Bedrock's historic core is thirty-three acres of vines dating back to 1886. Found among the old rows is some of California's earliest true Syrah. There's also Carignane as thick and stately as an apple tree, and both the Italian grape Refosco, known in earlier times as Crabb's Black Burgundy, and the French grape Mondeuse. (In another of those viticultural tangles, these last two were once thought to be the same.)

Reclaiming Bedrock has been a long process for the Petersons. Slowly they have been going back to loosen what was once virtual hardpan, compacted from the use of heavy tractors, and to revive soils worn out from heavy chemical use—what Twain-Peterson describes as "the nozzlehead farming that was out here before." His spader couldn't make it more than four hours in the field before the dense soil and rocks overwhelmed it, sending it to the shop for the day.

Bedrock is coming full circle. Sitting across a row from the gnarled old specimens is a tidy patch of young St. George rootstock vines. Even old vineyards need to be revived, and so Twain-Peterson has replicated the vineyard's old footprint of head-trained vines—the plants growing upright like small trees, rather than being tied to a wire trellis. Each of these babies sits in a small dimpled mound of dirt, allowing them to be hand watered. "The whole vineyard was established dry-farmed," he says, "so obviously it can be done."

These vines, with their bushlike shape, have mostly become a relic of Old California, although they are enjoying a small resurgence. The handwork required to farm them can cost more than tending to other types of vines, but there are also benefits. They can more easily offer grapes partial shade, which can keep them from burning or overripening.

For that reason, Passalacqua takes a similar approach with nearly all the Zinfandel that Turley now uses. He sees in this method the ability to intepret a vineyard's potential, without the overweaning farming that can obscure greatness.

"That's why old vines are so fascinating, because what were your tools?" he explains. "They had a horse wagon that they could pull through the vines and irrigate, they had sulfur they could throw out of a bag, and that's it. Man can fuck up a great site."

The Myth of the Estate

There is a deep dilemma in the New California equation: Those that have the land often don't make the wine. And increasingly, those who make wine have not only no land to grow grapes, but little chance of ever affording any.

A good share of the blame goes to California growing ever more crowded and real estate growing more scarce. A bit also goes to Proposition 13, enacted in 1978, which capped property assessment increases so long as an owner didn't sell. The net effect of Prop 13—not just for vineyards but for most properties—was to hold down property taxes, even as California real estate spiked in value. That was designed to benefit longtime landowners; it created a more stable market and preserved family vineyards. By holding assessments well below market value, Prop 13 artificially dampened the market. The tradeoff for stability was a nearly insurmountable barrier for young vintners to buy land.

Only in places like Napa County, home to the country's most expensive agricultural land, did

such rules of capital function differently—although not necessarily for the better. High taxes were usually a trifle to the sort of deep-pocketed buyers who targeted Napa. And any tax benefits for Napa's longtime vineyard owners were, as county assessor John Tuteur succinctly put it, "outweighed by the gains to be made from selling."

What does it take to buy land now? I put the question to Tony Correia, one of the state's veteran vineyard appraisers. We start at the top of the heap, in Napa. The costs can be staggering. Ovid Estate, three hundred acres high on Pritchard Hill in eastern Napa, cost at least $22 million to launch. The ambitious Dana Estates project, founded by Korean tycoon Hi Sang Lee, required an estimated $25 million. Chinese investors, wooed by Napa's prestige, have dived in, buying properties like Sloan Estate, a rapid-fame project in Rutherford.

Perhaps this was the high-dollar endgame of California wine's destiny. In Napa, land restrictions and cost had essentially capped the chances of new vineyard development almost as stringently as in Bordeaux or Burgundy, where new plantings are functionally nonexistent and extant vineyard land can top $500,000 per acre. But in Correia's view, Napa costs have already reached a tipping point.

"You're looking at, roughly speaking, $300,000 an acre," he says. "If you sit down and try to pencil out your return on that, you have to be launching your wine at $200 a bottle or so. Even then, you're taking enormous risk that you'll be able to do that consistently, that you'll never have a bad weather year. From a business standpoint, it really is not a good investment. But I'm always amazed that I see people going in and doing just that."

Napa in particular made it tough to acquire a new vineyard. In 1968 the board of supervisors approved an agricultural preserve, the first in the nation, which limited development in the valley and set a minimum lot size of twenty acres (eventually raised to forty), helping to ensure that vineyard land wouldn't be subdivided. Later ordinances limited hillside plantings, imposed a ten-acre minimum requirement for new winery properties, and required new properties to use mostly Napa-grown fruit. While all these hemmed in development, they also made the prospect of owning a true estate in Napa a rich man's game.

In some ways, buying your way into Napa had become passé by the late 2000s. Big money had for years been flowing farther afield. After acquiring Cabernet label Merus in 2007, Bill Foley—"William P. Foley II, Vintner," according to his website—chairman of insurance giant Fidelity National, went on a sustained buying spree, grabbing up the longtime Santa Barbara property Firestone, and Sonoma stalwarts Sebastiani and Chalk Hill. Stewart Resnick, whose business empire included Teleflora and Fiji Water, was awash in water-to-wine jokes when he acquired first Paso Robles's Justin Vineyards, then Landmark in Sonoma Valley. By 2009, the great recession began to force winery after winery onto the market.

Surely there must be a frontier left? Correia suggests a few areas, including Mendocino in the north of the state, or perhaps San Luis Obispo County, the center point between Los Angeles and San Francisco. But small vineyards are hard to establish in those spots; there's not enough geographic cachet to cover the costs of launching a winery. Monterey's Salinas Valley might be an option, but there you'd compete for land with deep-pocketed vegetable farmers (and middling prices for Monterey County grapes). Even in the Central Valley, almonds and pistachios are as lucrative as grapes. "There are no bargains anymore," Correia says.

With few exceptions, the new guard have little ability to change their landless fate unless they partner with a big-ticket investor—which at least a few have. In 2012, for example, Gavin Chanin founded a new project with investor Bill Price, who owned established vineyards like Durell and wine labels like Kosta Browne.

"Our whole tradition is screwed up," Steve Matthiasson tells me one day. "One person should be growing the grapes and then taking them into the cellar and making wine out of them." Really, though, the wine geography of California had stopped making sense a long time ago.

IN THE FIELD

New California's winemakers weren't going to let inconvenient economics stop them. There were plenty of ways get their hands in the dirt—even if it meant paying to do the farming themselves.

At first that might seem like a bourgeois fetishist's proposition: please, let me *pay you* to toil in the field. But consider the extent to which great wine is reliant on near-obsessive farming. If that's your goal, why pay a grower to do commodity work? It was a lesson learned in Burgundy, where two old practices aided land-poor *vignerons* (farmers who both work the land and make wine). The Burgundians engage both in *fermage*, a straight lease, that let *vignerons* keep the fruit they grow, and *métayage*, a sharecropping of sorts, with the landholder often paying costs to farm and maintain the land, but also keeping some of the fruit or finished wine.

California had good reasons—and not just economic ones—to adopt versions of these practices. If once winemakers were content to buy grapes as a commodity, the new guard hopes to control decisions about the work in the field: the yield per vine, the use of chemicals, the amount of pruning and leaf pulling. These values are increasingly important, not just for them but for their customers. Buying grapes has become more than just a transaction; it comes with ethical weight.

"I mean," Anthony Filiberti says one day, "what's the point? I've never understood the point of showing up at a custom crush facility, and then watching the grapes get crushed and handing off a work order. Why do it if you're not interested in doing the whole thing? It's funny how many winemakers just want to show up and taste wine from the barrel."

Along with partners David Low and Webster Marquez, Filiberti runs the Anthill Farms label. From the outset their wines were well received, but all three partners, particularly Filiberti, felt uncomfortable simply making wine without taking responsibility for farming, even if their winery was just a borrowed space in a Sonoma County warehouse.

Certainly they were conversant with the warehouse model. The three met as cellar rats at Williams Selyem, the famous Sonoma Pinot Noir house. If their contemporaries accepted whatever fruit contracts they could get, checked on the vineyards a few times during the season, and then awaited bins on the crush pad, the Anthill gang wanted full immersion.

Filiberti had spent time in Oregon, where land costs made it more plausible for winemakers to buy land. He became the designated farmer of the group starting in 2004, when they found a tiny vineyard in Mendocino's Anderson Valley. The hands-off owners were a Silicon Valley couple, Donna Abbey and Dan Harris, whose two acres were being neglected. So the Anthill boys fired the vineyard manager, bought their own backpack sprayer, and offered to farm for free the first year.

The next year they took over the vineyard lease, with an unusual arrangement: they paid nothing to lease the land, but they would pay all the farming costs or work it themselves, and then paid half

LOMPOC

In 1998 a veteran winemaker named Rick Longoria moved his barrels and equipment into a corrugated metal warehouse in an industrial park on the outskirts of the town of Lompoc, on the far western edge of Santa Barbara County. Once the flower-seed capital of the world, Lompoc was now mostly a satellite community for the nearby federal prison and Vandenberg Air Force Base.

What Lompoc had in its favor was that it was only fifteen minutes or less from the vineyards in the heart of what would become known as the Santa Rita Hills, soon to be Santa Barbara's new haven for Chardonnay and Pinot Noir. When he first moved in, Longoria's neighbors were about what you'd expect: a facility for storing hospital records, an auto repair shop, a tortilla maker, a bike manufacturer. But soon he had different company. In 1999 Greg Brewer, a former French instructor and assistant winemaker at Beckmen Vineyards, and Steve Clifton, a former rock musician and wine retailer, moved their own budding label, Brewer-Clifton into a nearby space. They opened a tasting bar, inviting visitors into their warehouse world.

So the Lompoc wine ghetto was born. Other wineries had tried this model before, but here was a wine region willing to stake its reputation not on estates in the vineyards, but on a concentration of *garagistes* working in close quarters. It was ultimate proof that the warehouse model worked.

the typical price for high-end Pinot Noir grapes. Other marriages of convenience soon materialized. At the Comptche Ridge Vineyard, they struck a classic sharecropping arrangement with brothers John and Mark Weir. Filiberti stopped by most afternoons to help direct the vineyard crew; half the wine went to the Weirs, the rest to Anthill.

At the Demuth Vineyard next to Abbey-Harris, the couple who owned the old dry-farmed site could no longer physically work their land. "I would come here and hire the crew out and then just take the money off the bill at the end of the year," Filiberti recalls. (He now works for Demuth's new owner, Peter Knez.) Always, Anthill went in with something to offer—either cash or sweat equity. In turn, they could control their crop.

Such arrangements were perhaps the new guard's best shot at breaking another California habit: a longtime cycle, ever since the early twentieth century, of least-cost pricing for grapes. Prices were often dictated by large wineries and co-ops, or by grape brokers. Growers hoped to maximize their crops for yield, not quality—at least until the next grape shortage came along and their leverage returned.

This is why, when young California winemakers began looking for vineyards, they realized that sustainable pricing was their other opportunity to change the conversation. At the Story Vineyard in Amador County in the Sierra Foothills, Tegan Passalacqua found a parcel of Chenin Blanc that had been planted on its own roots in 1979 and dry-farmed since then. Where the owner had been getting $400 per ton, Passalacqua offered $1,200. He and his wife drove up to prune the vines themselves.

BUILDING THE MYTH

This split between the field and the cellar was puzzling to Old World vintners. If we lack an English equivalent for the term *vigneron*, someone who both grows grapes and makes wine, the French don't have a word for "winemaker"; they consider it to be a New World presumption that a crafter of wine would be removed from the key agricultural task of growing grapes.

In fact, both before and after Prohibition it was relatively rare in California for a single estate to make wine from its own land, save for the occasional grand property like Inglenook, which was founded in 1879 by sea captain and trader Gustave Niebaum, one of the country's richest men at the time.

Most of California's twentieth-century wineries relied on grapes from all over, although they happily bought land when they could. Louis M. Martini once trucked in large volumes of purchased fruit, but in 1938 he also bought the Sonoma mountain property he would dub Monte Rosso, and in 1942 he acquired two hundred acres of the Stanly Ranch in Carneros. Even businessman Lee Stewart, whose tiny Souverain winery would become an early model for artisanal California, was a regular buyer of grapes, including for one of his surprise hits, a table white made from Green Hungarian grapes.

Only when the pioneers of the late 1960s and early '70s appeared, many of them escapees from corporate life, did the prospect of an estate become a distinct goal. Historian Charles Sullivan traces this trend to 1961, when Joseph Heitz, having worked his way through the valley's cellars, scraped together enough cash from investors to buy an old vineyard near St. Helena.

By that time the corporate world was intruding into the world of winemaking. What Sullivan describes as the Big Five of midcentury Napa—in addition to Inglenook and Martini, there were Beaulieu Vineyard, Beringer, and Charles Krug—began their decline when, in 1969, liquor giant Heublein acquired both Beaulieu and Inglenook. Two years later the Beringer family sold their winery to Nestlé. But, for the most part, Napa was still a farm community. Land was affordable enough that purchasing one's own estate remained a possibility, at least for people like Donn and Molly Chappellet, who planted 110 acres on Pritchard Hill, or Bob Travers, who with his wife Elinor bought the old Mayacamas Vineyards property high on Mount Veeder.

Yet Heitz's most famous wine, the Martha's Vineyard Cabernet, was made from purchased fruit. And while Robert Mondavi had acquired a large swath of the To Kalon Vineyard (with help from an investment by Seattle's Rainier Brewing), even by 1984 his winery controlled the vineyards for only 35 to 40 percent of its grapes. Indeed, the Chardonnay from Chateau Montelena that won the Judgment of Paris came not from its Calistoga estate, but from a mix of grapes purchased both in Napa County and from Sonoma's Alexander and Russian River Valleys. Even in California's crowning modern moment, the notion of the estate was a fancy.

HOMES FOR THE LANDLESS

Why, then, should California winemakers worry about the estate? The mentality of the *garagiste*—a moniker heisted from Bordeaux for those making wine in their garages—fit the state perfectly. After all, it was in California in 1938 that Bill Hewlett and Dave Packard split the $45 monthly rent for a garage in Palo Alto, developed an audio oscillator there, and decided to form Hewlett-Packard, and it was here that in 1976 Steve Jobs and Steve Wozniak began constructing the first Apple computers in Jobs's parents' bedroom. (Jobs and Wozniak had worked for a much larger Hewlett-Packard, no different than the way young winemakers pay the bills with a day job at another winery.)

Their wine counterparts would be Burt Williams and Ed Selyem, who in 1979 began making wine in a garage in Forestville, producing Zinfandel from Leno Martinelli's old vines on Jackass Hill. They bounced around for a bit without the required winery operating bond, but after a warning from federal regulators they went legit, using a series of facilities in Sonoma. "We used to think," Williams says, "we were the most mobile winery in the world." In 1983 they moved into another garage, this time in Graton, in western Sonoma, and they finally had a home of sorts. Over five years there they made a 1985 Pinot Noir from the Rochioli Vineyard that won the sweepstakes in the California State Fair wine competition, catapulting them to fame.

Eventually one of their growers, Howard Allen, a fourth-generation Californian who had planted Pinot Noir on Healdsburg's Westside Road, right next to Rochioli, offered to build them a winery in 1988, so long as it could pay for itself in ten years. He wouldn't have to wait that long. In 1998 the wildly successful label was sold to investor John Dyson for $9 million.

By that point Williams Selyem had become the defining name in California Pinot Noir—without owning a single vine or hanging a tasting-room shingle. Echoing their Silicon Valley brethren, they had shown that a different path was not only possible but profitable.

"There were a couple of times we could have bought acreage and put in a vineyard, and there were a couple of times we probably could have bought a vineyard," Burt Williams tells me, recalling his work with Selyem. "But we were both busy a lot. He was busy with the list and maintaining the sales, I was busy making wine. . . . So we felt like we had our hands full. Having a vineyard? That would have just been more work, more work we didn't need."

Soon Williams Selyem's warehouse model was widely copied. Pockets of no-frills wineries appeared throughout the state, many in wine ghettos like the Eighth Street corridor near Sonoma's airport and in the Santa Barbara County town of Lompoc (see Lompoc, page 80).

Napa tried a different approach. Many fancy Cabernets of the 1990s were launched without a physical winery, either because the cost of construction was prohibitive or because, frankly, there was no need to spend the money to make only eight hundred or so cases of wine. Instead vintners turned to shared spaces known custom-crush facilities, the first notable one being Napa Wine Company in Oakville, founded in 1993 almost across from Mondavi's winery in a building that had formerly housed Inglenook's large-scale production. These facilities took advantage of a loophole in regulations that allowed many wineries to operate under a single roof. The model drew top winemaking consultants like Helen Turley and Heidi Peterson Barrett. (They soon, however, discovered custom crush's big downside: winemakers were often forced to issue work orders, with the actual work done by cellar technicians, which sometimes led to costly mistakes.)

The arrival of new custom-crush facilities like the Ranch, developed in 2007 by winemaker Joel Gott in an old wine factory near St. Helena, added more space for winemakers to ply their trade. But this option came with a steep price tag, as Napa custom-crush fees remained around $35 to $45 per case, even if the winemaker did the work. Most new winemakers in Napa would have to charge nearly $30 per bottle—and often more than $60—just to break even.

LIVING IN THE CITY

If you were going to be relegated to a warehouse anyway, why not settle in the big city?

That was, in fact, a very old idea in California. In the late nineteenth century San Francisco was filled with winemakers, brokers, and wine warehouses; the 1893 city directory included more than 120 entries under "native wines." The Sonoma winery Gundlach Bundschu ran a block-long facility in San Francisco, destroyed in the city's massive 1906 earthquake. After the quake, the giant California Wine Association constructed its Winehaven facility across the bay from San Francisco in the city of Richmond, shipping some five hundred thousand gallons per month and claiming the title of the world's largest winery for more than a decade.

San Francisco revived the concept in the 2000s (see The Lure, and Lessons, of San Francisco, page 84), with at least half a dozen wineries springing up within the city limits. Warehouse space could be found in the city's southern industrial areas for around $1 per square foot. If the surroundings seemed like a set for Karl Malden in *The Streets of San Francisco*, at least the price was right.

But it was the other side of the San Francisco Bay that enjoyed the real renaissance in urban winemaking. If Burt Williams confirmed the viability of the warehouse model, Steve Edmunds created a template for a winemaker's urban survival in 1985 when he established Edmunds St. John in a narrow building on Camelia Street in west Berkeley. Other urban pioneers, like Peter Brehm's Wine and the People, and Richard Rotblatt's Bay Cellars, had previously set up facilities in the East Bay. But it was Edmunds who discovered the true value of working far from wine country.

After working in wine retail and as a mail carrier, Edmunds wanted to make wine. Being in Berkeley liberated him from the usual strictures of Napa or Sonoma. Rather than dabble in the Cabernet and Chardonnay that was flooding California at the time, he could pursue his notion of creating California's equivalent of a Côtes du Rhône–style blend. The wines of southern France held a gravitational pull, seeing as the store opened by importer Kermit Lynch, who familiarized many Americans with Rhône wines, was just a few blocks away.

Not far away Kent Rosenblum had established his own facility near the old naval facility on Alameda, the island city just off Oakland. Rosenblum became the other great beacon for city winemaking. His winery was, for instance, where winemaker Chris Brockway got his start by working in the tasting room. Then the Omaha, Nebraska, native got a cellar job at JC Cellars in Oakland, working for Jeff Cohn, who himself was Rosenblum's winemaker. Cohn moved to a warehouse near Oakland's revitalized Jack London Square, which he shared with Mike Dashe, whose Dashe Cellars makes a subtle style of Zinfandel and Grenache. Although Rosenblum's label was purchased in 2008 by liquor giant Diageo, which shuttered its winemaking in

THE LURE, AND LESSONS, OF SAN FRANCISCO

Logistically, San Francisco was a perfect location for vintners to set up shop: it was easy to access, and directly between the North and Central Coasts. But it might have oversold the grand wine dream.

Nothing better exemplified the potential—and pitfalls—of urban winemaking than Crushpad. In 2004 entrepreneur Michael Brill unveiled a five-thousand-square-foot facility in the industrial Dogpatch neighborhood of San Francisco. Clients around the country could have wines made to spec. But Crushpad courted both neighborhood enthusiasts and larger commercial clients. As it grew to some forty-five thousand cases made annually, its protocols grew heavy-handed; bins were heavily sulfured and fermented with the same yeast to prevent a microbial traffic jam. Serious wine types shied away.

In February 2010, after bragging about the virtues of community winemaking, Brill suddenly announced that Crushpad would leave for Napa to take a sweetheart rent deal. That deal, however, only lasted a year before Crushpad decamped for the Sebastiani facility in Sonoma. "For me," Brill told me in his defense, "it was always more about what we did than where we did it."

A year later, its new winemaker had departed and its assets were auctioned off.

But some of Crushpad's alumni never gave up on San Francisco. Bluxome Street Winery, established amid the dot-com offices in the city's South of Market neighborhood by a former Crushpad winemaker and a former client, opened near where dozens of wineries once flourished at the turn of the twentieth century. Dogpatch Wine Works was founded by other Crushpad vets a few blocks from the original location. Both provided an opportunity for commercial wineries to again thrive in the heart of the city.

Alameda, Kent and his daughter Shauna relocated their new Rock Wall label about a mile away, next to the Alameda naval station's abandoned runways.

The East Bay, in other words, had created a cozy little wine community. In 2006 Brockway quit his day job and set up shop on Camelia Street in west Berkeley, in the same 1,400-square-foot space Edmunds had leased in 1985, which in turn was where Travis Fretter, one of the state's *garagiste* pioneers, made wine in the 1970s. That corridor near Fourth Street would become its own wine magnet. Tracey and Jared Brandt located their Donkey & Goat winery around the corner from Broc Cellars.

Did dreams of the estate persist? Sure. But land wasn't getting any cheaper. And in Edmunds's case, convenience won out. His wife had a psychology practice in Berkeley and their kids were settled in school. "It just didn't make sense," he says, "to move any closer to where the grapes were."

Chris Brockway in his Berkeley facility

The Table Wine Dilemma

For all the progress the New California has made with its top wines, it has one big remaining challenge: table wine, the everyday bottles that constitute what most drinkers know from California, is still largely the domain of Big Wine. This is hardly unique to California. Throughout the world large companies dominate the wine industry on a volume basis, leveraging the same economies of scale that have allowed Big Food to put a fatal squeeze on small farmers.

Although modern consumers are far more concerned about the origins of their food than they once were, keenly eyeing the source of that organic spinach, their concern goes out the window when it comes to wine. Big Wine has discovered what I sometimes call the Whole Foods gap: most consumers, even if they are the type to shop at that particular upscale grocery store and obsess about the origins of their food, simply couldn't care less about where their wine comes from or how it was farmed.

This, perhaps more than anything, has been the great victory of the vino-industrial complex, the dark edge of Brand California. Why should wine cost more? The rise of wines like Charles Shaw—Two Buck Chuck—advanced the proposition that California wine not only could, but should, be had for less than $5 a bottle. Anyone who thought otherwise was a chump.

Brand California soon enveloped not only truly cheap wines like Two Buck Chuck but also a sea of fancier wines, bottles like Kendall-Jackson's Vintner's Reserve. Often these were industrially made but marketed with the patina of an artisanal product.

Still, a loyal opposition has emerged to Brand California, led by those who believe that making wine isn't simply about pursuing ambitious, expensive wines. Here was the New California's evolutionary thinking: not only could you admit that you made cheaper wines; your own talents with fancier fare became a key selling point. Indeed, the talent required to make those fancier wines came with not just the opportunity, but also a responsibility, to make everyday wines as well.

This inspired projects like the Cep label, made by the trio that runs the Peay estate on the Sonoma Coast, brothers Andy and Nick Peay and winemaker Vanessa Wong. Initially Cep was a way to utilize Pinot Noir and Syrah grapes that didn't make the cut for the Peay wines, but the label soon expanded to include a rosé and Sauvignon Blanc made from purchased fruit. The Peays were coy at first about linking Cep to their day jobs—it was the sort of thing known in wine circles but not officially disclosed—but ultimately they embraced the connection.

The Lioco label embraced this table-wine mandate from the start. Created by partners Matt

Licklider and Kevin O'Connor to explore California's potential for terroir-driven Chardonnay, Lioco was in fact largely financed on the backs of two simpler wines: a prolific (up to ten thousand cases) Sonoma County Chardonnay, blended from a wide mix of vineyards, and the Indica red blend, which was sourced from old Mendocino vineyards and named for that county's other prime agricultural product. Steve Matthiasson accomplished something similar in 2012 with the white Tendu, sold in a one-liter green bottle more frequently used for Austrian table wine.

Once, well-known wineries were eager to make honest table wines. In the early days of fighting varietals, good fruit sources for cheap wines weren't hard to find. But many of these wines spiraled down in quality as the lust for expansion required ever-larger volumes of grapes. A project like Mondavi's Woodbridge started out with fruit from outperforming Central Valley sources, like Borden Ranch in eastern Lodi, but soon enough quality suffered.

The solution? They turned to the arid stretches of the central San Joaquin Valley. Once a source for cheap jug and fortified wines, this would become the irrigated, chemically farmed heart of Brand California.

Wineries like Lioco chose a different path. Indica, for instance, was based mostly on old-vine Carignane from Mendocino. Carignane's lack of reputability made it affordable, a grape that New California's winemakers could leverage rather than chasing dreams of making cheap Cabernet. Tendu was based on Vermentino that Matthiasson farmed in rural Yolo County, north of the town of Davis—a spot exploited by Brand California, here reclaimed for a more intimate project. Wines like Indica and Cep had another purpose: to help finance more rarified single-vineyard bottles. This was, if anything,

old wine industry economics, something that had been learned by the Europeans and the early Californians alike.

At the same time, these wines transcended economics. They were based on a moral prerogative that good winemakers should not only pursue greatness but make humble wines as well. It was the chance for winemakers to reclaim California from industrial farming and cynical marketing.

THE FAMILY WAY

Forget economics for a moment. The table wine dilemma hinges first on the matter of ambition. In fact, it is quite possible for a small winery to make honest table wine and compete with the Constellations and Gallos of the world.

That is precisely what the Bilbro family, owner of the Marietta Winery, has been doing for more than three decades, since Chris Bilbro quit his job at the Sonoma State Hospital and in 1978 converted a rented cow barn near the northern Sonoma town of Geyserville into a makeshift winery.

"When everybody else was trying to go high-end, my dad consciously said, 'I'm going to go Monday through Thursday night, because not everybody just has wine on their table on Friday night,'" recalls Jake Bilbro, who now runs the business with two of his brothers, Scot and Sam. "Everybody shoots for the 100-point score. That's never been a place he's even wanted to go."

The Bilbros' great contribution to the California roster is their Old Vine Red, known for its impressive consistency as much as anything else. A non-vintage blend, released in sequentially numbered lots a couple times each year as demand requires (by 2013 they were approaching Lot No. 60), it is a throwback to the Sonoma wines of yore, the sort of jug wines made just up the road in the town of Asti, where Italian Swiss Colony once operated its empire. But Marietta follows the same two branding elements that Bronco's Fred Franzia, father of Two Buck Chuck, considered mandatory in selling the modern equivalent of jug wine: Old Vine Red is closed with a cork and sold in a 750 ml bottle.

Typically, such a wine would be made in a factory, using huge fermentation tanks and processing equipment to sculpt endless lots of fruit into a semblance of drinkability. But it's immediately evident how much Old Vine Red trumps mass-market competitors that cost only a couple of bucks less. It tastes like a classic old-fashioned California table red, robust in that Zinfandel way, but a far cry from the generic and sugary confections against which it competes. This isn't a wonder of tannin powder or grape concentrate; it's just simple old-fashioned blending.

If the Bilbros operate in a realm divorced from the cold numbers of corporate wine, it's hardly a mom-and-pop operation. Each lot of Old Vine Red is around twenty-five thousand cases—so, below the level of Yellow Tail, which produces five hundred thousand cases for a single release—but more than enough to satisfy its nationwide customer base.

One of the family's more brilliant strokes has been not to price itself too low, to stay away from the bottom shelf in the supermarket. Their price tends to be, say, $2 more than a much larger brand like Ménage à Trois (an industrial wine, if not a corporate one, controlled by the Trinchero family, which also pioneered white Zinfandel). The difference is crucial—though here I can practically hear Fred Franzia carping that the extra two bucks would buy you nearly a whole bottle of Charles Shaw. There's also enormous price stability. In 1992 Old Vine Red was about $7; twenty years later it was around $12, just about keeping up with the rate of inflation.

Like their industrial competitors, the Bilbros lean on the power of Brand California. But Old Vine Red is hardly a Central Valley concoction. It is made almost entirely from a handful of vineyards in Mendocino County, a strategy that once worked for the Fetzer family (which sold its familiar label to liquor giant Brown-Forman).

While Fetzer, Glen Ellen, and nearly every other combatant in the fighting-varietal wars of the 1980s chased the usual fodder—Chardonnay, Cabernet, and Merlot—the Bilbros never wavered from their plan, which was straight out of 1950s Sonoma: creating a basic table red based on the classic field blend of Zinfandel, Petite Sirah, and Carignane.

To that they added old Italian varieties held over from the North Coast's farming legacy: Montepulciano, Negroamaro, Nero d'Avola, Sangiovese, Barbera, and more, much of it from the sixty-acre Fox Hill Vineyard on the Talmage Bench, between the Mendocino towns of Hopland and Ukiah. Not tied down by either varietal or vintage restrictions, the Bilbros can finesse each lot to their standards. Tellingly, Big Wine has taken a similar tack in recent years, marketing blends like Gallo's Apothic Red.

Thus emerged a sustainable strategy in an unstable grape market. While bigger companies often dumped grape contracts at will, the Bilbros were remarkably loyal to their growers. Because Marietta is such a tiny operation, Chris or one of his sons would typically visit each farmer.

"When times were really good, we were able to keep our grape sourcing in line, and when times were really bad and Diageo and Constellation were up in Mendocino paying $400 a ton and screwing growers, we were able to keep our sources," Jake explains. "It may not be the high and it may not be the low, but it's consistent, and they know they're getting paid the day after."

For that matter, they could work with farmers who owned just six or eight acres, too small to be an effective contract for Big Wine. What would have been unworkable for a larger winery worked perfectly for the Bilbros.

"So," I ask Jake, "you're banking on reverse economies of scale?"

"Exactly."

This matter of fruit costs is another dark edge to Brand California. Grape pricing is always cycling through boom and bust, which is why, in the mid-2000s, the small print on popular California brands like Redwood Creek or Pepperwood Grove revealed origins in Italy, Germany, and Chile.

The Bilbros weren't immune to price fluctuations, so when the opportunity came to purchase the large McDowell Valley ranch outside Hopland in eastern Mendocino, they grabbed it. Between that and a nearby property they had purchased on the Talmage Bench, the Bilbros achieved that elusive California goal: Old Vine Red could become an estate-grown wine.

AIMING FOR THE MIDDLE

Chris Brockway seems an unlikely choice to be a table wine maven. Cooped up in a narrow Berkeley building full of concrete tanks and old wooden upright casks, he is a thoroughly urban creature. Having tended bar at San Francisco's hipper-than-thou wine bar Terroir, Brockway seems more conversant with the oddities of the Loire Valley—*Romorantin! Menu Pineau!*—than California.

In 2004 he launched his own label focused on fancier fare like Pinot Noir, but Brockway became increasingly taken with the minimalist winemaking he encountered in France's lesser-known appellations. He spurned commercial yeasts and enzyme additives, set up a decidedly low-tech cellar, and shifted his focus to more unusual fare: organically farmed Picpoul from Paso Robles; seventy-year-old vines of Valdiguié, the red grape long known as Napa Gamay, from Solano County; and carbonically fermented Carignane from 120-year-old vines in the Alexander Valley.

These were largely throwaway grapes for their growers. Who's out hunting Valdigiué grown near the bedroom community of Farfield? That's precisely why Brockway gravitated to them, especially after considering that planting his own vines might cost up to $35,000 an acre. It was a lesson from the French, whose new wave had gravitated to lesser-known corners of the Loire and Languedoc, where good soils and older vines could be farmed without hewing to the country's beloved but time-worn appellation rules.

"But how do you justify it in California, where there's some old plantings, but mostly new plantings?" Brockway asks me as we sit in his postage stamp of a tasting room. "You head where it's been handed from generation to generation and is obscure."

In Brockway's case, that meant a ceiling for grape prices at $1,200 or $1,500 per ton, far less than he had paid for fancier fruit. It was enough to rise above the mediocrity of $500 production grapes but cheap enough to keep his prices around $20 per bottle, and thus in competition with similar overseas efforts like Chinon or Dolcetto. Just as important, Brockway began to put his wines into reusable kegs, to be poured at local restaurants, which further cut the price (see Keg Wines, at right).

But this work also was underwritten by Brockway's other project. In 2006 he partnered with Brian Terrizzi, who runs the Giornata label on the Central Coast, to make an inexpensive Cabernet from the Margarita Vineyard outside Paso Robles under a label they dubbed Broadside.

Terrizzi, who lives near Paso Robles, is known for his boots-on-the-ground scouting for good fruit deals. He and Brockway endured the recession by making a nuanced single-vineyard Cabernet, a rarity at around $20—all the rarer because they added no yeasts, bacteria, or acid in the cellar and used almost no new oak, instead underscoring the variety's natural flavors. With its striking black-and-white label, Broadside carried itself as a serious wine—even if it was from generally underappreciated Paso. The strategy allowed them to grow to ten thousand cases, adding a Chardonnay and Merlot.

But what really made the Broadside Cabernet work was Margarita. Located 19 miles from the town of Paso, on the southwestern edge of the Paso Robles appellation, the vineyard is close enough to the ocean and at a high enough elevation—around 1,500 feet—to enjoy a crucial cooling influence. Part of the old Santa Margarita rancho, its soils are a compelling mix of shale, sedimentary rock, and calcium-rich former seabed spread across more than 750 acres. Initially it had been found by keen-eyed vineyard scouts for the Robert Mondavi Winery, which leased it in 1999. They dubbed it Cuesta Ridge, intending it as a key engine for Mondavi's Central Coast expansion. But five years later, with Mondavi having been acquired by Constellation,

KEG WINES

In the late 2000s California vintners began to provide restaurants wines to serve on tap, using a modern version of the keg systems that are widely used for beer. This had been tried in the 1980s by companies like Anheuser-Busch, but now small and reputable wineries were leading the charge.

While one company, Free Flow, specialized in kegging up both clients' wines and its own blends, the real interest was in emergent labels like Lioco, Broc Cellars, Wind Gap, and Scholium Project, which worked with San Francisco restaurants to create wine programs built around serving local, artisanally made wines. In Los Angeles, a handful of spots offered something similar. Soon enough keg wines appeared in New York.

Kegs were utterly logical: they required no glass for bottling and were easily reusable, although restaurateurs sometimes struggled with operating the keg systems. The kegged wines were meant for immediate drinking, and sometimes wine directors actually helped to fine-tune the blends. That was the case at San Francisco's Frances, where wine director Paul Einbund sold house wine from the tap for $1 per ounce.

Other efforts to reduce packaging included the reusable canteens of local wine made by Kevin Kelley's Natural Process Alliance label. But kegs found a particularly loyal user base, especially because they often featured wines, like Wind Gap's white Arinto, that were made only for the tap.

the company kicked Margarita back to its owners right in the midst of a grape glut.

Brockway and Terrizzi's timing was perfect. They could harvest good Cabernet at three or four tons per acre, no different than a Napa vineyard making wine at more than twice the price.

Broadside became a cost-effective snapshot of California Cabernet, nothing to age but several notches above Brand California.

But why would a winemaker, after building a reputation for more prestigious wines, take on the difficulties of crafting a cheap one, especially if it meant blending disparate lots of grapes from across the state?

Enter Bob and Jim Varner, who built a reputation as masters of Chardonnay, made from individual blocks of their Spring Ridge Vineyard, in a pristine slice of the Santa Cruz Mountains. Varner Chardonnay is routinely among California's best, which makes it even more curious how much time they spend on their other project: the Foxglove label, which produces about twenty-five thousand

cases annually of under-$15 Chardonnay from Central Coast fruit, as well as some Zinfandel and Cabernet. With all that, they still make most of their own sales calls.

In their cellar, located in the town of Portola Valley, south of San Francisco, the Varners hew to an update of traditional nineteenth-century Burgundian winemaking, which means fermentation in oak barrels, minimal stirring of lees, and even a hand-operated barrel winch that replicates an archaic French design. But Bob is also frequently scooting down to San Miguel, a nondescript town 170 miles south near Paso Robles, to mind their batches of Foxglove.

The brothers view Foxglove as their bigger challenge. Spring Ridge is tiny enough that they

Brian Terrizzi in his cellar

The New California Wine

can hand weed it. But Foxglove requires a logistical dance, wrangling ton after ton of fruit purchased from three counties. From Santa Barbara County, places like the El Camino Vineyard in Los Alamos add aromas and acidity. That's mixed with grapes from a Chardonnay vineyard in eastern Paso Robles, whose old vines are undervalued by its Big Wine customers, and grapes from a vineyard near Greenfield in the Salinas Valley, with a similar cumulative ripening potential to the Varners' fog-licked Santa Cruz vineyard, which provides fresh citrus flavors.

They soon realized that to set themselves apart from the glut of cheap California Chardonnay, their most important work would take place in the winery, not in the field. Whereas most cheap, mass-produced Chardonnay relies on lots of oak chips (using new barrels is too expensive), the stirring of lees to bulk up anemic fruit, and tweaks of chemistry, the Varners still insisted on very much the same minimalism that they demand for their expensive wines. So they decided to use their shortcomings to their advantage.

Realizing that much of the Central Coast was warmer than what they considered prime Chardonnay land, they decided to treat Foxglove more as a Rhône-style white. Its richer flavors could be highlighted simply through aging in steel tanks. While they inoculate with commercial yeast the huge tanks of wine they ferment in San Miguel, a nondescript town north of Paso Robles—"seventy-two thousand gallons worth of wine I can't screw up," Bob says—he is adamant about blending the grapes for the result he wants rather than tweaking the wine with added acid or concentrates.

"You can do anything you want in that type of wine, but it never comes out the same," Bob says. "You can deacidify, add concentrate and Mega Purple, but it just takes away the natural beauty of what's down there. To me, nonintervention means sorting out the starting conditions so that there's nothing to intervene in. We get a kick out of doing it just by blending."

A BID FOR HUMILITY

Economically speaking, none of the work the Varners did on Foxglove was necessary. They could have stuck with their own tiny Santa Cruz world. But having imported French wine, the brothers were conversant with European vintners' moral expectations that wine must serve thirsts both great and humble. As Wells Guthrie puts it, "There's not much of that in America."

Guthrie and I are sitting in the lounge of Spruce, a San Francisco restaurant that, with its blue-blood clientele and clubby interior transformed from a 1930s car barn, is perhaps not the obvious spot to talk about cheap wine. While Spruce's wine list is full of $300 Meursault, he is drinking a bottle of Jean-Marc Roulot's Bourgogne Blanc, the basic wine made by one of that village's greatest talents.

A Florida native raised in Southern California, Guthrie might resemble a mellower James Spader. His Copain label primarily traffics in expensive Pinot Noir and Syrah that wouldn't be out of place on Spruce's list. But increasingly Guthrie has affordability on the brain, which brings us to his Tous Ensemble wines.

This project began, as they often do, with bills to pay—in Guthrie's case, for a new winery near Healdsburg's Eastside Road. But Tous Ensemble was also intended to fulfill a need for wine with a little less ambition. And, perhaps because of his own time in France, where he apprenticed for

Rhône vintner Michel Chapoutier, Guthrie felt the nagging moral pull to do more than make wine solely for the rich.

At first he simply redirected some of his Pinot Noir, cast-off lots from his top vineyards. But over time Tous Ensemble grew to produce four thousand cases, made largely from flatland sites in Anderson Valley, the site of most of his vineyards. The fruit might be less intensely flavored, but the vineyards are far cheaper to farm. There's no new oak and less cellar aging, both of which save money.

"It's like a Bourgogne Rouge," Guthrie says, referring to Burgundy's basic level of table wine. "We're not trying to make it anything it's not."

Guthrie and I share a view about the gap between the ambition of American vintners and that of their Old World counterparts. In California today you choose to make either expensive wine or cheap wine. But this wasn't always so. Robert Mondavi truly believed he could put his name on both a $125 Reserve Cabernet and $8 Woodbridge and let consumers embrace the full value chain (a good belief, even if it wasn't entirely successful). At Stag's Leap Wine Cellars, Warren Winiarski launched his second label, Hawk Crest, for similar reasons.

But ambition had to reign. In the cult-wine era of the 1990s, it was considered unseemly for celebrity winemakers to lend their name to cheaper fare. They had to shroud themselves in exclusivity. If you were Bill Harlan, positioning Harlan Estate as Napa's grand cru at $400 a bottle, your idea of a second label? The Maiden, a relative bargain at around $150 a bottle.

Compare that to Europe, where Burgundians make Bourgogne Blanc and Rouge—and not just negociant houses but *vignerons* all the way up to Jean-François Coche, whose Coche-Dury Corton-Charlemagne might now be the world's most expensive white wine at $1,800 a bottle. In Bordeaux, second- and even third-tier wines are omnipresent, if ever less affordable. In the Rhône Valley, Jean-Louis Chave makes not only his exquisite Hermitage but also a Mon Coeur Côtes du Rhône for around $20; the same is true for Domaine des Tours wines from Châteauneuf-du-Pape's legendary recluse Emmanuel Reynaud, of Château Rayas.

The reason, or at least one of them, is that when the wine market goes into one of its cyclical soft phases—as it does about every five to seven years—you don't want to be left holding only the fancy stuff. Hence Guthrie started leasing his own vineyard land a few years ago to support Tous Ensemble. Since he was paying up to $5,000 per ton for Pinot Noir at the top of the market, his vineyard mortgages, which work out to about $2,500 per ton, still manage to be more cost-effective—although it exposes him to the risks of being a farmer.

"We almost cut our fruit costs in half," he says, draining his glass of Roulot. "Eliminating anything in the middle makes it better. You have one less person to placate. In any business, you don't need to be a rocket scientist to figure out if you can cut your cost of goods by 40 percent, you're going to do it."

MADERA WILL PROVIDE

"What do you want me to tell him?" asks Ernie Dosio. As president of Pacific Agrilands, one of the Central Valley's larger grape-farming companies, Dosio is instrumental in pumping grape juice through California's heart.

Grape broker Erica Moyer, my host for the day, shoots him a glance. "The truth."

The truth is that these sturdy vines of French Colombard we're looking at, the workhorse white of France and California alike, the rows planted a generous eight by ten feet apart and stretched along a trellis more than five feet in the air, can provide twenty-five tons or more per acre, at healthy sugar levels, more than enough to make a mild and palatable table wine. Those numbers are mind-boggling by the standards of the coast, and of fine wine. A robust Sauvignon Blanc vineyard might give you seven tons per acre. A productive Cabernet vineyard might offer five. These are like vines farmed on a different planet.

But then, this might feel like another planet to someone used to Napa's charms. It's late August, and we're somewhere between the city of Madera and neighboring Chowchilla, just east of Highway 99, the Central Valley's drab lifeline, with its constant flow of produce-filled tractor-trailers.

"When they say you can't raise good grapes in Madera," Dosio tells me, "they're full of shit."

What had I expected here? Monster vines, perhaps, planted in a wasteland and stripped down to do nothing more than ripen endless bunches of grapes. The vines—not just Colombard but Zinfandel (primarily for white Zin) and Syrah—are productive, sure, but they also look healthy, or as healthy as a vine can look when pressed into steroidal service. The ground is barren dirt. In peak heat it can radiate back up to the vines at over 120 degrees Fahrenheit—we are in an irrigated semidesert, after all—but aside from their mammoth size, they look far more vibrant and adapted than many vineyards I've seen in, say, Sonoma.

This is Berenda Ranch, first planted to vines in 1984 as tomatoes, tree fruit, and the other produce of Madera County became less profitable. More vines were planted in 2004. Now there are dozens of acres of new Colombard saplings grafted to high-vigor Freedom rootstock lining the dirt roads. It turned out to be a savvy move in the increasingly impoverished Central Valley, where the economy is in a constant torpor; unemployment in Madera County hit 17 percent at the depths of the recession.

On average, fruit from Berenda might cost $300 per ton. But the land, never expensive, is essentially paid for. Even now, farmland in the area costs only perhaps $17,000 per acre. And Dosio keeps his annual farming and delivery costs between $1,700 and $2,000 per acre. With an average yield of about twenty tons? That's about $4,000 net revenue per acre. With about 1,500 acres planted on the property, there's potentially $6 million a year. Whoever said you make a small fortune from a large one in the wine business should make a pit stop in Madera.

"We make our numbers easily," Dosio tells me, steering his gleaming white pickup down another row of Colombard. "Consequently, we make a lot of money."

A SOLID EARNER

This bounty is being pulled from the official soil of California, San Joaquin sandy loam, which is great for large-scale farming but relatively devoid of organic matter. There's hardpan two feet down, hard enough to require a Caterpillar D11, a huge mining bulldozer, to break it up. Thanks to machine pruning and harvesting, Dosio only needs day laborers in the vines once or twice per season. They move fast, snipping at each vine a couple of times to tidy up its structure. The cost: $50 per acre.

Dosio's life has been governed by wine's unromantic side. He grew up in Escalon, a small San Joaquin town southeast of Stockton, and learned to farm in Lodi. By the time he graduated Fresno State in 1973, wineries were starting to prune mechanically, although farmers hadn't quite begun working with drip irrigation. They routinely sprayed or flooded their fields with massive doses of water.

This particular ranch is owned by the Ace Tomato Co., a major tomato packer up in Manteca that's a sort of absentee landlord. But Berenda is a solid earner. And this is just one of Dosio's many projects; he farms large-scale operations throughout the valley. In fact, Dosio's father was Gallo's first in-house field man, working the stretches of the San Joaquin Valley to bolster Ernest and Julio's ever-expanding empire. It's no surprise that Dosio feels at home here, even when a top grower-relations official for Constellation Wines drives up in his own shining white truck. These are Dosio's key clients: Constellation, Gallo, the Wine Group, McManis (a huge Central Valley operation that's a sort of indie foil to Gallo), and Delicato. The full roster of Big Wine.

"You want to see what $250,000 looks like?" Dosio asks. We drive by a small clearing in the vines filled with a set of pump equipment. Without access to water from the Madera Irrigation District, the ranch has to find its own, which means a $250,000 well dug nearly every year to a depth of nearly a thousand feet to access moisture in the flood plain. This does not leave Dosio particularly sympathetic to his counterparts in the western San Joaquin Valley, where signs along the interstate conspiratorially lament a "Congress-Created Dust Bowl." "They're babies over there," he says.

As for farming, don't ask Dosio about organics ("an excuse to do a shitty job of farming") or the sort of managed vine stress—holding back water

and so on—about which coastal growers obsess. From his end, the vines here at Berenda are healthy, productive, and in balance.

Of course, his definition of balance includes systemic herbicides, fertilizers, and that constant trickle of water, which delivers into relatively dead soil all that is required to make the vine not only grow but explode. The two things these grapes hold inside them for sure are water and sugar. The sugar comes from photosynthesis. The water? Check the well.

But Dosio takes a particular pride in his vineyards' relative health. His solution for extending the life of a vine? Keep it well watered and nourished—by admittedly artificial means. His vines may not be fancy, but they have endured. His tools can be as old-fashioned as urea, a traditional fertilizing source of nitrogen, or as modern as abscisic acid, a plant hormone originally used with table grapes that helps hasten color development. ("Two days after you put it on, the grapes are jet-black.") Thus Dosio has a point when he notes that even well-farmed coastal vineyards have a planned life span of only twenty years. "We know," he sniffs, "that the people in Napa and Sonoma have been able to kill vineyards consistently over the years."

It's getting toward noon, the temperature approaching 100 degrees, as Dosio drives me over to his oldest Colombard block. The trunks are thicker, the vines a bit more unruly. Planted in 1982 on their own roots, these have endured the vine-wilting disease eutypa as well as nematodes and even phylloxera. Despite all that, they keep reliably pumping out eighteen tons per acre.

"These are pretty ugly old ladies here," Dosio says, lifting up a bit of canopy to reveal massive green clusters dangling underneath. "But they're pretty good hookers."

"THE ABYSS"

I had asked Moyer, a partner in Turrentine Brokerage, one of the state's biggest grape brokers, to guide me through California wine's back forty. Brokers perform a quiet but vital service, matching up wineries that need extra fruit with growers who can help—and they also work in reverse, selling off a winery's excess product. Lately, the Constellations of the world seem to be doing both. Brokers, at least in Northern California, are typically tight-lipped about their clients. If you make expensive Cabernet, you don't want to have to talk about those trucks quietly arriving from Lodi. But Moyer's territory encompasses the San Joaquin Valley, which has her working according to a very different (but lucrative) set of economics than her Napa and Sonoma counterparts. California's current wine industry could barely function without it. Yet this part of the state is effectively uncharted, and almost never seen, by fancier wine types. Moyer calls it "the abyss."

We meet at a Starbucks in the morning Madera sun. She views viticulture in her territory as Dosio does—a pure commodity business, filling bottles to slake thirst. Terroir? Please. Here land is discussed in districts, the state's official designations for grape pricing. We're right in the midst of District 13, which also includes Fresno and parts of Tulare and Kings Counties. To the south is District 14, which wraps in Kern County and ekes out even lower prices than workhorse 13. If you're lucky you might land in District 11, Lodi, where Chardonnay nabs an extra $100 per ton. It all gets channeled into Brand California.

These days Brand California's clout is stronger than ever. For all the interest in sourcing grapes from overseas, smart wine companies like Gallo and Trinchero currently find it more efficient to purchase grapes at home, which is why plantings are booming from Bakersfield to Lodi. In just the two-year period of 2010 and 2011, counties like San Joaquin, Madera, and Fresno, as well as coastal San Luis Obispo, each added over fifteen hundred acres of vineyards.

The Colombard grape is the unmentioned workhorse of the California wine industry. At best, the grapes grown here might be quietly blended to stretch the economics of cheap Chardonnay or Pinot Grigio grapes, which by law must account for at least 75 percent of a wine if it is going to be labeled with one of those varietal names. Just as likely, however, they will become a product like Mountain Chablis, perhaps at the huge Almaden facility next door, its massive tanks towering in the distance. They also might be distilled into one of the many generic brandies or sherries that were Madera's unheralded output for at least half a century.

Or, like the grapes hanging just above my head in a giant patch at the middle of the ranch, they might not become wine at all. We're standing under a sprawling vine of Rubired, one of the great successes of UC Davis grape breeder Harold Olmo. Olmo crossed the Portuguese variety Tinta Cao with Alicante Ganzin, itself a cross of inky Alicante Bouschet and an obscure *V. rupestris* variety. The resulting grape, released in 1958, was intended for Port-style wines, but it had adopted Alicante's great trait as a *teinturier*, or dark-juiced grape variety that could be used to darken wines with insufficient color.

More recently Rubired has had another purpose, which explains its rise to become California's sixth-most-prolific red wine variety. It's the main component in the grape concentrate Mega Purple, devised by a division of Constellation as a way to add color and sweetness to generally cheap red wines—although it is also added to more than its share of expensive bottles. If you haven't encountered this term in your wine studies, that's because Mega Purple is the third rail of California winemaking, one of those not terribly scrupulous additives that is widely used but never discussed. Because it is made of grapes and used in modest amounts, and because wine labeling laws have massive loopholes, Mega Purple has quietly found a happy home in California, and it provides a modest income stream for Constellation, seeing as it now sells for up to $200 per gallon.

That is the exact fate of this patch of Rubired, grown at a robust twenty-three tons per acre (in 2011, Rubired sold for an average $319 per ton, or about $7,300 per acre) and destined for Constellation—mostly for concentrate, though some might become kosher wine. I pluck a couple berries. The taste is indistinct, like a mild red table grape. Though it must be grown far riper than the Colombard, to a minimum of 23 Brix, it's an easy variety to grow, resistant to mildew, and mostly just needs a light dusting of sulfur. If there's no glory in this endless row of swarthy green vines, there's also surprisingly little risk.

"This," Dosio says, "is why we say we farm commodities."

ONCE AND ALWAYS

How can this not be the remnant of another era of California wine, of the charmless days after Prohibition's repeal? French Colombard pumped into generic white wine, or used to bulk up cheap fighting varietals? It's not even as au courant as Triplett Blanc, a newly released cross of Colombard and

Vernaccia Sarda. Another insubstantial but productive grape, Triplett Blanc had one major purpose: to be even more productive than Colombard. And it is, sometimes hitting thirty tons per acre.

Commodity grapes have grown more important than ever. For all the popularity of Chardonnay and Pinot Noir, Brand California would crumple without vineyards like Berenda. Its rows contain the stark fiscal core of California winemaking. Its profits make those obsessing over their Pinot Noir in Sonoma look like schmucks.

And that long driveway leading to the nearby Almaden plant? It's a reminder that California's old wine ways haven't quite faded away. Mountain Chablis? Carlo Rossi? Hearty Burgundy? They aren't rated or acknowledged by the fine-wine trade. Yet these wines—millions of cases worth—remain. The same base materials that go into them—the anodyne flavors that could be Colombard or Thompson Seedless, a grape pervasive in the south San Joaquin Valley equally suited for eating or fermenting—are thriving.

And here is another great lie of California wine. Chardonnay at $8? Merlot at $10? Each bottle is stretched to its fiscal limits, grown on the cheap and bulked up by even cheaper grapes by an industry that leverages every farming trick in the book, that uses every bit of geographic obfuscation it can muster.

Dosio himself has mastered every step of this chain. If you've had a bottle under $15 in recent years, chances are he or one of his counterparts had a hand in it. Madera is his big-scale success, but he also farms Chenin Blanc in Clarksburg, harvested at seventeen tons per acre and sold for $450 per ton. There's Riesling in Thornton, a crossroads between the delta town of Walnut Grove and the Lodi airport, and dozens of acres of the Tannat grape, which will be made into a Port-like wine, then be blended back into table reds to add color and sweetness. He even farms Pinot Noir in the delta, another of those quiet farming puzzles that explains the existence of $10 Pinot.

Brand California's requirements are changing in his favor. Those superripe grapes, with the soft, jammy flavors that once attracted drinkers? Farmers no longer want to deal with the risk of dragging out the growing season. Dosio already has seen Gallo and Constellation pushing up their pick dates, willing to do more cellar work—anything from adding concentrate to blending to various technical means of removing the green-tasting flavors caused by grape compounds known as pyrazines. "I think the wineries know they can't piss off growers anymore," Dosio tells me. "I think you're going to see them take grapes at 1970s ripeness and do more in the winery."

If coastal California has bet on being the public face of wine, there is little to draw anyone here to Road 24, amid the featureless Central Valley plain. And so Dosio has one last rhetorical question.

"Where's the wine business?" he asks me, then grins.

"You're standing in it."

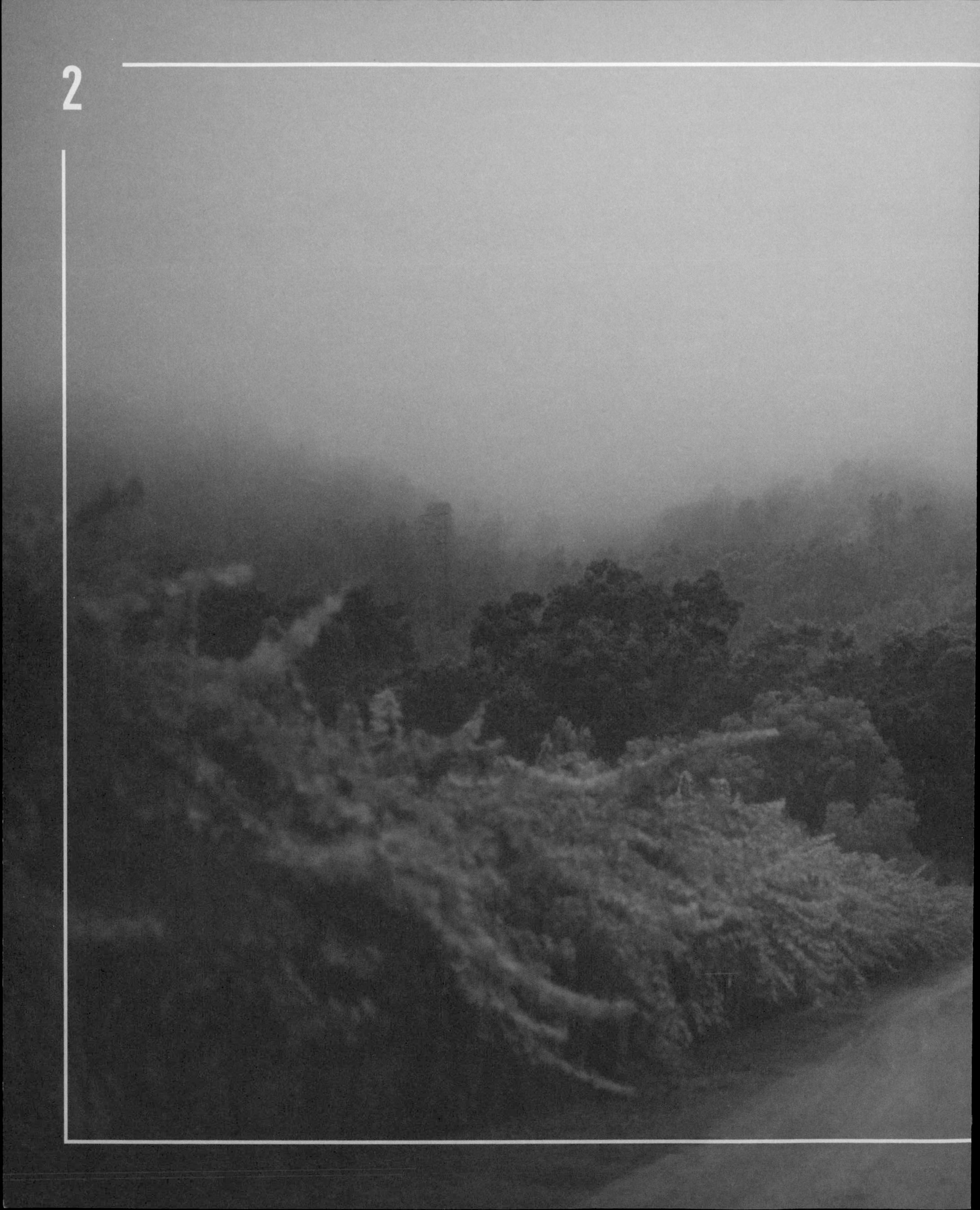
2

THE NEW TERROIR:
A CALIFORNIA ROAD TRIP

The Meaning of Place

Terroir is that most confounding of wine ideas— and nowhere more so than in California. It is more than just a sense of place; writer Matt Kramer once described it as "somewhereness"—the belief that place not only matters, but makes all the difference. California believes in this notion of "somewhereness," too—but it's a sad truth that terroir here has become primarily an economic consideration, arguably more so than anywhere else in the world. Bordeaux has its hierarchy of terroir, but the more crucial hierarchy there involves the rank of its producers. In Burgundy, Cistercian and Benedictine monks divined nuances of place, working over centuries to assess where the truly great soils could be found. California's efforts have been both hastier and far less pious.

This is in no way to dismiss California's terroir. Visit the steep parcels of the Monte Rosso Vineyard high above Sonoma Valley, where Emanuel Goldstein and Benjamin Dreyfus first established vines in iron-rich volcanic soils in the 1880s, and then taste modern-day Cabernet and Zinfandel from that spot, with their quintessentially dense tannins and warm spice, and realize that great sites were uncovered a century ago without the help of soil pits, digital mapping, or hydrology studies. The successes of the earliest California winemakers were often a result of trial and error, and often the application of lessons learned from the Old World. Nevertheless, nineteenth-century pioneers homed in on spots like the To Kalon Vineyard, which Hamilton Crabb happened to establish on one of the sweetest, best-drained spots along the western Napa Valley benchland. Just to the north in Rutherford, ship captain and trader Gustave Niebaum in 1879 began acquiring the plot he would call Inglenook, another perfect benchland spot that would go on to produce some of California's finest wines, both in Niebaum's day and decades later.

Cynics (including me, at one point) sometimes interpreted the overwrought nature of modern Napa Cabernet as a sign that the pioneers were wrong. But in the end, as Napa has circled back to revisit the style that made it famous in the 1970s, it has become evident that the century-plus legacy of winegrowing on the western Napa bench was no fluke. This is a near-perfect place for wine.

Even so, the notion of distinctive terroir in California is a relatively recent one. When California came home triumphant from the Judgment of Paris in 1976, its wine having trumped the French (for all their terroir-driven haughtiness), more attention was paid to the general quality of the American wines than their exact provenance. A few of the wines, like the 1971 Ridge Monte Bello and the 1970 Heitz Martha's Vineyard, were acknowledged for their specific origins (in the Santa Cruz Mountains and Oakville, respectively), but those were exceptions: the winning 1973 Chardonnay from Chateau Montelena wasn't even made from a

single county's fruit; it was blended from vineyards in Napa and Sonoma.

At the time, vintners paid little heed to specific geography, at least until 1978, when the federal government created American Viticultural Areas (AVAs), which at least partially regulated what place names could appear on a bottle. AVAs were meant to bring some consistency to what had become a Wild West of labeling. By drawing specific boundaries, they offered more precision than the state or county names that prevailed at the time. But they also were intended to ensure that American wines accurately represented their geography.

Unfortunately, the arrival of the appellation system brought a muddle of politics to the matter of terroir. In some cases, the creation of an appellation was relatively straightforward, as in the case of Napa Valley's approval in 1981. (Or so it seemed. Now there is some question as to why certain portions of Napa County were excluded, and others, like the warm Chiles Valley and Pope Valley areas in eastern Napa, were included.) More than thirty years after the Napa Valley appellation was designated, vintners are still battling over the valley's specific subappellations—smaller designations that can be nested inside larger AVAs.

If the American appellation system seems erratic or freewheeling, the lack of rigor was deliberate. While European wines must be grown solely in their area of origin to be labeled with an appellation, only 85 percent of grapes in an American bottle must come from the appellation on its label. And unlike in Europe, there are no regulations on farming practices or which grape varieties can be harvested. Certainly this has allowed California winemakers much-needed freedom to innovate— all while the Europeans have often tied themselves in bureaucratic knots. But it also opened up

the process to an increasingly cynical approach to wine geography. Marketing began to drive more and more of the appellation process. Secure your naming rights; grow the grapes later. Today regions are approved by federal regulators even when they barely contain a producing grapevine.

Early cracks in the appellation system could be seen when the three-million-acre North Coast AVA was approved in 1983, encompassing the counties of Napa, Sonoma, Mendocino, Lake, Marin, and Solano. That was followed in 1985 by the creation of the Central Coast and South Coast AVAs. These reflected some broad geographic terms used at the time. In an era when varietal wines were beginning to surge, the prospect of a labeling a Cabernet as from the North Coast or a Chardonnay as from the Central Coast was more appealing than simply talking about it being from California. But it also reflected the schism in modern California winegrowing: on one side were the industrial inland vineyards of the Central Valley, used primarily for cheap table wine; on the other were the fancier aspirations of coastal farmers, who rightly believed their wines could command a premium.

This coastal obsession reached its apotheosis in 2000, when Kendall-Jackson and other large wineries tried to create an omnibus California Coast appellation that would enfold all their vineyards in the North and Central Coasts, and even wrapped in the Southern California coast—a move that would have offered a valuable dollop of branding for megabrands like Kendall-Jackson's popular Chardonnay. The attempt failed to pass muster with the government, but by that point other ways of invoking the coast had been floated, like Beaulieu's creation of the BV Coastal brand. And there was the growing power of the all-encompassing California AVA. Brand California had by then become a potent marketing tool—flush with images of coastal hill-sides that too frequently were used to sell wines that hailed from the flat stretches of the inland desert.

AN ACT OF WILL

Defining California terroir, then, has as often as anything become an act of will. Which terroir has intrinsic potential and which is a gimmick? In the Old World, determining the answers to these questions took place—often imperfectly—over decades and centuries. In California, however, it is far tougher to ask questions about a sense of place with the proper humility required to find the right answers. Which appellations are sensible and useful? Which have been contrived by a lust for profit? A legitimate hunt for terroir has become clouded in a rush of economic ambition.

That's where soil hunters like Tegan Passalacqua come in. Passalacqua has some distinctly retro philosophies about farming. He believes many vines should be head trained, grown bushlike, without a wire trellis. Farming should be organic. Varieties should often be interplanted, as they were in old field blends.

Some of that might be extreme, but his views on winemaking, inspired by his stint working for South African vintner Eben Sadie, are minimalist for a reason: he believes that great grapes, grown in an appropriate place, should rarely require a wine-maker to fix things later with additions of yeast, acid, or water—makeup, essentially, that covers up the deficits of mediocre terroir.

This view is the very opposite of California's pre-vailing ideas about viticultural manifest destiny—that we should be able to grow what we want, where we want it, make the soil bend to our will.

"There are areas that you can and can't plant," Passalacqua says. "And when there are areas that don't want to take a grapevine, you're just going to exacerbate the problem."

While some of his fellow Californians might bristle at this view, Passalacqua's credentials are certainly impeccable. He oversees more than thirty-five vineyards across California, mostly for Turley Wine Cellars. At least once a week during the growing season, he traverses a wide swath of northern California—often in an eleven-hour, 350-mile loop—in addition to making routine hops to Paso Robles and elsewhere. In just eight months he put thirty-three thousand miles on his car.

These trips allow Passalacqua to engage in the vineyard version of management by walking around. But it also leaves time for some deliberate wandering, in the hope that the next great piece of soil might be around the corner.

"I think it's just curiosity," he tells me one day. "Over the years, people don't show up on time. I could just sit there and listen to the radio. But I want to poke around."

This has led Passalacqua to many long-forgotten sites, and it has turned him into a sort of informal vine archivist. In 2010 he cofounded the Historic Vineyard Society, to maintain a register of the state's great old sites (see Historic Preservation, page 261).

For him, studying old vines is simply a means to discover the lessons that were learned in the era before industrial agriculture, to understand what made a site like To Kalon great more than a century ago. Old vines are an antidote to the belief that humans can trump terroir. They provide a road map to the successful decisions of the past—and those decisions can help vintners begin to sketch a new map for California wine.

Contra Costa County

The winter sun is still rising as Passalacqua and I cross the Carquinez Strait near Suisun Bay and turn east toward the Contra Costa town of Oakley. Contra Costa is the northern apostrophe on the Bay Area, connecting Alameda County—Berkeley, Oakland, and beyond—to the Sacramento River delta. On its western side it is quintessential California suburbia, full of subdivisions and nondescript malls, plus the massive Chevron refinery on the edge of San Pablo Bay. As you move east, Contra Costa evolves into a humbler exurban patchwork, a mix of smaller homes with the remnants of a once-thriving agricultural industry.

We're on our way to one of the spots Passalacqua has hunted down; it sits behind a Carl's Jr. restaurant, down a back lane littered with plastic bags and an abandoned couch. "People out here are either crazy religious or meth heads," he says.

The Del Barba Vineyard, on a north-facing sandy swale by the highway, resembles a slightly ragged sandbox. Its patchwork of knobby century-old Zinfandel and Carignane vines, huddled close to the ground, is marked by holes where phantom plants have been pulled out.

The site is typical of Contra Costa: a tough old parcel that survived through the resolute stubbornness of the area's old, mostly Portuguese growers, who kept an eye on vines in between day jobs. As large companies cancelled their contracts for grapes grown here, Passalacqua and a handful of other new patrons appeared. The Evangelho Vineyard, which has been tapped by Morgan Twain-Peterson of Bedrock and Bonny Doon's Randall Grahm, himself an early vine hunter out here, includes interplanted white vines of Chasselas and Palomino amid its old Zinfandel and Carignane.

Great farming is a rarity in Contra Costa— more than a few vineyards look like they've survived a holocaust—but Passalacqua is trying. Squeezed between subdivisions, the Salvador Vineyard, with 110-year-old Zinfandel vines grown on thirty feet of sand, has been converted to organic farming. On my last visit a few years ago, the Zin trunks sprouted amid seemingly lifeless soil. Then Passalacqua began visiting the vineyard's owner, Steve Gonsalves, every week. Now a verdant cover crop spreads through the sandy rows. And Salvador has become one of Turley's prized single-vineyard wines. "They came across with the attitude 'we want this vineyard to prosper,'" Gonsalves tells me later.

I begin to sense an odd symbiosis. Gonsalves considers Passalacqua a savior: he's the guy who came, paid a fair price, and kept a vineyard from being gobbled up by urban sprawl. For Passalacqua, guys like Gonsalves are the link to saving California from an ocean of indistinguishable wine. For a few hundred dollars more per ton, Passalacqua can ask for great farming. That's a rarity in these parts, perhaps because Contra Costa has always been trapped between the glamour of the coast and the stark efficiencies of Central Valley farming. For years it has had visitors—whether reliable ones like Kent Rosenblum or big companies like Diageo (which bought Rosenblum's label in 2008)—who show up to grab fruit and depart. But rarely have these visitors helped elevate Contra Costa's fortunes.

As we cruise Oakley's back roads, the Fuji-like peak of Mount Diablo looming in the background, another point comes up. The whims of wine fashion seem to have gravitated to the stark landscapes of southern France, or Santorini, or the Canary Islands. Contra Costa has the same old vines, the same potential. Yet even Passalacqua, evangelist that he is, is struggling to shine a light here. He's had a few bites, from people like Abe Schoener of the Scholium Project, who has made one Mourvèdre from Del Barba and another from the Pato Vineyard, near the delta town of Antioch.

CONTRA COSTA COUNTY

VINEYARD AREA/TOTAL AREA: 1,878 acres/ 458,202 acres

MAIN GRAPES: Zinfandel, Carignane, Mourvèdre

AT A GLANCE: A treasure trove of old, productive vineyards that have survived for up to a century or more

THE PROMISE: Long a quiet source for good grapes, now being discovered by young, talented winemakers

THE RISK: Encroaching development, low grape prices, and subpar farming

Even so, this is one slice of California that never seems to make it into the conversation. Perhaps, instead of Black Rock City, the wine-hipster contingent should board a magic bus for Antioch?

"Out here," Passalacqua concludes, "the community has no idea what it has."

Sonoma

David Hirsch's vineyard might as well be at the end of the earth. Certainly it is at land's end, astride the next to last ridge, north of the Russian River's mouth, before California slides into the Pacific Ocean.

Hirsch's domain, seventy-two acres of mostly Pinot Noir vines on what once was a sheep ranch, sits atop a vast geological kaleidoscope, an extreme example of the Franciscan Complex that runs along the San Andreas Fault, which sits just west of his land. It is a mystery writ in earth.

The nearest town, a half-hour's drive away, is the tiny forest hamlet of Cazadero, just north of the Russian River watershed. With eighty inches of rain annually, constantly lurking fog, and microclimates that can shift as much as twenty degrees in a short walk, the only sure thing here is wild inconsistency. Yet for more than three decades Hirsch has been trying to decode this wild jumble of subsoils—everything from porous sandstone to

Harvest at Hirsch Vineyards

nearly impenetrable clay. Today it comprises dozens of subblocks based on soil changes that occur as frequently as every twenty feet. "We gave up trying to master it," Hirsch told me. "We just sort of settled in and got comfortable with the uncertainty and the complexity."

Getting to Hirsch requires a dramatic journey any way you do it. In my case, I head northwest through the rolling cow country outside the Sonoma County town of Petaluma, past the nubby grazing lands near the hamlet of Valley Ford, where the signs for family-style Italian dinners are the last bastion of unreconstructed Sonoma. From there you weave north, pushing deep into the Russian River watersheds, following the river's path along its final few miles west to the sea. Here's where it gets dicey: you have to turn inland again and climb Bohan-Dillon Road toward the coastal ridgetop—five more miles of switchbacks, past George Bohan's vineyard, the site of the first modern planting in this part of the California coast, in 1971. The pavement ends, a goat wanders nearby, and a dirt road slices through forest glades, filled with that dry conifer smell that California exudes.

While the coast is always bathed in fog and chill, the temperature rises back into the seventies as I drive the route one day, the pure September sun above. I pass a patch of exceedingly well-groomed vines, with bird netting draped on top and several signs warning away visitors; these are the Marcassin vineyards of Helen Turley and her husband John Wetlaufer. Finally, there is a hand-drawn paper sign stapled to a post. It would say "Hirsch," but the paper is folded back; only the "H" is showing.

How did Hirsch, a Bronx native who never quite lost his hometown accent, and never quite finished his studies at Columbia, find his way to this corner of the world? His trip west began in 1968, when he headed for Mexico and wound up in Santa Cruz. He went into the clothing business, and in 1978, following "an intuition that California was getting too crowded," Hirsch paid $425,000 for these scraggly parcels near Fort Ross, which at the time were torn up by timber harvests and sheepherding. He thought he would plant trees, but in 1980 an old Santa Cruz vintner friend, Jim Beauregard, convinced him to plant a bit of Pinot Noir.

This was an improbable plan at the time in the rural, poor, slightly hippie-ish hills of far west Sonoma. To the extent that anyone was thinking about soils for wine grapes back then, these seemed too eroded and thin to be of much value—and not just because of the years of timber harvest and grazing. This part of the coast sits at a confluence of multiple water systems, including the drainage of the Gualala River, and is home to sometimes colliding weather patterns that dump buckets of rain on the ridges. All that gave the vineyard what David calls its "gestalt."

Although to some extent the history of wine in Sonoma has always involved a push out to the coast (even in the 1970s, the relatively cool Russian River Valley was being explored as a spot for Pinot Noir rather tho Zinfandel it once had grown), many growers deemed western Sonoma too cold for red wine. At the time, the hills just west of Highway 101, nearly 20 miles inland, seemed remote enough. Only a few brave souls ventured farther west, like the Bohans, who had lived near the coast for generations; or Donnie and Linden Schatzberg, who established their Precious Mountain site in 1973 in the hills above Cazadero.

Hirsch's grapes were initially just a cash crop, sold to wineries as a side business, but after he left the clothing business in 1987 and moved up to the ranch, he hired a vineyardist named Eve-rardo Robledo to graft some old Riesling plantings over to Pinot Noir, using vine material purchased from Jeffrey Patterson of Mount Eden Vineyards. Robledo never left; today he runs Hirsch's vineyard operation.

In 1994, after years of selling his grapes to large wineries at commodity prices, Hirsch finally found a market for his fledgling Pinot plantings. Promi-nent winemakers began to make Hirsch-designated wines, and Hirsch's vineyard was reborn as a sym-bol of conquering the extreme coast.

Even then, Hirsch felt the soils hadn't quite revealed themselves. After a wet season in 1998, when rain mildewed the shallow roots of vines planted in hardpan, he realized that his prior farm-ing ways, dabbling in topsoils without considering the complications of his site, had been a mistake. Over the next eighteen months he commissioned soil pits and rebalanced the mineral content in the ground. This fine-tuning would continue for years. Driving down vine roots to access the full complex-ity of the soils, in part by giving up routine irriga-tion, would be the only way to produce wines that could exude their Hirsch-ness, their specificity.

THE CONSTANT CHALLENGE

By the early 2000s, using the coast of Sonoma to explore the extremities of farming, in particular for Pinot Noir, had become an increasingly popu-lar decision. The reason can be found in the pileup of soil at the edge of the coastal ridges, a result of tectonic activity from the San Andreas Fault, the collision of the Pacific and North American plates, which provides volcanic and metamorphic material like serpentine and greenstone, and the uplifted

remnants of ancient seabed from the Pacific, which contributes sandstone, marine fossils, and more—all of it part of the Franciscan soils that dominate the hills of the Northern California coast. The fault is particularly prevalent a few miles from Hirsch, as it resurfaces near the town of Jenner after a run underwater.

But the sheer size of the Hirsch Vineyard makes it an outlier in this corner of Sonoma; it is big enough that its assembly of parcels has been compared an entire Burgundy village. Such sweep-ing scale is no big thing to the east, in Russian River Valley. But in far western Sonoma, there's lit-tle choice but to plant small. South of the river's mouth, the Cobb family's Coastlands Vineyard managed to establish fourteen acres on the hills above Bodega Bay, which outsized Ted Lemon's Haven Vineyard on a nearby ridge, with just five of its ten acres actually in vine.

Even now the coast remains a frontier. Though there's heat and sun on the coastal ridgetops, at lower elevations, around six hundred or eight hun-dred feet, there is a constant battle with chill and the relentless wind from the ocean, which can dis-turb flowering and other aspects of vine growth. This marginality makes the wines here particu-larly compelling, but it also makes farming a nightmare—one magnified by the remote loca-tion, which means there are few trained vineyard hands nearby. It is a drive of an hour or more to any town of size.

Then there's the cost: planting a vineyard on the coast costs between $60,000 and $100,000 per acre, excluding land costs, which makes it poten-tially more expensive than even in Napa. This means it must be either a generational commit-ment or one borne by deep-pocketed investors like Peter Michael, the British-owned winery in Knights

Valley that reportedly spent upward of $25 million to resculpt land near Hirsch and its neighbor, Flowers Vineyard and Winery—or about $1 million per vineyard acre. Even the most ambitious economics of Pinot Noir make that a tough deal. And should you still be inclined to throw money at the hillsides, there's little land left for planting. While the original pioneering took place on depleted rangeland or timberland, a combination of conservation efforts meant to protect watershed quality and the salmon population have made any big new plantings unlikely.

In trade for the hardship is the possibility of greatness. That's what drew brothers Nick and Andy Peay to the tiny coastal town of Annapolis to plant their own estate in the late 1990s. Even by extreme Sonoma Coast standards, Peay occupies a chilly slice of the world. While vineyards to the south like Hirsch and Flowers sit above the inversion layer, this slice of the coast is lower—around six hundred to eight hundred feet—which means it's mired in the fog belt and precipitously chilly.

If discovering a spot like Hirsch was a happy accident, the Peays deliberately explored the Pacific coast for a location with an excruciatingly long growing season, somewhere that flirted with the edge of ripening ability. In the 1990s, land in this onetime timber area could be had for $4,000 per acre, less than a tenth of what it might cost today. Returning from a camping trip in Humboldt County, Andy stopped by an old 280-acre weekend retreat outside the town of Sea Ranch. Its weathered 1906 farmhouse still stands on the same rise today, and if you stand on the porch of that farmhouse on a winter day, feeling the wind in your bones and watching the fog sweep in from the Pacific, the extremes that drew the Peays here are evident.

In a way, these conditions are what have always drawn people out to Sonoma's far west. In the 1980s, after searching without luck for vineyards in the Green Valley area, in the southwestern corner of Russian River Valley, Burt Williams and Ed Selyem heard about a vineyard called Summa a bit farther toward the coast. They visited, tasted some homemade wines, and contracted for fruit in 1988. Their reasoning was simple: coastal fruit would ripen later than their Russian River mainstays, allowing them to use the same equipment for two rounds of fermentation, and thus make a bit more wine.

Summa, which sits southwest of the town of Occidental, is in that elevation range where mildew and rot are constant concerns. Farming must be impeccable. In good years like 1991 and 1995, it made one of Williams Selyem's top wines, but often it would be dumped into a Sonoma Coast blend. "It was always a problem vineyard," Williams recalls.

Things were a bit easier at David Cobb's nearby Coastlands Vineyard, which Williams Selyem began using in 1992 to make a wine that marked the ascendency of the Sonoma Coast. Eventually, Coastlands would become a symbol of how better farming, and the passage of time, helps turn a marginal spot into an established one. David's son Ross has become a great student of the coast, having worked as a viticulturist for Williams Selyem and as winemaker at Flowers, along with making wine for his family's label, Cobb. Over time he has continually pushed up his own pick dates, which are now far earlier than those of clients like Williams Selyem. "They typically pick about three weeks later than us," Ross tells me.

THE BIG LIE

The most unstable aspect of wine here might be how the coast itself is defined—because, in a way, the Sonoma Coast is one big lie.

It's not the coast itself that's a lie, of course; there it is, running from the cove of Bodega Bay in the south, growing rugged as it approaches the mouth of the Russian River, and downright wild as it stretches north to Mendocino. No, the lie is in the bureaucratic entity known as the "Sonoma Coast," a monstrously convoluted appellation approved in 1987 by the federal government. The appellation was created in an era when the word "coastal" had supreme clout in California wine, so much so that Jess Jackson and Robert Mondavi, among others, petitioned unsuccessfully starting in 1998 for the creation of a "California Coastal" appellation that would encompass their many holdings along the entire length of the state's coast.

The Sonoma Coast was a similar gerrymander, largely the work of Brice Jones of Sonoma-Cutrer. When Jones was drawing up the proposal for the Sonoma Coast appellation, he needed to sweep in the far-flung vineyards that constituted Sonoma-Cutrer's empire, which ranged from Carneros to some far-flung spots near the coast. Such an entity would allow him, for example, to label his wines from the Les Pierres Vineyard near Carneros with an "Estate Bottled" designation (in order to do so, a vineyard has to be in the same appellation as the winery). It would allow him to sell "coastal" Chardonnay in large quantities. The Sonoma Coast was thus was born of a moment of bureaucratic haste, although Jones maintained to me that the official AVA, although large, is "true to the purpose of having appellations." (He also asserted that "the only appellations that mean anything to consumers are Russian River Valley, Sonoma Coast, and Napa Valley.")

The Sonoma Coast has been a mess ever since. It stretches across 750 square miles, from the Napa-Sonoma boundary on San Pablo Bay to the far northern reaches of Sonoma's actual coast near the hamlets of Annapolis and Gualala. Along the way it engulfs most of Russian River Valley and the Sonoma portion of Carneros—all told, nearly half of Sonoma County.

Could a vineyard high on a ridge near the Pacific Ocean have more than a passing commonality with one fifty miles southeast, in sight of San Pablo Bay and Napa County? In terroir terms, it verges on the preposterous, which is why for a decade there has been a distinction made between the Sonoma Coast, political entity, and the "true" Sonoma Coast, where pioneers farm the county's remote western stretches.

In 2010 a group of winemakers in that more extreme slice of Sonoma dubbed themselves the West Sonoma Coast Vintners. To demarcate their region, the westernmost portion of the county, they drew a line more or less along Highway 116, which slices through what was once old Gravenstein apple country. The name was a bit of finesse—a way to avoid clashing with their fellow vintners over which vineyards were planted along the "true" coast. As Carroll Kemp, owner of the Red Car winery and one of the group's founders, judiciously put it to me, "We didn't want to build something that inherently in the name started putting people down."

The true coasters wanted foremost to differentiate their corner of the world from places farther east, such as the Lakeville area—a swath near Carneros where rolling hills rise up from the bay—which might be a sweeter choice for Chardonnay and Rhône-native varieties than for Pinot Noir.

But the delineation of the west Sonoma Coast region was not merely an attempt to credit the "true coast." It was also an effort to begin fine-tuning the nuances of its terroir. The hope was that the Westies could ultimately to subdivide, or at least bring order to, the bureaucratic blob that is the Sonoma Coast. They began to carve out smaller, seemingly distinct areas—like the Sebastopol Hills, which touches the western edge of the Russian River Valley appellation, hoping to differentiate it from nearby towns like Occidental and Freestone, as well as some very different areas north of the Russian River itself.

Each has its own particular soils and climate—enough that some of the true coasters had lobbied for their own subappellations. Slowly, they began to get them. In 2011, after nearly a decade of opposition from Jones and the Hartford Family Winery, a Fort Ross–Seaview appellation was approved by federal regulators, delineating coastal ridges north of the river around Cazadero that include Hirsch and nearby sites. Other subappellations remain on the drawing board: one for Freestone-Occidental, another for the area around Annapolis, and still others for the Sebastopol Hills and the Petaluma Wind Gap area, south toward the Marin border.

THE RUSSIAN RIVER PUZZLE

The geographic complications of the Sonoma Coast pale in comparison to those of the Russian River Valley. Once, that term might have been used to mean any part of the patchwork of valleys that dominate Sonoma and Mendocino Counties, but in time it has come to represent Sonoma's grand wine engine.

Currently the Russian River Valley embraces nearly 170,000 acres, thanks to an expansion in 2011 of more than 14,000 acres near the appellation's southern edge. The expansion was pushed through largely by Gallo, which hoped to include its 400-acre Two Rock Vineyard, near Cotati, inside the appellation, a move that would have given it a big source for Russian River–branded wines—and one that drew the ire of at least a few smaller Russian River growers. ("They argue that it's part of the Russian River watershed. Yeah, so's Ukiah," Rod Berglund of Joseph Swan Vineyards told *Wine Spectator*.)

But that was just the most recent expansion. In 2005 the federal government signed off on a thirty-thousand-acre expansion that growers claimed more accurately represented the limits of fog incursion, which had become the area's frequent talking point. In part this allowed for some expansion to the south and west, but it also swept in much of the entire area around the city of Santa Rosa, one more typically associated with warmer-climate grapes. Since 1983, the appellation has slowly been swallowing up ever more of Sonoma County.

Russian River's growth spurts kept leading me to the same conclusion: its sprawl has less to do with geography than it does with the need to constantly feed the industry that Russian River Pinot Noir has become. Much like Napa Cabernet, it is no longer a wine defined by its geography, or any specific sense of place. It is a brand.

A few years ago climatologist Greg Jones presented comparative data to the American Society for Enology and Viticulture that showed Russian River Valley to be the warmest spot on earth producing fine Pinot Noir, with an average of 2,642 degree-days Fahrenheit during the growing season, enough to place it closer in spirit to Cabernet

country than other Pinot regions. However, it's difficult to talk about a single climate for such a large region, and the western reaches of Green Valley, once a key spot for sparkling wine, are hardly the same as Santa Rosa's Chalk Hill or eastern Healdsburg. Indeed, degree-days Fahrenheit can range from around 2,400 on the western side to more than 3,500 at times on the eastern side—enough to simulate the Central Valley, or at least Calistoga, in northern Napa. Though rain occurs primarily in the off-season, Jones's data also showed that Russian River receives more than almost any other Pinot region—including Burgundy.

Yet the various valleys astride the Russian River have long been planted with grapes. These valleys were part of a flourishing wine industry in the nineteenth century, before the land was turned over to other fruit crops, particularly the Gravenstein apple. Indeed, author John Winthrop Haeger notes that an 1891 publication lists more than three hundred grape growers in the area, accounting for about seven thousand acres. The dominant red grape? Zinfandel.

In the 1960s and '70s a handful of pioneers dabbled in Pinot and Chardonnay here. Starting with farmer Charles Bacigalupi and then his neighbor Joe Rochioli Jr., a handful of pioneers planted small quantities of Pinot along Healdsburg's Westside Road, much of it destined for sparkling wine or, in Rochioli's case, Gallo's Hearty Burgundy. It would be another twenty years before Russian River Pinot began its grand boom. But the momentum of California wine in the 1990s, plus distinct praise for Russian River wines (over those of Carneros) and its evolution into an easy-to-know spot for Pinot aficionados—at a time when it became fashionable to plant Dijon clones in California (see page 68)—added up to an explosion of young vineyards on often fertile soils.

I had always been puzzled by the presumed greatness of Russian River Valley wines. Chardonnay grown here could be interesting, although it was often unfocused and oak-laden, but the persistent ripeness of Pinot fruit throughout much of the appellation—indeed, the typical descriptions of Russian River Pinot, brimming with dark fruit and cola flavors—was enough to make me ask whether Russian River Valley was the right place to be growing Pinot Noir.

Yet over the years I had encountered some glorious wines from Russian River Valley. There were examples from Tom Dehlinger, for instance, although the fact that he also made fine Syrah and Cabernet from his property was an early tip-off that area's climate wasn't as Pinot-friendly as it was often described. Dehlinger had planted Syrah in 1989 to take advantage of what he described to me as "a dual-purpose climate"—one that offered windows of ripeness for both grapes. On the rare occasion I tasted an early Williams Selyem Pinot, the wines were deep and luscious without being lavish. They offered instant evidence of why a Russian River land rush had taken place.

"WE DON'T HAVE TO WAIT FOREVER"

I couldn't puzzle out Russian River's shortfalls. Was it the proliferation of sandy loam known as Goldridge soil, a word uttered by the area's Pinot producers as a road sign for quality? (Ted Lemon of Littorai, whose Pivot Vineyard is on Goldridge soil, surmised that the depth of this particular soil type and its ability to retain water determines the wines' relative quality: "You can kind of turn those things around and say, well, is any old limestone soil . . . going to produce great wine? And of course the answer is no.") Or perhaps the problems I had noted

SONOMA COAST

VINEYARD AREA/TOTAL AREA: approx. 7,000 acres/ 480,000 acres

MAIN GRAPES: Pinot Noir, Chardonnay, Syrah

AT A GLANCE: A sprawling area that encompasses much of Sonoma County. Its remote western slice, including subdivisions like the 27,500-acre Fort Ross–Seaview appellation, produces some of the best Pinot Noir in California. The eastern portion may prove to excel for varieties like Syrah.

THE PROMISE: Exceptional Pinot Noir and Chardonnay from some of the state's most distinctive soils, with the best vineyards in relatively marginal climates near the Pacific coast

THE RISK: Geographic confusion, overripeness, and limited expansion possibilities near the coast

with Russian River Valley Pinots were the result of yield-minded growers, possessed of heavier clay-rich soils, pushing for a far larger crop than Pinot Noir had typically been able to offer—one reason why the area initially had appeal for sparkling wine.

The person to ask, of course, is Burt Williams, who still lives in the heart of Russian River Valley, just a few miles from where Westside Road follows the river. He lives in Hacienda del Rio, the same tidy cabin in Forestville that he first moved to in 1962.

We discuss a few of the wines we like from the area, including those from Dehlinger and Porter Creek. "I prefer cherry and berry flavors," Williams tells me. "But you know, Tom Dehlinger, I think, would always pick a little later and make plummier, deeper kind of wines. I love Tom's wines. He's a great winemaker. Just different from my style."

You realize, I ask, that these wines are now considered aberrant examples in Russian River Valley?

"Really?"

Mind you, Williams had an equally good reputation for Russian River Zinfandels, including those with robust alcohol from the Martinelli property in Windsor (his isolate of Zinfandel yeast even became one of the most successful alcohol-tolerant commercial yeasts in California). How had Williams's ethereal wines morphed into the modern-day jam piles that Russian River was now churning out?

Ted Lemon later suggested one theory: "Burt was able to seek out vineyards that had distinction, because either they were basically what Rochioli was, an old Italian vineyard that benefited from vine age. Or he knew how to look for stuff that was not getting all the irrigation, or was older."

Or perhaps the answer wasn't nearly so complicated. There were pockets of Russian River Valley made more interesting by their relative coldness, like the Green Valley area. (That, however, didn't stop some Green Valley winemakers from excess.)

But on balance, the enormous size of the Russian River appellation and its relative heat—enough not just for Zinfandel but also for Cabernet Sauvignon—combined with the typical California luxury of a long, dry fall, had added up to a perfect combination. It was the right spot for winemakers who viewed Pinot as just another beverage to sell down the retail chain, for an industry built upon the usual formula for over-the-top ripeness, lots of fancy oak, and wines built on a principle of shock and awe.

"I think they were picking way too late. I think they were picking way too ripe," Williams tells me. "I was always very concerned with the acidities of my wine, so I tended to pick early."

He laughs for a moment and then pauses. "We don't have to wait forever on these things. And I wanted to make wines more in the style of the Old World. I wasn't interested in making blockbusters."

Sierra Foothills

The distance from the California coast to the foothills of the Sierra Nevada mountains is modest; the drive from San Francisco to Amador or El Dorado County takes less than three hours. Indeed, just past the state capital of Sacramento, the land rises up from the hot floor of the Central Valley into high grasslands, then into the wooded hills that mark the mountains' start. Wander past the flatlands of Lodi and you'll soon cross into the first miles of Calaveras County, where you might find the Ghirardelli family's vineyard full of one-hundred-year-old Zinfandel vines and a scrubby little parcel of the white grape called Burger, vines whose grapes were once shipped by rail down to the city for home winemakers. The foothills' local wineries are always keen to remind city dwellers—usually with little success—that they're only a quick day trip away from the coast.

If the actual distance from the coast to the foothills is modest, the cultural distance is enormous. Indeed, as a wine region the foothills don't entirely feel as though they are of California. They are the state's *other* wine expanse, discovered and then forgotten again and again—first during the Gold Rush, when dozens of wineries sprang up throughout the Mother Lode, then again in the 1970s. The area's 2.6 million acres stretch from North Yuba to Mariposa County, an enormous but mostly unexplored spine that extends through much of California's northern half. As 1970s Napa was preparing to trounce France at its own game, Amador County Zinfandels, unabashedly big and Californian, drew a more rustic sort of attention, promoted by coastal wineries like Sutter Home and fans like Sacramento wine savant Darrell Corti.

But as the coast dominated California's story line in the 1970s and 1980s, the foothills largely disappeared from the conversation. While many of its wineries enjoyed an itinerant business, their tasting rooms drawing crowds from Sacramento and Reno, the wines themselves languished. They were rarely made by expert hands and were usually left out of the critical spotlight.

In the mid-2000s, clues began to surface about a small renaissance. Winemakers saw the same things that drew their predecessors in the early 1970s: a bounty of old vines and the untapped possibilities of the same geological jumble that drew Gold Rush miners.

If Zinfandel had once been the magnet that attracted winemakers to the area, it turned out that Grenache was the key to this latest quiet revival. Believers in Rhône-native grapes had been toiling in the foothills for more than twenty years, and over the course of several years in the late 2000s I encountered exceptional specimens here from labels like Favia and Donkey & Goat. When I inquired, one name kept surfacing again and again: Ron Mansfield.

"I kept hearing a little buzz here and there about Grenache," Mansfield explains as we drive in his pickup through the hamlet of Camino, nestled at 3,100 feet near the El Dorado County town of Placerville, which is known as much for its apple orchards as for its grapes.

Mansfield has become the foothills' Johnny Grapeseed. In 1978, freshly out of school, he landed in Placerville to help with an irrigation study. This familiarized him with local soils, and soon he began growing peaches, pears, and cherries. (His Goldbud Farms still ships picture-perfect specimens around the country.)

But Mansfield also realized the potential for wine, and eventually he made the Rhône connection. Despite obvious differences between the foothills and lowland Rhône, there are parallels in climate and crucial similarities in soil composition—particularly the presence of granite, a rarity in California but commonplace in the Rhône, as well as sand, which Grenache loves. For that matter, the hills are above the fog and clear of most of the coastal cloud patterns. They enjoy a long and almost uniformly sunny growing season, but without the brutal heat of the Central Valley down below.

These qualities had been evident as early as the 1860s, when the first vineyards were planted here, and they were rediscovered just over a century later by pioneers like John MacCready of Sierra Vista Winery. In the late 1980s the Perrin family of Châteauneuf's Château de Beaucastel weighed the possibility of planting in El Dorado County before founding their Tablas Creek project in Paso Robles. And the hills were a draw for Rhône-minded scouts like Bill Easton of Domaine de la Terre Rouge and Steve Edmunds of Berkeley's Edmunds St. John.

Edmunds was glad to find Syrah growing here, and he even tried farming his own vineyard, but the roster of Rhône-inspired grapes didn't fully satisfy his curiosity. So he persuaded a vineyardist working with pear grower Bob Witters to plant Gamay Noir, the grape of Beaujolais, at 3,400 feet, in granite soils similar to those of southern Beaujolais (Beaujolais is just north of the Rhône Valley).

That vineyardist? Mansfield, of course.

I ask Mansfield to show me around the foothills' new iteration. In El Dorado and Placer Counties, a happy band of soil and climate can be found along the American River Canyon, a sweet spot for Rhône-native grapes. The canyon tempers the heat and offers excellent air drainage to keep grapes cool and dry. It's possible to taste the radical differences in soil and elevation in El Dorado wines—even those from exuberant young-vine fruit. Grenache from the slate-packed 2,700-foot-elevation Swansborough site, one of Mansfield's pet projects, is gutsy but floral. One from the Gold-bud site surrounding Mansfield's office is delicate and beautifully perfumed, full of lavender and fennel seed.

As we traverse both sides of the canyon, I can't but notice the prevalence of head-trained vines trellised to a single wooden stake, a tradition in both the Rhône and old-time California. I ask my guide.

"You mean, the Mansfield vertical cordon?" he jokes.

A sort of modern head training—less sprawling than in the old days, but without the manicured nature of the coast—seems to suit the hills' rambunctious nature. While the foothills have no shortage of subpar viticulture, these more unruly plantings are deliberate: they help to temper the abundant high-altitude sunshine. Since foothill wines have never been shy on ripeness, more sensitive varieties like Syrah are routed to north-facing slopes; sun-loving grapes like Grenache and Mourvèdre face south.

The Sierras typically enjoy a thermal updraft each morning from the Central Valley to the west, reversed by a cooling afternoon downdraft. This helps temper daytime heat and offers the possibility for great flavor and moderate alcohol levels—if the fruit is picked at the right time. That's a big if in a region that prides itself on growing a high-acid grape like Barbera to well over 15 percent potential alcohol.

Red Grenache may be outshining the area's traditional Zinfandel and Barbera plantings, but Mansfield and others have realized that whites can excel here too. Mansfield seems to be leaving a trail of Grenache Blanc and Vermentino everywhere he goes, in addition to Marsanne, Picpoul, and even Italian grapes like Fiano. In nearby Amador County

the Verdelho grape, native to Portugal, is staging a modest rally.

These plantings were irresistable to talented winemakers near the coast. But another thing drew them inland: prices for grapes grown in the foothills remain a bargain by Napa or Sonoma standards. El Dorado Grenache, for instance, went for $1,538 a ton in 2009, about half the cost of grapes in Napa.

A TRICKY BARGAIN

The region's status as a bargain alternative to the coast, as well as the influx of coastal winemakers, can be a touchy subject in a region where raw possibility often outpaces local talent. It is why, for instance, Napa viticulturist Ann Kraemer kept a low profile after leaving her career managing vineyards for Shafer and Domaine Chandon to purchase an Amador parcel in 2001 with her family. She meticulously planted the site, Shake Ridge, to everything from head-trained Zinfandel to Counoise, applying her Napa-trained brain to the "geological chaos" of this area. Quietly, she began selling fruit to notable Napa clients like Annie Favia and Andy Erickson of Favia and Helen Keplinger of Keplinger Wines. In an area with a bit of an inferiority complex, it was crucial to fend off talk of viticultural carpetbagging.

There's less hesitancy on that front in Fair Play, a town southeast of Placerville that is believed to be the California appellation with the highest average elevation—all its vineyards are between two thousand and three thousand feet. There you'll find Skinner Vineyards. Other foothills wineries may invoke the Mother Lode for effect, but Skinner has a concrete link to California's gold-mining past: founder Mike Skinner is the great-great-great-grandson

The mountains' relative solitude attracted an avant-garde, like Hank Beckmeyer and his wife, Caroline Hoel. Their La Clarine Farm, not far from Fair Play in the town of Somerset, takes back-to-nature farming to its apotheosis, for better or worse. They embrace not only biodynamics but even the more esoteric beliefs of Japanese philosopher Masanobu Fukuoka, whose hands-off approach is evident in La Clarine's 3.5 acres of midget vines set amid a teeming patch of sage, wild thyme, and Indian paintbrush; there are no vine trellises and no weeding. Caroline keeps busy with her herd of goats, from which she has made a fine set of cheeses.

"We've got little, tiny, small vines that don't take much water, which is good, because there's not much water around," Hank tells me as we stand atop a knoll. "It's more of an experiment, and labor of love-slash-hate."

"Slash-hate, yeah," Caroline adds.

The couple are using the same roster of winemaking techniques that have caught the attention of wine minimalists in cities like New York and Quebec. La Clarine Farm, then, has become more of a darling in Soho than Somerset, as it taps into a particularly current set of wine interests: skin-fermented white wines that come across as orange; the barest use of the preservative sulfur dioxide.

La Clarine Farm shares a spirit with other outposts like Renaissance Vineyard, nearly sixty miles north in North Yuba, whose dense, tannic wines easily improve over a decade. Its winemaker, Gideon Bienstock, also makes wines for his own Clos Saron label, which demonstrates a similarly minimalist take in the cellar—no added yeast and almost no sulfur dioxide.

The attention from afar has created a Faustian bargain of sorts for the foothills. A handful of vintners have rejected the chance for outside acclaim,

of James Skinner, a Scottish miner who in 1860 turned his gold into one of the foothills' first wineries.

The modern-day Skinners not only built a sleek new facility that might look more comfortable in ritzy Healdsburg; they also hired a winemaker from the coast, Chris Pittenger, who had done stints at Williams Selyem and Marcassin in Sonoma and Torbreck in Australia.

Skinner, like other wineries in the area, sees in Grenache the opportunity for greatness. From the Sumu Kaw Vineyard, Pittenger gets an expression heady with the scents of chamomile and cocoa powder. But he sees even more possibility in Mourvèdre—"It's more representative of place than Pinot is"—and a roster of Rhône-native whites.

preferring to sell rustic wines to a local crowd. But, increasingly, this new attention is proving too tempting to spurn. As we drive past the Barsotti property in Camino, owner Gael Barsotti—whose family is better known in the area for making fruit juices—asks Mansfield about a shipment of newly arrived Gamay Noir vines. The Barsotti planting will cement this little area as California's ground zero for Gamay.

It all keeps fueling the foothills' happy bout of exploration. Several months later, I return with Tegan Passalacqua for a winter visit. He has discovered no end of promising leads: Zinfandel that dates to 1920, impossibly thick Mission grape vines dating to the 1860s, and new plantings of Rhône-native grapes like Grenache. Later he finds another source of sixty-year-old head-trained Grenache in the town of Loomis, in Placer County, twenty-five miles northeast of Sacramento; its fruit has unusual high-acid chemistry that's reminiscent of the Spanish region of Priorat. Turley has also bought the old Karly winery in Amador's Shenandoah Valley, so Passalacqua is back up often, not only hunting existing vineyards but cross-referencing the possibilities of unplanted land with his encyclopedic knowledge of soil types.

We stop at a limestone road cut and crumble off a bit of stone. It puts Passalacqua in a frame of mind for alpine French grapes like Poulsard. At another turn there's a granitic rock face where he envisions contoured terraces of the Spanish grape Mencia, much as it's grown in Ribeira Sacra. Near a mining operation he finds shards of llicorella, the black schist that helped make Priorat famous.

"To me, this is the future of California," he says. "How can it not be? You just need a bunch of whack jobs to come in and plant this, and maybe their grandkids could prosper."

SIERRA FOOTHILLS

VINEYARD AREA/TOTAL AREA: 5,700 acres/ 2.6 million acres

MAIN GRAPES: Zinfandel, although Rhône-native reds like Syrah, Grenache, and Mourvèdre, as well as Rhône-native whites like Vermentino and Grenache Blanc, are gaining ground. Gamay Noir is an unexpected highlight.

AT A GLANCE: An enormous region, stretching across eight counties, from Yuba in the north to Mariposa in the south, although relatively few vineyards have been planted. The geology of what was once gold country continues to deliver. After a blip of attention in the 1970s followed by general disregard, the area is again being discovered by top winemakers.

THE PROMISE: Complex soils, especially along parts of the American River where granite is present, which are perfect for wine; a moderate climate with intense sun; new plantings and forward-thinking viticulture

THE RISK: Distance from major urban centers, often combined with years of subpar winemaking, have denied the foothills the exposure they might have gotten closer to the coast.

Santa Cruz Mountains

The Peter Martin Ray Vineyard sits two thousand feet above the town of Saratoga, on the outer rim of Silicon Valley. On this site, Martin Ray, the Saratoga-raised stockbroker whose wines were as legendary as they were uneven, planted his own vines. Down below the valley is bustling, but there's an eerie calm up here. Duncan Arnot Meyers surveys a sloping pasture of vines. Each vine is lashed to a ramrod wooden post, the field full of them, as the morning fog unfurls below.

On the other side of a dirt path sit the trellised rows of Mount Eden Vineyards, once part of Ray's property until fights with family and investors cleaved the two. This more unruly parcel in which we're standing is owned by Peter Martin Ray, Ray's adopted stepson. Its orchardlike patchwork of vines is planted in clay veined with shale and limestone: four acres of Cabernet Sauvignon, three of Chardonnay, and a little less than that of Pinot Noir. The attaching of vines to the tops of the wooden stakes is a seemingly archaic style of pruning that vineyard manager Rick Anzalone was taught decades ago in the vineyards of the old Sacred Heart Novitiate, a few miles below in Los Gatos. The spacing is generous—"You could basically play football in this vineyard," Meyers points out—and though the vines look like a relic from another century, these plantings date only to the late 1970s.

Come harvest, the fruit will be picked into five-gallon paint buckets and old wooden boxes still stamped with Martin Ray's name. And, as though we needed more evidence of how California's progress stands still here, Peter Martin Ray, now pushing eighty, soon rides out on an old Caterpillar tractor and plow, its coiled steel tines predating the cold war.

Anzalone shrugs. "Trying to pull some of these guys into even the mid-twentieth century is like pulling teeth."

UNDISCOVERED COUNTRY

The Santa Cruz Mountains run along the San Francisco peninsula south from San Francisco, sitting astride what once was referred to as the Santa Clara Valley and skirting the city of Santa Cruz before tapering off near the Salinas Valley. The appellation with the same name is a lobe-shaped chunk of the coast, defined by elevation (down to four hundred feet on its west side, eight hundred on its east), and encompassing a large swath of north-central California's coastal area, down to the farming town of Watsonville.

This is not the simplest place to make wine. The boundary of two tectonic plates creates dramatic soil inconsistencies, and constantly shifting microclimates mean no two watersheds have the same weather. As Jeffrey Patterson, who runs Mount

Eden Vineyards, put it, "The appellation's confusing, and it always will be."

Somehow the Santa Cruz Mountains remain California's great undiscovered country. Certainly in the case of Mount Eden, there is precedent for greatness. Vintner Martin Ray's plantings here were the outgrowth of his work just to the south, on the site where Paul Masson ascended the hills and constructed his own La Cresta property in 1896, hoping to make the finest sparkling wines in California. In 1936 Ray bought Masson's winery and adopted the Masson brand.

The Mount Eden wines can be difficult at times—the Chardonnay can take a good five years to really unwind—but I always remind myself that these wines, and many others in the mountains, are not simply impressive; they are historic, with an untrammeled lineage that survived California's keen attempts to erase its past.

It is this history—and the somewhat archaic farming methods used here, which might have chased others away—that drew Meyers and Nathan Roberts to this location. Saratoga isn't a cool spot for Pinot Noir per se, but at two thousand feet the climate is modulated; the vines are older and infected with leaf roll and other viruses, which slow their ripening. The mountains' idiosyncrasies are marked by the lone orange flag at Peter Martin Ray that delineates where Pinot Noir switches to Cabernet Sauvignon. These two very different grapes have somehow happily coexisted here since Ray's era. And the mountains have been juggling these dual inspirations, of Bordeaux and Burgundy, for more than a century.

Quite literally. Paul Masson filled his vineyards with Pinot Noir and Chardonnay cuttings he had sent from France, hoping to make a sparkling wine to rival Champagne, while nearby, at his La Questa vineyard, in 1883 Emmet Rixford planted varieties in the same proportions as they were planted at Bordeaux's Château Margaux. Not only did the La Questa planting endure, but it enjoyed a similar fate as Mount Eden: its vine material filtered through California before returning home to the Santa Cruz Mountains via plantings at Ridge's Monte Bello.

Certainly the mountains aren't remote; a drive from San Francisco takes barely more than an hour. But even after a century's worth of accolades, they remain largely inaccessible and mysterious. The closest thing to a main road is vertiginous Skyline Boulevard, which weaves along the mountains' summit. "The history of the Santa Cruz Mountains," as Charles Sullivan puts it, "is simply replete with outstanding producers, most of them idealists."

Sullivan, who authored a definitive history of local winemaking, *Like Modern Edens*, points to the mountains' inaccessibility as both their boon and downfall. The relative isolation protected them from the fads that besieged the rest of the industry, but it also made fame elusive. The terrain also makes viticulture a financially dicey proposition since it's hard to find more than a few contiguous acres to farm. Hence, although their appellation is half the size of Rhode Island, the mountains contain just 1,500 acres of vineyards.

Yet the dramatic geology keeps bringing new explorers. At 2,700 feet, Ridge's Monte Bello Vineyard, home to its most famous wine, enjoys an exotic remnant of limestone amid a mix of soils that are part of the Franciscan Complex, the geological mélange found up and down the Northern California coast. Not far away are very different parcels of sandstone and shale. Credit goes to the constant grinding of the North American and Pacific tectonic plates along the San Andreas Fault, which bisects the Santa Cruz Mountains. These jumbled soils drew successive waves of pioneers—first those like Masson and Osea Perrone, then Martin Ray and other midcentury pioneers like David Bruce, the dermatologist who arrived in 1961 seeking a great site for Pinot Noir, and of course David Bennion and his fellow scientists at nearby Stanford Research Institute, who founded Ridge. It was somewhere they could focus solely on the substance of wine, rather than its trappings.

Much farther south, the appellation encompasses the southern edge of the Santa Clara Valley. Not far away, along the highway near Hecker Pass, on the road to the garlic capital of Gilroy, you can find 1910 plantings of Grenache at the Besson Vineyard, a site still used to good effect by Bonny Doon's Randall Grahm and two former Doon acolytes, John Locke and Alex Krause, who founded the Birichino label.

Yet Santa Cruz often has struggled to make wine as good as its terroir. Even Martin Ray was known for his wines being as temperamental as he was. Great vineyards are often hobbled by uneven farming or hacky cellar work, leading one Santa Cruz pioneer to say he was drawn to the area because he could "taste the terroir through all the crappy winemaking."

"WHY DO YOU HATE MONEY"

At the right time of year the roads in the Santa Cruz Mountains are full of the scents of bay laurel and pungent eucalyptus. This, to me, is the quintessential smell of California. Near the summit, you finally get a glimpse of expansive, almost overwhelming, views of the valley below. It always happens when I pull into the parking lot at Kevin Harvey's Rhys Vineyards, high above the town of Los Gatos at 2,360 feet.

Newcomers are always ascending the mountains, but few are more studious than Harvey, who turned an estimable fortune from his other career as a successful entrepreneur in the software wars into seed money for a grand exploration of Santa Cruz's potential. Inspired by a Pinot Noir planting in his backyard in Woodside, nine miles to the north, Harvey began scouting local soils, found several promising parcels, and planted them so densely that even a Burgundian would scratch his head. This forces competition for nutrients and often lowers yield.

We stand in his cellar—a massive vault dubbed "the rebel base," although Mssrs. Solo and Skywalker never had it so good—and scrutinize a detailed soil map. It simply proves how inconsistent the ground can be in the hills. But Harvey remains guided by a single thesis: shallow, rocky, infertile soils make the most timeless and profound wines. They, arguably more than California's generally luxurious climate, create a tremendous opportunity.

"We're at the edge of fertility, not the edge of ripeness," he tells me. "In Burgundy, the deeper the soil, the more early drinking the wine. California will one day realize the same thing."

Few have made this point with such fervor. This is not to dismiss Harvey's obsession with climate—the Rhys Vineyards website includes an online tool to compare temperature curves everywhere from Los Gatos to the Italian commune of Barolo—but he is driven by dirt, to the point that he stops his truck on occasion so we can pick away at a bit of exposed hillside.

Harvey's five established vineyards in the Santa Cruz Mountains (plus another in Anderson Valley)

are each a snapshot of geologic time. His westernmost site, Alpine, sits at around 1,400 feet, with just eight miles of warped ridges separating it from the Pacific. Its sandstone and shale soils are part of the four-million-year-old Purisima Formation, one of those mineral-rich uplifts from the ancient seabed. It makes perhaps the meatiest and darkest of Harvey's Pinots.

Alpine's soils are youthful compared to the eleven-million-year-old Monterey shale and volcanic ash at his Horseshoe site, less than a half mile east, a spot that yields a more studious, ethereal wine—and yet has the requisite warmth to ripen Syrah. If Alpine Pinot is brooding, Horseshoe Pinot always manifests the reticence and sagelike aromas that prompted winemaker Jeff Brinkman

Kevin Harvey

The New California Wine

to describe it, approvingly, as "the nerdy girl with glasses."

Both sites are relatively fertile compared to the depleted soils of Harvey's Skyline Vineyard, almost atop the rebel base and one of the state's highest-elevation Pinot vineyards. Farming here is demanding and wildly expensive. And Skyline's two acres of steep slopes, a mix of fractured sandstone, limestone, and mudstone, are so densely planted, at about seven thousand vines per acre, that its vines yielded only enough fruit for only 660 bottles of wine in 2009. Which explains a revealing harvest moment that stuck in Harvey's mind: "One guy comes out of the vineyard and says, 'Why do you hate money?'"

It may be less that he hates money than that he shares an obsessiveness demonstrated by only a handful of like-minded Pinotchiks, people like Calera's Josh Jensen or Aubert de Villaine of Domaine de la Romanée-Conti. Harvey, along with Brinkman and his vineyard chief Javier Meza, is on a mission to better comprehend the mechanics of timeless wine.

"With the focus on wine styles in the past twenty years," he says, "the money didn't flow to figuring out where our best terroirs were."

DOWN IN CORRALITOS

The mountains' isolation holds one other treasure, this time in their southern stretch, near the tiny hamlets of Corralitos and Aptos, about a fifteen-minute drive east of Santa Cruz proper. Thirty years ago this area enjoyed a boomlet when an earlier generation of arrivals tried their hand at Chardonnay and Pinot Noir. But those early ambitions soon petered out, and the area's grapes came to be sold mostly for low-bid prices.

The worn, pine-shaded bungalows and storefronts of Corralitos are a welcome holdover from sleepy midcentury California. It is the sort of crossroads, full of long afternoon shadows, where you can, without irony, buy a packet of handmade beef jerky.

The area had as much potential as its counterparts slightly to the north, maybe more. But what it needed was an evangelist. It found that in Prudy Foxx.

Foxx has become Santa Cruz's vine whisperer of sorts—discovering neglected plantings, improving farming, and matching grapes to the right winemaker. An Indianapolis native, she started out working for the agricultural extension office in Monterey. As she traversed the Salinas Valley and felt the wind ripping down its length, she often wondered how grapes could possibly ripen there. She began growing wine grapes in Washington State in 1982 before returning to California in 1989. She soon became a guru for Santa Cruz vintners, some of whom were living the last dregs of the 1960s and wanted to fine-tune what could charitably be called a freewheeling approach to farming.

Corralitos and its environs quickly became her sweet spot. In the sloping hills just a few miles from the slow curve of Monterey Bay, well-exposed slopes are planted amid evergreens at an elevation between five hundred and one thousand feet. A mix of morning fog and coastal breeze provides a constant tempering influence. That, plus moderate bay weather and sandy and clay loam soils, give Pinot Noir and especially Chardonnay from the area an intense mineral signature and subtle structure. (Rhys Vineyards' Harvey was drawn to buy an old apple orchard near Corralitos in order to plant his own vineyard.) If farming suffered as Corralitos faded from the map, the lack of attention also gave

Foxx the chance to make changes without her clients constantly fretting about the bottom line. "The people I work for, for the most part, do not derive their living from the vines," she tells me. "I think the potential of the fruit is so outstanding that it's great when someone with really great talent gets their hands on it."

Foxx is determined to get the southern Santa Cruz Mountains back on the map, mostly by functioning as a sort of matchmaker between nearby vineyards and a band of mostly Sonoma-based vintners, including Pax Mahle and Kenny Likitprakong, along with a handful of local producers. These sites are less a frontier than a hidden remnant of old California, forgotten in a back corner of a little-known appellation.

She drives me out to the Woodruff site, an undulating parcel of thirty-year-old dry-farmed vines bought in 2001 by Peter and Barbara Woodruff and revived over the course of a decade. Woodruff is another of the tiny spots in the hills tapped for revival, its old vine rows wrapped around a hill contour and barely escaping shade from nearby trees. Likitprakong, who makes wines under the Ghostwriter label, already knew it from his time working for the Hallcrest winery in nearby Felton. He was drawn back during a hunt for exactly what the area can provide: more aromatics and acidity than robust fruit.

SANTA CRUZ MOUNTAINS

VINEYARD AREA/TOTAL AREA: approx. 1,500 acres/ 408,000 acres

MAIN GRAPES: Pinot Noir, Chardonnay, Cabernet Sauvignon

AT A GLANCE: Just outside San Francisco and home to some of the state's defining vineyards, this is one of California's most historic yet least-known wine areas.

THE PROMISE: Complex soils, thanks to the San Andreas Fault, and microclimates that can perfectly grow a wide range of grapes

THE RISK: Often overlooked in favor of more famous regions, antiquated viticulture, and inaccessibility caused by mountainous terrain

Foxx is less interested in adding new vineyards here—the hills aren't especially hospitable for planting—than tidying up established ones like Trout Gulch, which was first planted on pure loam in the late 1970s. Often she goes in and shortens canes—the area's unruly farming can produce sprawling fifteen-foot vines—and tweaks the trellises, improving the flow of air and sunlight to the grapes. There's always something to improve.

"Nobody calls me," she concludes, "because they're happy."

Lodi

The town of Lodi has been California wine's sturdy packhorse since the 1800s. Perched at the head of the San Joaquin Valley, it enjoys both the heat of the Central Valley and a tempering effect from the Sacramento–San Joaquin River delta to the west.

That has made Lodi a difficult place to understand at times. It can be plenty hot, and yet it still enjoys at least a whiff of coastal chill. Its partisans constantly tout this latter characteristic, presenting a case that Lodi should stand out from the vast expanse of inland California. That may not be the easiest thing to achieve: what began as a crossroads to not much of anywhere has become a massive winegrowing region, with more than ninety thousand acres of grapes across a half million acres.

The road east to Lodi takes you straight through the delta. Either you can drive along Highway 12, an unbending stretch of asphalt that shoots past Travis Air Force Base, across countless low-lying islands and the sloughs that vein them. Or, for a scenic detour, you can follow Highway 160 up through the cornfields of Contra Costa County and tiny delta towns like Walnut Grove. Either way, you enter Lodi on its suburban west side, a flat-toned mix of fast-food restaurants and car dealerships.

The delta is an odd place, below sea level and preserved by an intricate series of levees, a no-man's-land filled with seed crops and boat docks, always brimming with more than its share of water—a rarity in a state with an unquenched thirst. A trip through the delta inevitably brings a dose of the surreal. On one visit, Scholium Project's Abe Schoener and I were delayed at a Walnut Grove drawbridge as a pirate ship (really a replica schooner, but this tale has grown in the retelling) sailed by underneath.

One day Tegan Passalacqua and I take Highway 12 through the delta to see, among other things, the Bechtold Vineyard, a parcel of old Cinsault vines planted in 1886 by Joseph Spenker, and still kept in the family by his great-granddaughter Wanda Woock Bechtold and her husband, Al Bechtold. Perhaps mostly by oversight, Bechtold has been farmed organically through the years, a true rarity in Lodi.

At first it's hard to believe that the Bechtold Vineyard, with its irrigation canal for a neighbor, is Lodi's nascent star. It is a sandy lot of knobby, sprawling vines of Cinsault, a red grape generally disregarded not only in California but in its native Southern France. And yet Bechtold's rows are capped with signs that display an impressive set of winery names: Scholium, Bonny Doon, Turley.

If Cinsault isn't the stuff of legend, it is reliable, suited to Lodi's warmth, and something different for a winemaker to play with, which is probably why Randall Grahm, thanks to a tip from UC Davis, uncovered the site and became entranced. It's also how a forgotten patch of Lodi has become the

source for several wines of the moment. There is Turley's El Porrón, a Beaujolais-style version mostly intended for restaurants that was one of Passalacqua's quiet successes, as well as Scholium's Rhododactylos, a blanc de noirs that shows the faintest shimmer of color.

Kevin Phillips, one of the area's most prolific grape growers and Bechtold's current handler, now has a waiting list for fruit that once could barely find a home. This was a happy accident of the recession: interesting fruit landed in the hands of the buyers who could shine a spotlight on Lodi. "It's a complete 180 from what is typically a California and especially a Lodi style, which is big, dark, jammy fruit bombs," Phillips tells me.

The Bechtold Vineyard tells us something more. It is the tale of Lodi in a snapshot. Somehow it survived—frankly, that should be Lodi's mantra—escaping decades of production winemaking and the tendency to plow under interesting parcels or turn them into efficient little grape factories meant to fill unremarkable bottles on the supermarket shelf.

Again and again, Lodi dirt has delivered—whether it has been for large concerns like the California Wine Association or the Wine Growers Guild, which churned out table wine in the early 1900s; for growers shipping Lodi grapes east by railcar to be fermented in Prohibition-era basements; or for 1970s table-wine players like Robert Mondavi's Woodbridge.

This, however, doesn't mean that these soils have been respected. Leaving aside the laments expressed in the Creedence Clearwater Revival song—"Oh Lord, stuck in Lodi again"—this is one of those stretches of California that have quietly done their part while certain fancy valleys near the coast take the credit (often with a bit of Lodi fruit blended into the bottle).

Recently Lodi—aided by the Lodi Winegrape Commission, which delivers its message with an efficiency rare for local wine organizations—has taken a stab at propping up its own name. Among its achievements was to devise Lodi Rules, California's first third-party wine certification for sustainability, and one of the few around the state to show real teeth.

More than anything, the area had a proliferation of great old-vine Zinfandel vineyards. In some cases they were swept up by labels like Turley, which has remained loyal to its Dogtown site on the east side of Lodi, in the Clements Hills area, even though it yields barely a ton per acre in a good year. For many years Lodi's old vines went into service for white Zinfandel; it's not too much to say that if it were not for white Zin, some of California's best old vineyards might have been lost.

The hunt for terroir is still relatively rare in the northern San Joaquin Valley; there's little economic incentive to explore the possibilities of the soil when the area's history has mostly been defined by cheap wine. But some small pockets of curiosity have been unearthed. East of Lodi, near the crossroads of Victor, lies a small bend in the Mokelumne River with a patchwork of old Zinfandel parcels interspersed with tidy new plantings of whatever seemed popular at the moment.

Passalacqua and I drive through Victor and turn north. He believed in Lodi enough to put down his own money to buy the Kirschenmann Vineyard just north of Victor, a parcel of 1915 Zinfandel vines sprinkled with the usual field-blend supporting cast, including—he proudly points out—an errant vine or two of the grape once dubbed Crabb's Black Burgundy, now better known as the Friulian red variety Refosco.

Kirschenmann is barely separated from a 1915-era parcel purchased by Michael McCay, one of the few Lodi natives to make vineyard-designated Zinfandels from sites across the region, in an effort to show the diversity of Lodi soils. Nearby are a handful of other old-vine parcels like Schmiedt, old Zinfandel planted in 1918, and Jean Rauser's Carignane vineyard, planted in 1909, or even the Mokelumne Glen Vineyard, a jumble of mostly Teutonic varieties like Kerner and Dornfelder—planted on deeper sandy soils near the Mokelumne River.

"There's eight old-vine vineyards in this little pocket," Passalacqua tells me. "I'm clearly biased, but there's something to it." Vineyards like these have endured in Lodi through sheer will—and by quietly sitting on the sidelines during the many contentious battles between growers and wineries in Lodi.

Markus Bokisch at Vista Luna

BOTH SIDES

The town has always been a growers' stronghold, one where farming grapes was the first order of business. If ambitious consultants have appeared recently, most of the winemakers who previously showed up in Lodi were employed by the large concerns that came looking for bottom-dollar fruit—and plenty of it. "The vast majority of people in Lodi are still happy growing production grapes for production wines," says Markus Bokisch, "and it really has to be that way, because you have ninety thousand acres to farm."

Bokisch is that rare farmer who finesses both sides of the equation. He is one of the area's most prolific vineyard managers, farming 2,500 acres, yet he has also pioneered some of its most terroir-driven efforts, including the Belle Colline Vineyard near the border of Calaveras County, and his own Bokisch Vineyards label, which uses Lodi as a vehicle to explore Iberian varieties like Albariño and Graciano.

Bokisch discovered the area in 1989 while working as a viticulturist for Napa's Joseph Phelps Vineyards. At the time, he was looking for affordable Carignane grapes, one of the old California workhorses. But it also struck him that Lodi was something of a blank slate. After a trip to the south of France, Bokisch came to the conclusion that just because the area had been viewed as a simple workhorse didn't mean that it didn't offer an outstanding opportunity. "Lodi is like the Languedoc," he says. "It's the stepchild of the American wine business."

That's what drove him, with four other partners, to establish the Belle Colline Vineyard on an old depleted ranch spread in Lodi's Clements Hills area. Clements Hills is a curious corner of Lodi, rolling grassland at the far east of the region near the border of Calaveras County, where the land begins rising into the foothills and the glaciated, cobbly soils are packed with the volcanic runoff of the Sierras. If Lodi's west side is defined by rich, loamy soils fed by irrigation canals, it's on the east side of Highway 99—the main artery of the San Joaquin Valley—where the land begins undulating and compelling soils appear.

Bokisch and his partners wanted to explore the complex soils in this eastern part of Lodi, to plant the same varieties—Tempranillo, Syrah, Mourvèdre, and more—in both volcanic-ash tufa in the flats and in Redding loam soils on the knoll tops. The ground was left untilled even during planting "to make sure we were expressing the pure terroir," Bokisch says.

Of course, the very notion of talking about soil in Lodi still seems alien, probably because table-wine farming typically views soil as nothing more than a medium for holding roots. That might help explain why Lodi has long had a reputation as dramatically fertile ground, so much so that Leon Adams wrote in *The Wines of America* that "grapevines grow to enormous size in its deep, sandy-loam soil, washed down from the mountains for centuries."

Or perhaps not. "The soils aren't fertile, they're fertilized," Passalacqua retorts. "Don't tell me with seventeen inches of annual rain, and soil with less than 1 percent organic matter, it's fertile."

Even in the midst of industrial vineyards, which make up the bulk of Lodi's plantings, you can find tea leaves that predict what might be. Ten miles northeast of the Mokelumne cluster, and due north of Clements Hills, sits the Borden Ranch area. If Lodi is California wine's little-discussed trump card, Borden is its best-kept secret, ever since Sutter Home and Mondavi discovered its volcanic soils in the 1970s. Now Borden is home to large plantings by California's biggest players.

This is also where Bokisch particularly wanted to explore his Catalan heritage with Spanish-native varieties. The idea wasn't so outlandish. Given the state's Mediterranean climate, nineteenth-century vine researchers gravitated to Spanish and Portuguese grapes. If Chardonnay could thrive all across the state, why not Verdelho or Tempranillo?

These varieties have become Bokisch's calling cards. More than that, really. In a region where production Cabernet rules, they are a demonstration of what could be if only there was the desire to experiment, a trait that Lodi has never been quick to embrace.

Bokisch farms 1,000 acres in Borden Ranch, a large chunk of the 2,500 he manages around Lodi. That includes his twin properties, acquired on a lowball bid to Prudential's land-management division.

On one side of a road is Vista del Sol, home to high-yield plantings of typically low-yield grapes like Pinot Noir, grown for big names like Treasury Wine Estates. Yielding more than six tons per acre, or twice what Sonoma might produce, this vineyard is how cheap Pinot ends up on the bottom shelf. Nearby are similar plantings of Cabernet Sauvignon and Pinot Gris.

Across the road is Vista Luna, Bokisch's laboratory of sorts. He has planted the usual Zinfandel and Petite Sirah, but also whites like Albariño, Verdelho, and Grenache Blanc—all part of his Spanish inspiration. His customers include some fashionable wineries, like Neyers Vineyards, Scholium, and Acha, the project from Napa winemaker Mark Herold. Like Bechtold, Vista Luna has gained a quiet cachet, even if it sits just across a dip in the terrain from grapes that go into faceless bottles. We

LODI

VINEYARD AREA/TOTAL AREA: 90,000+ acres/ 458,000 acres

MAIN GRAPES: Chardonnay and Cabernet Sauvignon (for lower-quality wines); also old-vine Zinfandel and other field-blend varieties; Iberian varieties like Albariño, Verdelho, and Tempranillo

AT A GLANCE: The reliable workhorse of California wine, providing inexpensive grapes for more than a century but rarely getting its due

THE PROMISE: Its old vines and a newfound respect for its soils hold the possibility of a rebirth. In 2006 the massive Lodi AVA was divided into seven subappellations: Alta Mesa, Borden Ranch, Clements Hills, Cosumnes River, Jahant, Mokelumne River, and Sloughhouse. At the time it seemed like overreaching, but as the various soils and sites have been explored in more detail the distinctions appear more valid.

THE RISK: Massive vineyard production for inexpensive wines, uneven winemaking, and a local industry bias toward overly flashy wine styles

stand between the two, at the gap between fame and anonymity as far as vineyards go, and consider Lodi's complicated fate.

"Nothing against Napa. I just never could have done this there," Bokisch tells me. "Lodi is like a big open canvas. And other people are going to paint pictures I can't even dream of."

Anderson Valley

Unless you're up for a stomach-turning trip over the mountains, Anderson Valley in western Mendocino County can be reached by one real road in and out: the tortuous two-lane strip that is Highway 128. One of my first trips to wine country after landing in California was along this route. Unless you're coming by sea—or at least the coastal route—you depart the northern Sonoma town of Cloverdale and climb through the hills, a series of switchbacks leading to a twisting descent through scrubby woods and pasture, a thirty-mile trek back into the North Coast's unimpeded solitude.

By the time I cruised through the tiny town of Yorkville (population 139) I was struck silent. Amid the redwoods, live oaks, and sandstone road cuts of southern Mendocino was the California I had always dreamed of: remote, untrammeled, edged with sunshine on the dry grass of sheep meadows. It reaffirmed why Thomas Pynchon set *Vineland*, his paean to the aftermath of the 1960s, in this valley.

Anderson Valley has always had a touchy relationship with the outside world. In the nineteenth century the residents of its largest town, Boonville, devised their own language, Boontling, to confound what they called Brightlighters, those from the outside. Even now it remains blissfully free of the trappings of prosperity, save for the faintly hippie charm of the restored Boonville Hotel and some unusually good fruit galettes baked daily at the Boonville General Store. Still, wine grapes have had to contend with the valley's other, far less licit crop.

While the valley began growing wine grapes in the early twentieth century, it also grew a reputation for being too cold and unreliable for viticulture, so much so that when the earliest modern vintner in these parts, Pasadena cardiologist Donald Edmeades, arrived in 1963, he painted "Edmeades' Folly" on a sign in tribute to those who frequently reminded him that the valley couldn't possibly ripen wine grapes. But it was the Louis Roederer house of Champagne that redirected the valley's fortunes, starting in 1981, when company president Jean-Claude Rouzaud decided to roll the dice on this heretofore unknown, and inaccessible, corner of California—albeit one that, with a reputation for being too cold to make still wine, would have spoken to a Champenois heart.

At the time, many French Champagne houses were seeking a California outpost. While Taittinger and Mumm headed for the relative sure bet of Napa, Roederer took the gamble, setting up shop on 580 acres in a remote and poor slice of Mendocino that was notorious for chasing away outsiders. Though Mendocino's logging industry was in collapse, the French found themselves paying above market value for land. But by 1988 their vineyards were established and the first wine was released. Along with a sparkling wine made by John

Scharffenberger (whose brand was sold to luxury conglomerate LVMH and then ultimately to its neighbor, Roederer), Roederer put Anderson Valley into play.

The Champenois also brought vine material from France, particularly cuttings of Pinot Noir that excelled for sparkling wine. Back-to-landers who came to the valley in the 1970s, like Ted Bennett and Deborah Cahn of Navarro and Hans and Theresia Kobler of Lazy Creek, were largely focused on Alsatian varieties like Riesling and Gewürztraminer. However, by the 1990s it was becoming evident that Pinot would help to change the valley's destiny, even more so than marijuana.

The early plantings of Pinot Noir, mostly on the flat land on either side of Highway 128, showed promise. But Anderson Valley remained one of those quiet California secrets well into the 1990s. In this remote Mendocino nook protected from the sea but drawing the coastal chill, the fog encouraged the purest imaginable expression of Pinot: bright red fruit, a foresty aspect, and a mineral tension that was increasingly lost in riper wines from further south. As Pinot elsewhere grew burlier, Anderson Valley was the funky opposition.

THE DEEP END

Paul Ardzrooni is driving through the rows at Ferrington Vineyard, just outside Boonville. Originally from near Fresno, Ardzrooni found himself up in Anderson Valley in 1989, and over time he became the valley's vineyard maven. He now farms more than 500 acres here, a large chunk of the valley's 2,250 vineyard acres. Ferrington is of note for being the first Pinot Noir vineyard in Anderson Valley whose name was specifically designated

The Demuth Vineyard

on a label, when Williams Selyem released a Ferrington bottling in 1992. Ted Lemon of Littorai quickly followed suit; in 1993 he chose the One Acre parcel of a vineyard called Deer Meadows as a vineyard designate, specifically calling out its origin on the label. The fact that two prominent winemakers had singled out Anderson Valley parcels marked the start of a new era. "Ted believed in this appellation almost before anybody else," Ardzrooni says.

Pinot became the big draw in Anderson Valley as the love for all things Alsatian faded. In the midst of Ferrington Vineyard, Ardzrooni and I examine ripe clusters of Gewürztraminer, aromatic even on the vine and brimming with both sugar and precious acidity. But in 2010 there were just 85 acres of this variety in the valley, down from 122 five years previous.

While sparkling-wine houses mined richer, lower-lying soils, the Pinot growers began shifting their focus to the hills, where the already-successful Deer Meadows was located. In 2007 and 2008, Peter Knez, a senior executive at the investment firm Barclays Global, acquired Dear Meadows's neighbor, Demuth, and another of the valley's cherished parcels, the Cerise Vineyard, both located on the eastern slopes above Boonville.

It's a tricky neighborhood to grow grapes. Cerise sits amid eight hundred acres of undulating hills, reaching up to 1,150 feet, above a Roederer vineyard on the valley floor; yet just sixty acres have soil stable enough to plant. Demuth, sitting above at 1,750 feet, is even tougher. Planted mostly to old Chardonnay with a bit of Pinot mixed in, it might yield 1.25 tons per acre in a good year. I took it as an unusually upbeat sign that Knez's wines were reminiscent of classic Anderson Valley wines from twenty years earlier; his acquisition capped a long buying spree in Anderson Valley. Through the

1990s, a series of Napa outsiders, including Duckhorn, charmed their way into the valley, looking for ways to expand their empires into Pinot Noir as the grape was becoming increasingly fashionable, the source for ever flashier wines. By the late 2000s the land grab had drawn other influential outsiders, wineries such as Ferrari-Carano and Cliff Lede, who acquired smaller local properties. Anderson Valley no longer stood clear of the trappings of Pinot's gilded age.

The valley's so-called deep end, as it winds northwest toward the coast, became the new frontier. Kevin Harvey of Rhys Vineyards in the Santa Cruz Mountains had expanded his terroir quest to Mendocino, planting a parcel, Bearwallow, so densely (nearly eight thousand vines per acre) that even a hand tiller could barely squeeze through. Across the highway, Wells Guthrie of Copain and Ted Lemon got Ardzrooni to develop a new vineyard, Wendling, farmed using a mix of organic and biodynamic methods.

Thus Anderson Valley's big twist: if big-name arrivals pushed the area toward the drabness of modern Pinot, at volumes that spoke more to a need for a line extension in a Napa tasting room (Duckhorn's Goldeneye label makes more than ten thousand cases of their basic Anderson Valley wine), a handful of outsiders had become the defenders of the area's best virtues. While Navarro and a handful of other locals had built loyal followings, the valley's real fame was due to the presence of Brightlighters—micronegociants like Williams Selyem and its descendants, labels like Radio-Coteau, Lioco, and Anthill Farms, to say nothing of Copain and Littorai. All sought to make a more nuanced style of wine. This set them apart not only from Napa arrivistes, but also from locals who aspired to the bulkier style of Pinot of the mid-2000s.

Burt Williams completed that circle when, in 1998, he bought his own land and planted the twelve acres of the Morning Dew Ranch. Having shined a light on Anderson Valley from the outside, a Brightlighter had come to set down roots.

A NEW MENDOCINO FRONTIER

As Anderson Valley juggled its identity issues, a new frontier was being established in the hills that separate it from the sea. High on a ridge, at 1,250 feet just three miles from the coastal town of Elk, Jason and Molly Drew finally located their own chunk of California with which they could pursue their Pinot dream.

The couple, who run Drew Family Cellars, grew up together in the town of Los Altos and carved a path through the California wine industry before coming north and hunting land of their own. After looking for years, the Drews finally discovered an old twenty-six-acre organic apple orchard, planted in 1960 on the rickety road between Philo and Elk. They began removing apple trees and putting in 7.5 acres of vines, mostly heritage selections.

While the Mendocino Ridge appellation had been established in 1997 among the area's ridgetops—a line drawn at 1,200 feet elevation—the area never quite caught the expected attention. Perhaps it was simply a matter of time, for high in the Mendocino hills could be found soils—a mix of San Andreas metamorphosis and lifted seabed from the Pacific below—that were similarly complex as those just south at the edge of Sonoma County. The Drews were doing something that was not so different from what David Hirsch and the Peay brothers had done when they made their pioneering treks to the coast to find old Sonoma timberland. They

wanted to explore terroir early on the curve. But unlike some of the early Sonoma pioneers, they had spent two decades in wine, which helped them to know exactly what to look for.

While Jason has a particularly good sensibility for the old tension-filled Anderson Valley style of Pinot, the Drew parcel is less reminiscent of the valley below and more like those weather-beaten vineyards of Sonoma Coast's far edge, with their grand collision of soils. Its proximity to the sea often makes it ten degrees cooler than in Anderson Valley below—and leaves it fully exposed to the heavy precipitation that buffets the North Coast. As Molly Drew puts it, "We are the rain shadow."

ANDERSON VALLEY

VINEYARD AREA/TOTAL AREA: 2,244 acres/ 56,000 acres

MAIN GRAPES: Pinot Noir, Chardonnay

AT A GLANCE: The once-hidden heart of unre-constructed California Pinot country, and a little-known sweet spot for sparkling wine, now entering the spotlight

THE PROMISE: Some of the most compelling soils in Northern California, with a climate that promotes moderate ripeness and a minerality that infuses the best wines

THE RISK: Development by large wineries and a growing divergence in wine styles

Santa Rita Hills

The city of Lompoc is one of the world's least likely wine destinations. To get there you head due west toward the ocean from the quiet Santa Barbara County town of Buellton. There are two roads to choose from, through two parallel valleys: to the north, Highway 246 runs relatively straight through the Santa Rita Valley, while Santa Rosa Road takes a winding route to the south. Separated by a set of transverse hills, these two valleys make up what is officially called the Santa Rita Hills.

Whichever road you take to Lompoc, you're deposited in a no-nonsense town in the far west of the county, an area that once served mostly as a satellite community for nearby Vandenberg Air Force Base and as home to a federal penitentiary.

Santa Barbara County is always banking on a next great thing, and it found that outside Lompoc. Once upon a time, farther to the north, the Santa Maria Valley was set to be Santa Barbara's haven for Pinot Noir. More recently, the Ballard Canyon area of the Santa Ynez Valley, between Buellton

and the town of Los Olivos, has banked on Rhône-inspired dreams. But the Santa Rita Hills, stuck like a coda onto the western end of the Santa Ynez Valley, offers a particular sort of hope. That turned Lompoc into a magnet for vintners, who set up in an industrial park on the east side of town, a spot dubbed Lompoc's wine ghetto.

I meet Sashi Moorman at his office in the ghetto. Once this was a cozy little outpost for the ambitious and half crazy, hunting greatness in the dirt near land's end. Now it has matured. And as a new generation of winemakers has come up, they have brought a quiet tension to the corrugated sheds. Lompoc's fame may have arrived during the era of Big Flavor. But Moorman and a handful of counterparts are vocal proponents of a style of wine far different from that of his neighbors at, say, Sea Smoke. He's certainly comfortable with the neighborhood dissonance: He and his wife, Melissa Sorongon, even built a bakery in the ghetto, complete with a hand-operated Austrian wheat mill and a wood-burning oven. They planted wheat nearby, right next to some of his key vineyards, to make locally grown bread flour.

He takes me out to Sweeney Road, in the south valley, to visit the Memorious Vineyard. Memorious sits at the hills' far western end, where an open corridor allows wind to whip in relentlessly from the Pacific Ocean, just six miles away. As Santa Rita gained attention through the 2000s for dramatic—and often dramatically ripe—Pinot Noir and Chardonnay, there arose a need to better understand its sweet spots. The hills' western terminus particularly became a focus of interest. "We've seen in the past ten years a push to the west," Moorman told me, "a push to the ocean."

Indeed, when I visited in 2007, vintners in Santa Rita's midsection insisted that their plantings,

of crumbly diatomaceous earth, an agglomeration of fossilized algae that's the local answer to Burgundy's cherished limestone. The complex geology explains the drive to plant: twelve thousand stunted specimens of Pinot Noir across three acres, mostly Mount Eden– and Calera-clone selections dating to 2007. This daring flag was planted by Evening Land Vineyards, a well-capitalized if tumultuous project that also invested in Oregon and Burgundy before being sold to Domaine de la Côte, a label founded by Moorman and sommelier Rajat Parr (who together run the Sandhi label) plus other investors. The Memorious planting stands at the area's western edge, in defiance of the very boundaries the appellation's founders constructed.

"When they drew these lines," says Moorman, the winemaker for both Domaine de la Côte and Sandhi, "they actually never thought they could plant it."

But plant they did. Not only did Moorman and his counterparts choose these barren south-facing slopes, but he even chose this as a location for a slightly wacky long-term experiment. He has been harvesting grape seeds to plant in the hopes that they will cross-pollinate and that natural selection will eventually yield new, California-appropriate grape varieties. Sometimes breeding has been done in the lab through classical fruit genetics, but it has almost never been done in the field, even if unintentional cross-breeding led to many of the world's more useful grapes (Chardonnay, for instance). This is probably because only one in several thousand seeds is likely to take. Bonny Doon's Randall Grahm is attempting something similar in San Benito County, south of Santa Cruz, as part of his quest for a "vin de terroir." But considering that grapes have about a one in ten thousand chance of cross-breeding in the wild, both projects seem quixotic.

particularly for red grapes, sat at the western edge of viability. Yet a westward push has continued in recent years, such that any day I expected to hear of Pinot Noir grown in a colonel's backyard at nearby Vandenberg. (In fact, cold isn't an issue so much as a lack of winter dormancy, which allows the vines to rest and reset for the new season. It is a crucial, if little discussed, fact: Santa Rita has a relatively mild year-round climate.)

None of this makes the Memorious Vineyard a hospitable spot for grapes. One destablizing dagger of wind through the vineyard, a blast directly from the sea, and I begin to question the sanity of planting vines here. But the attraction is the soil. Memorious juts out on a shelf composed of shale, positioned amid stark white hills composed

Add in the difficulty of the remote, wind-beaten location, which leads to an annual farming cost of $12,000 per acre (about double the typical Central Coast cost) and the need for saintlike patience to establish a vineyard (about twice as long as elsewhere), not to mention the failure of several neighbors to do just that, and you can see why Moorman talks in almost crackpot terms of wanting to farm this particular corner of the world. "You'd have to have someone dedicated to let it take a generation," he explains.

A FORTY-YEAR CIRCLE

Of course, Santa Rita Hills has always hinged on crazy dreams. In 1970, disillusioned after serving in the Vietnam War, Richard Sanford began driving the back roads along Santa Barbara County's transverse mountain ranges, hoping to find somewhere to farm. A geographer by training, he knew how rare the hills' alignment was. Most of California's coastal ridges parallel the coastline, but southwest of the city of Lompoc, near Jalama Beach, the coast, which has been winding south for hundreds of miles, takes a jagged turn east toward the city of Santa Barbara. In turn, the nearby hills run west to east, providing an unusual direct channel for coastal fog and wind to sweep inland. The series of valleys in between provided the Santa Barbara area with several climates ideal for winegrowing, and the ocean's cooling effect in particular offered some promise that Santa Rita, then simply the western fringe of the rural Santa Ynez Valley, would suit varieties like Chardonnay and Pinot Noir.

In the 1970s, most vineyard investment in the county was either for tax havens, thanks to a set of agricultural tax breaks available at the time, or

moves by big Central Valley growers to expand their holdings to the coast. At the time, the belief was that Santa Barbara was too far south for a delicate grape like Pinot Noir, at the time really more a hobbyist's indulgence than anything serious in California. But Sanford, who had been entranced by the wines of the Burgundy commune of Volnay, was encouraged by friends like Richard Graff, whose Chalone Vineyard pioneered similar ground north in Monterey County. He optimistically pulled a century's worth of weather records from sites along the length of the transverse hills.

"I did a comparative climate study and noticed that there is a dramatic difference. In fact, it is about a degree a mile as you go east or west," he tells me one day as we sit at his Alma Rosa Winery. "I located a climate about two to four miles wide that was in the area I wanted to locate in, and that climate was pretty much parallel to the ocean all the way from Edna Valley down to here."

So Santa Barbara had a sweet spot for wine grapes. But wine was barely part of the local economy. Mission vines had thrived nearby a century earlier, but by the 1970s the soils of Lompoc were planted mostly with garbanzo beans and barley, and they were also notably used to cultivate flower seeds (Lompoc was once the flower-seed capital of the world). It was the versatility of this very climate band that had allowed seed companies like Burpee and Bodger to become a major industry there.

In 1971 Sanford and business partner Michael Benedict located a north-facing slope about eight miles east of Lompoc that contained an ancient landslide. Its clay loam soils were part of the shale-rich Monterey Formation, which veins through much of central California, and were spiked with weathered chert, a form of hard quartz. These were denser, more complex soils than those near the gravelly riverbed of the Santa Ynez River, which flowed down below. The two purchased six hundred acres and planted a range of grapes, from Pinot Noir to Riesling. In 1976 they produced their first commercial harvest in the ranch's old barn, which at the time had only gas lights for illumination.

The 1976 Sanford & Benedict Pinot Noir became a California benchmark for the grape, particularly after Robert Balzer, perhaps the state's most influential midcentury wine writer, published an article titled "American Grand Cru in a Lompoc Barn." (Sanford's prospects were less sunny; in 1980 the partnership fell apart, and a series of sales and turnovers left the vineyard controlled by the influential Terlato Wine Group. Sanford himself founded another winery, Alma Rosa, which filed for bankruptcy in 2012.)

Not only was Sanford & Benedict in precisely the right location for ripening Chardonnay and Pinot Noir, but the vineyard became the spiritual core of a new winegrowing region. In the 1980s, vintners such as Au Bon Climat's Jim Clendenen flocked to buy fruit, both from here and also from the Santa Maria Valley to the north.

But the rise of Santa Rita didn't happen in a vacuum. By the 1990s, northern areas of Santa Barbara County (and particularly the Tepusquet area in the north, near the Santa Maria Valley) had become a haven for Chardonnay, driven by big players like Mondavi and Kendall-Jackson. Further south and inland, the warmer Santa Ynez Valley was becoming a haven for Rhône-native varieties, even Cabernet and Sauvignon Blanc.

For nearly two decades the western slice of Santa Ynez near Lompoc was lumped in as part of the larger Santa Ynez Valley appellation, but in 2001, tired of their vineyards being grouped with Cabernet plantings to the east, locals persuaded

the federal government to carve out the Santa Rita Hills as its own winegrowing area. (Five years later, fearful of reprisals from Chile's massive Santa Rita winery, the government shortened the name to Sta. Rita Hills.)

Appellation politics being what they are, the area encompassed the two valleys on either side of the Santa Rita range. Sanford had focused on the south valley. The more accessible north valley is full of sandy soils from ancient sand dunes that run along Highway 246—a source for generous, if perhaps more obvious, wines—although a few spots, like the Clos Pepe Vineyard, sit on denser clay soils.

In the south valley, Sanford & Benedict was soon joined by many notable plantings, including Sea Smoke, Mount Carmel, and Fiddlestix. Most gravitated toward Pinot Noir and Chardonnay, and to a lesser extent Syrah. (An exception was Manfred Krankl, the quirky owner of the Sine Qua Non label, who planted his Eleven Confessions Vineyard—for Grenache, primarily—on ranch land slightly east of Sanford & Benedict.) Some vineyards tapped the mix of clay, shale, and white diatomaceous earth on the hillsides; others were planted near the

riverbed in richer soils. Precisely where the interesting soils begin remains a matter of sometimes pointed debate. But most prominent vineyards were installed within a few miles of Sanford & Benedict, well within Sanford's original climate belt.

RIPENESS AND REVIVAL

By the early 2000s, Santa Rita's great talent had become apparent. Its temperatures rarely exceed 80 degrees, which means the cumulative heat during the growing season lands around 2,400 to 2,600 degree-days Fahrenheit, making it a cold-climate area in line with Burgundy or colder parts of western Sonoma.

But if it doesn't get hot, it also doesn't get terribly cold. Mean temperatures hover between the mid-50s and mid-60s into November, which allows growers to leave their fruit on the vine past Halloween with little fear of rain or freeze. Acidity levels in the area are often dramatically high when grape sugars are at moderate levels. This unusual chemistry left some winemakers unsettled—although it didn't impact Sanford's ability to make exceptional wines, and vintners like Moorman considered it the area's great strength. Whatever the cause, winemakers began to luxuriate in that long, cool, dry fall; they would leave grapes on the vine for an extra three or four weeks. And as they waited for acidity levels to drop, the sugar levels rose vertiginously high.

Was this a matter of necessarily waiting for "full flavor development" in the grapes, as vintners might insist (with a wink), or merely a justification for Big Flavor ripeness? Either way, this much was clear: long hang times, and resultant alcohol levels often north of 15 percent, led to a supersizing of the wines that was critically applauded, which in turn led to the wines getting even riper.

Dramatically big Chardonnay and Pinot from names like Loring, Brewer-Clifton, Melville, and Sea Smoke helped to equate Santa Rita with a huge, plush style. Detractors would quip that you could identify the local Pinot because it tasted like Syrah. (The Sea Smoke wines grew to bombastic levels, which were underscored by the addition of the words "California Grand Cru" to their label.) Soon enough, argues Jim Clendenen of Au Bon Climat, Santa Rita was chockablock with "people who thought they were replicating Sanford & Benedict, when they were doing nothing like Sanford & Benedict."

It wasn't long before the area would see a quiet resurgence of its pioneering style. Starting in 2005, Adam Tolmach of the Ojai Vineyard, Clendenen's original winemaking partner, experimented with earlier harvests, moving up pick dates for some of his vineyard lots. Other winemakers, notably Moorman but also Gavin Chanin of Chanin Wines, began picking grapes as much as three or four weeks earlier than their counterparts. Santa Rita, Chanin points out, gets a growing season of at least 120 days, "which is already a solid 30 percent more than Burgundy ever gets. That just drives me nuts."

Santa Rita had become another battleground for the Big Flavor fight. And some began to wonder whether, as Santa Rita was carved out of the larger Santa Ynez Valley, the time hadn't come for further subdivision. Should the starker western edge receive its own designation? Perhaps the differences between the southern and northern valleys should be acknowledged?

Moorman has become Santa Rita's Svengali of sorts. Not only does he have his hands in Domaine

de la Côte and Sandhi (plus wines for Stolpman Vineyards and his own Piedrasassi label), but he happily jabs at those who believe the area's terroir is suited for ripeness rather than the intense minerality and freshness that marked Sanford's early wines and more recent efforts like those of Sandhi. He insists that the only way forward is through a modern reconsideration of those 1970s ripeness levels, and a repudiation of Santa Rita's more recent, heavy-handed times. "Here," he says, "you will die if you don't change."

Is there really a widespread, Road-to-Damascus conversion under way? Perhaps not. Money can still be made on the big-footed Santa Rita style. Some of those with the deepest commitment to the area, like the Melville family, which bet big on the northern valley, are not ready to budge.

"Balance, in my eyes, with no disrespect to my colleagues, has nothing to do with numbers. In a way it belittles the craft," Greg Brewer, who makes wine for both Brewer-Clifton and Melville, as well as his own dramatically ripe Diatom Chardonnays, told me. "These people say, 'Oh, here's this wine, it's 13.2.' To me, it's like saying, 'Oh here's my girlfriend, she's blonde.' Or, 'Here's my girlfriend, she's five foot ten.'"

Santa Rita, then, is a crucible for California's larger debate over high ripeness, and whether it obliterates a signature of place. In some spots, there was little chance of determining an answer to that question. Sea Smoke's vineyards, for instance, seemed like some of the area's most promising. But both their wines and those of the few wineries that bought their fruit had lost the ability to telegraph anything more than Big Flavor.

And yet, at the same time, nearby vineyards in the south valley, like Wenzlau and Mount Carmel, began selling their grapes to wineries with more

SANTA RITA HILLS

VINEYARD AREA/TOTAL AREA: 1,700 acres/ 30,720 acres

MAIN GRAPES: Pinot Noir, Chardonnay, Syrah, Grenache

AT A GLANCE: A remote corner of Santa Barbara has proven to be an extraordinary spot, given its cool average temperature, shale-laced soils, narrow climate band, and wind presence that's a result of transverse hills that provide a corridor to the ocean.

THE PROMISE: Wines with a mineral intensity and high acidity almost unrivaled in the New World

THE RISK: Overripeness and low yields

restrained aesthetics. A legitimate hunt for terroir had resumed where wines like Sanford & Benedict's 1979 Pinot Noir had left off. During a 2012 visit I finally got a chance to taste one of the last remaining bottles of this particular wine. Its soaring acidity helped to preserve it over the years. If its fruit was in a twilight, the wine had endured.

"I think there was a purity in those early wines that perhaps became compromised," Sanford tells me. We're back in his meeting room. "And maybe we're returning to that purity now. I think, frankly, they hijacked Pinot Noir for a while, suggesting that it should be Syrah-like, it should be big and fat and thick. People who were making wine that way were applauded for it. After all this time, it's coming back to reason. And that's very exciting to me, all this balance and elegance coming back."

Paso Robles

Halfway between San Francisco and Los Angeles, Paso Robles has for the past twenty years been trying to refashion itself, to distance itself from the Central Coast's long tradition of cattle farming and fine tri-tip barbecue, to become California's great other wine destination.

The results have been mixed. A onetime cattle town that still hosts the Mid-State Fair, complete with its popular Livestock Pavilion, Paso has picked up a curious case of ambition. In the 1970s, the town had a scattering of Zinfandel and Cabernet Sauvignon, and it became an early outpost for Rhône-native grapes, primarily after the Estrella River property put in one of California's first modern Syrah plantings. By the early 1990s, perhaps two dozen wineries were in the area; two decades later, it was approaching two hundred, driven by relatively cheap land and a boomlet of critical attention for its brash, often over-the-top red wines.

As evidenced by the mechanical bull that visiting French vintners were induced to ride, Paso was not wine country for wusses.

So the Luna Matta Vineyard, tucked into two-thousand-foot-elevation hills of the Santa Lucia Range west of the city of Paso, is slightly off-message. Its 242 acres, with 36 acres of grapes, have become a laboratory of sorts for more studious farming in the Central Coast sun.

The July day on which I've come is blistering hot, a reminder that Paso exists on a climatic see-saw between the coast and the interior, one that has led to more than its share of confusion about a wine identity. By late morning the temperature gauge on my car is approaching 100 degrees; under the vine canopies it's nearly 120.

This is Paso heat, the sort on which its typically jammy, thick wines thrive. (A profound swing from day to night temperatures is often cited as Paso's strength, although the second half of the equation only seems to provide motivation to abuse the first half.) Certainly it offers the opportunity for compelling wine, thanks in part to dazzlingly complex soils that often include limestone, a rarity in California. However, Paso has prided itself on being all things to all vintners—a haven for Zinfandel, a spot where inspirations from Bordeaux and the Rhône can happily collide—while being party to another of those ripeness arms races. Its most successful wines have been ripe and almost ribald, and newcomers rarely diverge from this template.

"There's this thought here," Stephy Terrizzi tells me, "of, whatever you do, don't think for yourself."

Anthony Yount

THE ITALIAN JOB

Stephy and her husband, Brian Terrizzi, have become poster children for diverging from Paso's party line. Thanks to her work at Luna Matta, Stephy has become the area's great alternative vineyardist; if you want something besides Big Flavor, you call her. But what actually drew the couple to the area was the opportunity to work with Italian varieties, specifically Nebbiolo. While studying winemaking at Fresno State, Brian got a tip from a vine nursery that it could be found in Paso—and he found it at Luna Matta. Planted starting in 2001, the vineyard combined some of Paso's usual Rhône-native fare with Italianate varieties that included not only persnickety Nebbiolo, the base material for Barolo and Barbaresco, but also Sangiovese, which had a not particularly glorious history in California, and the Aglianico grape native to Campania.

Planting Aglianico, an import from the hot hills outside Naples, made sense, but Nebbiolo? It's at home in fog-shrouded Piedmont, in communes like La Morra and Verduno—and rarely successful anywhere else. Brian, however, points out that I'm not thinking about it right. At the northern tip of Italy, in the Lombardian foothills of the Alps, the area of Valtellina is a small banana belt that not only ripens the grape but has summer temperatures that can more than rival Paso—hence the name of one of Valtellina's rockiest and most famous subregions. "Inferno," Brian says, "is called Inferno for a reason."

Luna Matta is a great place for a laboratory, with its rows of head-trained Grenache on 40-degree slopes. If farming in Paso is usually about maximum sunlight, here's a case study in fending it off. The Terrizzis had to find a way to keep fruit shaded while it was still ripening, so they grew an extra cane on each vine just to provide shade and positioned the trellis crossarms asymmetrically to provide what Stephy calls a "comb-over," an extra bit of leaf canopy on one side of the vine that can shade the fruit. "It's constantly figuring out how Mother Nature screws you, and then fixing that," she says.

Luna Matta and its neighborhood along Peachy Canyon Road also have some great natural benefits, key among them the presence of calcareous soils, with granite, quartz, and shale mixed in, and a lot of clay that the couple found reminiscent of the commune of Barbaresco. ("The amount of clay that sticks to your shoes?" Stephy says. "You have stilettos by the time you walk out of there.") The highly basic nature of those calcium-rich soils—they have a pH of 7.8 to 8.1—retains great freshness in the grapes, such that Brian has never had to acidulate one of his wines.

And because the Terrizzis, as well as Luna Matta's owners, John Ahner and Jody McKellar, happen to be fervent believers in organics, Luna Matta has similarly become a spot for some curious experiments in alternative farming, like the use of weevils that only consume star thistle, an invasive weed that threatens to crowd out vine roots.

CHASING MR. SMITH

Such astute vineyard work is still a rarity in Paso, which is why we can't go much farther without discussing the cult of Justin Smith. Smith is the owner of Saxum, the winery he launched in 2000 after splitting off from an earlier project, Linne Calodo, which he founded with his college roommate, Matt Trevisan. Smith's roots go farther back, to 1980, when his parents planted the James

Berry Vineyard, which has become the area's most famous site.

Saxum has become Paso's beacon, not least because its 2007 James Berry was named *Wine Spectator*'s wine of the year in 2010, a rarity for a Rhône-style blend from California. This award was interpreted as a sign that Paso had finally come of age after years trying to prove itself as a worthy alternative between Napa and Santa Barbara.

Smith, then, has become the local guru and soothsayer, trying to help friends with farming and, for a handful of ambitious projects, lending his assistance and name. In a way, Smith created a road map to fame, one widely copied in Paso: massive, heady Rhône-inspired wines that approach 16 percent alcohol—a level permissible in part because of those limestone-rich soils, whose alkaline nature helps preserve freshness. Even if some critics have found his winemaking style too exuberant, they still respect his farming and attentiveness. The man is constantly in his vineyard.

Similarly, just north of Luna Matta, Tablas Creek Vineyard remains a key part of the Paso tale. The Haas family, which founded the import firm Vineyard Brands, and the Perrin family of Château de Beaucastel in Châteauneuf-du-Pape, discovered a 120-acre limestone-rich site amid the walnut-dotted hills of western Paso in 1989 and determined it should be ground zero for a Rhône invasion in America. They not only planted a vineyard but also arranged for the Perrins' nursery to ship over the full roster of varieties allowed in Châteauneuf, as well as others, to be cleared through quarantine and propagated. Thus Tablas Creek became not only a mother lode for vine material, but also distinct in Paso—like Smith—for an obsession with great farming. (And with fastidious cellar practices; their wines have always been fermented with indigenous yeasts.)

Now the Terrizzis, resolved to redefine their adopted home, have joined the roster. They began planting their own new vineyard next to their house outside the town of Templeton. It's farther inland than Luna Matta, atop a 1,400-foot hill, but the soils are similarly calcareous, and it's hit by two wind funnels: from the Templeton Gap, which begins near the coastal town of Cambria and sweeps inland, as well as from the Cuesta Grade to the south near the town of Atascadero. They put in not only Nebbiolo but also the white grapes Friulano and Trebbiano and cuttings from the original California planting of the Friulian grape Ribolla Gialla.

Brian even bought a couple of clay amphorae—the must-have wine tool of the moment—to help perfect a white blend made under the couple's label, Giornata. It is all evidence of their attempt to prove that the area's identity is still up for grabs.

"I hope," Brian tells me, "guys like you don't give up on Paso."

A WESTWARD TRIP

When I meet Anthony Yount, it's at his day job at Denner, founded when Denver businessman Ron Denner came west to buy property in the arid foothills of the Santa Lucia Range and planted vines in 1999. Denner had owned Ditch Witch of the Rockies, a chain of dealerships for trenching and excavation equipment. If dirt had made him a living in the mountains, so it would near the coast.

The Denner edifice is subdued by Paso's often gaudy standards, more National Park Service than Renaissance fair, but it's still an imposing facade behind an imposing gate. Here, at least, that first impression is deceiving. "We're trying to fight that perception that the quality of your wines is inversely proportional to the quality of your driveway," Yount tells me as we taste wines in his spotless laboratory.

Yount studied agricultural finance at nearby Cal Poly in San Luis Obispo. Then, after tasting at Denner as part of a wine trip he took for his twenty-first birthday, he interned there before returning in 2010 as winemaker. He mounted a quiet stylistic upheaval, dialing back the wines to show more of their innate Paso-ness without betraying the luscious fruit in which the area exults. The first step, of course, was to start picking earlier. "The vines," he explains, "are giving us more character at lower sugar."

This is a risky business in Paso, especially as Denner's next-door neighbor is none other than the James Berry Vineyard. But Yount wasn't fazed. Smith himself was starting to retrench his style, and Yount began switching from new oak barrels to concrete tanks, which he found added length and finesse to the wines, as well as older wooden puncheons—oversized wine barrels. We walk into the cellar and he pours me a sample of Grenache, heady with rich raspberry flavors, from a small concrete barrel. Then we taste a bit of the same wine in a neutral puncheon. There's a bit more tension and perfume—just the right counterpoint.

Yount is a happy warrior in a truly promising part of Paso, the Willow Creek area. The presence of James Berry next door, with its ancient limestone-rich seabed full of shell fossils and whalebones, provides further evidence. Denner's acreage occupies the same rolling hills, an old dry-farmed barley field grown on the same ancient seabed, full of sandstone and calcareous shale. Smith even helped his new neighbors farm at first. Willow Creek sits near the western edge of Paso's appellation boundary,

where the small adjoining York Mountain area begins, enjoying the cooling influences of the Templeton Gap, which allows marine weather through from the nearby Pacific.

Yount takes me up on a rise behind the winery to survey the neighborhood. Nearby, in addition to James Berry, from which Yount buys Roussanne for his own Kinero label, is the Black Seth Vineyard, a source for Nick de Luca's Ground Effect; as well as the Ledge Vineyard from Mark Adams, Smith's assistant winemaker, which includes own-rooted Grenache planted on sand; and the new Jack Creek Vineyard, astride the western boundary of the Paso appellation.

At Denner, Yount planted a Garnacha clone from Priorat, Spain, to diversify his roster ("It is tannic as shit, and I love tannin in Grenache") as well as some Carignane, a grape largely disregarded here. The vines are hand tilled, with no herbicides used and only compost for fertilizer.

The problem with farming in Paso, Yount explains, is that most wineries—following the model that first won the area acclaim—hang too little fruit on each vine, turning each plant into an efficient little sugar-building system, propelled by the hot days and cold nights that help lengthen the growing season. "They wonder," he continues, "why they can't pick before 32 Brix if they want to get physiological ripeness."

To that, add what Yount calls "classic, textbook Davis winemaking," including the routine acidification of grape musts, which is crucial in protecting superripe wine from microbes and bacterial flaws like pediococcus. This is often followed by deacidification as the wine is nearly ready. This one-two shuffle allows winemakers to avoid filtering their wines.

Paso has other problems, particularly its long battle to subdivide the Paso Robles appellation, which, at more than 650,000 acres, is one of California's most sprawling. An initial proposal to divide the east and west sides of Paso met such vocal opposition that federal regulators were forced to withdraw it. Another, more precise division into numerous subappellations was floated, but it too languished.

But subdividing Paso's sprawl is merely a distraction in the real hunt for the area's terroir. Yount drives west, up Highway 46 toward the coastal town of Cambria. We climb over the top of the Santa Lucias and down into the hovering fog. About three miles shy of the coast, amid rolling coastal grassland, we encounter the Bassetti Vineyard, a planting of mostly Syrah that Denner uses in its Dirt Worshipper bottling. The Bassetti family are fourth-generation Cambrians who previously grew hay for cattle and now also grow flowers and herbs for wreaths. But Yount has been helping them to replant (he added Grenache) and use better trellises, all meant to optimize a typically dry-farmed site that, at around three hundred feet, soaks up the Central Coast's marine chill. Yount considers the damp air. "I don't think it topped out at 80 today."

Certainly he isn't first to find this spot. John Alban, one of the early Rhône-minded pioneers, helped Ellis Bassetti plant the first seven acres of vines in 1998. Steve Edmunds discovered Bassetti as a Syrah source for his Edmunds St. John label in the early 2000s. For all the talk in Paso about its west side, and the proximity to the sea, most vintners are mum about this drive out Highway 46. Yet the highway's path, which more or less follows the Templeton wind gap, is an express route to the Central Coast's frontier.

We continue into the town of Cambria and then double back the long way, along Santa Rosa Creek Road, the old route to the coast. The road switchbacks up from Cambria across the top of the Santa Lucia Range, a typically serene drive through a quintessential Central Coast landscape. Grassy cattle pasture is dotted with exposed boulders and broad wildflower fields.

This is familiar territory for me. Several years earlier, returning to San Francisco from Paso, I decided to take the coastal route north. To get there I followed Santa Rosa Creek for a scenic detour. After cresting the mountains and wondering if I would ever reach Cambria—it's a desolate, slow fifteen miles of switchbacks—I finally wound my way down toward the water. As I sank into hovering fog, the familiar sight of a vineyard appeared to my right.

I slammed on the brakes and hunted for a mailbox number to jot down. Eventually I found one and sped on toward the coast road. When I got home I looked up the address and located Stolo Family Vineyards, founded when Orange County cabinet manufacturer Don Stolo and his wife, Charlene, in 2002 bought an existing vineyard on a site that decades earlier had housed a dairy run by Swiss immigrant Salvatore Berri (and, during Prohibition, Berri's hidden winery and grappa still). Later, I met the Stolos' daughter, Maria Stolo Bennetti, at a San Francisco dinner. She was stunned that I had actually laid eyes on their vineyard.

Even on that first trip, the landscape near Cambria felt as familiar as it had on a previous trek to the Sonoma and Mendocino coasts: a well-situated hillside bathing in marine weather. Despite any fretting about coastal chill and damp, the

Stolos routinely ripened Syrah into the high 14 percent alcohol range.

Despite its steep slopes, the Santa Rosa Valley is slowly being filled in with vineyards. Along Santa Rosa Creek Road, you'll find adventurers like Susan and Jamie Spitzley of Boulder Ridge, who planted Syrah and Pinot Noir—the collocation of those two always an auspicious sign—in the mid-2000s. Their organic patch sits on a ridge directly across from the original farm store where Linn's, a Cambria mainstay, sells its famous olallieberry pies. To the south of Highway 46 there's similar terrain along Old Creek Road, which winds through hills and grasslands past the Whale Rock Reservoir to the coastal town of Cayucos.

Yount and I are back on Highway 46, but soon we veer off again and climb York Mountain Road, past the old York Mountain Winery, which in 1882 was founded as the first commercial cellar in the area. York Mountain later enjoyed brief attention, enough to win its own appellation in 1984 before fading away in the din of California's expansion. (The winery is being reborn under a new name, Epoch.)

Yount guns his pickup and takes me farther up the mountain. We wind up a dirt road into a clearing of high grass at nearly 1,800 feet. Here Yount and his girlfriend have moved into their own house on twenty-five acres. They're planting a few acres of head-trained Grenache, plus Syrah, Mourvèdre, and a grab bag of white grapes. The sandstone and mudstone soils are similar to what's farther east, although it's cooler and wetter here, with forty-two inches of rain annually compared to half that down at Denner. Yount intends to plant the herbs needed for biodynamic work so that his vines can

PASO ROBLES

VINEYARD AREA/TOTAL AREA: 26,000 acres/ 614,000 acres

MAIN GRAPES: Syrah, Grenache, Mourvèdre, Zinfandel, Cabernet Sauvignon

AT A GLANCE: One of California's largest appellations, and one long stuck with an identity crisis. As a new generation of winemakers arrive, the fine-tuning of terroir may finally occur in earnest.

THE PROMISE: Abundant sunshine and limestone-rich soils (a rarity in California), with a variety of climates that support emergent grapes like Nebbiolo and Grenache Blanc—and emerging vineyard area in the coastal hills to the west

THE RISK: Winemaking quality, inconsistent farming, and geographic sprawl

be treated with preparations grown right on the property.

We watch the sun cresting over the Pacific. The volcanic plug of Morro Rock, at the entrance to Morro Bay, is fogged in below, and from here it's evident how marine air is sucked through the Santa Lucia Range's various watershed gaps, tempering the inland heat. Here atop York Mountain, in a mostly forgotten spot, is just enough land for a generation of pioneers like Yount to adopt.

"It'll take us twenty years to get vines in the ground," he tells me. "But I'm young enough that I can wait twenty years."

Ventucopa

Angela Osborne pulls her worn blue Mercedes, dubbed Blue Velvet, off the 101 just north of the city of Santa Maria. From this exit, Highway 166 climbs east into the desolate Sierra Madre Mountains.

Lino Bozzano is waiting for us, coffee in hand. A big, wide bear of a guy, Bozzano was raised in the Central Valley, went to Cal Poly San Luis Obispo, and ended up managing vineyards not far away, for the Laetitia Vineyard in the Arroyo Grande Valley. We pile into his massive SUV and head east for nearly fifty miles, climbing up the county's spine through the Los Padres National Forest.

After the better part of an hour we clear the pass and empty into a narrow plain, the Cuyama Valley, bounded by the Sierra Madres on one side and the Caliente Range on the other. This is high ranchland, often above two thousand feet. We pass through the farming town of New Cuyama, its faded post office a snapshot of the 1950s, and turn south onto Highway 33, California's oil thoroughfare, a taut

ribbon of a road that bisects ranch land and occasional fields tended by Grimmway Farms and Bolthouse Farms, the state's two carrot kingpins.

Our destination: Ventucopa, California, population ninety-two. The town lies near the headwaters of the ambitiously named Cuyama River, which, with an annual rainfall of only about ten inches, is usually just a dry riverbed. Chaparral-dotted hills rise into the national forest on either side. Hungry bikers sometimes pull off at The Place ("Est. 1929 Ventucopa, Elev. 2999'," according to a carved wood sign) for an elk burger and a beer.

Otherwise the valley is left in isolation. It's just thirty-three miles to the sea, in a straight line south toward the city of Santa Barbara, but this is the essence of high desert. Ventucopa sits by the intersection of four counties: coastal Santa Barbara, Ventura, and San Luis Obispo; and inland Kern, the lower end of the San Joaquin Valley and the southern terminus for California's sea of inland vineyards. The town of Ojai is a fifty-mile drive to the south, while the oil city of Bakersfield lies seventy miles northeast over the mountains. Ventucopa doesn't quite belong to either world.

"It's so easy to go for the low-hanging fruit," Bozzano tells me. "You go to Napa, or you go to Paso. And you overpay for dirt. It takes a lot more to come out somewhere like here."

I've come here because of Osborne's Grenache, dubbed A Tribute to Grace after her maternal

The New California Wine

grandmother. Grace was a transformative wine for me, a reminder that Grenache—usually the heart of robust, gaudy bottles—could have all the subtlety of a persnickety thing like Pinot Noir. Osborne's 2008 Grace, a nearly evanescent wine filled with scents of fenugreek and tamarind, and made even lighter by the grape bins being rained on while they awaited the press, was a wine that never should have existed. It was grown in an outback vineyard here called Santa Barbara Highlands, which gives the impression of a cool coastal ridge but in fact bakes under the sun at more than half a mile high. The light is so intense that by 10 a.m., with the temperature climbing north of 90 degrees, it already feels like 110.

A native New Zealander, Osborne first heard of these highlands while working in a San Diego wine shop, where she was saving up to make her own Grenache. In 2007 she paid the vineyard a visit with her mother. As they crested the mountains from Ojai, they fell silent as they witnessed an empty tan landscape dotted with green, a hidden world in California's mountains.

"There's a quality to the light in New Zealand that I've never seen anywhere else in the world," Osborne tells me. "I think that's the first time I had light strike me the same way, when I saw the Highlands. It is such a humbling place."

The first time I tasted Grace, Osborne's reference was clear: Château Rayas, one of Châteauneuf-du-Pape's legendary estates and certainly its most mercurial. Rayas's wines, grown on a cooler patch of pure sand that stands out from the warm, rocky stretches of Châteauneuf, is weightless and subtle in a place where wine is usually thick and dark.

When I first met Osborne, she didn't immediately cop to the Rayas connection, but it became clear over our long conversations that it had been

on her brain since her first vintage—indeed, since her first taste of it in the wine shop where she worked. Her recent years had essentially been one long meditation on the purity of Grenache.

But how could that possibly involve Ventucopa? In addition to grapes, the town sports an occasional alfalfa and apple crop as well as a big planting of pistachios from the Santa Barbara Pistachio Company, which also runs Ventucopa's equivalent of a general store. The area reminds me of nothing so much as a more dramatic version of the eastern Washington desert, where vineyards are also dropped into a neutral, dry landscape. There, as here, with just eight inches of rain per year, farmers can essentially create their own weather.

The tale of Ventucopa's vineyards begins with a guy named Larry Hogan, a rancher who moved here in 1981. He opened a restaurant and bar called Sagebrush Annie's, which remains, complete with a now dilapidated rodeo stadium behind it. But he also noticed similarities in climate and temperature to parts of Napa Valley. That seems improbable at first, but Cuyama Valley gets a mix of hot days and frigid nights, with the elevation balancing the sun, such that it receives a similar number of degree-days Farenheit as Calistoga—the altitude, perhaps, differentiating it from the San Joaquin to the east. The presence of Cabernet and Chardonnay at Highlands is primarily the result of California's endless thirst for cheap table-wine grapes. But for Rhône varieties like Grenache, it is a blissful spot. Hogan planted a few hundred acres of vineyard and began making wines under the Barnwood label.

Ultimately, though, Hogan was more rancher than vineyardist. He sold the majority of his land to the Laetitia label, based near the coast in Arroyo Grande, keeping some forty acres for himself. Now mostly a bar, Sagebrush Annie's remains one of

Ventucopa's few businesses. Hogan still makes wine, including a heady Cabernet, under the Sagebrush Annie's label. "All my wines are gold-medal wines," he tells me one night (along with anyone else who wanders by) as he hosts a party in the fading mountain light.

And Ventucopa itself? It lingers in a strange place between serenity and sadness, between the *om shanti* of Ojai and the banging oil wells of Bakersfield. Perhaps it's that ghost rodeo sitting behind Sagebrush Annie's, a handful of floodlights and bleachers framed by steep sandstone cliffs. Now Ventucopa is Bozzano's playground. He showed up in 2004 as a triage viticulturist, stepping in when Laetitia wanted to abandon the whole spread. But the vines were less than seven years old, so he persuaded his bosses to let him keep farming the high-elevation loamy sand soils.

Bozzano also wanted to expand, so he turned to the mesa on the valley's west side, three hundred feet higher, which had extra clay and alluvial runoff and more precipitous wind. It's an appealing spot, in an extreme way. Up here the vines grow spindly, and the harshness of the ground is, if anything, a boon to the Mourvèdre—"Maw-ved," Bozzano intones, in that flat Central Valley accent—and head-trained Grenache that he is planting on a newly cleared parcel.

Still, it is not a particularly sane place to farm. "I always tell people 'Cuyama,' in Chumash, means 'valley of lost fortunes,'" he explains. "If you're going to come out here and think you're going to make all this money, you've got to be creative."

But somehow the Highlands has muscled on, mostly by selling a lot of fruit from nearly 750 acres into the great pool of table-wine grapes. It is not a small place, or a glamorous one. As I stand alongside a rod-straight stretch of Highway 33, the

SANTA BARBARA COUNTY

VINEYARD AREA/TOTAL AREA: 16,580 acres/ 1.75 million acres

MAIN GRAPES: Chardonnay, Pinot Noir, Syrah, Grenache

AT A GLANCE: Known for its coastal growing regions, Santa Barbara hosts a great diversity of grapes—everything from Chardonnay to Friulano. Large wine companies determined much of its early history, leaving it to the current generation to fine-tune its geography and explore farther inland.

THE PROMISE: A wide array of growing conditions and potentially suitable varieties, with tens of thousands of acres still to be explored. The Ballard Canyon area near Los Olivos has potential not only for Rhône-native varieties but also warmer-climate white wines and Cabernet Franc. So does the Happy Canyon area in the eastern Santa Ynez, also an emerging area for such grapes as Grenache and Sauvignon Blanc. The Los Alamos area shows particular promise for aromatic white grapes, including Riesling. And remote areas like Ventucopa underscore the diverse possibilities for viticulture throughout the county.

THE RISK: Low grape prices, large plantings on mediocre soils, lingering geographic confusion

vines seem to fill the valley to the very edges of the veined hard-sand hills beyond. It's a thriving spot for wine in the midst of a moonscape, where talk of cattle quickly mixes with that of Nicolas Joly, the biodynamic maverick. In terms of wine, Ventucopa resists affiliation. It belongs to nothing but itself. That it can produce so remarkable a wine as Osborne's is a reminder that the whole truth about California's terroir is far from being discovered.

3

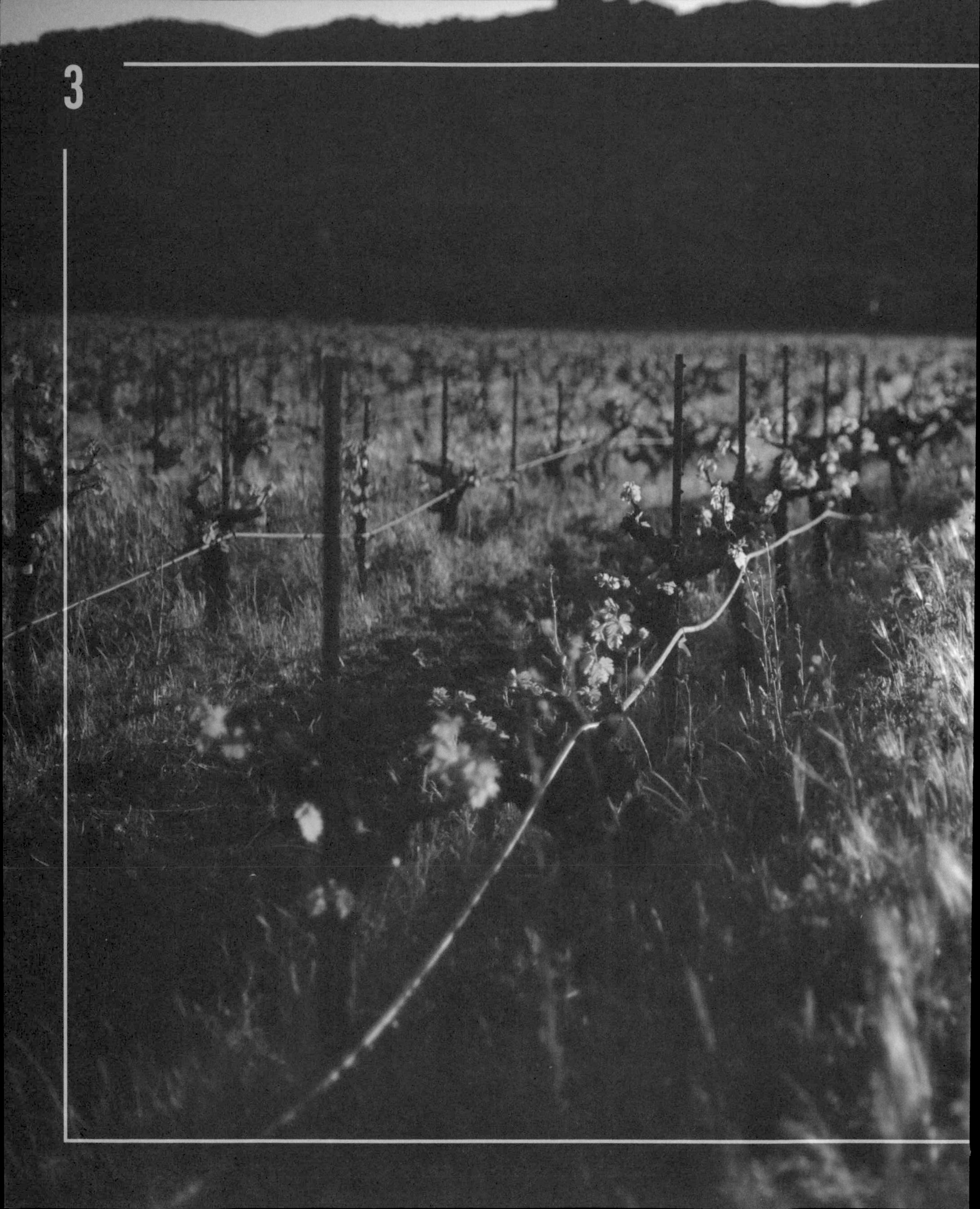

WINES OF THE NEW CALIFORNIA: A GUIDE

HOW TO USE THIS GUIDE

In the chapters that follow, I have categorized each of the wines listed by price. Of course, wine prices are constantly changing; however, my hope is that the four price categories I've established will give you a sense of comparative value. Many California wines are priced at a premium, especially when compared with wines from other regions. Often, the wines listed in this book have prices that reflect their small-scale production.

Because they're produced in limited quantities, some of these wines are in short supply, and are sometimes most easily purchased from the wineries themselves. (See the List of Producers on page 288 for winery contact information.)

Finally, you may notice that the wines are listed without vintage information. This isn't to imply that vintages don't matter in California—they very much do, and increasingly so, especially as the evolving styles among the state's producers complicate the topic. I've tried to include wines here that I believe will represent themselves well across multiple years.

$	$20 and under
$$	$21 to $40
$$$	$41 to $80
$$$$	Over $80

How Producers are Listed

This guide is not intended to be an exhaustive list of producers, but rather a curated selection of wineries and wines that reflect the best of New California.

Each chapter includes "Top Producers," a list of those who are making benchmark wines that warrant in-depth discussion. It includes wineries in each category that are likely to guide California's wine styles in the future.

Wines and winemakers in the "More Notable Wines" sections are also of excellent quality— and equally worth seeking out. In some cases, a producer may be listed in this section because its wines are in extremely limited supply or are priced at a notable premium; because its reputation is still being established; or because it is better known for making other varieties. On that last point, many producers appear in multiple places. If they have other focuses—for example, Syrah in addition to Pinot Noir—they are often listed in both chapters.

The vineyards used in making the wines listed in the following chapters can be found in the Maps section starting on page 274.

Pinot Noir

David Hirsch's diary recalls the day: January 9, 1994. On that winter morning, three winemakers gathered to walk his land: Burt Williams, whose Williams Selyem wines were already becoming legend; Ted Lemon, whose Littorai label had begun to sprout wings; and Chardonnay prodigy Steve Kistler, whose talents had expanded into Pinot Noir.

Hirsch had since 1980 been growing a patchwork of grapes, first contemplating Riesling, then planting Pinot Noir at the suggestion of Jim Beauregard, an old friend from Santa Cruz. Pinot had become David's specialty; in 1988, he added cuttings taken off Mount Eden Vineyards in the Santa Cruz Mountains, which had one of the state's longest Pinot lineages. But mostly Hirsch's fruit went to nondescript customers, blended into wines like Kendall-Jackson's larger efforts.

As Williams, Lemon, and Kistler—the three Pinot kings—surmised, this was a waste of grapes. Even in 1994, the quality of Hirsch fruit stood out. And the utter improbability of the vineyard, high

on a precipitous ridge above the Pacific Ocean, in an environment suitable for *King Lear* ("Blow, winds, and crack your cheeks!"), prompted an obvious question: why the hell would anyone want to grow grapes here?

The answer, of course, was that the complexity of the soils had turned Hirsch's lark of a project into a grand meditation on terroir. Hirsch himself has spent most of three decades on this ridge, struggling to understand his site in a studious, relentless way.

Whatever the three men saw that January day, their hunch that they should journey to the outer reaches of the coast soon paid off. Whether in the Williams Selyem or Littorai lineup, the Hirsch wines have always stood out, showing just a bit more intensity, a bit more drama. David soon acquired a rarified set of clients. The Hirsch name quickly became a *ne plus ultra* for California Pinot Noir.

A SEARCH FOR RELEVANCE

But progress takes time. It would take another fifteen years or so after that 1994 visit for what Hirsch and his daughter Jasmine call "the pursuit of relevance" to reach critical mass—in no small part because the modern quest for significance in Pinot was largely sidelined by Big Flavor.

Throughout the 1990s California witnessed a Pinot Noir boom. A combination of young vineyards featuring Dijon clones (see page 68) and a preference for ever-deeper extraction and late, ripe picking blurred terroir to the extent that, in most wines, any reflection of the soil was lost, even as Pinot arrivistes loudly proclaimed otherwise. If Big Flavor was frustrating in other wines, it was

absolutely intolerable with Pinot. The grape's historic purpose was a meditation on great soils. Its very nature required a far subtler and more deliberate touch than the attempt to make what Kosta Browne's Michael Browne called "a delicious beverage."

By the late 2000s, a raft of producers had emerged in fundamental opposition to Big Flavor, joining a handful of true believers like Ted Lemon, who quietly persevered through the ripeness years. Rather than offering lip service, they legitimately understood the purpose of Burgundy's exacting drive to comprehend the specifics of place—and the inevitable torture that accompanies a true love for the grape. Californians had long laid claim to the "Burgundian" approach, to the point of farce, but this group of new winemakers—Chanin Wines, Rhys Vineyards, Anthill Farms and so on—embraced the substance of terroir rather than just the word. Their wines tended to display lower alcohol levels and the refined structure that presaged the ability to age. And yet, while they paid homage to the classic tension of top Burgundies, they also exuded Californian fruit. As Vanessa Wong of Peay Vineyards put it, "We can't make Burgundy here. We're not in Burgundy."

THE STYLE MESS

Prior to the wine boom of the 1970s, great California Pinot Noir had been virtually a myth. Despite being responsible for some of the occasional successes, like a 1947 Pinot from Beaulieu Vineyard, even André Tchelistcheff, the dean of Napa winemakers, believed that most of these had been happy mistakes, and that truly proper sites for the grape hadn't yet been discovered. (As evidenced by his quote that "God made Cabernet Sauvignon whereas the devil made Pinot Noir," Tchelistcheff clearly had existential issues with the grape.) It was Cabernet and Chardonnay, not Pinot, that led the revolution of the 1970s. "The accepted wisdom in 1975," Calera's Josh Jensen told me, "was that Pinot Noir in America was no good, and it would never be any good."

That's what Burt Williams concluded, too. Despite finding an occasional standout, including Richard Sanford's early wines at Sanford & Benedict in Santa Barbara County, Williams's own winemaking began out of frustration with the lack of consistency among makers of California Pinot: "I surmised that what they were doing was, they were doing it right by accident one time."

Nearly three decades later, a new Pinot generation faced just the opposite challenge. Great vineyards were out there—the wines of Williams Selyem and Calera proved it—but winemakers could detect little distinction in most bottles. "One thing that struck me," recalls Gavin Chanin, "was how undifferentiated and un-terroir-like the high alcohol, high-oak wines were." But then, Chanin's palate had been honed by his mentor: Jim Clendenen of Au Bon Climat, whose subtler style developed in the 1980s. And Clendenen's wines were assailed during the Big Flavor years as not Californian enough.

The war over Pinot Noir had begun long before Big Flavor arrived. In 1984, Sonoma winemaker Forrest Tancer wrote, "For years Californians have felt that Pinot Noirs should be dark, robust wines in the same style as some California Cabernets or Zinfandels, but Pinot Noirs, in spite of their richness, are not wines of tremendous color or tannin. Their style is in their complexity, their subtlety and shading, strengths that we are striving hard to bring out in California."

Among the strivers were Calera's Jensen and Chalone's Richard Graff, who wanted, if not to replicate Burgundy in the New World, at least to aim to create wine with similar complexities. Williams had by that point cofounded Williams Selyem, not just out of frustration with the state of California Pinot Noir, but also because the Burgundies his uncle had served him when he was a teenager had become too expensive to buy.

Whatever brawn had been displayed in the past, such as the 1970s beasts from Ken Burnap's Santa Cruz Mountain Vineyard, it would be dwarfed by the early 2000s by the normalization of what Ted Lemon would call the "flamboyant" style. Labels like Loring, Aubert, and that ultimate example of irrational exuberance, Kosta Browne, favored among Pinot novices, quickly attracted partisans for their brash wines.

A BATTLE FOR BALANCE

Soon enough came the counterreformation, an attempt to restore Pinot's good name in California. The wines that emerged from the newer producers of the late 2000s were almost reactionary in their shyness; complicated and quiet, they revealed the best of Pinot's meditative ways. More crucially, they emerged from a belief that you cannot even begin to have a discussion about Pinot Noir unless your wine can truly show an interpretation of a specific site.

Of course, there wasn't a serious Pinot maker in the world, including the extract overlords, who didn't claim to offer just that. But the new Pinotists exposed the gap between words and deeds—and in doing so, created a particular culture clash. This gap was never underscored better than at a

tasting in March 2011, at an event called the World of Pinot Noir during a discussion of alcohol and "balance"—a polite way to quietly reference the style wars. One panelist, Sandhi's Rajat Parr, was served a wine from another panelist, Adam Lee of the Siduri winery, a bête noire of the lower-alcohol set. Parr had kind words for Siduri's 13.6 percent Cargasacchi Vineyard bottling, at which point Lee revealed that he had switched the wine with a 15-percent bottle from Russian River Valley, presumably to poke at Parr's skepticism about high-alcohol Pinot Noirs. It was intended to be a gotcha moment. Had Parr, revered for his blind-tasting abilities, been duped by Lee—whom the *New York Times* dubbed the "gadfly in the Pinot Noir"—into endorsing the flamboyant style? At that moment a battle flared over the notion of balance—a term that encompassed not merely rising alcohol levels, but the simmering philosophical clash over Pinot's true purpose.

This battle was highlighted during the three cool vintages of 2009, 2010, and 2011, when ripeness was elusive in California and making a big, high-extract Pinot became a feat of winemaking necromancy. But by then, many wineries had no option. They had become trapped into making unsustainably big wines, and many examples from these colder vintages tasted hollow—victims of a Big Flavor salvage attempt. Burgundy, too, had dabbled with turning up the volume—specifically through the 1980s work of consultant Guy Accad, who advocated extended cold soaking of must (and heavy additions of sulfur dioxide) before fermentation. Accad's method was an omen of California's flashy style.

Ripeness, more than anything, is the new Pinot generation's line in the sand. Picking grapes at sugar levels of 22 Brix is now considered far more acceptable than picking them at 25. Acidities must be far

WHOLE-CLUSTER FERMENTATION

Increasingly, California winemakers are fermenting red wines using whole grape clusters rather than removing the berries from the grape stem, or rachis. Although this practice has found recent converts, whole-cluster fermentation is in fact a traditional practice—essentially the default means of making wine until destemming technology arrived in the early twentieth century.

The practice regained favor mostly for Pinot Noir, but also for Syrah and Grenache, and even Cabernet in a few cases—although the larger industry takes an often dismissive approach to what it calls "MOG": material other than grapes. Whole-cluster usage remains hotly debated, not only in California but in France as well. While top domaines like Domaine de la Romanée-Conti now rely heavily on the practice, other Burgundian masters, like Henri Jayer, insisted that stems have no place in winemaking. But the current fondness for whole clusters among New Californians echoes a similar interest—and a similar debate—among the state's earlier pioneers. In 1977, Chalone's Richard Graff asserted that "unless Pinot Noir is fermented with the stems it doesn't have any tannin or much body."

Winemakers find a number of virtues in leaving the berries on the stems: a silkier texture; a spicy, coniferous aroma; more structural tannins; more juice movement during fermentation to keep the wine fresher; the presence of more whole berries (which can add complexity and promotes carbonic maceration, the process in which carbon dioxide helps break down the fruit and promotes fermentation inside the grape itself); and lower peak temperatures and final alcohol levels. While the process, in part because of the presence of potassium in the stems, can raise a wine's overall pH, many find the whole-cluster process actually seems to boost freshness. Often winemakers opt for a partial use

higher than in the past, in part because the addition of acid is frowned upon if not outright verboten. "I doubt we'll ever go and taste an old wine and say, 'Shit, I wish I'd picked this a week later,'" says winemaker Sashi Moorman, who harvests his fruit around 21 Brix. "That says everything. That is the struggle. No matter what, in California you're probably always going to pick it just a little too ripe."

Fermentation for most new Pinots is done with indigenous yeasts (a near-default practice in Burgundy), and whole grape clusters are increasingly used in fermentation (see Whole-Cluster Fermentation, above). Freshness is essential in these wines, along with less use of new oak, less extraction, and a more cautious use of an extended, Accad-style soaking of grapes.

PUZZLES OF PLACE

California's relationship with Pinot geography is as complicated as its struggles with style. Consider the Russian River Valley of the mid-1970s, populated by growers like Joe Rochioli, Tom Dehlinger, and Davis Bynum but still newly planted to Pinot and better known for white grapes and Zinfandel. At the time, wine authorities Bob Thompson and Hugh Johnson asserted that for Pinot, "the Sonoma Valley is considerably more proven than the Russian River watershed." In the meantime, other promising areas had often been disregarded, like the Corralitos area in the southern reaches of the Santa Cruz Mountains.

of stems, depending on the ripeness of the vintage.

Critics of whole-cluster fermentation argue that stems absorb pigment, making for a less intensely colored wine, and that unripe tannins in the stems can add greenness to the wine (although this often depends on the clusters and how they are handled). Conventional wisdom a few years ago was that stems had to be slightly brown if they were to be included, but Californians increasingly witnessed their Burgundy counterparts using bright-green stems.

But who could be expected to sort everything out in just three or four decades? It's a remarkably short amount of time to unravel the geographic mysteries of a grape that confounded Burgundy's monks for centuries. California's Pinot geography is embryonic—although some choices have seemed more reasonable than others. Calera's Jensen had a method to his mad quest for limestone that would approximate Burgundy's soils. It took him two years to find land in the most unexpected of places in 1974, when he planted his flag on three million tons of limestone in San Benito County.

Frequently, though, the momentum to declare a sweet spot for Pinot has been too strong to stop. Plantings boom. Rather than a long courtship between grape and place, California has too often forced a shotgun wedding.

Was there particular logic in, say, Monterey's Santa Lucia Highlands becoming a Pinot epicenter—aside from grower Gary Pisoni's early fondness for the variety? Similarly, the sheep-grazing lands of the Carneros District between Napa and Sonoma were perhaps an obvious choice for Burgundian varieties—at least when viewed through Napa's narrow midcentury lens. When Tchelistcheff looked south to make Pinot Noir, he turned to Carneros as Napa's coldest area, the best convenient option. But he also believed California's sweet spot for the grape hadn't yet been unearthed—and that it certainly wasn't in Carneros.

TOP PRODUCERS

* * *

ANTHILL FARMS

The trio that founded Anthill in 2004 got their start in a stronghold of Pinot expertise: as cellar rats at Williams Selyem. Anthony Filiberti was raised in Sonoma County, apprenticed at Oregon's Bergstrom, and now also farms vineyards in Anderson Valley and makes the wines for Knez (see page 188). Kansas native David Low attended UC Berkeley before migrating to wine; he also is assistant winemaker at Papapietro Perry in Dry Creek Valley, the same spot where the Anthill wines are made. Webster Marquez came west from cellar work in Virginia; in addition to this label he also makes wines for San Francisco's Bluxome Street Winery and other clients.

The three joined to make cool-site Pinot Noir and Syrah (and, in 2007, an excellent Cabernet) from a handful of sites, including their own leased spot, Abbey-Harris, outside the Mendocino County town of Boonville. The name Anthill refers to their communal work—and the burden of making wine while keeping down other day jobs.

While the Anthill wines have never used much new oak, perhaps 30 percent, earlier vintages came across as sweeter and more immediate. More recently, the wines have gained subtlety, transparency, and more aging potential, showing the distinction of the trio's excellent sites. A loyal following, including a roster of fans who migrated from their alma mater Williams Selyem, tend to make new releases vanish almost upon release.

THE WINES: With Filiberti biodynamically farming this tiny two-acre parcel at 1,100 feet elevation, the **Abbey-Harris** ($$$) is typically the most woodsy and tense of their bottles. The **Peters Vineyard** ($$$), a mix of Pommard and 777 clones, comes from a northern slope of the Petaluma Wind Gap, which is beset by constant morning fog. The wine evokes raspberries still clinging to the bush. The **Tina Marie** ($$$), grown in Sonoma's Green Valley, might be the most approachable, while the exotic **Campbell Ranch** ($$$) is grown in a chilly spot at 750 feet elevation in Annapolis, just a few miles from the sea. Its exoticism—one description: "It smells like walking into L'Occitane"—can be polarizing. The **Comptche Ridge** ($$$) is grown north of the Anderson Valley, and there is also an outperforming **Anderson Valley** ($$) blend in some vintages. There has been wine from the Demuth site in past years (Filiberti farms Demuth for owner Peter Knez), along with Syrahs from **Campbell Ranch** ($$) and

Peters ($$), and an occasional **Sonoma Coast** Syrah blend ($$).

CALERA

If it seems counterintuitive to file Josh Jensen and his wines with the avant-garde, the fact is that Calera, one of Caliornia's defining Pinot Noirs, has maintained a continuity of style. If his style doesn't seem so revolutionary now, it's because it took a few decades for tastes to catch up to his.

Mr. Limestone's particulars have been well covered, both here and elsewhere. A native of Orinda, east of Berkeley, he went to Oxford for a master's degree and ended up a cellar grunt in Burgundy, where he became entranced by its calcium-rich soils. He returned home to California and spent two years hunting up and down the state, pouring hydrochloric acid on the ground in hopes of uncovering the limestone that would allow him to conduct his grand experiment in soil. He hunted in vain, poring over Bureau of Mines surveys and pestering county assessors while trying to make ends meet, even reviewing restaurants for the *San Francisco Chronicle* under a pseudonym.

Finally, pay dirt. In 1974 he acquired a 324-acre parcel high in the Gavilan Mountains, a former lime quarry in San Benito County east of Monterey, and got to work.

Fast-forward nearly forty years and the arid, mountainous planting atop Mount Harlan— now all certified organic—has become one of California's defining sites. Jensen's wines, fermented with indigenous yeasts in an old multilevel mine facility that facilitates true gravity-fed winemaking, are legendary for their ability to age over decades. Although Jensen once called the crusher-destemmer a "doomsday machine," he has capitulated to its use, although Calera wines predominantly use whole-cluster fermentation. And while Jensen's wines have grown bigger through the years (they flirt with 15 percent alcohol, especially in a low-yielding year), they are the epitome of balance and precision.

THE WINES: Perhaps the most impressive achievement among the lineup is his **Central Coast Pinot Noir** ($$), of which he routinely makes around ten thousand cases, blending at least a dozen vineyard sources, including the Besson site in Santa Clara County and the Talley Vineyard in the Central Coast's Arroyo Grande area. Among his single-vineyard wines, it's a matter of preference. **Jensen Pinot Noir** ($$$), from 13.8 acres planted in 1975, is the most stoic and long-lived, with intense tannins and fruit. **Reed** ($$$), also from a 1975 planting, is a bit less austere but still dense in its dark fruit, while **Selleck** ($$$), from another original parcel, is lighter on its feet. **Ryan** ($$), named for longtime vineyard manager Jim Ryan, is from younger vines, suitable for an earlier-drinking bottle, as is the newer **De Villiers** ($$). Jensen's remarkably detailed back labels, which list more stats than a baseball card, are a model of forthrightness. Finally, there is a **Mt. Harlan Chardonnay** ($$) and **Central Coast Chardonnay** ($), plus a **Viognier** ($$) and a rare **Aligoté** ($$), an exceptional version of Burgundy's lesser-loved white grape.

DOMAINE DE LA CÔTE

This project in the Santa Rita Hills was born out of the ambitious Evening Land Vineyards, which was founded in 2005 with an impressive slate of investors, including Hollywood producer Mark Tarlov and New York restaurateur Danny Meyer. After tumultuous staff changes, Evening Land backed out of Southern California and sold the vineyards to Sashi Moorman, its winemaker in Santa Rita, plus Sandhi's Rajat Parr and a number of investors.

The ownership may have changed, but the land—more than sixty acres worth—and the winemaker remain the same. The property includes some of the area's most intensely farmed vineyards, all on south-facing slopes in Santa Rita's south valley; the three-acre Siren's Call parcel was planted on its own roots at an astonishing seven thousand vines per acre. Twenty acres of Chardonnay, a block called River's Fall, were planned for a lower parcel near the Santa Ynez River.

THE WINES: There is a **Tempest Pinot Noir** ($$$) using fruit from the eight-acre Memorious and other parcels, as well as **Bloom's Field** ($$$), from a six-acre parcel planted to alternating rows of Swan, Calera, and Mount Eden clones, and **Siren's Call** ($$$) and **La Côte** ($$$), the last of which is fermented entirely with whole grape clusters from a parcel that formerly was called Tempest.

DREW FAMILY

On the most remote of Mendocino County ridges, less than four miles from the Pacific coast and the tiny town of Elk, Jason and Molly Drew have carved out their own frontier for Pinot Noir. Their remote site, an old apple orchard, sits at 1,200 feet elevation above Anderson Valley (in the coastal rain shadow), where it receives up to eighty inches of rain annually, perhaps double that of the valley below. It is a similar setup to that found at the outer reaches of the Sonoma Coast, except the Drews have even fewer neighboring vineyards.

Jason did an early stint in Mendocino, at Navarro, before the couple headed to Australia, where he studied winemaking. Upon their return he carved an impressive path through Napa—at Joseph Phelps, Luna, and Corison—before landing at Santa Barbara County's Babcock. But the Central Coast wasn't the right fit: "The toughest thing for me when I was down there was to make a wine that had restraint." The Drews looked north again, settling their apple orchard in 2004.

Their wines have become some of Anderson Valley's most restrained and potentially long-lived specimens, reminiscent of old Littorai and Williams Selyem from the 1990s. No surprise, then, that Burt Williams sells fruit from his Morning Dew Ranch to the couple. It is their most standoffish, but also most complex, wine. In an era when Anderson Valley has chased the stylistic lure of Big Flavor, Drew is a beautiful reminder of its roots.

THE WINES: Drew makes a range of Pinots, including **Gatekeepers** ($$), from the Wiley and Akin Vineyards, and the **Talfryn & Calder** blend ($$$), a mix of high- and lower-elevation sites. But the **Fog-Eater** ($$$) is their calling card, a plummy, tension-filled snapshot of the appellation from a blend of sites in Anderson Valley's north end. For single vineyards, there is the **Valenti** ($$$), from the Mendocino Ridge appellation, and the more broad-shouldered **Weir** ($$$), from the Yorkville Highlands. And, of course, there's **Morning Dew** ($$$), their most cerebral and intense wine, from a mix of vine selections (Rochioli, DRC, and 828) off Williams's property east of Philo. When the Drews' estate vines have matured, they will be added to the roster. There's also, unexpectedly, a **Valenti Vineyard Albariño** ($$) and a wound-up **Valenti Vineyard Syrah** ($$) from that parcel on Greenwood Ridge near the Drews' property.

FAILLA

Ehren Jordan is a master of many wines, but increasingly he is defined by his nuanced Pinot Noir and Syrah. While Pinot has become a focus for him, the young double major in archaeology and art history from just outside Pittsburgh retains a particular fealty to the Rhône, ever since he toured the northern Rhône in 1991 and landed a two-year post in the cellar of Jean-Luc Colombo. That time in the Cornas appellation set his views about ripeness that have defined his work at Failla, which he owns with his wife, Anne-Marie Failla.

In California, Jordan got a job as a part-time tour guide for Joseph Phelps, talked his way into the cellar, and impressed executive Bruce Neyers (see page 271) enough that he hired Jordan for his own label—in part because of Jordan's ability to remember details with near-photographic precision.

At the same time, Jordan found his way into the graces of Helen Turley, doing odd jobs for her Marcassin label and for her brother's Turley Wine Cellars. Soon he was Larry Turley's winemaker too, a position he held until 2013. The two men quickly bonded, in part over their love of airplanes. Both were veteran pilots; Jordan can often be found traversing the coast in his Cessna 425 twin turboprop.

In 1997 Jordan married Anne-Marie, a childhood friend, and the Failla label (initially Failla-Jordan) was launched the following year. By that point Jordan was already assembling what would become an eighty-five-acre parcel of the true Sonoma Coast, an area he had familiarized himself with during his work with Turley. Eventually the label would gain its own home far from the couple's coastal vines: a large wine cave and tasting room south of Calistoga, on ten acres formerly owned by chef Cindy Pawlcyn. It hosts several custom-crush clients in addition to Jordan's own work, as well as a small vineyard.

In the cellar, Failla wines typically undergo spontaneous fermentation and receive varying amounts of new oak, although rarely more than 50 percent. Jordan has gained a reputation for being one of the first to pick his grapes, sometimes weeks before other clients at sites like Hirsch and Keefer Ranch. This has given his red wines, many of them made using a significant quantity of whole clusters, added precision.

THE WINES: On the Pinot side, there is an early-release **Sonoma Coast** ($$) blend, from mostly younger vines in some of the designate sites (Keefer Ranch, Hirsch) as well as fruit from other sources like Floodgate and Whistler. In terms of vineyard designates, Failla makes one of the defining bottles of **Hirsch** ($$$), relying on some of the vineyard's best blocks of Mount Eden and Pommard selections; a **Keefer Ranch** ($$$), perhaps the best expression of that richer-soiled site on the far western edge of Russian River Valley; a snappy **Occidental Ridge** ($$$); and an **Estate Pinot Noir** ($$$) that rivals their Estate Syrah in intensity, from the couple's densely planted dry-farmed vines near Hirsch on the coast. See also Chardonnay (page 201) and Revising the Rhône (page 233).

HIRSCH VINEYARDS

David Hirsch's site atop a ridge outside Cazadero has long been a Pinot mecca. Here David is benevolent ruler, constantly tinkering with and fine-tuning his parcels, tweaking the farming but always driving toward a level of intensity in the fruit that I often describe as "Hirsch-ness," an amping up of flavors and mineral intensity on the palate.

In 2002, after selling grapes for the better part of two decades, he determined the best way to better understand the nuances of his ranch was to make his own wine—and it had to be from a winery in its midst: "The wine just isn't complete if you don't have people living in the place where the vines are grown and the wine matures, where the grapes are transformed and the wine ages."

After a series of winemakers, Hirsch tapped Ross Cobb, whose family's nearby vineyards were another early western Sonoma Coast effort. Under Cobb, the Hirsch wines began to find a surer footing, becoming lighter in style and showing more evident signs of their origins. At the same time, Hirsch began a quiet conversion to biodynamic farming.

While there may be greater interpretations of the Hirsch site, these wines show a proprietor's vision of place—which might explain why David Hirsch still rises before dawn most mornings to attend to this extraordinary piece of California earth himself.

THE WINES: The **San Andreas Pinot Noir** ($$$) is Hirsch's mainline cuvée, a finely etched snapshot of the entire site—using dozens of different lots—with a structural backbone from Pommard selections (actually an unintentional interplanting of Pommard and Wädenswil) throughout the vineyard. The counterpoint of San Andreas's approachable fruit is the damp-forest aspect and stoicism of the **Reserve** ($$$$), a selection of top barrels (though with ever-less new oak). The real quest for place emerges in the **East Ridge** ($$$$), the most evanescent and tension-filled of the Hirsch bottlings, from blocks on the ranch's eastern aspect, and the **West Ridge** ($$$$), from the ranch's other portion, which shows more plushness to its dark fruit and a saline character. Finally, there's the **Bohan-Dillon** ($$), a second wine of sorts that had tapped some neighboring vineyards but is now an estate effort; it has a bit less intensity but plenty of earthy red-fruit complexity. See also Chardonnay (page 202).

LITTORAI

Ted Lemon's wines are an absolute paradigm of site-driven Pinot Noir. It would be facile to take his experience making wine at Burgundy's Domaine Roulot and draw an analogy to his work in California. But his wines speak with just as much specificity and detail as those made by Burgundy's best talents.

Winemaking at Littorai is precise but executed with a light touch. "It reminds me of what

Warren Buffett would say about a classic investment," Lemon says. "If you can't understand it, don't invest in it."

There is moderation in the cellar: the Pinot ferments mostly in steel (although with the occasional lot in upright wood tanks), it undergoes long fermentations using indigenous yeasts and native malolactic fermentation, and a portion of whole clusters are used, although they rarely exceed 40 percent. As much as Littorai wines almost never blip above 14 percent alcohol, Lemon is hardly a proponent of early picking. He has a surprising comfort with risk when it comes to waiting for optimum ripeness; a 2011 lot from the Hirsch Vineyard picked mid-September at 21.6 Brix had virtually identical chemistry—but 2 degrees less sugar—than different selections picked nearly a month later.

For this reason, it can be hard to root out a simple Littorai cellar philosophy. Lemon is obsessed with detail, but he rarely makes two wines the same way. Otherwise, he says, "you run the risk of making the wine in your head, and not the wine of the vintage."

THE WINES: Littorai's lineup arguably represents the purest showings of site signature in the New World. First, the two estate parcels: the **Haven Pinot Noir** ($$$), from five acres planted on an amphitheater of gravelly and sedimentary loam near Occidental, is Littorai's touchstone, while the **Pivot** ($$$), from its estate parcel outside Sebastopol, produces a profound, if young, chamomile-accented effort. But Lemon's exploration of the extreme North Coast simply begins with these two. There's the iris-scented richness of **Mays Canyon** ($$$), Lemon's name for the Porter-Bass Vineyard outside Guerneville. The **B.A. Thieriot** ($$$) outside Occidental, which Lemon farms himself, shows a clove accent and dense structure from a mix of Pommard, Swan, 828, and 114 clones. Littorai also makes arguably the finest interpretation of **Hirsch** ($$$), using a mix of clones 114, Swan, and Pommard from Hirsch's block 6, a parcel farmed first organically and then biodynamically. (This block was the Trojan horse that allowed Lemon to convince David Hirsch to take the whole vineyard biodynamic.) With a salted-plum intensity and forward tannins, Littorai's Hirsch might be California's apotheosis of matching site and interpreter.

On to Mendocino: After a long absence due to replanting, Littorai's **One Acre Pinot Noir** ($$$) from the Deer Meadows Vineyard above Boonville has returned, with its meaty, underbrushy aspects, the quintessence of Anderson Valley. There's also **Cerise** ($$$), planted just outside Boonville, and **Savoy** ($$$), between Boonville and Philo, a mix of Dijon and heritage clones that's redolent of cherry skins; plus **Roman** ($$$), from a hilltop site just above the Esterlina Vineyard, east of Ted Lemon's new Wendling planting near the hamlet of Navarro. Finally, Lemon makes two blended wines, a **Sonoma Coast** ($$) and a **Les Larmes Anderson Valley** ($$), both tremendous values. Buy them if you find them. See also Chardonnay (page 202).

RHYS VINEYARDS

On any given day, Kevin Harvey is likely to be caught talking about the many nuances of soil throughout the Santa Cruz Mountains, where he launched perhaps the most ambitious estate Pinot Noir project to come out of California in the past quarter century. Harvey has a point to prove: that the Santa Cruz Mountains and a few other places (he also farms in Anderson Valley) can compete to make some of the best wines in the world. He is proving this in a winery facility dug into a Los Gatos hillside, which is lined with some eighty small steel fermenters that can ferment tiny lots from each vineyard block, the better to assess their quality.

Harvey, along with his very thoughtful winemaker Jeff Brinkman and vineyard chief Javier Meza, achieve a stupendous complexity of flavor with their wines, which rarely rise much above 13 percent alcohol. He does this through a mix of moderate extraction, low-yield farming, significant use of whole grape clusters, and a modest amount of new oak.

But Harvey is not among those who believe that his farming methods, with a harvest typically in mid-September, is a matter of brinksmanship. "We have an extra six weeks that we could ripen Pinot if we wanted to," he says.

THE WINES: Any bottle of Rhys is worth getting your hands on, given their small production and long waiting list. More basic efforts, a **San Mateo County Pinot Noir** ($$$) and **Family Farm Pinot Noir** ($$$), can be enjoyed relatively soon after release. The **Alpine Vineyard** ($$$), from a steep younger-soil site based around Purisima Formation shale and sandstone, is always a bit more forward and blossomy, while the **Horseshoe Vineyard** ($$$), just half a mile from Alpine but planted on older volcanic and sedimentary soils, can be ferrous and reticent, a late bloomer. The often stoic **Home Vineyard** ($$$) comes from Harvey's original planting just outside the Santa Cruz AVA, less than two acres on sandstone essentially in his own backyard, while the **Skyline** ($$$), grown around the winery in a staggeringly dense planting of two feet by three feet, is coiled, packed with damp earth and porcini accents, and in need of a cellar stay. The **Bearwallow** ($$$), long a work in progress, has come into its own, full of the mineral and coniferous aspects that define

Anderson Valley and with very little wood signature ("It's so allergic to oak it's unreal," Brinkman says). See also Revising the Rhône (page 236).

MORE NOTABLE WINES

ALFARO FAMILY: After selling his Watsonville bakery to Sara Lee in 1998, Richard Alfaro turned his attention to wine, finding a seventy-five-acre apple farm in Corralitos, east of Santa Cruz. His fifty-six planted acres are mostly split between Pinot Noir and Chardonnay, with a bit of Merlot and Syrah thrown in, and in 2008 he planted a bit of Grüner Veltliner. After splitting from his business partner, Alfaro's wines seemed to lose some of their oakiness and become more nuanced, and they have become a great demonstration of what can be accomplished in this part of the Santa Cruz Mountains. The **Estate Pinot Noir** ($$) and **Lester Family Vineyard Pinot Noir** ($$) from a nearby site farmed by Prudy Foxx in particular show the intrinsic freshness that's a signature of the Corralitos area.

CERITAS: While Ceritas is arguably focused on Chardonnay, the Pinots from John Raytek and Phoebe Bass can be equally sublime—and their red-wine roster is growing. The wines are made with some whole clusters, receive no cold soak, and are fermented, as are the Chardonnays, using only indigenous yeasts. They are aged for up to eighteen months, typically in no more than 25 percent new oak. Their **Escarpa Pinot Noir** ($$$) comes from a 3.78-acre site first planted in 1978 on veins of schist and quartz. Raytek and Bass now farm the vineyard, near Occidental, themselves. The wine reveals the spice of stem inclusion, as well as dense fruit. The **Costalina** ($$$)—formerly called

Annabelle—from a blend of two sites in Occidental, shows a bit brighter, with approachable cherry flavors. The couple has also tapped the **Hellenthal** ($$$) site near Hirsch, Anderson Valley's **Hacienda Secoya** ($$$), and their own **Porter-Bass** ($$$). See also Chardonnay (page 194).

CHANIN: Gavin Chanin shows the same level of thoughtful restraint with his red wines as with his perhaps better-known Chardonnay. Chanin taps some well-known sources, which means his work is primarily that of reinterpreting familiar Santa Barbara vineyards. His **Bien Nacido Vineyard Pinot Noir** ($$$), using the famous site that put Santa Maria on the map, has a masterful red-fruit radiance, full of soy and moist earth accents that are often lacking from that site. Chanin also makes a **Los Alamos** ($$$) from his other major fruit source. See also Chardonnay (page 195).

COBB WINES: The Cobb family decided to make their own wine from their vineyard in 2001, and Ross Cobb's experience at Williams Selyem, Flowers, and now Hirsch make him a perfect interpreter of the far reaches of western Sonoma. The **Coastlands** ($$$) and **Diane Cobb: Coastlands** ($$$), both dusky-fruited and showing intense minerality, come from the Cobbs' Coastlands 15-acre plot overlooking Bodega Bay, with its mature vines—dating to 1989—and predominance of heritage clones. The latter is from 1.5 acres that Ross's mother Diane tended herself. They also buy fruit from several nearby parcels, including **Joy Road** ($$$), Terry Adams's 2.5-acre vineyard outside Occidental at 1,300 feet; the 2-acre vineyard **Emmaline** ($$$) outside Sebastopol; the 2-acre **Jack Hill** ($$$), above the Freestone Valley; and **Rice-Spivak** ($$$), 6 acres on Goldridge loam near Sebastopol

that's the farthest east of their sources and shows hints of that richer Russian River expression.

COPAIN: Copain's Wells Guthrie could get equal credit for his Syrah, but Pinot Noir helped define his current subtle style. For that grape, the base of the pyramid starts with about five thousand cases of **Tous Ensemble Pinot Noir** ($$), a bright fruit-driven effort from a range of mostly sandstone sites in Anderson Valley. Above that comes his **Les Voisins** ($$), again from a handful of Anderson Valley spots but with a bit of new oak and meant to be more intense and cellar worthy. As for his designates, the vineyards have been in flux, but the **Wentzel** ($$$), from a fractured sandstone site at seven hundred feet elevation, has a musky aspect, while his Kiser Vineyard in northern Anderson Valley is typically split into at least two wines: **Kiser En Bas** ($$$), from clone 115, and the electrifying **Kiser En Haut** ($$$), a mix of clones planted two hundred feet higher in the sandstone and clay soils. There's also a **Tous Ensemble Chardonnay** ($$) from the valley's Ferrington Vineyard. Additionally, Guthrie planted tiny amounts of the Jura grapes Trousseau and Poulsard outside his Healdsburg winery and debuted a **Russian River Valley Trousseau** ($$) with the 2011 vintage. See also Revising the Rhône (page 227).

DRAGONETTE CELLARS: This promising Lompoc label was founded by brothers John and Steve Dragonette and their friend Brandon Sparks-Gillis. Sparks-Gillis is a bright talent on the Central Coast, and Dragonette taps into Santa Barbara's best locations, including such Santa Rita sites as Cargasachi and La Encantada, and new ones like John Sebastiano, on Santa Rita's eastern edge. While the wines are eloquent, reining in their ripeness and oak would propel them into a far higher orbit. The blended **Sta. Rita Hills Pinot Noir** ($$$) might be the winner of the lot, perhaps because it gets a bit less oak, although whole clusters and use of older Dijon clones (113, 115) bring out a nuance in what might be the best bottling I've had of the **Fiddlestix Vineyard** ($$$). Their past work with the marginal **Cargassachi-Jalama** ($$) site just southwest of Santa Rita has been extraordinary. So too their **Syrah** ($$), the most subtle of their Rhône-focused efforts. There's also a fleshy **Sauvignon Blanc** ($$) from Happy Canyon.

GHOSTWRITER: Some of Kenny Likitprakong's formative winemaking years were in the Santa Cruz Mountains, which gave him the knowledge of the area to launch the Ghostwriter label. The style is almost breezy, with lots of buoyant red fruit. There are typically wines from the dry-farmed **Woodruff Vineyard** ($$$) and nearby **Aptos Creek** ($$$) as well as an **Amaya Ridge** ($$$) bottling from twenty-plus-year-old vines planted at one thousand feet; and a **Santa Cruz Mountains** ($$) appellation bottle, along with a **Santa Cruz Mountains Chardonnay** ($$). See also Back to the Future (Hobo/Folk Machine, page 271).

KNEZ: In 2007 and 2008, Peter Knez acquired two of Anderson Valley's most cherished parcels, Cerise and Demuth. This could have been another California ego indulgence, but the numbers whiz—chief of fixed income for Barclays Global Investors and an adjunct business professor at Northwestern—put his analytical brain to the task of comprehending Anderson Valley's nuances; he became, as he puts it, "obsessed that the potential of Pinot and Chardonnay in Northern California hadn't been fulfilled." He hired Anthill Farms' Anthony Filiberti to manage the operation, quickly turning Knez into an

exceptional addition to the area. The **Cerise** ($$$) and **Demuth** ($$$) Pinot Noirs perfectly frame those sites, both now farmed biodynamically. The wines are fermented with indigenous yeast and a healthy dose of whole clusters; if early vintages pushed oak a bit further, more recent ones have dialed it back. There's also an **Anderson Valley** ($$) blend from the two sites and pitch-perfect **Pinot Noir Rosé** ($) from Cerise. See also Chardonnay (page 202).

KUTCH: In 2005 Jamie Kutch traded a Merrill Lynch job on Wall Street for the allure of California. After being counseled by Michael Browne of Kosta Browne and spending a few vintages chasing Big Pinot glory, he got religion, so to speak, and began to rein in the style of his wines, turning to ever more marginal sites and dramatically lowering his alcohol content. The results have paid off, and Kutch's wines are now poised to join the ranks of California's most site-driven, complex Pinots. His use of grape stems has given the wines additional spice and finesse. Among the bottlings are the Goldridge-soil **Falstaff** ($$$) in the Sebastopol Hills, east of Freestone and an edgy **McDougall Ranch** ($$$) bottling, just north of Hirsch Vineyards. There's a **Sonoma Coast** blend ($$), and in 2012 Kutch began getting a young-vine parcel from Hirsch as well, which replaced his Savoy bottling from Anderson Valley. He's also planting a block at Mendocino's Alder Springs.

LARUE: Katy Wilson, who developed her winemaking chops at Flowers and Australia's Torbreck, took her San Joaquin Valley farm upbringing into account when moving into winemaking: she does everything herself, including driving her own fruit to the winery. Her young label, named for her great-grandmother, focuses on just one wine: typically a blend from three vineyards near Occidental and Sebastopol. The **Sonoma Coast Pinot Noir** ($$$) combines exotic dried-herb notes with fantastic clarity in its tart flavors.

LIOCO: This label's efforts with Pinot Noir echo those in making its single-site Chardonnay, although in the case of the Pinot, winemaker John Raytek uses mostly old barrels for aging instead of steel. When they have been able to get access to the fruit, Lioco's **Hirsch Pinot Noir** ($$$) is a standout for that site, in some years approaching the bottling from Littorai. There have been vineyard-designates from **Klindt** ($$$) in Anderson Valley and **Michaud** ($$$) in the historic Chalone appellation, though those are likely to change. Appellation bottles from **Anderson Valley** ($$), **Sonoma Coast** ($$), and **Santa Cruz Mountains** ($$) can be a great value. See also Chardonnay (page 197) and Back to the Future (page 271).

LONGORIA: Rick Longoria has worked in Santa Barbara since the 1980s, and having retrenched his style a bit, he is revealing the beauty of Santa Barbara's best vineyards, including Bien Nacido and Rancho Santa Rosa. His **Fe Ciega** ($$$), from his own 7.75-acre vineyard on a 350-foot-elevation mesa above the Santa Ynez River in the Santa Rita Hills, matches mineral intensity with brooding fruit. His mint-edged **Lovely Rita** ($$) also comes mostly from Fe Ciega.

LOST & FOUND: This tiny label shows the graceful promise of Russian River Pinots of yore, perhaps because of its principals, Joe Bartolomei and his sister Catherine, who run the Farmhouse Inn, a respected Forestville property, with Catherine's husband, wine writer Rod Smith. They run Lost & Found with master sommelier Geoff Kruth and winemaker Megan Glaab. The **Lost & Found Pinot Noir** ($$$) comes from the Bartolomeis' old Pinot parcel outside Forestville, planted to the almost archaic Jackson clone.

NATIVE9 VINEYARDS: James Ontiveros was the guy at his Cal Poly classes who always showed up dirty from working in the vineyard. But then, his family has been in California for nine generations, once holders of a land grant that now encompasses the Bien Nacido Vineyard. Since his family still owned land, he decided to plant it to heritage vine selections, and called on his college pal Paul Wilkins, then John Alban's assistant winemaker. The result was the **Native9 Pinot Noir** ($$$), which treads the line between magnitude and Santa Barbara finesse. (The pair's negociant project, Alta Maria Vineyards, enjoyed a promising start, although recent vintages have been uneven.)

NEELY (VARNER): In addition to Chardonnay (see page 200), the Varner brothers make several Pinot Noirs from dry-farmed blocks of their Spring Ridge Vineyard under the Neely label—excellent Santa Cruz Mountains expressions, if more immediate than their whites, aged in about 25 percent new oak. The **Hidden Block** ($$) from a small Dijon 115 parcel tucked at the north end of their property, is burlier and fruit-driven, while the **Picnic Block** ($$) and basil-scented **Upper Picnic** ($$), adjacent to their Chardonnay plantings, show a masterful density of texture.

THE OJAI VINEYARD: Having decided in the mid-2000s to dial back his winemaking to a more subtle style, Adam Tolmach has again found the beauty that brought him acclaim in the 1980s. There are several

Pinot Noirs, including versions from **Fe Ciega** ($$$) and **Kick-On Ranch** ($$) in Los Alamos, that show Santa Barbara's potential for subtlety. But he also makes Chardonnay and a heady, tense **Solomon Hills Syrah** ($$$) from a site in Orcutt near Highway 101. An unexpected addendum: Tolmach's **Sauvignon Blanc** ($$) from the low-yielding McGinley Vineyard in Santa Ynez remains one of the state's best examples of that grape.

PEAY: This estate in Annapolis, on the far edge of the Sonoma Coast, sits in a fog band that makes the ripening of its grapes precipitous. Yet its Pinots are plenty developed and ripe. The **Scallop Shelf Pinot Noir** ($$$), named for the marine fossils often unearthed in Peay's silty loam soils, is their benchmark for that variety, showing a heady spice and minerality. It is matched by the **Pomarium Pinot Noir** ($$$), which offers richer fruit and floral tones, and a somewhat newer offering, **Ama Pinot Noir** ($$$), which shows more low-hued flavors, akin to a muscular style of Burgundy. Beyond Pinot, the **Estate Chardonnay** ($$$) is a nuanced and long-aging, if slightly oak-weighted, version from lower blocks of the estate. The late-ripening fruit offers pear flavors and the vivaciousness their fog-shrouded Annapolis property can provide. See also Revising the Rhône (page 230).

PORTER CREEK: The Davis family bought their Healdsburg vineyard in 1979 and first made wine in 1982, in Sonoma's no-frills era—as demonstrated by the rustic cabin that doubles as Porter Creek's tasting room. But when Alex Davis began to take over for his father, George, he became entranced enough with Burgundy to enroll at the University of Dijon, where he apprenticed at the famous Chambolle-Musigny house of Georges Roumier.

Upon his return, Alex says of California, "I had to unlearn everything I learned here." He persuaded his father to farm biodynamically. Over time, as its Westside Road neighbors have sided with heft, Porter Creek and its vineyards have become the loyal opposition, producing wines with modest extraction and a silken texture. It is surprising the wines aren't better known. The **Estate** ($$) is a good younger-drinking introduction to the **Fiona Hill** ($$$), from a steep parcel dominated by tough clay soils; the **Reserve** ($$$) taps its steepest section. The **Hillside Vineyard** ($$$) is from a 1974 planting, one of the area's oldest. There's also a **Zinfandel** ($$) that shows a Pinot mind at work; same with a **Mendocino County Carignane** ($$) from 1950s-era vines.

RIVERS-MARIE: As the hand behind Napa labels like Schrader and Outpost, Thomas Brown has certainly basked in the glow of cult stardom, but it's hard to characterize his own label, which he runs with his wife, Genevieve Welsh. At times the wines embrace the ethereal nature of their stellar coastal sites: witness **Summa** ($$$$), **Silver Eagle** ($$$), **Occidental Ridge** ($$$), and **Gioia** ($$$), in addition to a **Sonoma Coast** blend ($$) and several Cabernets, all produced in miniscule quantities. At other times their wines seem more inclined toward glitz. Either way, Brown's reputation has created a tight market, with loyal fans clamoring for a spot on the mailing list.

SANDHI: Though Chardonnay might be Sandhi's core effort, the Pinot Noir made by Rajat Parr and Sashi Moorman is also redefining quality in Santa Rita. Mostly older oak is used, along with a high proportion of grape stems, often 100 percent. The bayberry-accented **Sta. Rita Hills Pinot Noir** ($$), from a handful of vineyards, delivers surprising finesse for the price, while the **Sanford & Benedict** ($$$), perhaps the best current effort from that iconic vineyard, mixes whole-cluster spice with a shocking minerality. Sandhi's **Bien Nacido** ($$$), with a floral, plummy aspect, is an outstanding example, although it underscores how Santa Maria Valley may struggle to keep up with Santa Rita in the future. Also from Santa Rita are rare bottlings from **Tempest** (part of Domaine de la Côte) and the **Wenzlau** ($$$) site near Sea Smoke, as well as a **Mt. Carmel** ($$$) and **Rinconada** ($$$) starting with the 2012 vintage. See also Chardonnay (page 198).

VAUGHN DUFFY: This young label, initially focused on the Suacci Vineyard on the western edge of the Russian River Valley, was founded by Sara Vaughn and her husband, Matt Duffy, who apprenticed at Siduri and also makes Pinot under the Easkoot Cellars label, which was founded by importers Emily and Stephan Schindler. The tense, moss-edged style of the **Pinot Noir** ($$)—typically from Russian River Valley—has taken an uneven turn or two but can be excellent, as can their **Sonoma County Rosé** ($). Bonus for their motto, echoed in their label artwork: "It takes a forklift to raise a wine."

WAITS-MAST: First inspired to make Pinot by a trip to a festival in Anderson Valley, Jennifer Waits and Brian Mast were among the refugees who were left homeless, cellar-wise, by the departure of Crushpad from San Francisco (see page 84); Jennifer even worked the sorting table there while pregnant with their daughter. They continue to make wine in the city, and Anderson Valley grapes remain at the core of their efforts. After tapping sites like Deer Meadows, more recently they've made wine from the **Londer Vineyard** ($$), with a subtle mix of 115 and Swan clones aged in 30 percent new oak; and a burlier effort from the **Wentzel Vineyard** ($$$), near Philo. All the fruit is destemmed, and fermentations—unlike during the Crushpad days—are with indigenous yeast.

ZEPALTAS: Wisconsin native Ryan Zepaltas came west in 1998, and ultimately he landed a job as assistant winemaker for Siduri while he launched his own label. He has retained that Midwest serenity, but, given the quality of his solo efforts, it's surprising he hasn't yet struck out on his own. The Sonoma Coast offerings are his best, including **La Cruz** ($$$), from the Keller estate in the eastern Petaluma Wind Gap, and the **Suacci** ($$$), from a chilly lower-elevation spot between Sebastopol and the Valley Ford area (he also makes wine for the Suaccis). He also makes a **Sonoma Coast** blend ($$) of barrel lots declassified from his single-vineyard wines. There's also a **Russian River Valley** ($$) bottling, richer but nuanced. The wines aren't shy on oak, often 50 percent new, but they show finesse and innate tension.

Chardonnay

After a long dark spell, a great third wave has arrived for California Chardonnay. In the words of Matt Licklider, co-owner of the Lioco label, the grape is "in the midst of a comeback tour," a return to its role as a vehicle for greatness. That was long its historical purpose: to help convey the uniqueness of place, both in Burgundy and in midcentury California.

How, then, I would always wonder, had it fallen into the state of crisis in which I found it in the mid-2000s? At that point, discussing the state's favorite variety would often as not draw curled lips. The "Anything But Chardonnay" (ABC) movement was well underway, and for obvious reasons: a dull, buttery, slightly sweet style of Chardonnay had become synonymous with California. A commercial success, perhaps, but Chardonnay had also become parody.

It was not always this way. First planted in California in the nineteenth century, Chardonnay was an obscurity until the 1980s, when, for many Americans, increasingly heavy-handed versions became synonymous with "white wine."

And what of the comeback tour? The new Chardonnay was born directly from the notion that if someone didn't reclaim Chardonnay—a grape that has spread over California like so much kudzu—from the Kendall-Jacksons of the world, there would be no chance of the grape returning to serious conversation about California wine.

In the mid-2000s, then, when faced with the sad state of Chardonnay, Licklider and Lioco cofounder Kevin O'Connor asked themselves the following: Could California make wines of consequence from a grape like Chardonnay? And could this most transparent of grapes produce wines that, instead of showing ambition in the cellar, do what Chardonnay does best, which is to reveal the possibilities of the land?

TO BURGUNDIAN AND BACK

This reconsideration of Chardonnay would complete a full circle for the grape in California. In 1953, former ambassador James Zellerbach planted a spot in the hills outside the town of Sonoma with Chardonnay and Pinot Noir, grapes he had loved during his time in Europe. Here, in fact, is probably where California's obsession with the term "Burgundian" was spawned; Zellerbach viewed his work not simply as a weekend lark but as an attempt to emulate the wines he loved from Montrachet and Clos de Vougeot. He spurned one bit of local advice: instead of using American wood, he sent to France for barrels, becoming the first California winery of that era to import new French oak. His wines were aged in barrel, the lees were stirred routinely, and, as of 1970, malolactic fermentation—the microbe for which was successfully isolated by Hanzell wine-maker Brad Webb in 1959—routinely took place in a portion of its Chardonnay, softening the wine and enhancing its body. All these techniques melded Californian sensibilities with how the finest white Burgundies were made and were a fine match for Hanzell's low-yielding vines.

At the time, though, Chardonnay was an after-thought, with just 150 acres in the state in 1960 by one estimate. It was of little interest to most, except for occasional partisans like Hanzell; the McCrea family, who planted it at Stony Hill in Napa using Herman Wente's old vine cuttings; or Martin Ray, following his own Burgundian dreams in the Santa Cruz Mountains.

Chardonnay got a more tepid reception from the state's viticultural high priests, Maynard Amerine and A. J. Winkler. Its quality could be very good, but they recommended it with hesitation, warning that yields were low and ripening came early "under the warm climatic conditions of California."

The Burgundy connection never wavered. Such influential winemakers as Steve Kistler and Zelma Long refined cellar techniques and increasingly bor-rowed parts of the Burgundy recipe, including not just the stirring of lees but also letting the juice turn brown as its more volatile components oxi-dized, leaving the fermented wine fresh and clear. Chardonnay became an increasingly significant wine through the 1970s, growing to 13,670 acres by 1981—then multiplying sevenfold in the follow-ing thirty years.

"THE VULGARITY OF THE TECHNIQUE"

These were the seeds of Chardonnay's undoing. If the use of oak barrels finessed California Chardon-nay, their use would become almost ubiquitous—to the great success of a barrel broker named Mel Knox, who in 1980 took over a small barrel-sales business from wine importer Becky Wasserman just as California began an oak binge. A defining—or damning—style was born in 1982, when a wine-maker named Jed Steele was hired by Jess Jackson for his new Kendall-Jackson winery. Either inad-vertently or with a need to salvage some difficult fermentations, Steele's first vintage of Kendall-Jackson Vintner's Reserve Chardonnay had a bit of sugar left, not enough to be distinctly sweet but enough to make the wine a bit more approach-able. Soon it was the most popular Chardonnay in the land.

Labels like Sonoma-Cutrer and Clos du Bois built on K-J's popularity, proclaiming the virtues of barrel fermentation in new oak, to say nothing of aggressive malolactic fermentation and vigorous lees stirring. What had begun as a mimicry of Bur-gundy turned into a buttery character, largely from a fermentation by-product called diacetyl, that soon became synonymous with American Chardonnay. When that style was hitched to California's other big trends of the 1990s, a rise in ripeness and a drop in acidity, Chardonnay's descent into travesty was unstoppable.

The real problem? The techniques pioneered by Hanzell were intended for the most intense, low-yielding grapes. But a widespread craving for sweet, oaky Chardonnay demanded shortcuts like using oak chips that imprinted the buttery style on cheap, underflavored grapes harvested at eight tons per acre or more.

"That," John Kongsgaard tells me, "is how you get the vulgarity of the technique."

After briefly working at Napa's Stony Hill in the 1970s, Kongsgaard arrived at Newton Vineyard in 1983, becoming responsible for Newton's wildly popular long-aged, unfiltered Chardonnay, which would become the It Chardonnay of the early 1990s. He and a handful of other holdouts—winemakers like Kistler and Mount Eden Vineyards' Jeffrey Patterson—stood by the prospect of a powerful, site-based interpretation. Others went in the other direction by aging wine in stainless steel and blocking malolactic fermentation—an interesting attempt to undo the excesses of others, but ultimately an overreaction (see The Steely Side, page 199).

These approaches were simply counterpoint to what Jim Clendenen of Au Bon Climat terms the "bombastic style" of Chardonnay. A Burgundy fanatic, Clendenen had remained true to the style of Chardonnay he crafted in the early 1980s. As buttery Chardonnays gained in popularity, he stuck by the grape's subtler charms, even when his stubbornness made him unpopular among his neighbors in Santa Barbara, a part of California that had become a major engine for cheap, overwrought Chardonnay. When the inevitable backlash came, true believers like Clendenen were buffeted in the ABC frenzy. "When it became fashionable to dislike Chardonnay," he says, "they were disliking one style of Chardonnay."

But traditional Chardonnay retained its loyalists, and they paved a path toward the grape's third wave. New winemakers held out hope that Chardonnay could speak clearly on its own again. There was, for instance, no reason to block the malolactic fermentation of fresh grapes picked at modest sugar levels. And using neutral barrels could provide a richness and durability that steel could not. The formula wasn't nearly as important as the base material. Or as Bob Varner, who planted his first Chardonnay vine in 1980, puts it, "It wasn't the techniques that were impressive. It's how connected they were to their grapes."

THE THREE-BOTTLE TOUR

In the north, a splendid guide is the **Lioco Demuth** (page 198) from Anderson Valley, one of California's finest sites for the grape (although the **Lioco Sonoma County Chardonnay** [page 197] is also a good introduction to its style). From there, move to Santa Cruz with the **Varner Home Block** (page 200), from the Varners' own-rooted parcel. Finish with a Central Coast choice, the **Chanin Bien Nacido** (page 196), which combines that label's thoughtful winemaking with one of the state's great pioneering Chardonnay sites.

TOP PRODUCERS
• • •
CERITAS

John Raytek and his wife Phoebe Bass have an intimate connection to Ceritas's top site: Bass grew up on the Porter-Bass Vineyard in Guerneville, which her family has farmed since 1980. Today she is now largely responsible for the farming herself. Raytek, who interned at Flowers, then worked for Rhys's Kevin Harvey and for Copain, has mastered the details of making North Coast Chardonnay as few others have. His attention to winemaking detail is astonishingly precise.

In the cellar, Raytek employs a similar routine as he does for the Lioco wines, which he also

Gavin Chanin in Los Alamos Vineyard

makes: using indigenous yeasts and malolactic fermentation, all in old barrels and often taking six months or more; twelve months of aging in old barrels on the lees, followed by several more months in steel; and little stirring of the wine during aging. The juice is typically browned, sometimes for up to ten days, before fermentation. The results are some of the purest examples of Chardonnay on the North Coast, wines with pristine tension and depth.

THE WINES: The **Porter-Bass Chardonnay** ($$$), from just over three acres at their home vineyard, is their calling card, with yellow raspberry fruit and a deep mineral intensity. Raytek also taps Charlie Heintz's well-known vineyard outside Occidental; Ceritas's **Charles Heintz** ($$$) shows a familiar honeyed element. A **Peter Martin Ray** ($$$) bottling comes from that Santa Cruz site. See also Pinot Noir (page 186).

CHANIN

It would be hard to find a better practitioner of the new Chardonnay than Gavin Chanin—and perhaps that's no surprise, as his mentor was Au Bon Climat's Jim Clendenen. Growing up in North Hollywood, Chanin intended to study art at UCLA. But Clendenen was a family friend, so the young student headed up to Santa Maria Valley to be a cellar rat, skipping quarters at school to work the harvest. When he turned twenty-one, with four harvests under his belt, Chanin did what any college kid would: he founded his own wine label.

Still, he insists, "None of my wines are flukes." His Chardonnay, typically fermented in old barrels, starts shy in its youth but soon shows a level of nuance that should soften the stance of even the toughest Chardonnay skeptic. Patience defines the Chanin wines through and through: often he raises his wines over fourteen months or more, letting them evolve with no more than a minimum of barrel work or racking. This reflects Chanin's view that a common gaffe among winemakers is looking for a wine to taste good just a few months into its aging. His approach adds a rigidity and twang that I find always marks the wines.

The other key? Picking at lower sugar levels, of course, especially in vineyards like Bien Nacido, where waiting for ripeness has been the standard practice. Chanin says, "People used to ask me how I get lower alcohols, and I just say I pick less ripe. But I don't think I pick early. I just pick on time."

THE WINES: Chanin's **Los Alamos Vineyard Chardonnay** ($$$), from a lime-rich site dating to 1974, shows tremendous power, focus, and corn silk accents from a lesser-known corner of Santa Barbara. His **Bien Nacido Chardonnay** ($$$) comes from some of the oldest vines on this 1973 vineyard, and it matches precision with distinct yellow fruit and a richer profile. See also Pinot Noir (page 187).

KONGSGAARD

John Kongsgaard's advice when the Chardonnay hopeful knock at his door for wisdom: "Don't write anything down, because you can't do this. You don't have my vineyard."

His Judge Vineyard is an inheritance of sorts from his family, which has old roots in Napa. The grapes were planted in the 1970s on the hillside land his grandparents bought in the 1920s. The Judge Chardonnay is nearly unique in California for matching tooth-rattling tension to an impressive size (it can push 15 percent alcohol in ripe years, but lately it has been dialed back). Sitting on the remnant of an old lava flow, the Judge's core of nine acres sometimes yields just seven tons of fruit.

But Kongsgaard's own talents also helped to define the exuberance of California Chardonnay in its preparody days. This brings us to what is known as his "death and resurrection" technique, derived from his 1980s trips to Burgundy, where he witnessed domaines like Bonneau du Martray and Lafon using hardly any sulfur dioxide in the first months after harvest, rendering murky wines with off aromas. Nearly a year later the wines would be fresh and clear. "They just don't worry about the wines going through some pretty severe places," he says.

After some experimentation he refined his technique by adding a small amount of sulfur dioxide to the grapes when they are crushed, but otherwise letting the juice turn as "brown as a grocery bag" before going into barrels to ferment. The wine ages at a painfully slow rate, with dying yeast scavenging the remaining oxygen in the wine. The stirring of lees—which can add texture but also can expose the wine to air—has a reverse effect here, actually protecting the wine from oxidation.

Over more than a year, the wine gets clearer and more structured. It is not the most approachable wine when young, but it has the same endurance as top white Burgundies. (There are other factors to Kongsgaard's process, including the exposure of nascent grape clusters to full sunlight early in the season.)

Kongsgaard founded his own label with his wife, Maggy, in 1996. Now his son Alex is increasingly taking over responsibilities in a new cellar, located atop Atlas Peak outside the city of Napa.

THE WINES: Kongsgaard wines often taste backward, showing fierce minerality and tension before any obvious California fruit. The **Napa Valley Chardonnay** ($$$) shows lemony brightness and oak but also a riveting tension. When young, the **Judge Chardonnay** ($$$$) is as powerful a wine as you'll find. Defined more by structure than flavor at first, it reveals deeply layered fruit and a clover-honey accent with air (or time). There's also a **Syrah** ($$$$) from blocks of Lee Hudson's vineyard that constitute some of Carneros's most interesting soils, along with a **Cabernet Sauvignon** ($$$$) now sourced from a neighbor's Atlas Peak vineyard, and **VioRous** ($$$), a limpid blend of Viognier and Roussanne.

LIOCO

Matt Licklider and Kevin O'Connor's project grew out of a "a six-year conversation," a long lament about the state of California wine that began in the alley behind Spago, the Beverly Hills restaurant. O'Connor was its wine director and Licklider a salesman of mostly French wines. Having concluded, as Licklider puts it, that "Chardonnay was going through a Fat Elvis phase back in the late '90s," they determined their mission: to discover whether California had compelling sites for wine. Chardonnay would be their primary vehicle. This was the beginning of Lioco—a portmanteau of the two partners' names.

Soon enough, Lioco's single-vineyard wines became New California icons, a hit at restaurants across the country. They were particularly notable for their clarity of flavors—as showcases for vineyards like Demuth, the old dry-farmed site in Anderson Valley, and for the historic Hanzell Vineyard in Sonoma Valley, which made its first designated fruit sale in a half century to Lioco.

To further this notion of transparency, the labels on their wine rival Calera's in their minute detail, with encyclopedic notes about fruit sources, harvest specifics, aromas, flavors, and even suggested food pairings.

Like other new Chardonnay pioneers, Licklider and O'Connor decided that their goal was not to clone the wines of Europe. Their wines would not be Burgundian. They decided on a winemaking style free of artifice, one that would turn the California style on its head: Chardonnay aged solely in stainless steel and typically fermented with indigenous yeasts—although their winemaking style eventually evolved to embrace a wider range of techniques. The wines increasingly went through malolactic fermentation to add weight and depth (see The Steely Side, page 199).

After a strong start followed by a series of wobbly vintages, the Lioco wines settled into a distinct, if less edgy, style. Initially the wines were made by Kevin Kelley, but after the 2010 vintage John Raytek of the Ceritas label took over. The label began fermenting some wines in neutral oak barrels before letting them age in steel, using a hybrid approach that made the wines less austere and more distinctive.

THE WINES: The **Sonoma County Chardonnay** ($), a larger-production wine (six thousand cases or more), is Lioco's essential calling card, made from a mix of up to a dozen vineyards that includes everything from Stuhlmuller in Alexander Valley to Ricci in Carneros. That often cracks the door for its single-site efforts. The **Charles Heintz Chardonnay** ($$$), from that notable and often damp site on Goldridge soils near Occidental, has been a key bottling, even with the occasionally funky dose of botrytis, the noble grape mold that's a catalyst for sweet wines like Sauternes but can be polarizing in dry wines. More recently, the **Demuth** ($$) bottling, from high above the Anderson Valley town of Boonville, has become a benchmark with its austere mineral aspect. The **Hanzell** ($$), richer and full of lemon-curd flavors, is flashier but has the potential for long aging that marks Hanzell's own wines. See also Pinot Noir (page 189) and Back to the Future (page 271).

MOUNT EDEN VINEYARDS

The history of Mount Eden is as famous as it is convoluted. The original site of Martin Ray's legendary winery in the Santa Cruz Mountains, it endured a series of ownership struggles in the 1960s and '70s before ending up, as of 1981, with winemaker Jeffrey Patterson in control. Patterson has remained ever since, living atop the two-thousand-foot-elevation vineyard outside the town of Saratoga.

The site's legacy of heritage vine material planted in tough shale soils has created a long string of some of California's most intense and age-worthy Chardonnays. This is one of the state's original focal points for the grape.

Here winemaking is old-fashioned and unhurried, performed in the old concrete cellar that Ray built. Juice is barrel-fermented in a mix of new and slightly used barrels, then aged for ten months. It is cellared for another two years after bottling. Even then it remains a deep powerhouse, such that a new Mount Eden release is often several years shy of beginning its drinking life.

THE WINES: The **Estate Chardonnay** ($$$), from six acres that ultimately date back to Ray's early plantings in the 1940s and '60s, is always opulently textured, full of stony accents. There's also a gentler, sometimes funky **Domaine Eden Chardonnay** ($$) from lesser barrels not used in the estate bottling, and a plusher, pear-flavored **Wolff Vineyard Chardonnay** ($$) from fifty-five acres in Edna Valley outside San Luis Obispo that dates to 1976. Additionally, the **Estate Pinot Noir** ($$$), from seven acres, brims with the ethereal blue-fruited quality that the Mount Eden clone often exhibits. And a 1980s replanting of old La Questa vine material gives the **Estate Cabernet Sauvignon** ($$$) a shaded, leafy aspect that characterizes the area's greatest Cabernets. It might be Mount Eden's great hidden asset.

SANDHI

An ambitious partnership (the name is essentially Sanskrit for "collaboration") between sommelier Rajat Parr, investor Charles Banks (ex–Screaming Eagle), and winemaker Sashi Moorman, this is the soul of the new Santa Barbara. They make exceptional Pinot Noir, but their real progress has been in Chardonnay, as they have retraced and expanded Richard Sanford's pioneering work in the Santa Rita Hills and also tapped the Bien Nacido Vineyard, those two locations providing a sort of continuum of Santa Barbara history. The trio seems determined to set the course for a new winemaking era in Santa Barbara, following pioneers like Au Bon Climat's Jim Clendenen. And Parr's influence has helped give the wines a wide audience among restaurants.

For those on a soapbox about oak: most Sandhi whites are fermented in five-hundred-liter French oak puncheons, predominantly new. Those add a whiff of wood presence but also the finesse on which Burgundy hinges—no surprise,

THE STEELY SIDE

As the late 1990s brought a backlash to the overwrought style of Chardonnay—you can only slip so far down a buttery slope—some California winemakers decided to reverse the trend toward aggressive winemaking. They would ferment and age their fruit in stainless steel and block malolactic fermentation, leaving the wine crisp and relatively neutral.

This wasn't a radical technique; UC Davis and other universities had for decades advocated it for making fresh white table wines. But, of course, Chardonnay wasn't just another white wine.

This new style of Chardonnay, branded with names like Metallico and Unoaked, was meant to draw back those drinkers who had adopted the "Anything But Chardonnay" mantra and had shifted to Sauvignon Blanc or Pinot Grigio, or perhaps to French or Italian wines. It was no surprise that these wines were—and still are—frequently described as "Chablis-style," even though that northern slice of Burgundy has its own fondness for oak.

By the late 2000s, the baroque style of California Chardonnay clearly needed to be dialed back. But too many mainstream winemakers tackled the symptoms rather than address the obvious problem: fruit picked far too ripe and then chemically tweaked. They kept the ripeness but enacted a series of half steps: picking ripe but blocking malolactic fermentation to give an impression of acidity; mixing barrel- and steel-fermented lots; acidifying juice to prevent spoilage and later deacidifying it to punch up the tropical flavors they sought. These hybrid styles could sometimes work—at Hanzell, for instance. But when applied to overripe or inferior grapes they seemed, like the austerity of the unoaked approach, primarily about triage.

Even those who had fully committed to the steel method, like Lioco, began to realize that the wines could be too hard-edged, that an approach conceived for young-drinking table wine might not be right. As Lioco's Matt Licklider explains, when the label was launched there were few good examples of oak use in California that preserved a transparency of flavor. But over time, they softened their stance. Lioco winemaker John Raytek began fermenting in old oak barrels for a richer texture before moving the wine to steel tanks. Licklider explains their logic this way: "Could we figure out how to put Chardonnay in a wood vessel and have the wine come out in a way that's not offensive to us?"

considering that Parr bends the ear of such vintners as Jean-François Coche and Chablis's Jean-Marie Raveneau. Moorman has set the bar for Santa Barbara 2.0 by using indigenous yeast, tiny amounts of sulfur, and minimal stirring or other handling of the wines in barrel, although they are always aged on their lees. Often picking three or four weeks earlier than their neighbors, with resulting alcohol up to 2 percent lower (around 12.5 to 13 percent), they are keen to differentiate themselves from many of their neighbors in the Lompoc wine ghetto. It's not an unconsidered choice; the chemistry of their wines is not unlike that of the wines that gave Sanford & Benedict its fame. Sandhi's partners are well versed in the full history of those wines.

THE WINES: As an appellation wine, the **Santa Barbara County Chardonnay** ($$), from a rotating mix of sources, is an excellent introduction. Accented by lemon pith and saline, it is made primarily in older oak. There's also a **Sta. Rita Hills Chardonnay** ($$)

that exudes the area's high-acid signature. Sandhi's **Bien Nacido Chardonnay** ($$$) brings out the oat and stony aspects of that more fertile site. The **Rita's Crown Chardonnay** ($$$), from a site on the south-facing slopes of the Santa Rita Hills near the Sea Smoke Vineyard, is always saline but on the fleshy side, while the **Bent Rock Chardonnay** ($$$$), from a north-facing parcel on the valley's opposite side, is honey-edged but almost astringent in its texture. The jewel here is the **Sanford & Benedict Chardonnay** ($$$), sourced from Mount Eden selections in the vineyard's oldest block, which shows an edgy lime-leaf character and impressive chewiness in its texture. It's a great example of Santa Barbara coming full circle. See also Pinot Noir (page 190).

VARNER

Minimalism reigns at this tiny winery run by twin brothers Bob and Jim Varner in the Silicon Valley–proximate town of Portola Valley. "The idea," as Bob Varner puts it, "is to be as simple as possible."

They have spent thirty years in relative isolation in the Santa Cruz Mountains, where they farm their Spring Ridge estate with a monklike devotion: less than 8 acres of Chardonnay plus some Pinot stretch across a 235-acre parcel of clay loam and porous sedimentary rock just below Skyline Boulevard, a spot once owned by William Randolph Hearst's attorney. The vineyard is dry-farmed and hoed by hand, and from it they coax three distinct wines from three different blocks, among the most exquisitely tension-filled, pristine examples of American Chardonnay.

The brothers' meditative approach comes from their long view of California. Jim was an early student of wine scientist Ann Noble (inventor of the much-loved and hated aroma wheel for sensory analysis) at UC Davis; in the late 1970s, he was already scouring Carneros and Sonoma for a cooler vineyard spot before finding a more affordable alternative in what was then a sleepy horse town in San Mateo County. Bob was studying genetics at UC Berkeley when he took a leave in 1980 to help his brother plant the vineyard.

Their approach has hardly wavered over the years: fermenting with indigenous yeasts, putting must into the barrel with a lot of suspended grape remains and spent yeast, stirring those barrels only rarely, and adding nothing beyond a bit of sulfur dioxide. Winemaking here evokes the nineteenth century, down to the hand-racking tool built for them by a craftsman in Burgundy to gently tip barrels without agitating the contents. It is good, clean noninterventionist winemaking. "No one touches a barrel but Bob," says Jim.

For contrast, the Varners also run the Foxglove label, which produces value versions of Chardonnay, Cabernet, and Zinfandel.

THE WINES: The Varners' three designate wines all have their own identity. The **Home Block** ($$), from a 2-acre parcel planted in 1980 on its own roots, is the most electric of the lot. The **Amphitheater Block** ($$), from 2 acres planted a year later, is similar but often a bit broader in its flavors. The 3.5-acre **Bee Block** ($$) is the most generous, with deep minerality but fleshier fruit. And the **Foxglove Chardonnay** ($), from a mix of Central Coast vineyards, is one of the great deals of California wine: steel-aged but with no malolactic fermentation, and showing a balanced ripeness that charms even skeptics. See also Pinot Noir (Neely, page 189).

MORE NOTABLE WINES

ARNOT-ROBERTS: Chardonnay is a side project for this prodigious duo and yet they clearly have a fondness for it. Typically it is fermented in steel and aged in old barrels, and undergoes at least some malolactic fermentation. They initially gained attention for a Napa bottling from the Green Island Vineyard, next to the salt marshes of San Pablo Bay, but that has been replaced by a marjoram-scented **Watson Ranch Chardonnay** ($$) from a nearby marine-sediment hillside planted in 1993. A **Santa Cruz Mountains Chardonnay** ($$), sourced primarily from old Wente-clone vines in the pure-loam Trout Gulch Vineyard outside Aptos, might be the more interesting project, as it shows the area's quintessential acidity and saline bite. See also Cabernet (page 217), Revising the Rhône (page 233), The New Whites (page 251), and Back to the Future (page 263).

AU BON CLIMAT: Jim Clendenen has a deep love for this grape (as well as Pinot Noir), and makes a wide range of Chardonnays, including his lavish Nuits-Blanches. The bottles particularly to seek out are from his Historic Vineyard collection, a curation of Santa Barbara County's top sites—including **Bien Nacido** ($$), **Sanford & Benedict** ($$), and **Los Alamos** ($$). But Clendenen's most compelling white might be his rare **Hildegard** ($$), a mix of Pinot Gris, Pinot Blanc, and Aligoté made in homage to a more ancient style of white Burgundy.

FAILLA: Ehren Jordan's label makes quite a number of relatively fleshy Chardonnays, increasingly fermented in a mix of mostly older barrels and concrete eggs (see Innovation in the Cellar,

page 254), which finesse the opulent style. In addition to a **Sonoma Coast** blend ($$) from younger vines, there is an ever-expanding roster of vineyard designates, including prominent sites like Hudson. Of particular note are the intensely concentrated **Estate Chardonnay** ($$$) and recent additions from the old vines of **Haynes Vineyard** ($$$), in Napa's Coombsville area, and the **Chuy Vineyard** ($$$), above Sonoma Valley. See also Pinot Noir (page 183) and Revising the Rhône (page 233).

HANZELL: Now run by president Jean Arnold Sessions, wife of longtime winemaker Bob Sessions, and with current winemaking by Michael McNeill, Hanzell is experiencing a glorious renaissance. Sonoma Valley isn't an obvious spot for this grape, and these are not everyone's Chardonnays: deeply oaked and powerful, they are grown on soil that might equally suit red wine. As such, I find them analogous to the whites of Corton-Charlemagne, powerful and flashy, with a whiplash of dark minerality.

If anything, the winemaking here has gained a lighter touch in recent years, although it maintains that hybrid California approach. Seventy percent of the fruit is fermented in stainless steel, with no malolactic fermentation; the remainder goes into new oak for full barrel fermentation and malolactic conversion. The two are combined, then aged in mostly older wood for a year. Grown at around seven hundred feet elevation outside the town of Sonoma, the **Hanzell Estate Chardonnay** ($$$) shows deep yellow fruit and some savory oak. A second wine, the **Sebella Chardonnay** ($$), has more modest mineral power and lemon-oil headiness. There is also **Estate Pinot Noir** ($$$$), aged in about half new and half once-used oak, and small lots of wine from James Zellerbach's original 1953 planting and other parcels.

HDV: This partnership of grower Larry Hyde and Aubert de Villaine, proprietor of Domaine de la Romanée-Conti, often gets less attention than it deserves. But under the talented winemaking of Stephane Vivier, the wines can reveal the great possibilities of Chardonnay planted in the right places in Carneros. In this case, that's Hyde's clay-loam site. The **HdV Estate Chardonnay** ($$$) is heady and richly flavored, perhaps showing more magnitude than restraint but more than supporting its frame. The more modest **De La Guerra Chardonnay** ($$$), with fresh quince flavors, should be better known.

HIRSCH VINEYARDS: Pinot Noir is the main focus here, but 2.5 steep hillside acres of block 10 have been in Chardonnay since 1994, grown with an unusual quadrilateral cordon, or four branches per vine, a technique David Hirsch was persuaded to try by Steve Kistler. Another 1.4 acres were planted nearby in 2002. From the two comes a tiny amount of **Estate Chardonnay** ($$$). After Hirsch experimented with a wide range of techniques, including the use of glass carboys, the wine is now barrel-fermented and aged, although it finishes aging in steel, a technique borrowed from Meursault's Jean-Marc Roulot. The technique enhances both textural breadth and an intense minerality. See also Pinot Noir (page 183).

KNEZ: Peter Knez's label has a tremendous resource to tap—Anderson Valley's Demuth Vineyard clone, with its thirty-year-old plantings of shot–Wente Chardonnay on a bizarro dual-rootstock combination meant to keep the vines alive as old phylloxera-plagued roots withered away. Made by Anthony Filiberti (Anthill Farms), the **Demuth Chardonnay** ($$) balances its share of oak when young with a stark saline depth and sheer juiciness. See also Pinot Noir (page 188).

LIQUID FARM: This young label established by Southern California natives Nikki and Jeff Nelson was intended to show the precision of Chardonnay from the Santa Rita Hills. The **White Hill** ($$), from a mix of vineyards including Bentrock, Clos Pepe, and Rita's Crown, is leaner and more precise, while the **Golden Slope** ($$$), which taps Zotovich and Rita's Crown, is plusher and more indicative of broad-shouldered Chardonnay from the hills' north valley. The wines receive little new wood, no acidification, and mostly indigenous yeast.

LITTORAI: While his work with Pinot Noir attracts the most attention, Ted Lemon could be just as well known for his Chardonnay from the Sonoma Coast. The opulent, apple-skin-flavored **B.A. Thieriot** ($$$) is from a vineyard at nine hundred feet overlooking the town of Bodega that Lemon leases and farms biodynamically. **Charles Heintz** ($$$), with its typical honeyed notes, uses that well-known source just east of Occidental, with its Goldridge loam soils. **Mays Canyon** ($$$) is Littorai's designation for the Porter-Bass site, specifically a north-facing parcel planted in 1999. A fourth Chardonnay, the **Tributary** ($$$), comes from Lemon's own estate parcel, the Haven. There's no particular formula for Lemon's cellar work with white wine, although there are some common practices: the juice is protected from oxygen at pressing and goes right into barrel for fermentation, and there's about one-quarter new wood, typically natural malolactic fermentation, little stirring of lees, and very little sulfur used in the course of about twelve months of aging. "Chardonnay is like the proof of immaculate conception," Lemon says. "You can do almost nothing and it can turn out brilliant." See also Pinot Noir (page 184).

MATTHIASSON: Steve Matthiasson draws on a range of sources to make Chardonnay, including his own intensely rocky plot in Sonoma, known as Michael Mara, which he shares with the Idell family. He sometimes mixes grapes at low sugar levels (21 Brix) with those at much higher levels (26 Brix), with the latter sweetening the blend. The **Michael Mara Vineyard Chardonnay** ($$) mixes a savory rye seed aspect with waxy fruit. There's also a more accessible freesia-scented **Linda Vista Vineyard Chardonnay** ($$), made in neutral oak from a vineyard leased just behind his house in Napa's Oak Knoll. See also Cabernet (page 218) and The New Whites (page 246).

RIDGE VINEYARDS: Chardonnay seems almost an afterthought for Ridge, but the grape has been planted in the complex soils of Montebello Ridge since at least the 1970s. The **Monte Bello Chardonnay** ($$$) remains one of the state's most powerful, evocative examples. Typically landing in the mid-14 percent range for alcohol and only made in certain vintages, it shows baby fat when young, with Ridge's inevitable deep accent of American oak. It endures sixteen months in barrel (the last few in old wood) and another twenty months of bottle aging, even longer than Ridge's reds. There's also an **Estate Chardonnay** ($$), typically from a lower block of Monte Bello, with twelve months in mostly American oak. See also Cabernet (page 216) and Back to the Future (page 272).

STONY HILL: One of California's Chardonnay mother sites, this estate on Napa's Spring Mountain has done the improbable, which is to make a name for itself by producing white wine in a red-wine zip code. They also make **Riesling** ($$) and **Gewürztraminer** ($$) from the estate. The **Estate Chardonnay** ($$$) is long-aging and heathery, with a lack of new oak that is almost quaint in this era. See also Cabernet (page 219).

TYLER: Justin Willett is among the new generation occupying the Lompoc ghetto and tapping Santa Rita's great sites. His wines are clean—almost too much so—but they exude the tension and purity the region does so well. The **Clos Pepe** ($$$) shows a sublime honeydew-skin texture from one of the rare clay parcels in the appellation's north valley. There's also a fully fleshed **Bien Nacido** ($$), along with a **Santa Barbara County** ($$) bottling mostly from Santa Maria Valley, plus a handful of Pinot Noirs from these and other Santa Rita sites—including Bentrock and La Encantada.

Cabernet

There's always a thrill that comes with drinking a wine made from grapes grown the year you were born. But there was a larger message in my first taste of the 1972 Robert Mondavi Cabernet Sauvignon.

From a soggy, grim vintage, this wasn't meant to be one of the greats. But four decades later, it remained alive, full of silken black fruit and a burnt-earth depth. Thanks were due in part to the talents of Mike Grgich, who would soon go on to draw the world's attention to California with a very different wine, the Chateau Montelena Chardonnay that stunned the world in the Judgment of Paris. But thanks also were due to Mondavi himself, who at that point in his career was driven by a swirl of ambitions: to chase the holy grail of wines made in Bordeaux, and to outdo his family's Charles Krug winery.

It has been a long path from that wine to Cabernet Sauvignon's modern kingship in California. In fact, Cabernet has always been a measuring stick for greatness, thanks to its primacy in Bordeaux.

Plantings at Monte Bello

And its history in California dates to the early 1830s, when pioneer vintner Jean-Louis Vignes imported Cabernet and other grapes from his native Bordeaux and planted them near where Los Angeles's Union Station now sits.

How did California Cabernet once taste? This is currently one of the great puzzles of California wine. We have good evidence from the 1970s era, but the question stretches farther back, to midcentury, when Inglenook's Cask Cabernet was a symbol of American determination, and, farther still, to the pre-Prohibition era.

Once Cabernet was simply part of a roster of grapes used to make wines like Inglenook's "Médoc-type Extra Claret," but with Frank Schoonmaker and others pushing the rise of varietal wine after Prohibition, Cabernet was finally free to be Cabernet. While its rise wasn't exactly dramatic—in 1956 there were just an estimated seven hundred acres, far less than was planted with Zinfandel and Petite Sirah—its pedigree rested in Bordeaux, making it the right yardstick by which to see how well California could stack up against France's dominant spot in the midcentury wine world. Cabernet was the obvious vehicle for measuring California's progress.

Those midcentury California wines were made to share as much as possible with their French counterparts. They were riper, perhaps, but were still very much what Californians called (once approvingly, then disdainfully, and now wistfully) "claret-style"—crafted in the image of Bordeaux. This was the era when Russian-born André Tchelistcheff, Napa's Cabernet master, presided over Beaulieu Vineyards' Georges de Latour, a pinnacle of Cabernet achievement. The wines were refreshing, and even when aged in the small oak barrels introduced by Tchelistcheff before World War II, they retained the same leafy edge, high acidity, and deep tannic structure essential to fine claret. It is no surprise that many such wines, like the 1959 Inglenook, thrive even today, despite being made without any technology more advanced than rudimentary redwood fermentation casks.

In the 1970s, the best wines remained lean, wiry, and amply tannic. Joe Heitz, for example, held back his Cabernet for nearly five years before release. As early as 1974, pioneers like Warren Winiarski of Stag's Leap Wine Cellars were fixated on freshness and finesse, wary that many California wines were becoming overly ripe and robust.

And then came Paris. But even afterward, the exuberance of post-Judgment wines was modest by today's standards, with alcohol levels rarely rising above 13 percent.

Bordeaux did not take its beating lightly. In 1977, the historic Château Margaux was purchased by a Greek-born retail magnate named André Mentzelopoulos. A year later he debuted his first vintage. Margaux had previously been the underperformer of Bordeaux's First Growths, but the 1978 showed a stunning improvement—in part because of heavy investment in equipment and facilities, but also because consultant Émile Peynaud had advised making the final wine using only a selection of the best lots. The turnaround work resulted in a rich and opulent Margaux, a nod toward California's friendlier flavors. But more than that, it was, frankly, evidence that the French realized that if California had once been pursuing them, the chase had now been reversed. "That began an arms race," says Tim Mondavi.

Even so, there was reluctance in California to push the style. In 1982, Gerald Asher noted, growers were typically paid for maximum ripeness; wineries began to offer a premium "to have the grapes picked at a lower concentration for the same price."

BEYOND CABERNET SAUVIGNON

If California is the land of Cabernet Sauvignon, much of that grape's success has been boosted by Bordeaux's other native varieties.

Mostly. One big loser has been Merlot, which is struggling back after a mid-2000s fall from grace. It's easy to place the blame on the movie *Sideways*, which underscored its milquetoast ways, but the truth was that Merlot had already devolved into a certain boringness before the film was released. Generally riper than Cabernet and with less tannin, Merlot had often become slightly sweet and anodyne, as much a generic term for "red wine" as Chardonnay had become for white.

This is not to discount the grape entirely. John Kongsgaard's 1990s examples from Newton were dramatic and age-worthy, as is the version from Mayacamas, a little-known gem. But

there's also the large empty field in front of Dominus Estate where Merlot once grew. Christian Moueix pulled it out when he decided, as others have, that the gravelly soils of the western Napa benchland were a better fit for Cabernet.

In its place, he blends in Cabernet Franc and Petit Verdot. These grapes, particularly Cabernet Franc, have enjoyed a long-overdue rise in Napa. Perhaps the best example at the top end is Dalla Valle's Maya, a red blend typically composed of a large dose of Franc. The grape has also rallied elsewhere, like Santa Barbara's Ballard Canyon.

This is not entirely a surprise. Even in 1892, E. W. Hilgard advised California vintners to "regard Cabernet Franc with special favor." But just a few years ago, it was still a backbencher. A ripeness-obsessed generation

either ignored it or grew it into raisins to make sure, as winemaker Robert Foley put it, that "you're out of the woods on cat piss, and out of the woods on geraniums and all those wonky flavors." Yet recent varietal bottlings, from Matthiasson, Broc Cellars, Cultivar, and others, demonstrate that Franc can shine well shy of 28 Brix.

And don't count Merlot out just yet. It excels in the cooler, clay-heavy reaches of the Carneros District and the heavier soils of Oak Knoll. And just two miles east of Dominus, in the heart of Yountville, Lou Kapcsándy Sr. planted the grape on the former site of Beringer's State Lane Vineyard. He immediately discovered the Pomerol corollary—similar soils, especially—that had eluded Moueix. "It is such hard clay," Kapcsándy says, "that you cannot put in a shovel and start digging."

The 1980s witnessed California ascendant and Bordeaux on the chase, not only in France, but also through projects like Napa's Opus One, founded jointly by Baron Philippe de Rothschild and the Mondavis. This was the decade when, critic James Laube wrote in 1989, "one could make a case that California Cabernet and Bordeaux are closer in quality and style than ever before."

Increasingly, the fresh herbal flavors in Cabernet were viewed as a flaw rather than the sign of quality they once had represented to claret-trained

palates. Outside Napa, Monterey County found itself drowning in Cabernet from that region's 1970s planting boom. The green and generally unripe flavors of its Cabernets were increasingly shunned.

Perhaps most importantly, the 1980s were a time when Cabernet—like Chardonnay—sealed its position as one of California's defining wines. By 1991 there were 34,176 acres planted, more than double a decade earlier.

"FOOD WINES"

Success brought other concerns for Cabernet producers. One of the biggest dilemmas was a move toward what were dubbed "food wines." In a 1985 column, Frank Prial laid out the problem in the *New York Times*: a rising American fondness for lighter, sweeter, and mostly white wine had created an identity crisis for reds, particularly Cabernet. Bordeaux and its partisans, notably the British, were happy to paint California Cabernet as too big and ripe.

"What sort of wine should it be, anyway?" Prial wrote, presaging later fights. "Big and rich and mouth-filling, with lots of body, color and alcohol? Or should it be lighter, leaner, more 'sculpted,' which is a word Robert Mondavi likes to use for this newer style of wine?"

A backlash soon followed against this latter approach. Robert Parker in particular, fresh off his enthusiasm for Bordeaux's ripe 1982 vintage, seemed keen on punishing those who emphasized restraint. In his scolding review of the 1982 Shafer Reserve Cabernet ("the wine's acidity is akin to a chastity belt"), he suggested that we "blame those anti-pleasure, puritanical and misguided food/wine fanatics."

This slap fight over ripeness and acidity has endured ever since. It is perhaps best underscored by what I'll call the 1947 Cheval Blanc Theory. That near-mythic wine, considered one of the best Bordeaux ever, was a freak of nature from a ripe vintage, with a high alcohol level for the time (around 14.5 percent), low total acidity, and a remarkable level of volatile acidity, a potential flaw that would never be allowed today. Estate director Pierre Lurton has called it a "happy accident." To a Bordeaux-loving palate, Parker's included, beset by too many thin, green wines, the '47 Cheval Blanc is a revelation: deep, unctuous, and full of ripe flavors ("Port-like" and "motor oil" are two frequently used descriptions). It was very much a precursor to California's late-1990s Cabernet style.

Wines emulating the '47 Cheval bolstered a belief that lower-acid, higher-alcohol, Port-like Cabernets were the pinnacle of achievement—the antithesis of underripe Bordeaux. (Parker later asserted that "most of the greatest red Bordeaux vintages of the last 100 or so years had extremely low acidity and very high pHs.") Its modern counterpart might be the 1997 Harlan Estate, which received a perfect score from Parker but has been the subject of concerns about overripeness and volatility.

In any case, the template for the next two decades was set. The 1990s would usher in Cabernet as the ultimate symbol of California's power—and, depending on your view, its tumble into disrepute. Starting in the late 1980s, a sea of young-vine Cabernet spurred by new money helped propel dramatic exuberance in Cabernet winemaking. Cabernet—and specifically expensive Napa Cabernet—was now more than just a wine; it was something to aspire to.

Along, then, came ever-higher scores—as Don Bryant of Bryant Family Vineyards put it to the *Wine Spectator*, "I am in the wine business to make 100-point wines"—and aspirational pricing. You had to charge like the winery you wanted to become. Even a relatively common wine like Caymus's yellow-label Cabernet spiked from $25 a bottle in 1992 to $70 four years later.

THE NEW STYLE

There remained holdouts for a more classic style, people like Cathy Corison, Ridge's Paul Draper, and Christian Moueix of Dominus.

"I feel kind of like the Lone Ranger," Corison told me at one point. "If I hadn't made wine for myself, I wouldn't have been able to be so stubborn about maintaining my style. But I believe that a house needs to stand for something."

After leaving Caymus in 1985, Randy Dunn established his own label as a nose-thumbing of sorts; its deeply tannic style was a repudiation of Napa's user-friendly tendencies. For that matter, labels like Mayacamas, the historic Mount Veeder winery, were known for being hard as nails but never wavered in their style, even as critical attention moved on.

But I wasn't the only one encountering wines like the 1972 Mondavi, or the 1993 Caymus, that demonstrated the virtues of California's earlier era. Younger winemakers were increasingly revisiting old vintages. Starting in 2010 they gained a library at which they could do their research when sommeliers Kelli White and Scott Brenner were hired from New York by Dean & Deluca owner Leslie Rudd to revamp the cellar at Press, his St. Helena steakhouse. The two soon established their mission: to build a ten-thousand-bottle cellar, the West Coast's largest restaurant collection of old Napa wines.

Soon all of Napa was turning out to taste aged versions of its mother's milk, wines that hadn't graced a restaurant wine list in a couple of decades, from the 1974 Freemark Abbey Bosché to the 1984 Heitz Bella Oaks. A place once reluctant to acknowledge its past was suddenly drinking it down.

Cabernet has the most distance to cover in returning from the brink of Big Flavor's excesses. But there is at least a step toward modest ripeness in the field through higher yields and less sugar-obsessed farming.

This has less to do with the interest in food wines of the 1980s than it does with the rekindling of a discussion about the distinction of great sites. Formerly Martha's Vineyard was known for the eucalyptus accent of its wines, and the Rutherford Dust Society trade group was named for the area's presumed signature. Stags Leap District prided itself on its suppleness and mineral edge (although its wines, which Warren Winiarski had described as "an iron fist in a velvet glove," had, for some of his neighbors, become confected enough to be more a timber-beam fist in a Fruit Roll-Up glove).

As obvious as it may seem, doing less in the cellar and more in the field has begun to regain popularity as a way to showcase Cabernet terroir. "If you don't inoculate, and you don't acidulate, and you don't do all those things, that's what you get," says Annie Favia of Favia Wines.

There might be no better evidence of this shift than Francis Ford Coppola's recent push to reclaim not only the Inglenook name (the former moniker of his Rubicon Estate) but also Inglenook's classic style. And Larkmead, one of the major post-Prohibition powerhouses in Napa Cabernet, has similarly returned, with a style that bridges cult wine muscle and a subtler, more classic approach. These shifts demonstrate, as Corison puts it, "that we're definitely making better wines in that style than they did in those days."

Which isn't to say the style has come full circle. At Continuum Estate, Tim Mondavi's new hillside-grown wines are far bigger creatures than his old Reserve Cabernets. (The Robert Mondavi Winery, now owned by Constellation, drove full-bore into ripeness; its wines now surge past 15 percent alcohol.) Continuum's wines seem to be making a compromise between Mondavi's old style and the excesses of Big Flavor. And Tim seems comfortable with that middle ground. "I've been around here long enough," he tells me, "to do what I think Napa Valley can do best."

TOP PRODUCERS
...
CONTINUUM ESTATE

Tim Mondavi and his family like to take visitors to a spot high on Pritchard Hill from which you can view their entire eight-decade history in Napa, from their famed Oakville winery and To Kalon Vineyard across the valley to Charles Krug up north past St. Helena, which Cesare Mondavi bought in 1943.

Continuity is important to this branch of the Mondavi family, hence their wine's name. But Continuum marks a big shift from the past. For one, it was conceived as a single wine made from a single vineyard, a departure from the Mondavi winery's omnibus habits. And it also marks a sort of stylistic peacemaking with Napa.

The winemaking is sure to be refined as Continuum completes its new estate winery, designed with help from UC Davis's Roger Boulton to incorporate eco-friendly techniques like rainwater storage. There are individual fermentation tanks for nearly every block, to better fine-tune quality, including expensive upright redwood vessels Tim struggled to justify buying in the days of the Robert Mondavi Winery. Maceration is long, often a month or more, and aging is in all new French oak, with frequent stirring of lees over twenty months in barrel to finesse the texture. The wine is a ripe creature, often topping 15 percent alcohol.

That might be an accommodation to Napa's current style, but it also reflects a move from the valley floor to stressed hillside volcanic soils that struggle to reach a yield of two tons per acre. "At Robert Mondavi," Tim says, "if the yields were less than three tons, they'd be yanked."

Sixty-two acres are being organically farmed across the 173-acre property; the oldest vines date to 1991, but there has been major replanting, in part to add more Cabernet Franc and Petit Verdot.

THE WINES: There has been an evolution in the **Continuum Red Wine** ($$$$). Early vintages used fruit from the valley floor, but it is now a mountain wine that relies on a high proportion of Cabernet Franc. By the 2010 vintage it was 92 percent estate fruit, with the layered aromas that Franc was meant to add. A second wine, **Novicium** ($$$$), is in limited release to mailing-list members.

CORISON

Every year like clockwork, for more than a quarter of a century, Cathy Corison's wines have offered proof positive that Napa can deliver a timeless, tension-filled wine. This track record has made her a folk hero among those seeking a reprieve from California's overwrought Cabernets.

Her work would become a line in the sand against Napa's ripeness. The Cabernets she made under the label she founded in 1987 became the anti–cult wines, demonstrating that Napa's steroidal style was largely manmade, the result of decisions in the cellar. But even the Cabernets she made before leaving her day job at Chappellet in 1989 spoke more with charm than muscle.

At times, the style seems imposed, a deliberate attempt by Corison to make Cabernet as she thinks it should be: the alcohol levels never exceed 14 percent, and the wines always deliver power with a porcelain touch. But that is achieved in part because Corison has mastered managing ripeness in the field, trimming away lateral shoots and extra grape clusters to finesse sunlight on the fruit and to slow down sugar accumulation. She's a critic of routine irrigation, especially as a means of prolonging ripening; her Kronos Vineyard, which surrounds her winery south of St. Helena, is organically dry-farmed, although its age and the presence of leaf roll virus (see page 71) rarely allow yields above one ton per acre.

Her winemaking remains guided by her training at UC Davis, and she uses relatively neutral inoculated yeasts and a modest amount of new oak. She hasn't acidified a wine since 1981, believing that it hampers its ageability. Mostly, she relies on her polyglot palate, which often gravitates to European wines. As California's style has evolved beyond heft, Corison has found a new generation

AGING

The classic California Cabernets of the midcentury as well those of the 1970s, have aged just fine, as have some of the so-called food wines of the 1980s. But will they endure as long as Bordeaux from the same era? Quite probably, or at least the best of them will. (Cathy Corison's early wines, for instance, are going strong after more than two decades.) This is a promising sign for the emerging, leaner style.

But what about the riper wines of recent years? It's a question that rankles many winemakers. "We've been debating whether Napa Valley wines will age for the past fifteen years," Andy Erickson told me, "but show me one that hasn't aged well."

Behind that lurks a larger question: how long does California Cabernet need to endure? Even critic James Laube, who supported his share of these riper wines, wrote in 2005 that "many, if not most, of today's wines are best drunk in their first five to 10 years of life."

It's also a matter of debate what it means to age with grace. A wine might survive for fifteen years, but does it get more complex and worthy with time in bottle? For example, I hadn't tried the 1997 Bryant Family upon release, but I did taste it a few years ago. It hadn't gone dead, but it was still so ripe and monolithic that I wondered, What was its purpose? Is aging California Cabernet simply an attempt to emulate the 1947 Cheval Blanc's Port-like qualities?

of fans who are rewarding her years in the stylistic wilderness.

THE WINES: Corison's **Napa Valley Cabernet** ($$$) comes from a blend of several vineyards along the benchland from Rutherford to St. Helena, including the famous Hayne Vineyard; it is always aromatic and fresh. The **Kronos Cabernet** ($$$$), from her estate plot, shares the style but shows the intensity of naturally low yields. Both reward a decade or more in the cellar. There is also a **Helios Cabernet Franc** ($$$) and, improbably, a dry **Corazón Gewürztraminer** ($$) from Anderson Valley.

DOMINUS ESTATE

Christian Moueix's effort to make a great American wine has fully matured in the three decades since he launched Dominus Estate in 1982 with partners Robin Lail and Marcia Smith, daughters of Inglenook proprietor John Daniel Jr. (The sisters sold their shares and Moueix was full owner by 1995.) Dominus, of course, benefits from Moueix's experience as the owner of Bordeaux's Château Pétrus, but more than anything it has the advantage of 124 acres of the Napanook Vineyard, on the site where George Yount planted Napa's first wine grapes in 1838. That site was later the source of some of Inglenook's finest vintages, which means it offers as unbroken a legacy of viticulture as California can offer.

Just over one hundred acres of Cabernet Sauvignon, Cabernet Franc, and Petit Verdot are planted on the gravelly and clay loam that defines western Napa. Moueix has always pledged to farm without irrigation, and the watersheds of the Mayacamas Range provide an abundance of moisture. The farming is essentially organic, with plowing to manage cover crop and soil tilth.

In the cellar, technical director Tod Mostero uses a relatively light touch, although there are diastolic pumps and one of the valley's recent must-have gadgets: an optical grape-sorting machine to ensure that fruit is handled gently, a system so impressively ordered that you almost root for a bit of chaos to appear. For such a stately wine, Dominus receives surprisingly little new oak—about 40 percent (and about 20 percent for Napanook, its second wine). Aging is typically eighteen months, with frequent rackings. This all takes place in Dominus's black monolith of a winery designed by Swiss architects Herzog & de Meuron, one of Napa's most impressive facades (although, sadly, it is closed to the public).

THE WINES: The **Dominus Estate Red** ($$$$) is among Napa's quintessential expressions, typically a blend with more than 80 percent Cabernet Sauvignon, filled out with Cabernet Franc and Petit Verdot. Certainly there is plenty of extract, and the wines have grown slightly bulkier over the years, but it always comes across as aromatic and subtle, ready for long aging. Their second wine, the **Napanook Red** ($$$), has become so good in recent vintages that it is almost keeping pace with its big brother.

FAVIA

Annie Favia and Andy Erickson are one of Napa's power couples. Erickson made Screaming Eagle for many years in addition to Dalla Valle, Ovid, and more. Favia worked for John Kongsgaard and Cathy Corison before spending a dozen years working for David Abreu, the cult-wine era's vineyard hero.

Favia is an opportunity for the two to finally have their own fun. They tap a handful of vineyards, predominantly in the Coombsville area, where they live with their two daughters. If Andy is the quiet, studious one, Annie is a constant ball of energy, proof that you can never keep a viticulturist from farming. Obsessed with biodiversity, she has filled their backyard with a chicken coop, honeybee hive, trellised raspberries, tea plants, and raised garden beds. The front yard? An acre of dry-farmed Sauvignon Blanc.

The wines tend to be relatively ripe but not overwhelming, and they receive a healthy dose of new oak. Fermentations are typically indigenous, and barrel aging stretches nearly two years, with another year in bottle. They also make a range of Rhône-inspired wines from the Sierra Foothills, which get less new oak and, in some cases, partial aging in concrete eggs (see Innovation in the Cellar, page 254) and semicarbonic fermentation for a lighter extraction. The Napa-based wines occasionally receive something similar, with grapes destemmed and cracked but left whole. And the couple extended their work in 2013 with Charles Banks' acquisition of historic Mayacamas Vineyards (see page 218).

THE WINES: The **Cerro Sur** ($$$$) is Franc dominant, from thirty-year-old vines on the Rancho Chimiles parcel above the little-known Wooden Valley area of eastern Napa, mixed with Cabernet Sauvignon. The **Cabernet Sauvignon** ($$$$) combines a range of Coombsville sources with fruit from Oakville Ranch. The **Linea Sauvignon Blanc** ($$$$), from their front yard, is picked around 23 Brix and aged in concrete eggs. The ripe **Leviathan** ($$$), which now includes Charles Banks (Sandhi, Wind Gap) as a partner, is a constantly changing blend of Cabernet, Syrah, and sundry other grapes—and a less expensive way to taste the couple's talents. See also Revising the Rhône (page 234).

INGLENOOK

Just a few years ago Francis Ford Coppola's grand Napa project was chasing Big Flavor, but by 2006 Coppola perceived a need to change course. In the fields, old vines were being torn out in favor of higher-yielding vines; Rafael Rodriguez, Inglenook's longtime vineyard manager, had been sidelined. The wines struck Coppola as too by-the-numbers, too far removed from both the Bordeaux

he enjoyed and Inglenook's classic midcentury Cabernet bones: "I felt there was too much science being employed. And I wanted more instinct."

To his credit, the director of *The Godfather* knew that he had one of California's most historic properties. Starting in 1879, Gustave Niebaum, a Finnish seafarer who had become one of America's richest men, devised a Rutherford estate to rival any of Bordeaux's top growths. He planted 250 acres using cuttings from Europe. His winery architecture was so forward-thinking that its use of cable-car cables was a precursor of rebar. In 1890, the *San Francisco Examiner* gushed that Niebaum had "performed a work of incalculable value to the State by demonstrating that California can not only produce wine, but can make a wine the equal of any in the world."

Niebaum's widow kept Inglenook afloat through Prohibition by selling grapes to neighboring Beaulieu Vineyard. By midcentury her son John Daniel Jr. was reviving Inglenook's original glory. The Daniel-era Inglenook produced an astonishing array of wines, from legendary Cabernets to varietal Charbono. That would all crash soon after Inglenook was sold in 1964 to United Vintners, then to liquor giant Heublein, which all but destroyed the winery's reputation, so much so that when Coppola made a public event out of knocking down Heublein's barrel-storage building in 2007, much of Napa came to watch.

Coppola had converted the property to organic farming by the 2000s, but Big Flavor was still the operative style. After a long talent search, he hired Philippe Bascaules, who had spent two decades at Château Margaux, to transform the wines into a style that Bascaules describes as "impressive, but not aggressive." Among Bascaules's tools: raising yields to about three tons per acre in order to better control ripeness.

Despite years of the Inglenook name being slapped on cheap jug wines, Coppola realized that its reputation had survived. In 2011 he bought the name from the Wine Group, planned a new gravity-flow winery, and rebranded the wines with a label reminiscent of Inglenook's old design. Coppola had bet around $50 million—probably more—on restoring the glories of an earlier era.

THE WINES: Bascaules's arrival marked a radical change in style, which was perhaps magnified by the cold 2011 vintage. The **Inglenook Rubicon** ($$$$) began to evolve into a more classically framed Cabernet, mixing a modern sensibility with aspects of the Daniel-era wines. The **Cask Cabernet** ($$$) follows suit; once it had been differentiated by its use of American oak, but it is becoming more a pure second wine, using a mix of oak sources (around 35 percent new, versus 75 percent for Rubicon). Bascaules's Château Margaux sensibilities are imprinted on the **Edizione Pennino Zinfandel** ($$$) too; its energetic flavors are reminiscent of that grape's serious-minded past.

KAPCSÁNDY FAMILY

Lou Kapcsándy Sr. escaped Hungary in the 1950s, came to America, played professional football, and developed a large Seattle construction business. He began importing Bordeaux, but in 2000 he took advantage of an opportunity to acquire Yountville's State Lane Vineyard. He then hired Helen Turley and John Wetlaufer to replant the phylloxera-era-ravaged site and make the wines.

This could have been the start of another cult wine, but Kapcsándy soon began to grok the lessons of Tchelistcheff-era Napa and decided to take a sharp left turn in style, aligning himself more with Bordeaux, and with the great old Beaulieu and Beringer Cabernets. He hired former Château Latour winemaker Denis Malbec, and soon his wines dropped about a percentage point in alcohol, to the mid-13 percent range. They now evoked the freshness of 1970s Napa Cabernet, albeit with more new French oak and more modern cellar work.

Winemaking at Kapcsándy is fastidious; workers stand elbow to elbow at one of the valley's most meticulous sorting tables. Farming of the sixteen acres is equally fastidious, if conventional. (Lou Sr.'s views toward organics are uncharitable at best.) Plantings are dense even by Napa standards, with around 2,600 vines per acre.

THE WINES: The Kapcsándy wines are marked by an earthy aromatic power and just the right mix of California fruit and Bordeaux rigor. The **Cabernet Sauvignon Grand Vin** ($$$$) is Kapcsándy's spendy aim—a successful one—to rival first-growth Pauillac, although the **Estate Cuvée Cabernet Sauvignon** ($$$$), all Cabernet from clones 191 and 337, has a brushy aromatic side that is in some ways a truer homage to classic Napa. There's also a Merlot-dominant **Roberta's Reserve** ($$$$), the ripest and spendiest wine (around $350) in the lineup. And Merlot composes a significant portion of the **Endre** ($$$), Kapcsándy's excellent second wine, along with Cabernet Sauvignon, Cabernet Franc, and Petit Verdot.

LARKMEAD

The history of Calistoga's Larkmead begins with Lillie Hitchcock Coit, she of San Francisco's Coit Tower, who originally settled on her parents' property here. By 1895 it had been taken over by Felix Salmina and his uncle John, members of an Italian-Swiss family who had migrated to Napa. After Prohibition the Salminas revived the label, and soon Larkmead wines were considered one of Napa's big four, along with Beaulieu, Beringer, and Inglenook. Starting in the 1930s, vine researcher Harold Olmo used the property for clonal research, making it ground zero for much of Napa's current vine material.

In 1948 the property was purchased by Larry Solari, president of United Vintners, the massive growers' co-op. The Solaris kept the land, but the Larkmead brand fell into disrepair until being revived for the 1998 vintage by the current owners, Kate Solari Baker, Larry's daughter, and her husband, Cam Baker.

Hence Larkmead has an unbroken lineage of Napa farming. Among the 113 planted acres are Friulano vines more than 120 years old, along with a diversity of Cabernet clones, sort of a continuation of Olmo's work. It has become a perfect integration of Napa's modern priorities with the best of its previous style, thanks in large part to winemaker Dan Petroski (Massican) and consultant Andy Smith (DuMol), who have successfully navigated a tricky path in regard to Napa ripeness. "We say we want to pick the day before the fruit is ready," Smith says.

In the cellar, the winemaking shows shades of 1978, albeit with more new oak and more modern fermentation vessels. Reds receive about three weeks of maceration, plus three-day soaks before and after. There is plenty of new wood, usually more than 50 percent, but it is always well integrated.

THE WINES: The estate **Napa Valley Cabernet Sauvignon** ($$$) is a quintessential bridge between new and old Napa, underscoring the mineral power of the gravelly soils; the all-Cabernet **Solari** ($$$$) steps up the oak a bit. Rounding out the reds are the Merlot-dominant **Firebelle** ($$$), a blended **Red Wine** ($$$), and a handful of rarer bottlings. The **Lillie Sauvignon Blanc** ($$$), fermented and aged in oak barrel and cask, is plush but focused, while the rare old-vine **Tocai Friulano** ($$) is one of Napa's most intensely mineral whites.

RIDGE VINEYARDS

Cabernet forms only a portion of Ridge's legendary heritage, but Monte Bello arguably remains America's classic wine. And Cabernet has defined Ridge's history. (For its work with Zinfandel and other legacy varieties, see page 272.)

Monte Bello is in fact a collection of four different ranches. Torre Ranch, founded in 1890, was the first. Revived in the 1940s by theologian William Short, it was acquired by Ridge's founders, four scientists from Stanford Research Institute, in 1959. The next, Osea Perrone's old 180-acre parcel near the top of Montebello Ridge, was initially acquired in 1968. Downslope is Jimsomare, originally the

property of Frenchman Pierre Klein, who came to the mountains in 1888. The nearby Rousten property completes the quartet.

Ridge's winemaker Paul Draper was drawn up the mountain in 1969 as a curious student who had ventured to Chile to make wine using old-fashioned means by following nineteenth-century Bordeaux texts in the original French. Winemaker David Bennion had his successor taste the 1959, a noncommercial first vintage made using a wooden grid to submerge the cap of crushed grapes under fermenting juice while he and his wife went on vacation—an old-fashioned technique that preserved hygiene in the must. Draper was further

The New California Wine

impressed by Bennion's 1962 and 1964 Monte Bellos, both made in old wood containers with indigenous yeasts, natural malolactic fermentation, and a minimum of sulfur.

Extractions are shorter now—grapes are pressed after a week or so—but this sort of deliberately unfussy cellar work has been the template for Ridge's winemaking ever since Draper's arrival, even as Draper maintains one of the industry's most elaborate in-house labs. Perhaps the biggest change has been the use of more new oak barrels. Always, the oak has been American, typically dried for two years.

With about thirty parcels to evaluate, Monte Bello winemaker Eric Baugher gathers with Draper and his team in February for a series of blind tastings of each lot. The best make it into a preliminary blend, with the process repeated in May. As Draper puts it, "We're saying, does this taste like the last fifty vintages of Monte Bello?"

THE WINES: The **Monte Bello** ($$$$), that rare American wine with an unbroken lineage of more than fifty years, is perhaps more relevant than ever to a discussion of Cabernet in California. Never creeping above about 13.5 percent alcohol, it always shows the signature of Ridge's high-altitude greenstone and limestone soils. As about 40 percent of Monte Bello lots are declassified, the **Estate Cabernet** ($$) remains a remarkable value, a perfect early-drinking companion to its big brother. Since 1974 Ridge has also had a steady interest in Merlot; its **Estate Merlot** ($$) is a consistent standout for that variety. There's also a **Torre Ranch Merlot** ($$$) from that original portion of the Monte Bello property. See also Chardonnay (page 203) and Back to the Future (page 272).

MORE NOTABLE WINES

ARAUJO ESTATE: Bart and Daphne Araujo came to wine well financed from another life; in their case, their money came from Bart's sale of A-M Homes, one of the nation's largest homebuilders. This could have been another case of deep-pocketed arrivals to Napa making undistinguished wine, but impeccable vineyard work and a desire to transcend the constraints of Big Flavor have made Araujo the rare effort to gracefully evolve beyond its cult-wine status (although its pricing is still at a cult level). The **Araujo Eisele Cabernet** ($$$$) shows the loamy richness that is a signature of Eisele's rocky soils and a perfectly finessed tannic structure. The excellent **Altagracia** ($$$$), a blended wine, provides less expensive access to an expression of mostly Eisele fruit. There's also **Estate Syrah** ($$$$), an exceptional **Sauvignon Blanc** ($$$), mostly aged in steel barrels, and occasionally Viognier.

ARNOT-ROBERTS: This duo has quietly built a track record for excellent Cabernets that defy conventional wisdom: they are made largely without the use of new oak and use a percentage of whole grape clusters, a technique more common with Pinot Noir. They have tapped two vineyards on the western slopes of the Mayacamas Mountains, which divide Napa and Sonoma: **Clajeux** ($$$$) and **Bugay** ($$$$), both of which both show those soils' red-spice aspects. Farther south, they also work with **Fellom Ranch** ($$$$), a Santa Cruz Mountains property adjacent to Ridge's Monte Bello. See also Chardonnay (page 200), Revising the Rhône (page 233), The New Whites (page 251), and Back to the Future (page 263).

BROADSIDE: This joint project from Chris Brockway of Broc Cellars and Brian Terrizzi of Giornata harnesses the wonders of the Margarita Vineyard outside Paso Robles. The limestone-derived soils give both the **Cabernet Sauvignon** ($$) and a more recent **Merlot** ($$) the sort of freshness and depth of flavor at relatively low alcohol that shame many heftier efforts. Fermented with indigenous yeasts and aged almost entirely in old wood, these are pristine expressions of outperforming soils. They also make a handful of Chardonnays, made in a mix of steel, old oak, and concrete eggs (see Innovation in the Cellar, page 254).

DUNN VINEYARDS: Randy Dunn's wines are a love-it-or-leave-it proposition. He is unapologetic about the fierce tannins in his wines, unapologetic about his use of reverse osmosis to modulate alcohol (often to below 14 percent), and unapologetic about his belief that most of his winemaking counterparts in Napa have gone to the stylistic dark side. The Dunn wines are also some of the most interesting, and long aging, in Napa—a perfect snapshot of Napa's Howell Mountain. As of 2009, both his **Howell Mountain Cabernet** ($$$$) and his (slightly) earlier-drinking **Napa Valley Cabernet** ($$$) come from his own estate plantings, slightly blurring the line between the two.

FOLKWAY: They may have grown up in the Central Valley, but Lino Bozzano, vineyard manager for Arroyo Grande's Laetitia, and his brother Anthony have created a label that pays homage to California's coastal reds. These two have a fine hand with Bordeaux-style blends from unexpected spots, especially the **Revelator** ($$), a blend of Merlot, Cabernet Franc, and Cabernet Sauvignon from two Santa Barbara vineyards (Bien Nacido and Santa Barbara Highlands), and a **Black Ridge Vineyard** ($$) red from the Santa Cruz Mountains that shows the best of Merlot's black-tea qualities. Bonus points for label drawings that would do Lewis Carroll proud.

MATTHIASSON: Steve Matthiasson's white wines garner more attention, but his work with reds might ultimately have a more crucial impact. Matthiasson is on a mission to show that Bordeaux-native varieties can ripen in Napa below 24 Brix. That doesn't dent the opulence of his **Napa Valley Red Wine** ($$$), always aged in about half new oak and dominant in Merlot grown on the alluvial soils of the Red Hen Vineyard. He also makes a miniscule amount of extraordinary **Cabernet Franc** ($$$), grown around his family's home and aged in old oak. Like his whites, it hovers gracefully between Napa and Friuli sensibilities. Ditto an inky **Refosco** ($$$) from his home vineyard. See also Chardonnay (page 202) and The New Whites (page 246).

MAYACAMAS VINEYARDS: The Travers family's vineyard high up on Mount Veeder, one of Napa's historic nineteenth-century sites, got a new chapter in 2013 when it was purchased by investor Charles Banks (Sandhi, Wind Gap). Bob Travers' early Cabernets were legendary but also massively tannic: the 1974 remains a drama queen nearly forty years later. Banks installed Annie Favia and Andy Erickson of Favia for what promised to be a decade-long revitalization. Despite initial concerns (Banks and Erickson were both Screaming Eagle alumni) the new team seemed determined to maintain the Mayacamas style, which was unique for Napa—more in the spirit of Barolo, with a short fermentation and two years aging in large, old American oak casks, then years longer in barrel. The property needed both new cellar equipment and replanting of several phylloxerated blocks. But as Erickson put it, "We'd be stupid to change anything really except the things that need to be addressed." While exact changes remain to be seen, the **Cabernet Sauvignon** ($$$) traditionally has an intensity and freshness unlike almost any other California wine, while the **Merlot** ($$), a rollicking mountain expression, has been one of Napa's brilliant secrets.

SNOWDEN: The Snowden family has had land outside Rutherford since 1955, a strip nearly a mile long on the hills east of the Silverado Trail, first planted in the nineteenth century. While much of the twenty-four acres of fruit is sold, the family keeps a bit for its own winemaking. Scott Snowden, a former judge in Napa's Superior Court, is a well-known valley presence, and this is a family affair, with particular help from his daughter, winemaker Diana Snowden Seysses. She splits her time between here and Domaine Dujac in Burgundy, the property of her husband's family. That Burgundy brain brings finesse to the tannins in her savory Cabernets, a model of what she calls "precision, rather than breadth." Hence fermentations with indigenous yeasts and at relatively cool temperatures, and less extraction than many counterparts. This provides both subtlety and magnitude to the **Reserve Cabernet** ($$$$), while a dose of Merlot helps plush up an earlier-drinking effort, **The Ranch Cabernet** ($$).

SPOTTSWOODE: Like Araujo, the Novak family's estate in St. Helena is finding a balance between modern Napa and its classic roots, which date back to 1972. Beth Novak Milliken, daughter of founder Mary Novak, now runs the winery without succumbing to fads—or to the valley's big egos. In the Novaks' favor is a forty-acre jewel of a benchland vineyard, farmed according to organic and biodynamic precepts; they even use horses to plow on occasion. That has given the **Estate Cabernet** ($$$$) a multidecade durability even amid its growing opulence, a tradition that continues under the hand of winemaker Aron Weinkauf, along with the second-label **Lyndenhurst Cabernet** ($$$), and one of California's best Sauvignon Blancs. See also The New Whites (page 253).

STONY HILL: After six decades in Napa, the white-wine-devoted McCrea family took the unusual step of introducing a **Cabernet Sauvignon** ($$$) in 2012. From relatively young, dry-farmed estate vines on Spring Mountain, its slightly exposed, fresh tannins are an homage to the restrained style of Cabernet from the 1960s and early '70s. See also Chardonnay (page 203).

TURLEY WINE CELLARS: This Zinfandel producer has always gone against the tide in Napa, refusing to make a Cabernet. No more. **The Label** ($$) is a tribute to older-style Napa Cab predominantly from a parcel of twenty-year-old vines at the back of Turley's estate near St. Helena. The concept came from Christina Turley, daughter of owner Larry Turley, who drew from her time working at New York's Momofuku to make reality of a sommelier in-joke: that Cab drinkers don't drink the wine, they drink the label. See also Back to the Future (page 269).

Revising the Rhône

This was supposed to be Syrah's time of triumph. It had been pushed diligently by its true believers for so many years, touted as a counterpoint to the everywhereness of Cabernet.

But the row of glasses in front of me, at a seminar held by the Rhône Rangers—a group of American vintners dedicated to the bounty of that part of France—tells a different story, of a different battle fought and won. What have we here? A bit of Picpoul, the tart white grape better known from the Languedoc, but this time from Paso Robles. A splash of Grenache Blanc. The red grape Counoise from El Dorado County. Cinsault from Lodi.

If the history of American Rhônelandia in the last three decades has been the history of trying to make Syrah a contender, today's Rhône-minded winemakers have embraced a far broader palette. The Rhône's great asset—its diversity—is on display in California as never before.

There is a new contender rising where Syrah has faltered. In a way, it's puzzling that Grenache wasn't California's grape of choice to begin with. Despite being one of the world's most planted wine grapes, it offered a nearly silent contribution in California, at least as a red wine, until recent years.

Certainly Grenache is not new to the state, having presumably been introduced in the late 1850s by Charles Lefranc of Almaden Vineyards, who pioneered wine in the Santa Clara Valley. (One theory has posited that much of what thrived was not true Grenache Noir but Grenache Gris, a palish mutation. But plantings of true black Grenache have been found dating to the early twentieth century and even earlier.)

If Syrah was viewed as nobility, a fine grape brought low by overplanting and bad winemaking, Grenache's history in the state was as scullery maid. Certainly it boomed in the nineteenth century, and then again after Prohibition, but it primarily had a reputation as a cheap throwaway grape. It was rarely vinified on its own in the midcentury except as a pink wine. This was hardly a California problem: Grenache's dual personality, as base material for everything from noble Châteauneuf to plonk, persists everywhere.

Fittingly, it was Almaden that pioneered Grenache rosé in the 1940s, and later the grape was occasionally used in light red wines, even in Beaujolais nouveau–style bottlings. But at a time when darker was better, it was condemned for its light color, as well as its relatively low acid and slightly sweet character. Decades of use in cheap table wines ultimately led to its fall from favor in the 1980s. Huge swaths of Grenache vines, mostly in

the San Joaquin Valley, were uprooted; its acreage was halved between 1994 and 2012, to 6,020 acres.

After more than a century, it is finally being recognized that the grape's presumed deficits are in fact its great charm. Grenache is finally receiving its star turn—in Rhône-inspired blends, of course, but also as a solo act. The arrival of not only high-quality clonal material from the Tablas Creek project but also smaller-clustered, tannic specimens brought in from Spain's Priorat area, plus the propagation of vines sneaked in by Edna Valley winemaker John Alban, have aided the spread of more intense, complex examples.

But where to grow it? For years, Grenache's sweet spot in California was elusive. There were long-standing examples like George Besson's vineyard dating to 1910 outside Gilroy, in the midst of the Santa Clara Valley, not far from Leblanc's early efforts. Besson's gravelly loam soils, at the tail end of the Santa Cruz Mountains, have been a source for several quintessential Grenache-based wines, including Bonny Doon's Clos de Gilroy. Something about the Garlic Capital of the World seems to do right by the grape.

As it turns out, rarely has there been a grape more suitable across California. Exceptional Grenache can be found in the remote high ground of Santa Barbara County; in the warm alluvial stretches of Calistoga's Frediani Vineyard; in the volcanic soils of eastern Lodi and up into the granite-marked terrain of the Sierra Foothills; even in remote stretches of eastern San Diego County. Its relatives, Grenache Gris and Grenache Blanc, are similarly becoming more prolific. The survival of nearly century-old Grenache Gris vines in the McDowell Valley area of Mendocino gives hope for the whole family.

SYRAH'S MOMENT OF CRISIS

And what of Syrah? It essentially launched the modern American Rhône revolution. After a brief nineteenth-century appearance, and quiet survival in a few fields like Sonoma's Old Hill Ranch, it was functionally lost until researcher Harold Olmo imported French cuttings in the 1930s. But its real tale began four decades later. In 1974, Joseph Phelps made a Syrah using an old Christian Brothers planting, and the following year Gary Eberle planted twenty acres at the Estrella River Winery near Paso Robles. But these were asterisks. In 1982, less than ninety acres were planted. Growth crept along for a decade.

Then, boom. By 1999, 10,298 acres were in the ground—two-thirds of them too young to harvest—and California Syrah would nearly double again in the next ten years. The grape clearly had the opportunity for greatness, as it was the base material for the famous wines of Hermitage and Côte-Rôtie. With Cabernet becoming a rich man's drink and Pinot Noir still in relative obscurity, by the mid-1990s Syrah seemed (at least to the Rhôneists) like a contender for California fame.

Just one problem. The grape's true home, whence those great wines hail, is only about a fifty-mile portion of the northern Rhône, a tiny swath of the Rhône overall. Far fewer places in the world than anyone had imagined could actually produce Syrah with the spicy aromas and depth that made it noble in France. (Australian research ultimately pinned this to a compound in the grape, rotundone, which provides a peppery aspect and appears to be more prolific in grapes planted in cooler climates.) Soon there was more Syrah planted in California than in the northern Rhône.

California had misinterpreted its geography, but, then again, it had little wisdom to follow. There had been virtually no research about where Syrah might thrive, and on the Winkler climate scale, the Rhône Valley was equated with the warm Region III—although that designation was more applicable to the sunny southern Rhône, not the north.

But the French also had misinterpreted Syrah. This was at least partly the result of a deep cultural gap between Burgundy and the Rhône. While Burgundy has often been considered a world away from its southern counterpart, it's perhaps only forty miles from southern Burgundy to the northern Rhône. Climate data show that Syrah and Pinot Noir share a proximate sweet spot; the northern Rhône's cumulative heat typically lands around 2,500 degree-days Fahrenheit, not much above the heart of the Côte d'Or. As climatologist Gregory Jones put it, "If you ask where the Syrah zones should be today, then Syrah should be planted in parts of Burgundy."

Ehren Jordan of Failla was one of those who initially labored under this misunderstanding. But Jordan had apprenticed in the northern Rhône and realized how cold it could be. He headed west to the remote, chilly Sonoma coastal ridges to plant his own dry-farmed Syrah vineyard. Far western Sonoma was considered marginal at the time for Pinot, much less Syrah. But, then, the northern Rhône is also marginal—"well north of the olive oil–butter divide," in Jordan's words. Its best spots, like the hill of Hermitage, provide warm exposures in a generally cold region.

A handful of Californians reached a similar conclusion by the late 1990s, but they were largely drowned out by the typical California shuffle: a great push to plant in warmer areas—and often to double down by drastically lowering crop levels. Syrah would be exuberant and big, its historical nature be damned. This became common practice in places like Paso Robles, which soon found itself ratcheting up sugars and thus alcohol levels, with young vines hanging far too little fruit.

By the late 2000s Syrah sales were sagging—in part because Pinot had lapped it, in part because of a desire to emulate cheap Aussie Shiraz, and in part because many Syrahs seemed too monotonous to justify $40 price tags. (The success of a few exuberant examples, like those from the Sine Qua Non label, further distorted ambitions.) In 2010, after two decades of boom, plantings dipped for the first time. Producers quipped that they could more easily get rid of a case of pneumonia than a case of Syrah, a not-terribly-funny joke punctuated by a Rhône Rangers charity event titled "Pneumonia's Last Syrah."

But the marginality message was finally sinking in. Vintners sought out the edge of ripeness—whether on the last stretches of the Sonoma Coast, where the Peay estate in the Annapolis fog barely ekes out 2,000 degree-days Fahrenheit in a cold year, or the Clary Ranch site in the Two Rock Valley area west of Petaluma, made famous by the 2008 Arnot-Roberts Syrah, an aromatic powerhouse that at 11.5 percent alcohol was even leaner than its Rhône counterparts. Syrah maven Pax Mahle reached the same conclusion in 2004 when walking his Majik Vineyard in the Sebastopol Hills, prime Pinot territory. "There the grapes were, in my hand, in my mouth, just about as ripe as a grape can get while still having freshness, and there it was sitting at 22 Brix," he recalls. "What am I going to do?"

He took the chance. Like the Clary Ranch, Pax's Majik became one of those transformative Syrahs, a wine that both nodded back to Bob Lindquist's 1980s efforts with his Qupé label and to its French inspirations.

This edgy style began to redefine the grape in California. Arnot-Roberts gave up its fruit from the Hudson vineyard in Carneros: not marginal enough. In Anderson Valley, Copain's Wells Guthrie and Drew's Jason Drew achieved as much quality with Syrah as with Pinot. While the Lakeville area, at the eastern edge of Sonoma, prided itself on Pinot and Chardonnay, it was inadvertently a haven for Syrah. Even on San Luis Obispo's foggy coast near Hearst Castle, the grape could more than amply ripen.

California might have less Syrah, but what remained would be far better.

DIVERSITY REIGNS

Perhaps Syrah needed that dose of humility in order to let the rest of the Rhône contingent flourish. Its moment of stress had precisely that effect. In addition to blends that nodded toward the southern Rhône, wines like Bonny Doon's famous Le Cigare Volant, there were blips of interest in the Rhône's lesser-known grapes: whites like Marsanne, which Qupé's Bob Lindquist planted in Santa Barbara in 1985, and red Mourvèdre, the native grape of Bandol. Roussanne, the other half of the northern Rhône's white-grape equation, made a quiet appearance, although interest lagged until better French clonal material was finally cleared into the country; even now fewer than four hundred acres are planted statewide.

Viognier fared slightly better, with plantings in the early 1980s by Ritchie Creek on Napa's Spring Mountain and by La Jota across the valley, and soon after by Calera's Josh Jensen, inspired by his two-day harvest stint at Château Grillet, the Rhône's tiniest appellation. Viognier made a significant splash, but it also fell prey to the Californian scramble to Chardonnay-ify every other white variety—drowning them with oak and aggressive stirring of the lees, both bad ideas for a grape that is already unctuous by nature.

Mourvèdre had been in California for a century, a staple for red field blends, albeit under another name: Mataro. When winemakers like Bonny Doon's Randall Grahm, or Kenneth Volk of Wild Horse, who in the early 1990s found a 1922 planting of Mourvèdre in the limestone-rich soils of San Benito County, surmised that the two were the same, they exulted in solving a key piece of the Rhône puzzle. The long-obscure Grenache Blanc became an unlikely star, and esoterica like Clairette and Vermentino found a new audience.

A grand bump in genetic diversity came from an effort by Paso Robles's Tablas Creek Vineyards, a partnership between the Perrin family of Châteauneuf's Château de Beaucastel and importer Robert Haas. Unimpressed by the vine material available in California, they began to import cuttings from France—Grenache, Mourvèdre, Counoise, Picpoul Blanc, and more—putting them through the US government's lengthy quarantine. The so-called Tablas clones provided a huge catalyst for the Rhône movement—although some winemakers still preferred either old California stock or imported suitcase versions like Alban's Grenache clone.

GROWING UP

Place began to matter in a serious way for the Rhôneists. The complex granite- and shale-rich soils of the Sierra Foothills, with their volcanic origins, became a sweet spot, affirming the years of evangelism by Sierra Vista's John MacCready and by Bill Easton of Domaine de la Terre Rouge, two of the area's Rhône pioneers.

The same is true of areas around western Paso Robles and nearby Templeton, which offered not only the degraded calcium-rich clay of the ancient seabed that had drawn Tablas Creek, but also shale, sandstone, and even pure sand. Sand and Grenache, in particular, were a perfect match—one that diligent students of Châteauneuf's Château Rayas had deduced. Farther south, Santa Barbara's Ballard Canyon area offered both sand and, at higher elevations, clay loam and gravel similar to that of Paso Robles. It was far enough inland to get a bit more ripeness than the Santa Rita Hills, although Grenache ripened just fine there, too.

With this fine-tuning of geography came more mature winemaking. If once Syrah was extracted and handled much like Cabernet, lessons learned from the Pinot world—and from the careful study of traditional Rhône producers—began to take hold. Though Syrah's skins were thicker than those of Pinot, the best winemakers began extracting more gently and often used whole clusters during fermentation (see Whole-Cluster Fermentation, page 178) to enhance the aromas—techniques that similarly refined Grenache's profile. (Syrah does need lots more oxygen in the cellar to prevent the sulfurous faults known as reduction, so it can be handled more aggressively than Pinot. Grenache requires just the opposite: little exposure to oxygen.)

THE THREE-BOTTLE TOUR

A Tribute to Grace Santa Barbara Highlands Grenache (page 226)—subtle, aromatic, and duly serious—is a fundamental reconsideration of that grape in California. Syrah, too, is finally getting in touch with its serious side. **Wind Gap Sonoma Coast Syrah** (page 232) is a perfect snapshot of that area's marginal wonders. Finally, **Donkey & Goat Sluice Box** (page 229), a blend of Grenache Blanc and Marsanne, shows both those grapes' beauty, plus the utility of partial skin maceration and, most of all, the dramatic minerality of Sierra Foothills whites.

The use of new oak, which had compounded Syrah's stylistic problems, began to recede. Small oak barrels were increasingly replaced either with larger wooden casks that imparted less flavor—a technique evidently inspired more by the southern Rhône than by producers like Cornas's Thierry Allemand, a patron saint of California Syrah producers—or with concrete vessels that helped enhance texture without adding oak flavor.

Ripeness levels began to drift downward as well, even with a grape like Grenache, which tends to accumulate sugar. Those game-changing Syrahs from marginal areas had uncovered a new audience—and sharpened the stylistic battle lines. Proponents of riper wines bristled, but the success of bottles from Arnot-Roberts and Peay quickly made it clear that California Syrah could find an audience, and that pneumonia need not strike.

TOP PRODUCERS
...
A TRIBUTE TO GRACE

Angela Osborne is on a mission to redefine the greatness of Grenache. Hers is a one-woman show, driven by her cellar experience at Central Coast wineries in Ojai and elsewhere. Grace remains a miniscule effort, producing fewer than a thousand cases, but Osborne's quick ascent and harnessing of the improbable terroir of Ventucopa, in remote Santa Barbara County (see page 164), has become a case study in focus—and winemaking that is by turns fastidious and defiantly spiritual.

Winemaking follows the delicate new school for Grenache: grapes left at least partially in whole

clusters, depending on the lot, mostly foot trod, fermented with indigenous yeasts, and aged in predominantly old oak barrels, although the addition of extra wines has necessitated the use of some tanks. Important winemaking tasks are often performed after Osborne lights a heart-shaped candelabra dubbed "the flaming heart of passion," and, as often as not, when the lunar cycle dictates an advantageous moment. Even without the spiritualism, this is a decidedly traditional, Pinot-like approach to Grenache. While the result may not have the deeper color of more forcefully extracted versions, Grace is not only a tribute to Osborne's grandmother but to the grape's ethereal side.

Grace's 2008 Grenache is particularly worth mentioning, despite it being rained on before fermentation; the rainwater actually balanced out the fruit's robustness—an elemental water addition, if you will. It became one of the most porcelain and transformative wines I've had from California: heady and aromatic.

THE WINES: The defining wine is the **Santa Barbara Highlands Grenache** ($$$), one of California's best examples of that grape, grown in high-elevation loamy sand and fermented with a high proportion of whole clusters in largely neutral wood barrels and puncheons. Osborne's fruit sources vary by year, so there have been additions of **Vogelzang Grenache** ($$) from Santa Ynez Valley and **Shake Ridge Grenache** ($$$) from Amador, and a **Santa Barbara County Grenache** ($$) combining the Highlands with the head-trained vines of Coghlan Vineyard in Happy Canyon, which is also the source for a direct-pressed **Rosé** ($$). In some years there is a high-wire blend of Graciano and Grenache, named in honor of Osborne's other grandmother, Marie.

Osborne also teamed up with Faith Armstrong-Foster (Onward Wines) to launch a label of more affordable table wines. Named Farmers Jane, after the book *Farmer Jane* by sustainability expert Temra Costa, it produces a **Field Red** ($$), a Chenin Blanc–focused **Field White** ($$), and a Grenache-Cinsault **Rosé** ($) from sources in Santa Barbara and Mendocino.

COPAIN WINES

Wells Guthrie started with a rare perspective: The Florida native, raised in Southern California, was a tasting coordinator for the *Wine Spectator*. Wanting to make wine himself, he and his wife headed off to the Rhône Valley, where he spent two years apprenticing to major producer Michel Chapoutier. Upon his return, he worked for Helen Turley and began to chase prominent vineyards, including James Berry in Paso Robles and Garys' in the Santa Lucia Highlands, founding his own label in 1999. Soon his wines, especially his Syrah, were critical darlings. Copain quickly rose to that rank of California labels with an elite mystique.

But Guthrie was increasingly dissatisfied with his own work, finding the wines outsized and tiresome. By 2006 he had decided to pick his grapes earlier. In the subsequent years, he focused more on Mendocino County, and in particular the Kiser Vineyard, in Anderson Valley's so-called deep end, which he established in 2000 as his calling card for Pinot Noir. As his perspective on ripeness changed, the Central Coast wines seemed anemic, and he decided to walk away from those sites and, in turn, lease more acreage in Mendocino County. In 2010 he split his custom-crush facility away from his winery and focused full-time on his own label.

The current Copain lineup is aged in mostly older oak vessels, including large six-hundred-liter demi-muids. Bottles from Jean-Louis Chave and Jura vintner Stephane Tissot on his office windowsill signal where Guthrie's cellar brain is at. He seeks ripeness levels close to 22 or 23 Brix, several points lower than his earlier efforts, uses more whole clusters, and has eased up on extraction. His less expensive wines are released relatively early, as part of a commitment to affordability, but his vineyard designates are often held back. (His 2009s were kept almost three years before release.)

THE WINES: In addition to Pinot Noir, Guthrie makes several tiers of Syrah, most of them late-released, in an aromatic and red-fruited style. Guthrie is particularly taken with the Yorkville Highlands area of Mendocino, south of Anderson Valley. His **Tous Ensemble Syrah** ($$) and **Les Voisins Syrah** ($$), both made in lots of several thousand cases and largely from shale and schist soils in several Mendocino vineyards, are aged in older oak barrels and demi-muids. His single-vineyard choices are also aged mostly in old oak: the **Baker Ranch Syrah** ($$$) from Anderson Valley, grown on sandstone, may be his most fine-boned; to the south, in the Yorkville soils of shale, mica schist and quartz, are designates from both **Hawks Butte** ($$$), at 1,200 feet, and the dramatic, exposed **Halcon** ($$$), at 2,500 feet, both with more roasted and inky flavors. One final nod to the Central Coast: a plummy **Brosseau Syrah** ($$$) from the Chalone appellation. On occasion, there is also **Viognier** ($$), although one of Copain's standouts, a James Berry Roussanne, is no more. See also Pinot Noir (page 187).

DENNER VINEYARDS/KINERO

What connects Denner and Kinero is their winemaker, Anthony Yount. At Denner, his day job, he has found a way to successfully bridge Paso's love for the exuberant with a dose of restraint, making some of the finest Central Coast Rhône-inspired wines.

In part, he has help from his Willow Creek neighborhood, a slice of Paso nestled into the Santa Lucia foothills near the Templeton Gap. Saxum's famed James Berry Vineyard is essentially next door. Denner's 108-acre vineyard on calcium-rich soils, formerly an old barley field, contains nineteen different grapes, everything from Cinsault to Vermentino, although Syrah and Grenache (and thirty-seven acres of somewhat off-message Cabernet) dominate. There's an increased focus on hand tilling and compost to nurture the vines, plus robust Garnacha selections from Spain's Priorat and the Estrella clone of Syrah to diversify the roster.

Since taking over in 2010, Yount has made quiet but important changes at Denner: aging in more large oak puncheons and concrete tanks, using more whole grape bunches, bringing forward the fresh exuberance of Grenache fruit, and adding in lots from other vineyards closer to the ocean that contribute complexity and lift. The alcohol levels have drifted down slightly, although in Paso that can be as much liability as benefit. But as Yount puts it, "There's a lot of talk nowadays about pendulum swings. My approach has always been, I don't want to be on the pendulum."

Kinero, meantime, offers Yount's extraordinary focus on the potential of white wines from Paso. Goaded into making his own wine by his former employer, Cris Cherry of Villa Creek, Yount focused on whites so as not to compete with Paso's dominant fare. He began with Grenache Blanc, and added Roussanne from James Berry.

THE WINES: Denner has two main bottlings, both named in tribute to Ron Denner's earlier career selling earth-moving equipment. The **Ditch Digger**

($$$) finds a perfect balance of whole-cluster spice with Grenache fruit (there's also Syrah, Mourvèdre, Cinsault, and Counoise), and the mix of neutral puncheons and newer oak shows a reasoned approach. In the punchier Syrah-driven **Dirt Worshipper** ($$$), with around 10 percent new oak, whole-cluster Syrah aromatics drive a broad raft of generous fruit that's never unseemly.

The Kinero wines are a study in contrasts. The **Alice Grenache Blanc** ($$) comes from small lots in a range of vineyards, including Luna Matta, Black Seth, and Alta Colina; fermented in steel and concrete, it highlights that grape's profound acidity and freshness (the fruit rarely exceeds 23 Brix) while showing a stony aspect and tremendous complexity. It might be the best example of Grenache Blanc in the state. By contrast, the **Rustler James Berry Roussanne** ($$) is briefly fermented on its skins and aged in a mix of Hungarian oak and concrete, which brings out its rich toasted-almond side. Finally, there's a **Talley Vineyard Chardonnay** ($$), a relatively sharp-eyed take on that well-known Arroyo Grande site.

DONKEY & GOAT

Perhaps a warehouse in zany Berkeley is the perfect spot for Jared and Tracey Brandt to stage their two-person campaign for California minimalism. The Brandts originally migrated to California (she from North Carolina, he from Utah) to work in technology, but in 2001 they managed to convince Eric Texier, one of the Rhône's most prominent non-interventionists, to let them intern with him for nearly a year.

It was their first real introduction to winemaking, and they came back to California with some retrograde ideas about cellar and vineyard work. Texier's resistance to thinning his vineyards and his adherence to biodynamic methods all struck the Brandts as eminently reasonable. As a result, they sought out vineyards that tolerated less pruning and irrigation, to the point of adopting a hands-off approach reminiscent of philosopher Masanobu Fukuoka for a Chardonnay they dubbed Untended.

This approach extends across a wide range of wines, but more than anything the Sierra Foothills have become their chosen spot, with grower Ron Mansfield their scout for everything from Grenache to Vermentino. Nearly everything is crushed by foot and fermented in tanks or neutral wood using indigenous yeasts, almost no sulfur dioxide, and no other additions. Jared did create a stir when he made verjus—tart juice from underripe grapes—from a Chardonnay vineyard to blend into wine as a natural acidity booster, a move radical enough that one winemaker sniped, "Next time I make a soup and it isn't salty enough, I'm just going to take a pee in it."

This was not an unusual reaction to the Brandts, whose winemaking minimalism has made them both emblems of a hands-off approach in the cellar and occasional lightning rods for criticism of that movement. They have also become popular figures among Bay Area wine lovers, who flock to their facility near Berkeley's Fourth Street, where they produce about three thousand cases of wine annually.

THE WINES: The roster is always in flux at Donkey & Goat (the name refers to two field animals the Brandts encountered in France), but their Rhône-tribute white wines, mostly sourced from El Dorado County, are excellent examples of type. They include a **Stone Crusher Roussanne** ($$) that sees partial skin fermentation to add texture, as well as a steely **Grenache Blanc** ($$) and **Sluice Box** ($$), typically a mix of Marsanne and Grenache Blanc that also receives partial skin fermentation. For reds, there's a heady **Broken Leg Vineyard Syrah** ($$) from Anderson Valley, plus the **Prospector Mourvèdre** ($$), **Thirteen** ($$), a southern Rhône–style blend that is renumbered each year (in 2010 it was Five Thirteen), and a **Carignane** ($$) from varying North Coast sources. They branched out beyond the Rhône with several Chardonnays, including the **Untended** ($$) from Anderson Valley, which is also a source for a **Pinot Noir** ($$), and **Isabel's Cuvée Rosé** ($$), a tribute to their daughter.

MARTIAN RANCH

Martian Ranch, a biodynamically farmed twenty-acre property in Los Alamos, is the brainchild of Nan Helgeland and her husband Brian, both long-time Angelenos (Brian wrote the screenplays for *L.A. Confidential* and *Mystic River*) who wanted a hands-on wine project. They combined their sons' names, Martin and Ian, for their remarkably catchy brand name.

Winemaking is overseen by Mike Roth (Grgich Hills, Demetria), who has incorporated some novel ideas into his craft, such as cropping grapes at relatively high levels early on to modulate alcohol levels. They chose some unexpected varieties—Grenache, Mourvèdre, and even Albariño—in a corner of Santa Barbara County that is better known for its rubber-stamp Chardonnay. (Kendall-Jackson is a next-door neighbor.) They also installed three acres of Gamay Noir, extending the migration of the key Beaujolais grape to Santa Barbara.

Roth adds au courant winemaking to this mix, including the use of indigenous yeasts, minimal use of sulfur dioxide, and semicarbonic fermentation for some reds. It remains to be seen whether the Martian Vineyard has soils compelling

Mike Roth

enough for profound wines, but the label serves a far more important purpose: it makes fashionable, thirst-quenching, and, crucially, affordable wines that serve a niche few producers in California are willing to tackle. Theirs is a model worth replicating.

THE WINES: There are both regular and semicarbonic fermentations of Grenache, the **Local Group** ($$) and **Ground Control** ($$), along with the funky-floral **Parallax Mourvèdre** ($$) and a **Red Shift Syrah** ($$), all of which are made in minimal-sulfur versions. Additionally, Martian makes a **Down to Earth Grenache Rosé** ($) from whole-cluster pressed grapes,

and two whites, a **Uforic Albariño** ($$) and **Mother Ship Grenache Blanc** ($$), both aged in a mix of steel and old barrels.

PEAY VINEYARDS

The two Peay brothers, Nick and Andy, and Nick's wife, Vanessa Wong, have become key celebrants of Sonoma's coastal extremes. In some ways their Pinot Noir (at thirty-four acres, to eight of Syrah) is their bigger engine, but at a time when truly finessed Syrah is rare, the Peays have an impressive affinity for the grape. They keep the faith in ways that flirt at the very edge of feasibility, seeing as theirs is one of the state's coldest sites, perpetually stuck in fog. Yet the wines always feel graceful and rich, never shy.

The fifty-one-acre Peay Vineyard outside the town of Annapolis was created from old pasture and timberland. Nick and Andy planted it themselves starting in 1998, and it's now effectively farmed organically by a full-time crew—a considerable expense considering that the property is a hilly forty-mile drive from their winemaking facility in the town of Cloverdale. Wong's winemaking experience at the Peter Michael Winery informs a style that's slightly oak-forward and pristine, and results in wines that need several years of aging in the bottle.

The three together form an essential partnership: Andy is the businessman, and a driving force behind Peay's second label, Cep. Nick is the nutty professor of the bunch, a savvy farmer who suffers no fools on topics like biodynamics ("intellectually fraudulent") and clonal selections. Vanessa is the cautious intellect, at home in the cellar. Peay's fans take great pleasure in their earnest and sometimes nerdy newsletters.

THE WINES: Two pure Syrahs typically come from their Annapolis estate, each from a combination of parcels. The **La Bruma** ($$$) always has the lighter touch, with accents of flowers and white pepper. The **Les Titans** ($$$), named for massive redwoods that rise from their property, is its counterpoint, brooding, chewy, and inky. There's also an occasional **Roussanne/Marsanne** ($$$) and **Viognier** ($$$), depending on yields, which are often less than one ton per acre. As for Cep, there is a **Sonoma Coast Syrah** ($$), plus rotations of **Pinot Noir** ($$), **Sauvignon Blanc** ($$), and a **Rosé** ($$). See also Pinot Noir (page 190).

SKINNER VINEYARDS

A key to improving Sierra Foothills winemaking has been to have a new local producer serious and ambitious enough to redirect the region's more rustic ways. The foothills found that in Skinner, located at 2,740 feet high up in remote Fair Play, the highest average-elevation appellation in California. The winery's ties to the past are deep: founder Mike Skinner is the great-great-great-grandson of James Skinner, a Scottish miner who in 1860 turned his gold into one of the Sierra Foothills' first wineries. But the modern, sleek facility atop a knoll is a grand departure from the foothills' otherwise no-frills tendencies. (Others have tried to fancy up the foothills, mostly in Amador, with far less success.)

A key factor was the hiring of Chris Pittenger from Sonoma. Pittenger did stints at Williams Selyem and Marcassin in Sonoma, and at Torbreck in Australia, and so he came to Fair Play with a measuring stick for seriousness—and a desire to be close to Lake Tahoe, especially during ski season.

Wines come from both nearby sites and young estate vines in two vineyards, one near the Skinner family's historic cellar location (White Oak Flats, located near the town of Rescue at around 1,300 feet) and another at the Fair Play winery (Stoney Creek, on granite soils up to 2,700 feet). For winemaking, a small portion of Grenache and Mourvèdre is fermented with whole clusters; wines are mostly aged in older wood, and increasingly in large casks. Pittenger's preference is for indigenous yeast fermentations, although there's inoculation for the malolactic process. The Skinners are also planting a small historic block of varieties used by their family's original facility: Petite Bouschet, Trousseau, Mission, Carignane, Zinfandel, and more.

The Skinner wines have a delicate side that reveals the minerality of Sierra soils in a way that few local wineries have managed. While many true believers in the Sierra are based near the coast, Skinner has raised the winemaking stakes in the mountains proper.

THE WINES: Skinner makes a wide range of Rhône-inspired efforts, although the most dramatic work can be found in the **El Dorado Grenache** ($$) and **El Dorado Mourvèdre** ($$), each using mostly neutral oak and a mix of estate and purchased fruit. On the white side, the **Grenache Blanc** ($$) is a standout varietal example, while the **Seven Generations White** ($$) deftly mixes Roussanne with Marsanne, Viognier, Picpoul, and Grenache Blanc. There is also varietal **Syrah** ($$) and **Roussanne** ($$) and a blended red **Eighteen Sixty-One** ($$), among others.

WIND GAP/PAX WINE CELLARS

Pax Mahle and his future wife, Pam, began their trek west in Massachusetts, from which they traveled to Scottsdale, Arizona, where they studied in the Master Sommelier program. But as Mahle grew disillusioned with that path, they headed for California, where he initially worked as a wine buyer for Dean & Deluca.

In 2000, at the urging of Copain's Wells Guthrie, the couple launched their own label, Pax Wine Cellars. They focused primarily on Syrah, as Pax had become a routine drinker (when it was still possible) of northern Rhône bottles from Marius Gentaz and Jean-Louis Chave. After an initial round with a consultant who advised adding enzymes and de-alcoholizing the wine, Mahle decided to take over winemaking himself, despite a lack of formal training. The Pax wines quickly became must-haves.

The bliss wouldn't last. Mahle became tangled in disputes with the winery's majority owner, Boston investor Joe Donelan, who in 2008 fired Mahle from his eponymous winery. But Mahle had already planned to launch an alternate label for some lower-alcohol wines from vineyards, such as Majik and Nellessen. And so began his second act, Wind Gap, named in tribute to the gaps in the coastal hills where his best vineyards were situated.

Soon he was sharing space in nearby Forestville with Arnot-Roberts, with whom he originally planned to partner on his new effort. Not only did Wind Gap benefit from Mahle's reputation (if not his first name, which he was barred from using on wines), but since he had renounced the routine use of acid or water additions and had focused on more marginal vineyards, his wines sent an appealing aesthetic message at a time when big-muscle Syrahs had begun to stall. His white wines and Pinot Noir, and his early adoption of concrete eggs (see Innovation in the Cellar, page 254) as a fermentation vessel, found equal favor.

Ultimately, Mahle won back the rights to his name. He revived the Pax label as of 2013, with a hand from investor Charles Banks

(Sandhi, Leviathan). Riper wines live there and under another label, Agharta, while his other efforts remain under Wind Gap.

THE WINES: It's a big roster. The Pax label focuses on Syrah, in particular from three riper sites: Mendocino's **Alden Springs** ($$$), **Griffin's Lair** ($$$) near Petaluma, and **Castelli-Knight** ($$$) near Healdsburg.

As for Wind Gap, its calling card is a **Sonoma Coast Syrah** ($$) that combines lots from Mahle's three vineyard designates: **Nellessen** ($$$) and **Majik** ($$$), both known to his early fans, plus **Armagh** ($$). There's a similar approach with Pinot Noir, a **Sonoma Coast** bottling ($$$), and occasional designates from such vineyards as **Gap's Crown** ($$$). There's also a **Woodruff Vineyard Pinot Noir** ($$$) and **Woodruff Chardonnay** ($$) from farther south, in the Santa Cruz Mountains, plus a **James Berry Chardonnay** ($$) from that Paso Robles site.

There are two old-vine reds, **Bedrock Vineyard Mourvèdre** ($$), from Morgan Twain-Peterson's vineyard, and a **Sceales Vineyard Grenache** ($$), grown on sand in Geyserville, both fermented using carbonic methods in a Beaujolais-Rhône mashup. There is also sometimes a tiny amount of **Ritchie Creek Blaufränkisch** ($$) from a site high on Napa's Spring Mountain. Also look for a skin-fermented **Windsor Oaks Pinot Gris** ($$) and a **Fanucchi-Wood Trousseau Gris** ($$), aged in concrete and bottled early from one of California's last sources of the grape. Bonus: Mahle makes a bit of Arinto, the salty Portuguese grape, from Monterey County, sold in kegs for local consumption.

MORE NOTABLE WINES

ARNOT-ROBERTS: Had this label not excelled with so many other wines, it would be known foremost as a Syrah house—notably because of the 2008 Clary Ranch, which set the current course. The **Clary Ranch** ($$$) from cold southwestern Sonoma remains their defining wine, rarely traveling north of 12 percent alcohol but full of heady pepper scents that have a Pavlovian effect on the grape's true believers. The **Griffin's Lair Syrah** ($$), from the Lakeville area at the eastern end of the Petaluma Gap, is denser and aloe accented. They have stopped designating their Alder Springs wine, but there's a meaty, young-drinking **North Coast Syrah** ($$) blended from several sites. See also Chardonnay (page 200), Cabernet (page 217), The New Whites (page 252), and Back to the Future (page 263).

BROC CELLARS: In addition to his work with other grapes, Chris Brockway shows a certain ingenuity with a wide range of Rhône-native varieties. There's a **Counoise** ($$) from Mendocino's Eaglepoint Ranch, a rare and friendly expression of this Rhône grape. See also the **Cuvée** ($$), mostly Syrah from the Santa Lucia Highlands' Fairview Ranch, perhaps as a commentary on that area's typical ripenesses, he names it according to the vintage's alcohol level (Cuvée 12.5, Cuvée 13.1). Additionally, look for a **Luna Matta Mourvèdre** ($$) from that Paso vineyard, a **Cassia Grenache** ($$) from a rotating variety of sources, a densely textured **Picpoul** ($$) from Paso Robles, and a skin-fermented **Roussanne** ($$). See also Back to the Future (page 264).

CLOS SARON: Israeli native Gideon Bienstock and his wife Saron Rice have been working the northern Sierra, specifically the North Yuba area, for nearly twenty years. Bienstock is the winemaker at nearby Renaissance Vineyards, with its long-aging Cabernet, but he also grafted and planted a small, organically farmed and densely spaced Pinot vineyard near their home in Oregon House Valley, a relatively cool spot in Yuba County. Their **Home Vineyard Pinot Noir** ($$$) is a feisty high-altitude effort. But Bienstock has gotten equal attention for his Rhône-inspired "Unique Cuvées." The **Out of the Blue** ($$) and related **Deeper Shade of Blue** ($$) blend are robust expressions of the Cinsault grape, blended with other components. There's also the Syrah-based **Heart of Stone** ($$); **Cuvée Mystérieuse** ($$), a nonvintage Syrah-Merlot mix; and their white blend, **Carte Blanche** ($$), previously from Renaissance until a fire claimed that vineyard (more recently it's a Lodi mix of Albariño, Verdelho, Chardonnay, and Petit Manseng). In all cases, the cellar work is minimal, with no additions, no commercial yeasts, and no more than a bare minimum of sulfur dioxide. The wines can be rustic and densely tannic, but can also be sublime.

FAILLA: Although Ehren Jordan's label has turned its focus toward Pinot and Chardonnay, the winemaker apprenticed in the Rhône, and that region remains his muse. The wine that perpetually defines Failla's efforts is its **Estate Syrah** ($$$), from dramatically low-yielding, dry-farmed vines that show that grape's adaptability to the Sonoma Coast's far edge. Often fermented entirely with whole clusters (and sometimes right in the barrels), it is always a dramatic, deep, long-aging wine. Sadly, Failla's Phoenix Ranch Syrah, from Napa's Coombsville area, is no longer made. It has been replaced by a bulkier **Hudson Vineyard Syrah** ($$$), also fermented with whole clusters and aged in about one-third new oak. Completing the Rhône side is a miniscule amount of **Viognier** ($$$) from John Alban's vineyard in Edna Valley. See also Pinot Noir (page 183) and Chardonnay (page 201).

FAVIA: Perhaps equally well-known for their Cabernet-focused efforts, Andy Erickson and Annie Favia also make several Rhône-style wines, including the Grenache-dominant **Rompecabezas** ($$$) and a **Lincoln Grenache** ($$$) from Ann Kraemer's Shake Ridge Ranch in Amador, plus the occasional lavish Viognier-based wine. See also Cabernet (page 212).

FOUR FIELDS: After serving as a guide to the Sierra Foothills' finest grapes for wineries such as Donkey & Goat, viticulturist Ron Mansfield and his winemaker son Chuck launched their own label to showcase the beauty of mountain-grown Grenache, in this case from the Fenaughty Vineyard and the family's own Goldbud Farms. Fermentation on the **El Dorado Grenache** ($) is typically indigenous, with ten months in neutral puncheons, which showcases the mineral intensity derived from many of the sites Ron Mansfield farms.

HOLLY'S HILL: Holly and Tom Cooper and their family began planting Syrah in schist-rich Josephine series soils on their steeply sloped Placerville property in 1998, adding a second vineyard in 2000. There's now Grenache, Grenache Blanc, Counoise, Mourvèdre, Viognier, and more. Whites are of particular note, including a **Viognier** ($) that's a perfect example of mineral expression in that grape. Also look for the **Roussanne** ($$) and a range of reds that include the Mourvèdre-dominant **Petit Patriarche** ($) and **Patriarche** ($$) blends, **Grenache** ($), and a rare varietal bottling of spicy **Counoise** ($). Wines

are made by the Cooper's daughter Carrie and her husband, Josh Bendick.

KEPLINGER: Trained at UC Davis and having worked her way through a roster of top Napa wineries, Helen Keplinger could have staked her claim to fame making Cabernet. But time working in Priorat piqued her interest in rocky soils and the grapes (Grenache, Mourvèdre) that traverse both sides of the Pyrenees. She found her happy place in the Sierra Foothills, although she also makes a range of wines from the North Coast. Of note are the Mourvèdre-dominant **Caldera** ($$$), from red soils in El Dorado, and the **Lithic** ($$$), a Grenache-Mourvèdre-Syrah blend from Ann Kraemer's Shake Ridge property. Both are aged in larger used oak vessels, mostly demi-muids.

KESNER: Jason Kesner, who managed Hudson Vineyards in Carneros before becoming assistant winemaker at Kistler Vineyards, is primarily known for his range of stylish Chardonnays; he's a sort of next-generation Steve Kistler, if you will. But he has a hidden winner in his **Old Vines North Coast Grenache** ($$$), from eighty-year-old vines at the McDowell family ranch in Mendocino.

LA CLARINE FARM: Hank Beckmeyer, a former musician for the band Half Japanese, returned stateside from Germany with wine on the brain. His wife, Caroline Hoel, whom he'd met in Munich, was keen to become a cheesemaker. They decamped for the Sierra Nevada, to the town of Somerset, to create a self-contained farm: vines and goats, cellar and dairy. But they also wanted to push beyond the usual farming methods—organics, even biodynamics—and aim for something closer to the minimalism espoused by Masanobu Fukuoka, author of *The One-Straw Revolution*.

Whether that will pay off for their tiny Home Vineyard remains to be seen; the vines have struggled to establish themselves. But Beckmeyer's work with a handful of nearby vineyards has resulted in a light-touch expression from the foothills. After initially using fruit from Lodi and elsewhere, he now relies on his mountain neighborhood for grapes.

With indigenous yeast fermentations, a minimum of sulfur dioxide, and aging in mostly large, older oak, Beckmeyer's winemaking speaks to a certain do-less school. The La Clarine efforts can be rough-edged and pungent at times—the risks of cellar minimalism—but when they succeed they can be revolutionary, as with their two Mourvèdres, both pure expressions of the foothills' complex soils. Either way, the wines are defiant and different, and are helping to rewrite the story of the Sierras. The **Sumu Kaw Mourvèdre** ($$) and **Cedarville Mourvèdre** ($$) are from nearby vineyards in Placerville and Fair Play, on volcanic Aiken series loam and granite, respectively. Both are heady carbonic-maceration interpretations of the Jura's style of lighter reds more than anything typically related to their base grape, and they hover around 12 percent alcohol. There's also an ethereal **Sumu Kaw Syrah** ($$); and the **Piedi Grandi Red** ($$), a blend unexpectedly dominant in Nebbiolo, is noteworthy. Also look for a **Home Vineyard Red** ($$), a **White Blend** ($$) of varying components, and a **Rosé** ($).

LAGIER MEREDITH: Few Californians are better equipped to discuss Syrah in the long view than Carole Meredith, the former UC Davis vine geneticist. Now she and her husband, Steve Lagier (a Robert Mondavi veteran), farm a small portion of the eighty-six-acre property on Napa's Mount Veeder they bought in 1986 and planted eight years later. This is the most intimate sort of winemaking: just the two of them making perhaps five hundred cases annually, using long cellaring and no new oak. The **Syrah** ($$$) is a monolith: packed with spice and demanding several years aging, it is also remarkably focused, making it one of Napa's best examples of the grape. Meredith's geneticist background got the better of her. Knowing that Mondeuse Noire is essentially an uncle of Syrah, she couldn't resist planting some to see how the two grapes responded to the same site. The **Mondeuse** ($$$) can be even more rambunctious and tannic than Syrah, a far cry from its counterparts made in Savoie, but it's also a perfect prism to comprehend Syrah itself. Meredith and Lagier also collaborate on the Chester's Anvil label with their neighbors Aaron Pott (Quintessa) and his wife, Claire. See also Zin's Mystery (page 258).

LEDGE: Mark Adams is a true Paso boy; he was born and raised there and knows it well enough to recall driving ATVs into a pond in his native Templeton. He migrated to Los Angeles, became a musician and sound editor, then returned and became assistant winemaker to Saxum's Justin Smith, a childhood friend. Ledge's **Adams Ranch Syrah** ($$$) comes from his family's forty-acre plot about a mile northwest of the Smiths' James Berry Vineyard, which was purchased in the 1970s and only partially planted starting in 2006. If this part of Paso is all about limestone, Adams's site is sandstone and sand, which allowed him to plant the vines on their own roots—mostly Syrah with a bit of Grenache and Mourvèdre. It's field blended and fermented with indigenous yeasts, using about one-half whole clusters, and aged in neutral oak. Zinfandel, a Rhône-style blend, and a rosé are also forthcoming. Like Denner, Adams offers a promising bridge between Paso's lavish ways and a more cerebral effort.

LEOJAMI: Ben Spencer, an assistant winemaker at Carmel Valley's Bernardus, and his wife, Nadine, a cookbook editor, founded this tiny Monterey-focused label before moving to Sicily in 2012. But they vowed to keep making wine in California. The **Pierce Ranch Grenache** ($$), an exceptionally perfumed version of that grape aged in older oak, highlights southern Monterey's little-known San Antonio Valley. There's also a **Viognier** ($$) from Arroyo Seco, and occasionally **Ræd** ($$), one of the sole American examples of Marselan, a cross of Cabernet Sauvignon and Grenache, in this case from the RBZ Vineyard east of Templeton.

LE P'TIT PAYSAN: This value-minded label from Ian Brand (former assistant winemaker at Big Basin, then at Chualar Canyon) taps mostly Monterey and San Benito fruit for modest, straightforward table wines. Look for the **Viognier** ($) and Grenache-dominant **Le P'tit Pape** ($$) red blend, a perfectly descriptive name for a mini-Châteauneuf.

QUPÉ: Bob Lindquist's history at this Santa Maria winery is the history of California's Rhône faithful. His Bien Nacido Syrahs have had fans for decades, as has the **Central Coast Syrah** ($), still a miracle of affordability. But of particular note is his **Marsanne** ($) from the organically farmed Ibarra-Young site in Santa Ynez Valley and fermented in neutral oak—without the lees, a lesson he learned from Hermitage's Gerard Chave, as they can add a

creamed-corn character. Blended with a bit of Roussanne, this is one of California's great age-worthy whites, improving over a decade or more and priced to suit Lindquist's evangelism. A more recent addition is the **Sawyer-Lindquist Grenache** ($$), grown in his biodynamic Edna Valley estate vineyard.

RHYS VINEYARDS: Kevin Harvey's grand exploration of Santa Cruz terroir isn't just about Pinot Noir. He also makes Syrahs that show the differences between soils and aspects in his nearby vineyards. Sandstone soils give the **Skyline Syrah** ($$$) a burnt-earth, inky character, while the sedimentary-volcanic soil mix for the **Horseshoe Syrah** ($$$) brings out that vineyard's more introvert, briny nature. See also Pinot Noir (page 185).

SALINIA: Obsessed with wine even when he was a high school student near San Jose, Kevin Kelley had a good teacher: wine historian Charles Sullivan, who taught his English class. After a stint at UC Davis, Kelley interned at Burgundy's Méo-Camuzet and was assistant winemaker to Copain's Wells Guthrie before launching his Salinia label in 2003. Kelley's devotion to minimalist practices gave birth to an ambitious project, the Natural Process Alliance, which sold mostly unsulfured wines in steel canteens for consumption within a hundred miles of his Santa Rosa facility. He also did a stint as winemaker for Lioco, although after a tumultuous few years he refocused his efforts on his own label, and in particular on the one wine that launched it: the **Heintz Vineyard Syrah** ($$$) from Charlie Heintz's Sonoma Coast site. Salinia has taken a more free-form approach to recent releases, which include **Mix** ($$), a red blend of of Syrah, Grenache, and more than a half dozen other grapes from Mendocino's Sun Hawk Vineyard; a **Saffron Haze** white blend ($$)

from Russian River Valley; and the **Taken Rustic** ($$) *pétillant naturel* (see Modern Sparkle, page 250).

TABLAS CREEK: The Haas family's grand effort has been a beacon for Paso and for the American Rhône movement. Their wines, both red and white, can be excellent, although in recent years the Tablas wines have been crowded by the competition. The **Esprit de Beaucastel Blanc** ($$), dominated by Roussanne with Grenache Blanc and Picpoul, aged in a mix of older wood casks (*foudres*) plus smaller barrels and steel, shows a keen understanding of the assemblage of Rhône whites. Both red and white versions of the value-minded **Patelin de Tablas** ($), which incorporate fruit from nearby sites mostly in the Adelaida, Estrella, and Templeton Gap areas, are solid responses to California's quest for a home-grown Côtes du Rhône.

TWO SHEPHERDS: Sonoma blogger William Allen channeled his wonkery into this eager young label. Particularly strong is the **Grenache Blanc** ($$), from the Saarloos Vineyard in Santa Ynez Valley, aged mostly in old barrels for eight months. The **Saralee's Vineyard Viognier** ($$), from a beloved Russian River site, is heady but precise, a prototype for how to get that grape right in California. There's also a **Syrah-Mourvèdre** ($$) blend, with Syrah from Saralee's and Mourvèdre from Livermore Valley; some single-varietal reds; and a rare **Centime** ($$), a skin-fermented mix of Marsanne and Roussanne. All the wines are fermented with indigenous yeasts and typically no cellar additions.

VESPER VINEYARDS: Husband and wife Chris Broomell and Alysha Stehly are on a mission, along with Los Pilares (see page 271), to showcase the potential of San Diego County. In Broomell's case it's personal: his family planted vineyards in the Valley Center and Pauma Valley areas during the late 1990s, when he was twelve. Stehly grew up down the road, although the two didn't connect until they were both making wine. (She attended UC Davis; he worked at Santa Barbara's Jaffurs.)

Initially Broomell made wine for his family's Triple B Ranches, but the couple wanted to highlight more obscure grapes than San Diego's tiny winemaking community was used to. They found Marsanne and Roussanne south in remote Ramona Valley, along with the same thirty-year-old Carignane in Pauma that the Los Pilares label uses. These wines do San Diego proud. The **McCormick Ranch Carignan** ($$) has a Seville-orange tanginess and the finesse of good Burgundy. There are two whites, the **Highland Hills Vineyard Alcalá** ($$), a deft combination of Marsanne and Roussanne, aged partially in acacia wood, that shows talent with two finicky varieties; and the Viognier-dominant **Steele Canyon Alcalá** ($$). They're also developing their own biodynamically farmed vineyard, Accipiter Ridge, in an old avocado grove near their Valley Center home.

the vineyard, stand in its midst, surveying it one August afternoon.

"It has always been here," Twain-Peterson tells me, "right in front of everybody's face."

WHEN BLENDS WERE BANISHED

When Bedrock and Arnot-Roberts, along with the Carlisle winery, began making old-vine white blends from Compagni Portis, they were not only reviving an essentially lost tradition; they were also making a larger point about the wisdom of California's white-wine legacy and the options for its future.

A diversity of white grapes has rebounded or appeared anew, challenging—if not threatening—the primacy of Queen Chardonnay. Again, it's worth noting that varietal whites like Chardonnay didn't become fashionable until after World War II, especially in the 1970s. Before then blends were the norm, often coming from a pleasant chaos of varieties planted in the field. In 1890, more than 65 percent of Napa growers were documented to be growing Riesling—although that was just an omnibus term for a mix of Sylvaner, Welchriesling, and more. Hence famous winemakers like André Tchelistcheff were forthright about the composition of a wine like BV Chablis, which was really a mix of Chenin Blanc, Melon, and Colombard.

But blends were increasingly considered inferior—cheap jug swill. Large swaths of grapes like Green Hungarian, once manifest in Napa, all but vanished. None of this is to say that those grapes made great wine. Even in the nineteenth century, some winemakers avoided Grey Riesling (aka Trousseau Gris) in their so-called Riesling blends, finding it devoid of character.

The New Whites

In a largely overlooked corner of the town of Sonoma sits a vineyard called Compagni Portis, and its six scrubby acres tell us a lot about the state of white wine in California. Compagni Portis is a true curiosity, nearly the last of its kind. Originally part of Agoston Haraszthy's Buena Vista property, its white soils rich in volcanic ash have yielded wine grapes since well into the nineteenth century.

Its current form, planted in 1954, is an interplanted muddle of white grapes now considered more historical than practical—Roter Veltliner, Trousseau Gris, Burger—along with the more typical Gewürztraminer and Riesling. Riper grapes like Gewürztraminer balance out tart ones like Burger, ensuring a decent vintage every year. So the vineyard has scraped along over the decades, generally disregarded but surviving even as Chardonnay took the throne.

Morgan Twain-Peterson of Bedrock and Duncan Meyers of Arnot-Roberts, both of whom harvest

For California to rediscover the virtues of white blends, and a broader roster of white grapes, is an affirmation of the past. Or perhaps California is simply catching up to the rest of the world. Elsewhere mixed whites are a noble tradition, as in Italy's Friuli (see Finding Friuli, page 242) or the field blends of Alsace, where vintner Jean-Michel Deiss controversially interplanted top vineyards to highlight site over grape. A wine like Deiss's Engelgarten, with its mix of Riesling, Pinot Gris, Pinot Beurot, Muscat, and Pinot Noir, has spiritual affinity with a place like Compagni Portis.

FRIENDS OLD AND NEW

Blends tell just one part of the New Whites tale. Many white grapes beyond Chardonnay have endured in California. Riesling has been here since the mid-1800s, as have Gewürztraminer, Chasselas, Sylvaner, and so on. While those sometimes went into blends, as with Compagni Portis, they also thrived on their own.

Once-discarded grapes are enjoying a quiet resurrection. Take Chenin Blanc. Some of California's great plantings have been lost to the whims of economics and taste. But the Loire Valley's great grape retains an obscure home in the inland area of Clarksburg, just outside Sacramento, in the river delta. Its current revival happened for the same reason that Clarksburg Chenin found a following among 1970s winemakers: it makes an affordable, friendly wine. A similar renaissance is taking place in Santa Barbara, with the old Chenin vines of the Jurassic Park Vineyard put to new use.

Then we have the curious case of French Colombard, one of California's workhorses. Though you're unlikely to find Colombard on a label, it remains California's second-most-planted white grape, with more than twenty-two thousand acres, almost all of it in the San Joaquin Valley. But Napa winemaker Yannick Rousseau, a native of France's Gascony region, discovered a parcel in Russian River Valley: thirty-five-year-old vines farmed by Butch Cameron, a trucker and fifth-generation grape grower, that had been used to bulk up a nearby winery's Chardonnay. (Another local producer, Woodenhead, uses the same fruit for its Colombard, called Halfshell White.)

Having grown up in Gascony, Rousseau understood Colombard's possibilities. He was happy to pay $800 a ton, well above the state average of $242. "In 2008, when I did my first vintage, my wife said, 'You're crazy to make Colombard,'" he says. "I don't think it was properly made or respected as a variety. So that's my mission."

Increasingly, though, the New Whites are defined by grapes that were never envisioned in the postwar era, when most vintners hoped to emulate the wines of France and Germany. Spain might have been a better inspiration, climatically speaking, for midcentury pioneers. Yet it's peach-scented Albariño, a finicky native of chilly Galicia, that is on the verge of a California breakthrough, rather than Spanish choices like Viura or Godello.

One unexpected starlet in California has been Ribolla Gialla, an obscure high-acid grape native to Italy's northern Friuli region. From a single planting in Napa's Dry Creek area, Ribolla has become a catalyst for change—and its ties to Friuli have inspired some of California's most revolutionary new white wines (see Finding Friuli, page 242).

Many other grapes are being added to the mix. In addition to a bevy of Rhône-native whites, there are also Italian grapes like Malvasia Bianca and Greco, part of a revived focus on what grows

best in a Mediterranean climate. Malvasia has in fact long been a quiet part of California's plantings. Even lowly Trousseau Gris has become a source for fashionable wines from Wind Gap and Jolie-Laide.

If these grapes seem marginal, it's worth remembering how quickly fashion can shift. Consider one grape that had just thirty-three bearing acres in California less than twenty years ago, with perhaps fifteen new acres planted each year. It was barely more than a blip on the radar.

The year was 1994, the grape was Pinot Grigio, and by 2011 it had blossomed to 13,292 acres, making it California's fourth-most-planted white variety. This is despite it being a grape, like Chardonnay,

that is indigenous to northern Europe and not particularly well suited to the climate.

"All the regions in California are totally different," says Matthew Rorick of the Forlorn Hope label, "and it's never made sense to me that California vineyards should grow Cabernet and Chardonnay and Sauvignon Blanc everywhere. With all the variations in temperatures and soils, it just seems to me that we would grow all sorts of interesting things well."

The embrace of California's abundant warmth by winemakers like Rorick has led to other ascendant grapes, like Verdelho, a Portuguese variety that's flourishing in Lodi and the Sierra Foothills.

Same with the fortunes of another Mediterranean grape, Vermentino, commonly found on Sardinia or the Ligurian coast. California examples of Vermentino have become manifest, particularly in places like the Sierra, where granite soils approximate the grape's Sardinian home of Gallura. While Vermentino in California began with pioneering but mild versions from labels like Uvaggio and Mahoney, it is getting more serious consideration from labels like Ryme Cellars, just as producers like Bisson and Giacomelli in Italy's Liguria elevated the grape there.

SAUVIGNON'S SALVATION

Amid this growing roster of white grapes, some of the best white-wine innovation is taking place with a grape long exploited in California: Sauvignon Blanc. It has admittedly been a victim of endless dumbing down. But Sauvignon Blanc's use as the base material for serious wine is less surprising when you consider its role in past innovations. In 1968, Robert Mondavi relabeled it as Fumé Blanc, made it in an oak-focused style, and launched a love affair with the grape.

The problem with Sauvignon Blanc? It is generally considered a cash crop, made for a quick buck, to the point that critics have doubted whether

FINDING FRIULI

California's white-wine revival hit its pinnacle with what can be called neo-Friulian wines. The northern Italian region of Friuli, which abuts Slovenia, is one of the few places in the world where whites are considered wine's most serious expression. This has made it a hotbed of innovation, with wines like Vintage Tunina, from vintner Silvio Jermann, who combined Sauvignon Blanc and Chardonnay with indigenous Friulian grapes like Malvasia Istriana, Picolit, and high-acid Ribolla Gialla. It was also home to Josko Gravner and Stanko Radikon, pioneers who revived the old practice of fermenting white wines on their skins, creating so-called orange wines, often aging them in large clay amphorae.

Friuli has become California's most curious inspiration. Credit George Vare, who decided, after a long career that included buying the Geyser Peak Winery and launching Luna Vineyards, to plant a Ribolla Gialla vineyard in Napa—a logical extension, perhaps, of his earlier work at Luna Vineyards, which, thanks to Luna partner John Kongsgaard, became a catalyst for white-wine innovation.

Vare's eight acres became a seed grant for pioneering winemakers, parceled out to a collection of Friuli devotees who participated in Vare's annual Ribolla Gialla symposium, producers like Massican, Arbe Garbe, and, of course, Steve Matthiasson.

"Ribolla truly tastes like rocks," Matthiasson says. "I was a Boy Scout growing up in Arizona and our scout leader would have us suck on rocks when we were hiking. So I loved the flavor of rocks."

Vare organized trips to Friuli for winemakers like Abe Schoener and Matthiasson. While others were enticed by skin fermentations and amphorae, Matthiasson was taken with producers like Miani, where Enzo Pontoni used super-low yields and a fair amount of new oak in a more stylish Friulian interpretation. The impact of Vare's efforts soon became clear: he had quietly laid the groundwork for a new era of white wines in Napa, and really throughout California.

California can make a truly great one. Serious past attempts usually paid less attention to the grape itself and more to a big dose of new oak and an even bigger dose of pretense.

Now comes a new wave. Versions of Sauvignon Blanc made at Spottswoode, in St. Helena, and elsewhere take advantage of the full range of more serious winemaking techniques (see Innovation in the Cellar, page 254). In some cases, the inspiration comes from Friuli, which explains the grape's presence in wines from Massican and Matthiasson. But vintners are also tipping their hat to the Loire Valley, and specifically to the work of Didier Dagueneau, who used the grape as fodder for experimentation with cigar-shaped barrels, long fermentations, and soaking juice on the grape skins to achieve greater depth.

Sémillon, Sauvignon Blanc's companion grape in Bordeaux, is similarly attracting new regard. It has long had fans like Terry Leighton of Kalin Cellars, whose late-released versions have their own devoted following. Now versions from labels like Forlorn Hope are underscoring its suitability for California's warmer stretches.

TOP PRODUCERS
* * *
ARBE GARBE

Enrico Bertoz and Letizia Pauletto have devised the ultimate California tribute to Friuli, perhaps because they both grew up in that region of Italy. Bertoz's father was the local tractor-tire dealer, which gave his family ties to many local vintners. So the couple, already high school sweethearts, found themselves working the harvest for local vintner Silvio Jermann.

Bertoz also knew the Nonino family, makers of some of Italy's top grappas, who connected him with Los Angeles restaurateur Piero Selvaggio. Bertoz worked in the wine cellar of Selvaggio's Valentino restaurant, where he discovered the wines of Manfred Krankl, whose Sine Qua Non was becoming a very different sort of California cult wine.

Bertoz worked two harvests for Krankl before he and Pauletto got married and moved to Napa. In 2007 they secured fruit from Russian River Valley for their tribute to Friuli, a mix of Pinot Grigio and Malvasia. In particular the couple began a shadow campaign to revive the fortunes of much-dismissed Pinot Grigio.

Arbe Garbe follows in the best Friulian traditions: grapes might be destemmed and soaked on the skins for more than a day to gain flavor and texture, then fermented in neutral oak. In 2010, the Malvasia was partially dehydrated in a cold room—a technique learned from Krankl—to concentrate flavors. Skillful blending puts those pieces back together in wines that are powerful, exuberant with fruit, and yet remarkably precise.

THE WINES: Their **Arbe Garbe White** ($$) is a constantly evolving blend, recently a mix of Pinot Grigio, Malvasia, and Gewürstraminer, the last of which replaced Ribolla Gialla given that grape's short supply. Its mineral kick balances a floral freshness and dense fruit. An increasingly successful offshoot is the varietal **Malvasie** ($$), with orange-blossom and olive accents, and a density reminiscent of the Carso region that bridges Italy and Slovenia. Pauletto and Bertoz also plan to make additional varietal white wines from old-vine vineyards, and as of 2013 were adding a red blend.

BOKISCH VINEYARDS

Markus Bokisch is on a quest to make Lodi a great place for Iberian varieties. In part, it's a tribute to his Catalan heritage, but he also once lived in Spain with his wife, Liz. And, thanks in part to his time as a viticulturist for Joseph Phelps Vineyards, he saw that grapes like Grenache (he calls it Garnacha) and Verdelho could thrive in Lodi's hot stretches in a way that Chardonnay couldn't.

Bokisch has become one of Lodi's most prominent vineyard managers (see page 140), but his own wines are also a fantastic snapshot of Lodi's abilities. His hand with whites is particularly deft, as evidenced in his two single-vineyard Albariños. He still sells much of his Verdelho fruit, but with these two grapes he has made a case for Iberian white grapes in California. And his red Garnacha stands to rewrite beliefs about Lodi's potential with subtle red wines.

THE WINES: Of the two Albariños, the **Terra Alta Albariño** ($), from volcanic-derived clay loam soils in the Clements Hills area of southeastern Lodi, is more focused and stony, while the **Las Cerezas Albariño** ($), from silty soils in the Mokelumne River area, is plusher. From the heavier soils of Borden Ranch comes **Vista Luna Garnacha Blanca** ($), a ripe, stately example of that grape, and the **Vista Luna Verdelho** ($). There's also the **Terra Alta Garnacha** ($) from Clements Hills, a radiant example of that grape in a warmer climate, plus his other Spanish tributes, **Tempranillo** ($$), **Monastrell** ($$), and **Graciano** ($$).

FORLORN HOPE

Matthew Rorick was drawn to water before wine: he surfed as a Southern California teenager, then served in the Navy during the First Gulf War. Afterward, he returned to Oceanside, near San Diego, and moved in with his grandfather David, a wine enthusiast. David Rorick encouraged his grandson to study enology, and backed it up with a deep cellar of old wines. Rorick made his way to UC Davis, but ultimately he decided to pursue a more minimal winemaking path: adding no yeast or acid, and using grape stems to ferment most of his red wines.

After stints in Chile and South Africa and a winemaking spell at Napa's Elizabeth Spencer label, Rorick focused on his own tiny project—turning out microbatches of whites like his densely textured Que Saudade Verdelho from the Sierra Foothills and reds like the Gascony Cadets Petit Verdot from the obscure Suisun Valley east of Napa, all of which he dubbed his "rare creatures"—fitting, since they're typically made in lots of less than 2,500 bottles.

The winery's name, incidentally, is a twist on *verloren hoop*, a Dutch term referring to soldiers chosen as the first wave in an offensive. While massive casualties were commonplace, survivors reaped significant benefits.

Rorick has become somewhat better defined by his white wines than his reds, including the Nacré Sémillon, a tribute both to Australia's Hunter Valley and to the long-aging examples from Kalin Cellars. Sourced from 1950s-era vines in Andy Hoxsey's Yount Mill Vineyard in Yountville, its fruit rarely surpasses 20 Brix, or 11 percent alcohol, to make a wine that is almost searing in acidity when young. Seeing as Hunter Sémillons can barely find an audience in the United States, Rorick's endeavor might take some championing. "There still might not be much money in it, but there's glory to be had," he says.

With his Que Saudade, Rorick has particularly elevated the Portuguese grape Verdelho, primarily known as a component of Vinho Verde but here tapping sources in Amador County and Lodi for an effort that rivals the most serious European versions.

THE WINES: The **Nacré Sémillon** ($$) exudes that grape's long-lived glinting green flavors along with with fig and mint accents. Released more than three years after harvest, it's a nearly electric foil for oysters. By contrast, the **Lu Oituna Torrontés** (¢), from the Silvaspoons Vineyard in Lodi's Alta Mesa area, is crushed in a basket press to preserve its young, blossomy aromas. The **Que Saudade Verdelho** ($$), typically from a site at 1,500 feet near the town of Plymouth, matches that variety's lime-rickey signature with deep nectar fruit. There's also the **Sihaya Ribolla Gialla** ($$), another expression from Vare; and an almost austere expression of dry Gewürztraminer, the **Faufreluches** ($$), a reference to please Frank Herbert fans. See also Back to the Future (page 270).

GROUND EFFECT

Dissatisfied with the heftiness of the wines he was making, Nick de Luca walked away from a prestigious job with the Dierberg and Star Lane labels to found his own tiny project, which would focus on the wines he wanted to drink at home.

De Luca's ability to find profound flavors in generally overlooked Chenin Blanc—in his case from thirty-five-year-old vines planted in the Jurassic Park Vineyard in the Foxen Canyon area of Los Olivos—is head turning. He initially blended it with Viognier, making a more serious iteration of the combo that Napa's Pine Ridge made famous.

De Luca coferments the grapes together, beginning in stainless steel before switching to neutral wood, aging for ten months on the lees to build texture. He insists that this switch of vessels helps to freshen the wine by keeping the lees healthy. "For me," he says, "lees are really the lifeblood."

THE WINES: The **Gravity Check** white ($$) began as predominantly Chenin Blanc with a bit of Viognier, although more recently it evolved into a mix of Chenin, Albariño, and Pinot Gris, the latter two from Edna Valley. The **Rock Garden** red ($$), aged in old oak barrels, combines Grenache, Counoise, and Syrah from Paso Robles near the Cuesta Ridge area, and de Luca added a **Never Say Never Syrah** ($$$), also from Paso, fermented with indigenous yeast and all whole clusters. In 2011 the latter landed at just 13.2 percent alcohol.

MASSICAN

Raised in Brooklyn, schooled at Columbia, and a veteran of the New York magazine business, Dan Petroski was an unlikely candidate to start making wine in Napa. But after a year interning at Sicily's

Valle dell'Acate winery, he came to California to apprentice with DuMol's Andy Smith.

Smith secured Petroski a day job making Cabernet for Calistoga's Larkmead. But Petroski wanted to find local, fresh white wines he could enjoy with a meal at day's end, so he launched Massican in tribute to the Italian whites he loved.

Petroski's wines find a happy balance between Italian freshness and California ripeness. His Gemina blend tends to be dominated by the flesh of Napa Chardonnay, while his Annia combines Ribolla with the floral intensity of Tocai Friulano from the Nichelini Vineyard in eastern Napa.

The wines are typically aged in a mix of steel and used oak, with malolactic fermentation blocked, then often filtered and bottled the following spring. While Petroski envisions his wines being consumed quickly, they will likely evolve and deepen with age.

THE WINES: Massican's defining wine is the **Annia** ($$), which fills out Ribolla's icicle sharpness with Friulano and Chardonnay. For contrast, the **Gemina** ($$), which is predominantly—and often exclusively—Chardonnay, offers a richer counterpoint. A **Sauvignon Blanc** ($$) shows an almost salty aspect that's rare for Napa, and there's also an occasional sweet **Passito** ($$$) from Sauvignon Blanc, as well as a tiny-production **Vermouth** ($$).

MATTHIASSON

More than any other wine, Steve Matthiasson's white blend has changed the conversation about Napa's potential, and about the possibilities for white wine in California.

The Matthiasson white combines elements of Bordeaux (Sauvignon Blanc, Sémillon) and Friuli (Ribolla and almond-accented Tocai Friulano). Matthiasson propagated Friulano in George Vare's

vineyard from 1800s-era cuttings off Calistoga's Larkmead Vineyard. They may not actually be Friulano; more likely they include an unidentified mix of other grapes. (What Californians call Tocai Friulano is in fact sometimes Muscadelle, Bordeaux's lesser-known white variety, in part because some called Muscadelle by another name, Sauvignon Vert, which is also a synonym for Friulano.)

Winemaking here is relatively straightforward, typically in a mix of tank and barrel, but Matthiasson is a strong believer in cofermenting white wines. His Sauvignon Blanc typically comes in earlier than the other grapes, so he begins to barrel-ferment it while awaiting the others. When they arrive, he presses those into a tank, adds the Sauvignon Blanc, and continues fermentation. The wine is not shy on oak, often being made in as much as one-half new wood, although many of the barrels are special ones from the producer Boutes that minimize oak flavors. In Friulian fashion, the fruit quickly absorbs the wood influence.

THE WINES: Dramatic and profound, Matthiasson's **Napa Valley White** ($$) often finds more depth after six to twelve months in the bottle. As the oak integrates, it shows rich citrus, the quicksilver edge of Sémillon and Ribolla, and a chervil-like nuance. Matthiasson also makes several rarities: an exotic varietal **Ribolla Gialla** ($$$), fermented on its skins in an old barrel in Matthiasson's barn; a varietal **Sémillon** ($$$) redolent of green olives; **Napa Valley Flora** ($$$), a dessert wine made from a rare cross of Gewürztraminer and Sémillon; and a **Rosé** ($$). See also Chardonnay (page 203) and Cabernet (page 218).

RYME CELLARS

Ryan and Megan Glaab both grew up in California, Ryan in the Orange County town of Ontario and Megan in Carmel. But it took a trip to Australia for them to meet. They first got acquainted when both worked at Torbreck in the Barossa Valley.

Torbreck's Dave Powell later helped Ryan get a job working for the iconoclastic Manfred Krankl at Ventura's Sine Qua Non. When Megan also returned to California, the couple settled in Sonoma.

Their first joint wine was red, a 2007 Aglianico. But Ryan was taken with the white Ribolla Gialla grape. In 2008 he visited Stanko Radikon in Friuli, and in another case of making California connections far afield, Radikon tipped him off to a guy in Napa—George Vare, of course—who was growing the stuff.

Yet it's a different Italian grape they have finessed: Vermentino. The two had the opportunity to buy some from Francis Mahoney's silt-and-gravel Carneros parcel. Since they had already made a skin-fermented Ribolla Gialla for their tiny label, Ryan proposed to do the same with Vermentino. "My wife said that was a terrible idea," he recalls. "She didn't think that we needed another orange wine."

Megan preferred to pay homage to the salty whites of Liguria and Sardinia, where the grape is native. So they each made their own, His and Hers, two radically different wines.

THE WINES: Fermented on its skins, the **His Las Brisas Vineyard Vermentino** ($$) is ripe and resinous. It's inspired by Friuli and Sardinian rebels like Dettori but shows restraint in the technique. The saline **Hers Las Brisas Vineyard Vermentino** ($$) comes from the same source, but the inspiration is different, with more traditional aging in

THE NEXT BIG THING?

Between the comparison of California regions to Mediterranean locales, vintners' worries about climate change, and the increasing popularity of grapes like Verdelho and Vermentino, there is momentum to find white varieties that properly speak California's language. That's why UC Davis researcher James Wolpert planted fifty-five new varieties, including such Sicilian whites as Grillo and Carricante, at the research station at Kearney, in the hot San Joaquin Valley.

His goal wasn't necessarily to find a great new grape for the San Joaquin Valley's large-scale farmers. Instead, Wolpert wanted to identify which grapes might be used for a bit of blending, or which might ultimately have the same warm-weather utility as Verdelho. He grew weary of witnessing how the state's grape researchers focused primarily on disease-free vines rather than exploring which new grapes might be appropriate for the climate.

Wolpert decided to move beyond Davis's Franco-centric habits and plant a grab bag of varieties, both red and white, that thrive in warmer countries, including the Sicilian selections mentioned above plus Trebbiano and Timorasso from central Italy, Godello from Spain, and Petit Manseng from France. For him, experimenting in the hot Central Valley is the way to reopen the discussion of which grapes might truly suit California—much as E. W. Hilgard did more than a century ago.

"Once we start on our warmest region for winegrowing, it might inform what Napa Valley might do if it gets warmer than it is now," Wolpert says. "I think there's a treasure trove of varieties there. All we need to find is a couple."

Abe Schoener

old wood using indigenous yeast. Their **Vare Vineyard Ribolla Gialla** ($$) modulates that grape with subtler skin contact than many versions. They also make a heady, bright **Cabernet Franc** ($$) from the Alegria Vineyard in Russian River Valley, as well as an occasional Cabernet and Aglianico. In 2011, they launched their second label, Verse, for Chardonnay and Pinot Noir.

SCHOLIUM PROJECT

No discussion of current California wine would be complete without talking about Abe Schoener (see page 15). While Schoener's wines initially were more experimental, and daringly high in alcohol, in recent years they have become more nuanced—less outré and more reflective of their origins.

This is not to say the Scholium wines don't retain their quirks: rather than a varietal name or even an appellation beyond "California," most wines receive a fanciful name, often a nod to Schoener's past as a classics scholar (witness the botrytized Sauvignon Blanc known as Cena Trimalchionis, or "Trimalchio's dinner," a reference to the *Satyricon*). But they also typically list the vineyard source, to highlight for customers the specificity of place.

THE WINES: There's no way to keep up with Scholium's endless process of reinvention. Perhaps the biggest constant in Schoener's lineup is **The Prince in His Caves** ($$$), deeply textured skin-fermented Sauvignon Blanc from Sonoma's Farina Vineyard; the prince referred to here is Alberico Boncompagni Ludovisi, the reclusive Italian nobleman whose white wines earned a rabid following. From the same site, the contrasting **La Severita di Bruto** ($$$) is a Sauvignon Blanc aged more conventionally in steel and neutral barrels. There also are several Verdelho-based wines, including the **Naucratis** ($$), at least partially from the Lost Slough Vineyard, below sea level in the Sacramento delta, the name a reference to an ancient city in the Nile delta mentioned by Herodotus, along with the **Wisdom of Theuth** ($$), a occasional version of Naucratis that's partially barrel-fermented and more intense. By contrast, the **Marcher sur la Lune** ($$) has been a more immediate Verdelho from Markus Bokisch's Lodi property. That fruit also makes up the core of the **Midan al-Tahrir** ($$), a blend from six vineyards and eight blend components, its name a tribute to the Cairo square.

The **Rhododactylos Rosé** ($$), also from Lodi, is in fact less pink and more blanc de noirs, made from ancient Cinsault vines in the Bechtold Vineyard and redolent of orchard fruit, with a name from Homer's *Odyssey* (it means "rosy fingered"). Back to the delta, there's the **Riquewihr** ($$), Schoener's high-octane Gewürztraminer tribute to Alsace, in a squat 500 ml bottle. Additionally there is the **Glos** ($$$), an old-vine Sauvignon Blanc from Napa; **FTP** ($$), a Pinot Grigio from Lodi's Kirschenmann Vineyard; and several Chardonnays (Michael Faraday, Chuy, and others). See also Back to the Future (page 273).

TATOMER

Graham Tatomer was taken enough with Austrian wine to convince Wachau master Emmerich Knoll to give him an apprenticeship. But his efforts are all about California, specifically Santa Barbara, and he also has worked for Brewer-Clifton and with Adam Tolmach of the Ojai Vineyard, who ultimately connected him with some of his best grape sources.

In addition to a couple of Grüner Veltliners—he taps the same Edna Valley fruit as the Zocker label—Tatomer's calling cards are a pair of serious Rieslings from the Highway 135 corridor in Los Alamos, the front stoop of Vandenberg Air Force Base. Often the wines show a phenolic depth that nods to Tatomer's time in the Austrian heart of white wine. These are among that rare California breed of Rieslings that welcome, and perhaps require, time in the cellar.

"It's just such a serious variety," he says, "that if you take it seriously, it will age."

THE WINES: The **Vandenberg Riesling** ($$) and designate **Kick-On Ranch Riesling** ($$) come from the same Los Alamos site. Both are dry and get extra time to settle in bottle, and the latter gets ten hours soaking on its skins and evokes something closer to a riper Smaragd in style, speaking in Wachau terms. To these have been added recent efforts from the **Sisquoc** ($$) and **Lafond** ($$) Vineyards, the latter first planted in 1972. There also is Grüner Veltliner, including a **Paragon** Vineyard ($$) bottling and more recently one called **Meeresboden** ($$)—meaning "ocean soil"—sourced from several vineyards, including the John Sebastiano site at the eastern edge of the Santa Rita Hills.

MODERN SPARKLE

California's pursuit of Champagne dates to the nineteenth century. By the late 1800s San Francisco was awash in home-grown sparkling wines made by Agoston Haraszthy and the Italian-Swiss Colony wine concern, and the pursuit of a Champagne analogue had sent Paul Masson into the hills above Saratoga, where he planted high-quality vine cuttings from France.

Masson and Korbel were among the few producers of sparkling wine to survive Prohibition, but love for wines made using the labor-intensive *méthode champenoise* waned until Jack and Jamie Davies launched Schramsberg in Calistoga in 1965. Another boost came when European Champagne houses started to establish California outposts, beginning with Moët & Chandon in 1973. By the 2000s, these long-established players had solidified their places in the market (and a few others, like Maison Deutz in Arroyo Grande, had faded away).

Today there is a quality schism. Some producers—including,

notably, **Roederer Estate**—are turning out excellent sparklers at relatively large volumes, while others have fallen into a sort of clock-punching stupor. Among California originals, **Schramsberg** in particular is stronger than ever. Not everyone has maintained their finesse, however: Sebastopol's Iron Horse, a pioneer of small-scale sparkling wines, has shifted toward bigger, more rough-hewn wines.

A handful of new sparkling projects have emerged since the late 2000s, perhaps none more ambitious than **Under the Wire**, launched by Bedrock's Morgan Twain-Peterson and his friend Chris Cottrell. Dedicated to batches of single-vineyard sparkling wine, it operates in the spirit of Champagne microproducers like Cédric Bouchard. Starting in 2011, they produced wines from the Brosseau Vineyard in the Chalone area and from Mendocino's Alder Springs, as well as a Lambrusco-style sparkling Zinfandel from Bedrock itself.

California has also ushered in a modest embrace of *pétillant naturel*, a style of lightly sparkling wine adopted from Europe's naturalistas. Rather than having sugar and yeast added to bottles for a Champagne-style second fermentation, these are bottled with enough of each to complete sparkling fermentation on their own.

"*Pet-nat*," with its sometimes beery yeast flavors, doesn't appeal to all comers, and it often requires an elaborate procedure to open the bottle so that it expels the built-up lees—similar to the Lunar wines from Slovenia's Movia, which needed to be submerged in water before being opened, making serving them something of a sommelier's party trick. But it has been embraced as part of California's artisan boom. A roster of bottles includes Salinia's **Taken Rustic** blend, reminiscent of Andrea Calek's polarizing Blonde from France's Ardèche; and **Lily's Cuvée** from Donkey & Goat, which comes complete with hand-drawn disgorging instructions.

VERDAD

In 2000, Louisa Sawyer Lindquist decided to create a label to highlight Spanish varieties in California, a counterpoint to the Rhône-inspired work of her husband, Bob Lindquist, who founded Qupé.

Two years later, the Lindquists found a rolling property in receivership in chilly Edna Valley, and soon they began planting Albariño, sagely predicting the state's embrace of this grape. With the harvest of their biodynamically farmed estate, the label's two Albariños became benchmark efforts for the variety in California.

Typically fermented with indigenous yeasts and aged in steel and neutral barrels, the Verdad whites show a textural weight and aromatic complexity that is so often missing in many examples from the grape's home in Rías Baixas. The Lindquists are in fact paving the way to make Albariño one of California's next great whites.

THE WINES: The **Sawyer-Lindquist Vineyard Albariño** ($$) is a serious bay-leaf-edged take on the grape that shows the virtue of great farming—and makes a strong case for Edna Valley as a stronghold for aromatic whites. The **Santa Ynez Valley Albariño** ($), from the organically farmed Ibarra-Young near Los Olivos (also a source for Qupé's Marsanne), is a more basic but refreshing wine. There's also Tempranillo and rosé.

MORE NOTABLE WINES

ACHA: Winemaking talent Mark Herold (Merus, Kamen) is covering new territory with his Mark Herold Wines portfolio, which also includes the Flux and Collide labels. Herold, a Panamanian native who studied biochemistry at UC Davis, is one of the most laboratory-focused winemakers in the state. This can lead to analysis-driven results, but it also results in wines like his polished, ripe **Blanca** ($$), made with 100 percent Albariño from Lodi's Vista Luna Vineyard, fermented in concrete eggs (see Innovation in the Cellar, page 254) and heavy on Riesling-like aromatics; and his **Flux Blanc** ($$), a mix of Grenache Blanc and Roussanne.

ARNOT-ROBERTS: While Duncan Meyers and Nathan Roberts have their hands in a lot of wines, their two more esoteric whites are quintessential examples of their style. Their **Vare Vineyard Ribolla Gialla** ($$) is edgy and precise, although it's gaining flesh as Meyers and Roberts increasingly use clay amphorae for fermentation. Their nervy **Compagni Portis Old**

Vine White ($$) shows the remarkable possibilities of a white field blend. See also Chardonnay (page 200), Cabernet (page 217), Revising the Rhône (page 233), and Back to the Future (page 263).

BEDROCK WINE CO.: While Morgan Twain-Peterson is on a crusade to bring glory to Sonoma's old red field blends, his work with white grapes produces equally complex and engaging wines. The **Compagni Portis Vineyard Heritage White** ($$), a plusher expression of that site, is a mix of Gewürztraminer, Trousseau Gris, Riesling, Berger, and Roter Veltliner. The **Cuvée Karatas** ($$) is Morgan's tribute to Bordeaux, a mix of 120-year-old Sémillon from Monte Rosso Vineyard and Sauvignon Blanc from Kick Ranch. Also look for a **Casa Santinamaria White** ($), a mix of Muscadelle, Chasselas, Sémillon, and more, from 1905 vines, and a rosé, **Ode to Lulu** ($), named for the proprietress of Bandol's Domaine Tempier. Twain-Peterson also makes the **Abrente Albariño** ($$), a project launched with Napa winemaker Michael Havens, who pioneered that variety on the North Coast. See also Back to the Future (page 264).

BIRICHINO: Bonny Doon veterans John Locke and Alex Krause have created this Monterey-focused label, and in addition to a **Veilles Vignes Grenache** ($$) from Gilroy's Besson Vineyard and some Pinot Noir, they have placed their bets on **Malvasia Bianca** ($), an example fermented in steel with deft lees handling that brings out the best of a grape long overlooked in California.

BLUE PLATE/PICNIC WINE CO.: Grant Hemingway of Napa Sauvignon Blanc specialist Mason Cellars founded this label with friends Zach Bryant and Jeff Anderson in 2010. Their breezy, apricot-edged

Blue Plate Chenin Blanc ($) revives the tradition of affordable Chenin Blanc from Clarksburg, in the Sacramento River delta.

BRACK MOUNTAIN: This ambitious Sonoma project combines estate land in Dry Creek Valley with purchased fruit under a wide range of labels (Origine, Fable, Daniel, and others). The winemakers are Dan Fitzgerald (formerly at Williams Selyem and Pellegrini Family) and Visalia native John Harley (Donum Estate). Their whites in particular are worth seeking out, among them the **Origine Sauvignon Blanc** ($), from the Louvau Vineyard near Santa Rosa, and the rare **Fable Sauvignon Vert** ($), from 1930s vines in Dry Creek Valley.

BRANDER: This Santa Ynez label has made its name on Sauvignon Blanc. Of note is their **Au Naturel Sauvignon Blanc** ($$), a tribute of sorts to Didier Dagueneau and the Loire Valley. Left on its skins for a day, then fermented in steel, it's polished and dense, with intense hay, mineral, and grapefruit flavors.

FIELD RECORDINGS: Andrew Jones's tiny label makes a range of red and white wines, but Chenin Blanc is their forte, both the old-vine **Old School** ($), another specimen from the Jurassic Park Vineyard, and an **Acacia-Aged** ($$) version.

GAMLING & MCDUCK: Aside from its show-poster design aesthetics, this tiny Napa label has developed a reputation for its Loire-inspired wines. In addition to a rare Cabernet Franc, the wine to look for is the **Jurassic Park Vineyard Chenin Blanc** ($$), from the same Santa Ynez source used by Nick de Luca, here fermented with native yeasts in barrel and aged for seven months in neutral oak.

HABIT: Los Angeles voice actor Jeff Fischer took on winemaking as his other career, with a focus on whites from the Santa Ynez Valley. Fischer is yet another partisan of the Jurassic Park site, and his **Jurassic Park Chenin Blanc** ($$) uses its old vines for a deep dried-apricot effect. There's also **Grüner Veltliner** ($$), from dry-farmed vines in Los Olivos, aged in steel; a stony **Sauvignon Blanc** ($$) from the Curtis Vineyard; and several red wines. His base in Los Angeles has given him a growing following among the city's restaurants.

JOLIE-LAIDE: As there has until recently been essentially one source for the lightly tinted Trousseau Gris grape in California (the Fanucchi Vineyard in Russian River Valley), it's hard to say it's a thing. But onetime sommelier Scott Schultz, an assistant at Pax Mahle's Wind Gap, banked his tiny label on it. That effort paid off with the 2011 vintage of the **Fanucchi Vineyards Trousseau Gris** ($$), destemmed and left on its skins for five days until it was "electric pink," according to Schultz. The color largely precipitated out, but the resulting wine had a textural bite and wintergreen freshness that has brought a reconsideration of a previously disregarded grape. Schultz was also expanding to Pinot Gris and a Syrah-based red.

KALIN CELLARS: The work of former microbiology professor Terry Leighton and his wife Frances, based in Marin County, has enjoyed a small but loyal following since Kalin's first release of Sémillon in 1979. Leighton also makes Pinot Noir, Chardonnay, and Sauvignon Blanc, but his calling card is the **Livermore Valley Sémillon** ($$), barrel fermented from 1880s-era vines on the Wente estate planted from cuttings thought to be from Château d'Yquem, with a bit of Sauvignon Blanc blended in. The twist? Leighton often releases the wine a decade or more after vintage. This would make him a lover of lost causes, but the wine ages pristinely, and Leighton has more than been proven correct in his lone view of what grape the deep, gravelly soils of Livermore (similar to Bordeaux's Graves area) can grow best.

LEO STEEN: Denmark native Leo Hansen left his sommelier job at Copenhagen's Kong Hans to explore wine in California. His label, founded in 2004, takes inspiration from its second word—both his middle name and the South African name for Chenin Blanc. His **Dry Creek Valley** ($) version, from thirty-year-old vines and aged in neutral wood, has gained a reputation as Sonoma's answer to the snappy dry Chenins of the Loire.

PALMINA: Steve Clifton of Brewer-Clifton and his wife, Chrystal, were married in Friuli, so it makes sense that even in the Pinot-loving heart of Lompoc they would carry a banner for Italianate wines. Palmina's whites from a range of Santa Barbara sources show a deep understanding of northern Italian source material, including one of California's pioneering bottlings of **Tocai Friulano** ($)— and an orange-wine version of that grape, **Subida** ($$)—plus an **Arneis** ($), **Malvasia Bianca** ($$), **Traminer** ($$), and one of the state's few compelling examples of **Pinot Grigio** ($). In addition there is a handful of reds—Nebbiolo, Barbera, Dolcetto— and, in the spirit of curiosity, **Lumina** ($$$), a sparkling Nebbiolo.

PARR WINES: In addition to Sandhi and Domaine de la Côte, Rajat Parr also relaunched his namesake label in 2013 as an umbrella to make "wines for a purpose"—curiosities from mostly old vineyards,

all priced for $30 or less. That includes **Chenin Blanc** ($$) from the Jurassic Park site and **Riesling** ($$) from the old Gainey vineyards in Santa Barbara, along with such sundries as Trousseau.

ROARK WINE CO.: Ryan Roark, who apprenticed in the Loire Valley and has worked for Central Coast winemaker Andrew Murray, tapped thirty-year-old vines near the Curtis Winery for his own Lompoc-based label. The linchpin is a masterful expression of **Chenin Blanc** ($), with just the right balance of spruce aromas and textural flesh. He also makes Pinot Noir, Cabernet Franc, and Malbec.

SCRIBE: The Mariani family, originally Yolo County walnut growers, purchased a 256-acre former turkey farm just outside the town of Sonoma, part of the property founded by Emil Dresel, who helped bring Riesling to California. (The remainder of Dresel's land became Gundlach Bundschu's Rhinefarm Vineyard.) While their project is still finding its footing, worth watching are an estate **Riesling** ($$) and **Sylvaner** ($$), tributes to the German varieties that once flourished in this part of the Napa-Sonoma interface zone.

SPOTTSWOODE: This esteemed St. Helena Cabernet house deserves credit for its **Sauvignon Blanc** ($$), perhaps the most serious effort for that grape in California. Made from a mix of Napa and Sonoma fruit, it exudes age-worthy complexity. (Credit owner Mary Novak, who prefers white wine.) Where once Spottswoode relied on Napa fruit, it now uses a mix of well-known Napa vineyards like Hyde and Tofanelli, plus Joe Votek's rocky Farina Vineyard on Sonoma Mountain, which is also used by Tres Sabores and Scholium Project. The real alchemy comes in Spottswoode's cellar,

White winemaking in California used to fall into two camps: simple efforts fermented in steel and released young; and elaborate barrel fermentations—typically for Chardonnay—devised to impart unctuous texture and oak flavor. But the world is more complex now. Indeed, much cellar innovation is directed toward white wine, including improvements on time-honored techniques.

Long lees time. Rather than stir lees, winemakers have begun to let the wines sit on them untouched through the winter as part of a long, cold fermentation—a move inspired in part by Didier Dagueneau's work in the Loire. Even Chardonnay masters are barely touching their wines once they go to barrel, a departure from the frequent lees stirring of the past. The result builds texture in a slower, but potentially more profound, way.

Steel barrels. These provide fermenting wine with a higher ratio of solids to liquid than a larger tank would, which results in a richer texture without oak flavor. First implemented around 1994 by Pam Starr, then the winemaker at Spottswoode, along with Selene's Mia Klein and Françoise Peschon of Araujo Estate, these have become a signature in high-end Sauvignon Blanc and other wines. Originally the barrels, which at around $800 cost a bit less than new oak, were designed to hold insertable staves that provided oak flavor without the expense of a new barrel. Winemakers just left out the staves. As with a wood barrel, the solids, or lees, can be stirred to enrich mouthfeel.

Concrete. California's current must-have gadget is the concrete egg pioneered by the French firm Nomblot. It can add more texture to wine than steel, in part due to a convective shape that churns the wine during fermentation. The eggs are now appearing in numerous cellars, including those of Wind Gap, Acha, and even Williams Selyem, for use with Chenin Blanc. A newer model made by Sonoma Cast Stone has gained attention as well.

Concrete vessels, whether large or small, have generally gained favor for their ability to add a subtle richness without wood influence or the austerity of steel. Manufacturers like Paso Robles's Vino Vessel are creating not only small concrete barrels but also cylindrical tanks and pyramid-shaped containers.

Skin contact. The process of soaking white wine on grape skins might be the most fashionable choice of all. After an extended soak the wine can fall into a category popularly called orange wine, popularized by Italian producers like Josko Gravner, who in turn borrowed the idea from the long Georgian tradition of making white wine as though it were red.

Some winemakers go full-on with the practice, including Wind

---

where about 90 percent of the wine is fermented in mostly stainless steel barrels, with the rest going into used and new oak, plus the occasional concrete egg (see Innovation in the Cellar, above). See also Cabernet (page 219).

Y. ROUSSEAU: Having grown up in Gascony, Yannick Rousseau wanted to celebrate the native bounty of his home. He found Russian River Valley fruit, which had once gone to sparkling wine house Korbel. He typically picks it in mid-October, then soaks it on the skins for about nine hours and partially ferments it in old barrels to enhance the texture.

Gap for its Trousseau Gris, Donkey & Goat for its Stone Crusher Roussanne, and Point Concepción for its Celestina. The last is Pinot Grigio made in the *ramato* style, borrowed from Friuli, which yields a wine closer in spirit to rosé. Others are using the technique for a day or less to subtly add flavor and texture without profoundly changing the wine. Again, this follows producers in

Friuli and elsewhere who prefer a less dramatic use of skin contact.

Amphorae. Skin contact leads to another technique that has been adopted by California winemakers: the use of clay amphorae, a technique revived in Friuli but ultimately based on the use of Georgian *qvevri*, a type of earthenware vessel that defined that country's winemaking style for thousands of years. As the

vessels caught on more broadly with European winemakers, including Austria's Bernhard Ott, they inevitably crossed the sea. Ryme's Ryan Glaab, Brian Terrizzi of Giornata, the Arnot-Roberts label, and Kenny Likitprakong of Hobo are among those experimenting. Likitprakong even had a local potter throw his vessel.

His **Old Vines Colombard** ($), with its mandarin and fern flavors, shows a side of the grape not often seen even in Gascony. He also makes more traditional wines (Cabernet, Chardonnay) and a Tannat as homage to Gascony's robust reds. Rousseau hopes to plant Petit Manseng, the grape of southwest France's Jurançon area.

Chris Cottrell and Morgan Twain-Peterson in the Bedrock Vineyard

Back to the Future: Zinfandel and Beyond

What's most curious about the New California is how much it echoes the bounty of Old California—all the way back to the days of the first Mission plantings. Grapes like Zinfandel, a constant through California's wine history, today are being embraced alongside varieties like Trousseau, which were all but lost on these shores until the past few years. In part, that's because the current diversity in California vineyards is perhaps unparalleled since before Prohibition. In the nineteenth century, the viticultural scouts of the time tested a wild diversity of grapes, everything from Italian Bonarda to Austrian Rotgipfler. E. W. Hilgard's work to catalog the grapes of 1880s California sounded more like a twenty-first-century wine shop—"Jura Type," "Austrian and Hungarian Type"—than the state's vine roster a half century later.

Most of these grapes vanished in the mists of Prohibition. A handful survived. Many more are now returning.

Carole Meredith's 2001 discovery, with the help of Ivan Pejić and Edi Maletić of the University of Zagreb, solved one of wine's great puzzles: What was the ancestral home of a grape that Paul Draper once termed the "true American"?

The discovery of Crljenak Kaštelanski was only part of the tale. Just nine vines of Crljenak had been discovered in Croatia, which meant that Zinfandel's past was effectively wiped out.

Over the next decade, Meredith and her fellow researchers added a significant chapter to the history. They discovered a grape in the Dalmatian hinterlands called Pribidrag, along with a ninety-year-old leaf specimen of a variety, Tribidrag, from an herbarium in the city of Split. When the researchers finally extracted DNA for testing, it revealed that the old dried leaf was, in fact, Zinfandel—and that Crljenak and Pribidrag were the same.

At the same time, historian Ambroz Tudor uncovered references to Tribidrag as far back as the early 1400s—and its wine had been significant enough to be referenced by name in trade with Venice across the Adriatic. "It wasn't a junk grape," Meredith says. "It had nobility to it."

Meredith and her husband, Steve Lagier, put their own skin in the game in 2009 by planting just over half an acre of Zin on their Mount Veeder property. In 2013, they brought her work full circle, releasing the first California Tribidrag under their Lagier Meredith label.

The Mediterranean is finally serving as an appropriate inspiration. The grapes of Italy, long considered a challenge to grow in California, have again gained currency. If onetime hopes for Sangiovese have faded, there is now optimism for a far wider set of choices: Nebbiolo, Aglianico, and Teroldego; Friulano, Ribolla Gialla, and Fiano. Varieties like Montepulciano have been here for decades, cherished by Italian farmers who simply wanted to farm what they knew. New ones like Schioppettino are just appearing.

Spain, too, has risen. Tempranillo remains a New World work in progress, one pushed along by devotees like Markus Bokisch. Now Albariño, Verdelho, and Graciano are gaining ground, along with the occasional Portuguese variety—like Alvarelhão, which found both an unlikely home in Lodi, and currency thanks to a version made by Forlorn Hope. Mencia, Galicia's answer to Cabernet Franc, will undoubtedly find a home in California before long.

A NATIVE SON

Through it all there has been Zinfandel, California's defining grape—perhaps its most mysterious, and often its most frustrating. Mysterious because Zinfandel's heritage has remained murky, and frustrating because of its struggle to be accepted into polite company. Nonetheless, the state embraced it as an adopted son, and for much of the twentieth century it was California's most planted grape.

For decades, it was believed that Zinfandel had vanished from the Old World. Indeed, it is likely California claimed it for that very reason. Had it been a Hungarian misfit, perhaps? That was the midcentury theory, thanks to a claim by the family of Hungarian-born Agoston Haraszthy, founder of Sonoma's Buena Vista Winery, that he imported it. Like many of Haraszthy's tall tales, this was disproved. It became evident that the grape migrated west from East Coast nurseries by the 1820s, well before he arrived in California.

But where was its true home? By the 1970s ampelographers saw enough similarities to assert that it was the same grape as Puglia's Primitivo (although Primitivo was long treated as a separate variety), and then they traced its likely origins even farther, to the Dalmatian coast.

Only in 2001 did vine geneticist Carole Meredith put the question to bed, determining it to be the obscure Croatian variety Crljenak Kaštelanski. Over the next decade she and other researchers went further, determining that Zinfandel was in fact a fine Croatian variety called Tribidrag that dated to the fifteenth century (see Zin's Mystery, opposite).

This discovery came just as Zinfandel's fortunes began to shine again. After decades of wandering in the stylistic wilderness, the grape acquired a more serious reputation. Wines from it reappeared that could offer the gravitas of the best Cabernet and the terroir potential of Pinot Noir.

These new Zinfandels—and some long-overlooked classics—have found a balance between nuance and what has kept Zinfandel beloved through the years: its exuberant, utterly American fruit. Perfecting that balance is a truly Californian mission.

CULTURE CLASH

The culture wars over Zinfandel were smoldering as far back as the 1970s. Through much of the twentieth century, the grape either was the material for jug wine or, more ambitiously, was made in what came to be known as the claret style, approximating Bordeaux in rigid structure and freshness.

Even good midcentury Zins had their shortcomings. They often were marked by dramatically high acidity and a need for long aging. Many—not just the claret style, but plump late-harvest bottles, too—never completed the malolactic fermentation that would soften their edges.

But they also thrived as California began its last great wine renaissance. Through the 1970s, Zinfandel was valued as a native treasure, a wine that only California could offer. Berkeley's Chez Panisse restaurant embraced the grape, commissioning it as a house wine first from Joseph Phelps and then Jay Heminway's Green & Red. Simple Zin nouveaus were bottled barely after harvest, meant to celebrate a humble tradition with a nod to Beaujolais.

Those uninterested in the claret style began craving ever-riper late-harvest Zinfandels, which often exceeded 16 percent alcohol, as wineries tried, in the words of Sutter Home's Bob Trinchero, "to out-Zinfandel each other." Trinchero was among those who had located old Zinfandel in the Sierra Foothills, mostly in Amador County. At the behest of Sacramento retailer Darrell Corti, he began bottling a more swaggering Zin, a deliberate counterpoint to the more popular style.

In 1972, trying to concentrate one of these wines, Trinchero followed Corti's advice: bleed some pale juice from the tank and ferment it as a dry rosé. Bingo. Three years later Trinchero repeated the effort, but the juice wouldn't ferment to dryness. He bottled it anyway and had a runaway hit. Soon white Zinfandel was an essential part of the California tale.

The big-footed mountain Zinfandels, and others like them, cleaved the Zinfandel world. Ridge's Paul Draper recalls when California "hit the New York market with high-alcohol wines, and the New York market just said, 'Forget it. I'm never going to buy a bottle of Zinfandel again.'" As the 1980s arrived, Zinfandel went into a downward spiral. But there was one bright spot: white Zin, which saved many old vineyards from destruction in the lean years.

The next decade brought hints of revival, perhaps none more important than the creation of

Larry Turley's Turley Wine Cellars in 1993, which soon was known for its late-picked and dramatically stylish wines. But this was the era of Big Flavor. A raft of massive new wines soon appeared, slathered with oak flavors and driven by a more-is-more approach. Zinfandel was recast as a populist beacon, the *America's Funniest Home Videos* of wine. The grape's annual celebration, the Zinfandel Advocates & Producers festival, became a sloppy bacchanal.

Zinfandel classicists realized they had to launch a counterstrike against Big Flavor, and the tide of anti-intellectualism that had attended it. They shared this mission with younger winemakers who wanted to celebrate California's defining grape. By 2011 the zeal had spread, with the arrival of wines like Broc's Vine Starr, which was bottled under 14 percent alcohol and meant to charm a skeptical audience.

This doesn't simply mark a return to claret style; modern Zinfandel is often heartier than that, and the grape itself tends toward ripeness. While Turley, of all wineries, now picks relatively early, the wines often still top 15 percent alcohol. But the wines have grown fresher and more distinctive than many of their counterparts—or even their own earlier efforts—as the cellar work has gained a lighter touch. For better or worse, their 15 percent wines are an honest 15 percent, at least compared to the Big Flavor Zinfandels, which arrived at the same alcohol level by picking grapes that had almost turned to raisins (think 30 Brix) and then dialing them back with water and acid.

Perhaps the best revivalist moment came when Christina Turley, Larry's daughter, engineered the release of a Turley white Zinfandel. If her family had been a big catalyst in reviving Zin's fortunes, why couldn't white Zin be part of that?

She succeeded in 2011 with a bone-dry floral pink wine akin to crisp Provençal rosé, which had been picked in early September from Turley's estate vineyards outside St. Helena. At 11.2 percent alcohol, it was not only the leanest thing Turley had made, but was also a shot across the bow of the flotilla of cheap white Zinfandels. It quickly sold out. As Christina explained, "We all love the idea of something with a good heart and a bad reputation."

THE SUPPORTING CAST

But Zinfandel's history in California was never just about Zinfandel. It always had good company in the field.

There has been Petite Sirah in the state since at least the 1880s. (Although it was often mistaken for Syrah, it is not; it is a grape called Durif, although Carole Meredith determined Syrah was its parent). Pets, as the old growers called it, had deep color and tannin, good yields, and acidity that allowed it to get quite ripe. It was, however, one of those grapes that more or less disappeared into the field with Prohibition. When it reemerged, with 1961 vintages from Livermore's Concannon and Chateau Souverain, it was mostly an asterisk, despite its fervent partisans. Its sturdiness and tobacco-chaw tannins made it a love-or-hate-it proposition.

The more impressive comeback has been for Carignane, long a down-and-outer, a Jake LaMotta that similarly hid in the fields during the fighting-varietal years. It has made a steady case for itself, in no small part because it has largely resisted California's spiraling grape costs. Its downside? Younger-vine fruit can be so devoid of character that winemaker Sean Thackrey once dubbed it "sweetwater." The rap is unfair, because old California

Frustrated by California's fading link to the past, several prominent vintners, including Morgan Twain-Peterson of Bedrock, Mike Officer of Carlisle, Ridge viticulturist David Gates, and, of course, Turley's Tegan Passalacqua, created the nonprofit Historic Vineyard Society in 2010. Their hope was that if they could create a registry of the state's old vineyards—currently more than two hundred are listed at historicvineyardsociety.org— it would draw attention to the state's little-known connection to the past. As Passalacqua puts it,

"It is agriculture. There is culture to it. It isn't agribusiness."

The registry is particularly strong in certain areas: Sonoma, Contra Costa County, and the Sierra Foothills. It includes Officer's own Carlisle Vineyard in Russian River Valley, dating to the 1920s, along with sites like the Evangelho Vineyard in Contra Costa, old field-blend grapes dating to the 1890s.

To qualify, a vineyard must have first been planted in 1960 or before, with at least one-third of the vines dating that far back. The year is key: it predates the meteoric rise of Cabernet

and Chardonnay as California's king and queen. Attention, the logic goes, will bring grape customers—and incentive for growers to keep vines in the ground. Unfortunately, the incentive stops there. California has no tax breaks to offer and no protections for old vines—aside, perhaps, from ill will. Famous grower Andy Beckstoffer drew the ire of his fellow Napans when he tore out Petite Sirah from St. Helena's Hayne Vineyard, one of the valley's legendary non-Cabernet plantings, to replace it with very expensive Cabernet.

---

specimens have survived since the Italian farming days, plants that naturally hedge its prolific growth and prolong ripening. They can provide the complexity—bright red fruit and a celery-seed spice— to allow Carignane to stand on its own.

Old head-trained Carignane, which is often located in places like Mendocino's Redwood Valley and Contra Costa County, is frequently more than fifty years old—the age at which it starts to make compelling wine. These vines once attracted pioneers like Bonny Doon's Randall Grahm, and more recently they have enticed a new generation of hopefuls like Lioco and Broc, which use it as the base for their affordable table wines.

They owe thanks to farmers like the Finnish ancestors of Alvin Tollini, whose Carignane vines in Redwood Valley have endured for more than

six decades. Mendocino is Carignane country. The Tollini family's first vines went in around the time Alvin's grandfather was born in 1915; phylloxera forced a replanting in 1948. Tollini's grandfather extracted a promise from his grandson: the land would remain his so long as the Carignane remained. Thanks to the new economics of table wine, it has.

LOOKING TO THE JURA

The truly unlikely resurrection in California has been Trousseau Noir. By 2010, New California winemakers could often be found uncorking bottles from Jacques Puffeney, Michel Gahier, or Jean-François Ganevat. As their predecessors in the

1970s craved Lafite Rothschild, California wine-makers had become obsessed with the wines of France's Jura.

The Jura, with its mountain slopes rising from the eastern side of the Bresse plain opposite Burgundy, had become an unexpected darling, as had its indigenous varieties, including red Trousseau and Poulsard grapes and white Savignin. The style of making reds in the Jura can be archaic but compelling; at times the wines are so barely extracted that they resemble rosé.

California wanted in. Duncan Meyers and Nathan Roberts of Arnot-Roberts had sorted through one of Europe's great ampelographic puzzles and come to a realization: the Trousseau grape in the Jura was the same as Bastardo, grown in the Douro region and one of Port's lesser-known grapes. That Portuguese lineage, and its utility in field blends, had quietly kept Trousseau in California since the nineteenth century. They soon located one of the state's few contiguous blocks of Trousseau Noir, in the Lake County town of Kelseyville, where the Luchsinger family had planted two acres in 2001 hoping someone might use it in Port-style wine.

Lake County, north of Napa, might not have been the ideal spot for Trousseau, but the grape had otherwise been lost except for a few Central Valley remnants. Arnot-Roberts's 2011 vintage galvanized Jura partisans across the country.

Their bottling earned enough attention to warrant new plantings, like a small one in the Bartolomei Vineyard near Forestville. Passalacqua negotiated with George Bohan, David Hirsch's neighbor on the Sonoma Coast near Cazadero, to graft over the roots of about an acre of Merlot to young cuttings of Trousseau; the variety seems to express itself as distinctly as Pinot Noir in the chaotic coastal soils. Outside Healdsburg, Copain's Wells Guthrie planted a small parcel by his winery. Using cuttings from Arnot-Roberts, Rajat Parr planted an acre in Santa Barbara's Stolpman Vineyard.

Poulsard, or Ploussard as the Jurassiens called it, had not seemed to survive the journey to California outside of some nineteenth-century plantings lost after Prohibition. But as Trousseau was having its moment, a few cuttings of Poulsard were surreptitiously carried over, quietly planted at Copain in Healdsburg next to the Trousseau, and installed as a tiny nursery block at Alder Springs Vineyard in northern Mendocino to propagate for future plantings in the Sierra Foothills and possibly elsewhere.

GAMAY'S UNLIKELY HOME

At the same time, California had a long fascination with the wines of Beaujolais, home of the Gamay Noir grape. In the 1970s, wines like Robert Mondavi's Gamay rosé were a familiar sight.

One glitch: Little of what was in California was actually Gamay Noir à Jus Blanc, the true specimen. Most was Napa Gamay, which turned out to actually be a grape called Valdiguié, a Languedoc native that arrived in one of those many fumbles of nursery work. Another grape, audaciously called Gamay Beaujolais, was merely a lowbrow Pinot Noir cultivar. At some point true Gamay was imported by grape researcher Harold Olmo, but little had actually been planted. By 2007, the other grapes' Gamay-related names had been banned from wine labels.

But true Gamay was enjoying a quiet retreat in the Sierra—and today is witnessing an improbable planting boomlet. El Dorado vineyard guru Ron Mansfield has become California's unlikely Gamay mogul.

The quest for true Gamay began in 2000, when Mansfield and Steve Edmunds of Edmunds St. John conspired to graft over four acres of vines in Bob Witters's vineyard at 3,400 feet near the town of Camino. The foothills share one thing in particular with Beaujolais: granite soils. Witters's soils were rich in clay, similar to southern Beaujolais, while nearby land owned by the Barsotti family has more decomposed granite and porphyry, similar to Beaujolais's northern hillsides. As much as California sniffed at soil analogues, here was a valuable one. Mansfield's plantings were tapped by several other vintners.

Even Valdiguié has gotten another shot. The grape survived in unexpected places like Mendocino's Redwood Valley, the Green Valley area of Solano County, and Calistoga's Frediani Vineyard, an improbable use for prime Napa land, and a handful of bottlings remained after 2007 under the grape's true name. Recently, ambitious versions have appeared from Broc Cellars, Folk Machine, and Forlorn Hope. These new versions do what the grape once did: offer a California companion to modest Beaujolais.

THE THREE-BOTTLE TOUR

Turley's Old Vines bottling may be easier to find, but if you can, locate a bottle of the eloquent **Turley Mead Ranch Zinfandel** (page 269). The **Broc Carbonic Carignane** (page 265) is a perfect mesh of old and new; he applies the semicarbonic technique used in Beaujolais on Alexander Valley fruit. Finally, in the spirit of the new, the **Arnot-Roberts Luchsinger Vineyard Trousseau** (at right) was the wine to make a case for that grape in California.

TOP PRODUCERS
• • •
ARNOT-ROBERTS

Duncan Meyers and Nathan Roberts, two hometown boys from a solid middle-class Napa upbringing, have become the very personification of New California's bounty. As they juggle everything from Cabernet to Trousseau, their work has helped to highlight the continuity between California's past and future. While they may believe in lower ripeness levels and the joys of esoterica, this isn't reactionary winemaking. It's simply a case of two native sons viewing California's bounty through their own prism.

It's also a reflection of the DIY ethos that pervades California's new guard. One day, lunch at their winery might be fennel soup and sardine *conserva* Roberts made the previous evening. They have a small drum roaster for their own espresso beans. Their wines are inevitably made in small quantities, often only a few barrels' worth. "There's a return to artisanally produced things, and smaller scale," Meyers says. "People have seen what a mass-production approach means."

In the cellar, fermentations are with indigenous yeasts, although not all wines go through malolactic fermentation. Typically they use old oak barrels and puncheons, and they handle all the work in their Healdsburg warehouse themselves. They are cautious, for sure, but certainly not radical. "I don't see our wines as extreme," Roberts says. "I consider our wines to be made in a classic style."

THE WINES: Aside from their Clary Ranch Syrah, the wine that has come to best define Arnot-Roberts's work is the **Luchsinger Vineyard Trousseau** ($$), from Lake County. Expect more Trousseau—and potentially Poulsard to match. There's also the surprisingly serious **RPM Gamay Noir** ($$) from the Sierra Foothills, made jointly with Sandhi's Rajat Parr. All these wines have a stylistic kinship with their Pinots, including the **Peter Martin Ray** ($$$) and **Legan** ($$$), from the Santa Cruz Mountains, and the **Coastlands Pinot Noir** ($$$), from the Cobb family's Sonoma vineyard. See also Chardonnay (page 200), Cabernet (page 217), Revising the Rhône (page 233), and The New Whites (page 251).

BEDROCK WINE CO.

It's almost silly to say that Morgan Twain-Peterson got an early start in winemaking. He made his first wine, a Pinot Noir, at age five.

With the sale of their Ravenswood label in 2001, the Peterson family was free to pursue their own path to quality—one built around the 152-acre Bedrock Vineyard near Kenwood, with its vines dating to the 1880s. Zinfandel is the key base material, but the Bedrock label's lineup of wine also includes Syrah, "mixed blacks," white blends, Cabernet, and more. Few wineries are such dedicated curators of the state's old-time bounty.

Twain-Peterson's studiousness and globalism (he is working toward his master of wine) informs his winemaking style, which has gained finesse in the past few years: slightly lower alcohol levels, less sweetness, and more distinct aromatic character. His winemaking is in the mode of his father Joel Peterson's best work: indigenous fermentations and malolactic conversion, a modest amount of new oak, and relatively early harvests.

This is not to say the wines are shy. They can be lusty and forward, are often released early, and rely on a healthy dose of big fruit. But they have made peace between that and their innate nuance.

THE WINES: Bedrock makes a wide range of reds, tapping not only its own vineyard but also a bounty of old-vine sites. The **Bedrock Heritage** ($$), formerly called the Bedrock Heirloom, is a mix of twenty-two varieties—about 60 percent Zinfandel, plus everything from Merlot to Mission—off the Petersons' own ancient vines. There's a range of other heritage red field blends, from such Sonoma sites as **Pagani Ranch** ($$) and **Dolinsek** ($$), as well as a stunning red **Evangelho** ($$) blend that incorporates a good dose of Carignane, and even mixed whites, from Frank Evangelho's Contra Costa site, plus a designate **Monte Rosso Zinfandel** ($$). There's also an **Old-Vine Zinfandel** ($$) from Sonoma Valley, a mix of parcels that's astonishingly good value, and a **North Coast Syrah** ($$), as well as the **Shebang** ($), one of the best red-blend values around. See also The New Whites (page 251).

BROC CELLARS

Chris Brockway—an Omaha, Nebraska, native—came to California via Seattle, studying first at UC Davis and then at Fresno State. After first aspiring to somewhat fancier wines, he soon realized his mission: to make less aspirational, more down-to-earth, and ultimately more interesting wines of the thirst-quenching sort that got little attention in the Big Flavor era.

From his cramped quarters in Berkeley, Brockway practices a relatively simple winemaking regimen. Fermentations are indigenous, with no additives and a minimum of sulfur dioxide—a radical change from his early yeast-happy training at nearby facilities. Often the fermentations take place in the winery's backyard, many in five-ton wood casks, otherwise in steel or concrete. He also works with Brian Terrizzi on the Broadside project.

Chris Brockway (left)

Of particular note is Brockway's work with the Vine Starr wines; the red has been a catalyst in bringing Zinfandel to a new audience. This is Brockway at his best, finding new pathways for California's heritage grapes.

THE WINES: Broc Cellars offers an eclectic and always shifting set of wines. The **Vine Starr Zinfandel** ($$) is typically from a range of Sonoma sources, including Arrowhead Mountain and Buck Hill, with a spice and lightness of step rarely found in the grape these days. Similarly, the **Carbonic Carignan** ($$), made using the semicarbonic technique used in Beaujolais on Alexander Valley fruit, shows a refreshing rooty side of the grape. Brockway turned to Paso Robles for his **Cabernet Franc** ($$), which shows a style more Friulian than Loire, and to Solano County for his **Valdiguié** ($$). There's a companion **Vine Starr White** ($$), usually some combination of Chardonnay, Roussanne, Grenache Blanc, and Picpoul. And following in Turley's footsteps, Broc released a slightly off-dry **White Zinfandel** ($$) in 2013. See also Revising the Rhône (page 233).

DASHE CELLARS

Michael and Anne Dashe have long occupied a curious position in Zin world, as voices of restraint that counter the push toward bigger, harder, more. Mike began making wine as an undergraduate at UC Santa Cruz. After working in the Santa Cruz Mountains, he got his masters from UC Davis before going to New Zealand and then landing in the lab at Château Lafite Rothschild. He returned home and became assistant winemaker at Ridge, where he honed in on Zinfandel. While running Ridge's Lytton Springs operation, he founded Dashe Cellars in 1996. Two years later he quit his day job. Anne, a French native, gravitated from her studies in Bordeaux to Napa, where she met Mike.

The Dashe style is subtle though not bashful; the Zinfandels, particularly from Dry Creek Valley, exhibit a continuity with Ridge wines, showing exuberant fruit at times, but also sometimes landing below 14 percent alcohol and exhibiting a certain serenity. Fermentations are indigenous, and increasingly the wines are aged in older five-hundred- and nine-hundred-liter oak puncheons and casks, providing structure with ever-less new wood presence. The Dashe Zins are of that style that rewards age.

Dashe may have attracted the most attention for Les Enfants Terrible, its line of lighter-styled Grenache and Zinfandel, often made in a Beaujolais-like semicarbonic style, with almost no sulfur dioxide and just five months in barrel. These wines, and their winemaking, became a modern prism for exploring the quieter possibilities of two usually robust grapes.

THE WINES: The **Dry Creek Valley Zinfandel** ($$), from several vineyards, is a perfect introduction to Dashe's restraint. The three single-vineyard Dry Creek choices: There's intensity but not bulk in the old-vine selections from the vineyards **Louvau** ($$) and **Todd Brothers** ($$), the former on riverbed soils and the latter on dense red soils near Geyserville. The younger vines of the **Florence** ($$) site show a surprising delicacy. As for the Enfants, look for two Zinfandels from Mendocino, one from Potter Valley's organic stalwart **McFadden Farm** ($$) and the other from the biodynamically farmed **Heart Arrow Ranch** ($$), plus a **Dry Creek Valley Grenache** ($$). In addition, Dashe makes a number of other red wines and a Riesling.

GIORNATA

In addition to her vineyard work and his efforts with the Broadside label, Stephy and Brian Terrizzi have taken on that most frustrating of California pursuits: interpreting Italy's grapes in the New World.

Many have tried and failed, most notably Piero Antinori, with his attempts to crown Napa as the next great spot for Sangiovese. The Terrizzis, however, have some advantages. For one, most of their wines depend on Stephy's own farming. And they are guided by persistent skepticism about the ripeness that pervades their home turf of Paso Robles (see page 156).

Also, they chose Nebbiolo as their holy grail—usually a foolhardy decision in California, but they perhaps have accomplished making the most successful Nebbiolo yet in the state, in part because they found a correlation in chemistry and composition between the soils of the Luna Matta Vineyard and Barbaresco's limestone-rich marls. In the cellar, fermentations are typically indigenous and the oak is restrained; a clay amphora has arrived for use on white wines.

THE WINES: Their three Italian varietal reds all come from Luna Matta: The **Nebbiolo** ($$), aged partly in newer Taransaud oak puncheons and partly in neutral wood, shows a brilliant skill with tannins, especially for that grape, while the **Sangiovese** ($$) has similar restraint, like a good Vino Nobile di Montepulciano. The **Aglianico** ($$) has the aggressiveness that marks many California versions of that Campanian grape. The flashiest might be their **Gemellaia** ($$), a Super Tuscan nod that blends Sangiovese with Merlot and Petit Verdot. They produce a handful of whites, too, including a **Vermentino** ($$) and **Il Campo White** ($), a remarkable value that's typically a mix of Moscato Bianco and Friulano. It has a Sangiovese- and Merlot-focused counterpart, **Il Campo Red** ($).

MARIETTA CELLARS/LIMERICK LANE/IDLEWILD

The Bilbro family is on a dual track to exalt California's old bounty. For thirty years—ever since patriarch Chris Bilbro followed in the footsteps of his mentor Bruno Benziger, who launched the Glen Ellen brand in 1980—their Marietta wines have been a quiet and affordable alternative to increasingly corporate table wines.

They expanded upon that mission in 2011, when son Jake Bilbro bought the Limerick Lane winery in Healdsburg. The estate, long known for its refined Zinfandels, was a perfect acquisition for the family and its no-frills winemaking style (little new oak, relatively early harvests, modest extraction). The following year the Bilbros expanded further, acquiring the McDowell Valley property in Mendocino, enough acreage to turn their Old Vine Red into an estate bottling.

With about five of its thirty acres of vines dating to 1910, Limerick has the benefit of heritage material as its base source—and further demonstrates that the eastern stretches of the Russian River area really are Zinfandel territory. When meshed with Marietta's everyday philosophy, the two together compose a snapshot of Sonoma's continuity.

THE WINES: The Marietta lineup is defined by the **Old Vine Red** ($), always designated nonvintage by lot number. More recently they have revived varietal bottles, including Zinfandel.

As for Limerick Lane, there's a **Russian River Valley Estate Zinfandel** ($$), and then several bottles that generally have been labeled by planting date: the nuanced **1970 Block Zinfandel** ($$); the **1934 Block** ($$$), with Trousseau, Negrette, and Peloursin among its minor components; and the sublime cardamom-scented **1910 Block** ($$$).

Finally, Chris's son Sam and his wife, Jessica, launched their own label in 2012, Idlewild, which focuses on lesser-known varieties: white **Arneis** ($$), **Grenache Gris** ($$), and a Syrah-based **Vin Gris** ($$), plus red Dolcetto, Carignane, and others.

MCCAY CELLARS

A Lodi resident and grape grower since the 1980s, Michael McCay started making his own wine commercially in 2007. If big and brawny is Lodi's hallmark, McCay sprinted in the opposite direction, making Zinfandels (plus some Cabernet Franc and Petite Sirah) that dial back oak and heighten fresh flavors. This is a rarity in a neighborhood where the wines receive enough wood to smell like a hickory fire.

McCay often describes his efforts as Old World in style; I'd say they are a clear-eyed interpretation of Lodi's great soils. The Zinfandels have an innate freshness, often with relatively low pH and bright flavors that evoke Lodi's earlier style with the grape.

McCay often ferments with indigenous yeasts (he finds they induce cooler fermentations and less volatility) and typically no more than one-quarter new oak. He views this as a means to his ultimate goal: highlighting the uniqueness of Lodi soils, using Zinfandel as the base material. It's a departure from the area's tendency to dump old-vine fruit into big-production blends: "There are a few hidden gems around Lodi that aren't ending up in one-hundred-ton fermenters somewhere."

McCay recently put money down on this proposition, acquiring an old 10-acre Zinfandel vineyard from around 1915 in the Mokelumne River area. Stocked with trunks of stumpy vines, it even hosts a few errant vines of Flame Tokay, once a local bounty eaten as table grapes or distilled into "Lodi scotch." He is equally bullish on other sites, in particular the Contention Vineyard, 1.5 acres from the late 1930s on Lodi's west side.

THE WINES: The **Jupiter Zinfandel** ($$), from a site in the Mokelumne area south of Victor, east of Lodi proper, is McCay's defining wine, with its perfume and cacao-bean scents; his **Truluck's** ($$), from vines between forty and eighty years old on Lodi's west side, is burlier and riper. His own estate parcel will be the source for a **Lot 13 Zinfandel** ($$). His **Contention** ($$$), from eighty-year-old vines, is the most polished, aiming for a Turley-style complexity. Additionally, there is a **Paisley** ($$) red blend of Zinfandel and Petite Sirah, the occasional varietal Petite Sirah and Cabernet Franc, and a **Rosé** ($) mostly from Carignane vines dating to 1909.

SANDLANDS

Tegan Passalacqua has made enough wine for Turley Wine Cellars and farmed enough vineyards that his own label is merely a logical extention of his endless curiosity. It reflects the core of his best work: a great curation of California's forgotten vineyard treasures—with the name intended "to describe the outliers" among the state's plantings.

The wines are made in the same transparent style as at Turley, using indigenous yeasts, little new oak, and essentially no manipulation aside from basic cellar handling of wine, although Passalacqua's wines tend to land slightly less ripe and often receive even less sulfur dioxide. (A 2012 old-vine Grenache from Placer County yielded less than two parts per million of free sulfur dioxide.) The reds get relatively light extraction and, again, mostly neutral oak.

But Passalacqua's true fascination is with Chenin Blanc, presumably because of his work in South Africa's Swartland area, a home for old head-trained specimens of that grape. He makes a version that's destemmed into a basket press in order to expose the grapes to oxygen. As he puts it, this "builds a tougher wine," which is then fermented in old barrels.

Increasingly, he is using grapes from the circa-1915 Lodi Kirschenmann site, which he purchased in 2012. After the sale closed, one of his fellow growers told him, "You're a farmer now. You don't retire. You die."

THE WINES: The reds begin with the subtle **Kirschenmann Zinfandel** ($$), as well as the **Del Barba Carignane** ($$) from Contra Costa and a **Trousseau** ($$) from the Bohan Vineyard, which reveals the minerality of its coastal roots. There are Rhône-inspired efforts, including a **Shake Ridge Grenache** ($$) from Amador that evokes high-altitude Spanish expressions, as well as a perfectly spicy **Soberanes Syrah** ($$), from the Santa Lucia Highlands and **Grenache** ($$$), from Placer County.

As for whites, the **Story Vineyard Chenin Blanc** ($$) is from old dry-farmed vines in Amador's Story Vineyard. Typically landing in the mid-12 range for alcohol, it has the verve of a Loire white like Savennières, but without the higher ripeness.

TURLEY WINE CELLARS

Few turnarounds in California have been so dramatic as Turley's. The wines were stars from their launch in 1993, when Larry Turley, a former ER doctor and founder of Frog's Leap winery, launched a new Zinfandel-driven label. His sister Helen was his first winemaker, and the early Turley wines were made in her unapologetically maximum-overdrive style, dosed with lots of new oak.

She would soon depart, and eventually winemaker Ehren Jordan—and later Tegan Passalacqua—would devise a far subtler protocol. That isn't to say the wines became shy; Larry Turley remains a fan of Big California—he once shipped cases of his wines to Europe so he'd have something to drink there—and Turley Zinfandels are as sizable as any, often surpassing 16 percent alcohol. But new oak is a rarity, fermentations are indigenous, and there are virtually no cellar additions. In many cases, picking has been moved up, sometimes by weeks, to get fresher fruit.

The wines have become some of the purest, most site-driven expressions of California around, expressed through the raw material of Zinfandel. This is driven in large part by a reliance on excellent vineyards, many of them more than fifty years old, and most farmed both without irrigation and according to organic principles. It is a revival of some of California's best resources, with an economic prospect: farm great grapes, and we'll sell the wine at fair value. This, perhaps more than anything, has become Turley's great mission.

With an estate winery at Larry Turley's house outside St. Helena—complete with a barn and chickens—plus a facility in Templeton, outside Paso Robles, and a new property at the former Karly winery in Amador County, Turley has established beachheads throughout the state.

THE WINES: With more than two dozen wines, which are still surprisingly affordable for mailing-list members, Turley's offerings are a catalog of old-vine bounty. Among the highlights: the **Dogtown Zinfandel** ($$), from Lodi's east side; the **Ueberroth Zinfandel** ($$$), from 1885 vines near Paso Robles that make one of Turley's biggest but highest-acid wines; the finessed **Salvador Zinfandel** ($$), from century-old Contra Costa vines; and the **Mead Ranch** ($$) from an old dry-farmed parcel near Napa's Atlas Peak, with its tobacco aromas and savory, nervy profile. Many of their wines have loyal followings, including both the **Rattlesnake Ridge Zinfandel** ($$) and the **Petite Sirah** ($$$) from Larry Turley's planting on Howell Mountain; the **Hayne Zinfandel** ($$$) and **Petite Sirah** ($$$), from one of St. Helena's oldest and best sites; and the **Library Petite Syrah** ($$), in fact a St. Helena field blend.

More recent additions include the **Fredericks Zinfandel** ($$$), from a 1940s-era parcel above Sonoma Valley, and the **Heminway Zinfandel** ($$), from Green & Red's vineyards. Additionally, there is the **Bechtold Vineyard Cinsault** ($) from Lodi, a wine initially called Porrón and intended as a Beaujolais-style restaurant drink, the **White Zinfandel** ($), and the more widely available **Old Vines** ($$) and **Juvenile** ($$) blends. See also Cabernet (page 219).

MORE NOTABLE WINES

BUCKLIN: The key asset of this label run by Will Bucklin and his three siblings is their Old Hill Ranch, founded in 1852 and with vines dating to 1885, making it one of Sonoma's oldest vineyards. The Bucklins' mother and stepfather, organic farmers Anne and Otto Teller, acquired the site in 1981. They meticulously plotted it vine by vine, and along the way they discovered such lost treasures as century-old Syrah, Grenache, Trousseau, and even an old rootstock variety, Lenoir. The **Ancient Vine Zinfandel** ($$) has that old-vine balance of density and lift, although it can require a bit of cellar time, during which the fruitier **Bambino Zinfandel** ($$), from a field-blend block planted in 1998, can be enjoyed. There are several other varietal bottles, plus a dry **Rosé** ($). While the oak can be a bit forward, fermentations are indigenous and the wines are typically unfiltered.

CARLISLE: A one-time software developer and home winemaker turned pro, Mike Officer is one of the most diligent students of California's vineyard legacy, and his own wines have gained distinct popularity—enough to allow Carlisle to move into its own winery facility in 2013. By that point, Officer and his wife Kendall were proud owners of their own heritage site, a mixed-blacks vineyard dating to 1927 in the Russian River Valley, which can go into a **Carlisle Vineyard Zinfandel** ($$$), as well as Officer's **Sonoma County Zinfandel** ($$)—the latter a remarkable value.

The Carlisle style can be determinedly big muscled at times, but Officer is a deft interpreter of a dizzying array of vineyard sites. His interpretation of **Monte Rosso Zinfandel** ($$$) is quintessential, as are his **Bedrock** ($$$) and **Rossi Ranch** ($$)

bottles. Carlisle partisans all have their own favorites, including Rhône-inspired wines from both Sonoma and the Central Coast, but of particular note are the Mourvèdre-dominant **Two Acres** ($$$) red and several whites, including Officer's own limpid interpretation of the **Compagni Portis** ($$) site and a **Grüner Veltliner** ($$) from Sonoma Mountain.

EDMUNDS ST. JOHN: Steve Edmunds's Rhône-inspired wines from vineyards like Fenaughty have had a following since the 1980s, but it is his work with Gamay that might become his greatest legacy. The **Bone-Jolly Gamay Noir** ($), from the Witters Vineyard, was his original effort, while the **Porphyry Gamay Noir** ($$) typically comes from the newer Barsotti planting, although the sources shift. There's also a **Bone-Jolly Rosé** ($). He makes several other wines, too, including the occasional white **Heart of Gold** ($), which exudes Sierra minerality through the prism of Vermentino and Grenache Blanc. Additionally, Edmunds and fellow vintner Don Heistuman make **AHA Bebame** ($), a blend of foothills Cabernet Franc and Gamay with an *Alice in Wonderland*–inspired label.

FORLORN HOPE: In addition to his panoply of whites (page 244), Matthew Rorick is pioneering several reds from unexpected grapes and sources. The **Suspiro del Moro** ($$), a rose-scented version of the Portuguese grape Alvarelhão, grown in the Alta Mesa area near Lodi, has become an improbable hit. Also look for the **Mil Amores** ($$), a blend of Portuguese varieties (Touriga Nacional, Tinta Roriz, Tinta Cão, and Trincadeira) from Amador's DeWitt Vineyard, plus an Amador County Barbera, **San Hercurmer delle Frecce** ($$), a Petite Sirah and even the Austrian grape St. Laurent; and finally, **Kumo to Ame** ($$), a rosé from Portuguese-native varieties.

GREEN & RED: Jay Heminway bought this Chiles Valley property in 1970, planted it two years later, and started making wine in 1977, in time for Green & Red to become the house wine at such Bay Area institutions as Chez Panisse and Swan Oyster Depot. Many of the thirty-one acres of mostly Sobrante series volcanic soils, in Napa's eastern stretches, have been replanted, but the wines remain as lusty and old-school as ever, aged in a mix of American and French oak. Among his Zinfandels, **Chiles Mill** ($$), from a northwest facing site around 1,200 feet elevation, is the classic, while the **Tip Top** ($$), from the highest of the vineyards at around 1,800 feet (with chert and greenstone in the mix), is shier. There's also a **Chiles Canyon** ($$), from a mix of vineyards, and an excellent Musqué-clone **Sauvignon Blanc** ($).

HOBO/FOLK MACHINE: In addition to his Pinot (see Ghostwriter, page 188) Kenny Likitprakong has a proliferation of other wines, including tangy **Branham Vineyard Rockpile** ($$) and **Dry Creek Valley** ($$) Zinfandels, and a **Sceales Vineyard Grenache** ($$) under his Hobo label; plus **Banyan Gewürztraminer** ($) and several value wines under the Folk Machine label, including a **Redwood Valley Valdiguié** ($$) and **Mendocino Tocai Friulano** ($).

HORSE & PLOW: Husband-and-wife winemakers Chris Condos (Vinum Cellars, Kathryn Kennedy) and Suzanne Hagins (Lutea) exhibit the great match of their talents in their affordably minded effort to tap older vines. The **Farmstead Red** ($) uses Carignane, Zinfandel, Petite Sirah, and other grapes from Dry Creek Valley and Mendocino for a layered table wine. There also are **Old Vine Carignane** ($$) and **Old Vine Grenache** ($$) from Testa Vineyard in Mendocino, along with a number of other varietal reds and whites, and an occasional **Harvester White** ($) blend.

LIOCO: In addition to focusing on Pinot Noir and Chardonnay, this Sonoma-based label put its early efforts into **Indica** ($), a Carignane-dominant table blend made primarily from Alvin Tollini's old Mendocino vines. More recently has come the **Sativa** ($$), a refined whole-cluster fermented Carignane-based companion from dry-farmed Mendocino vines at 1,600 feet elevation (the naming scheme should comfort Peter Tosh fans). It shows more polish, in the spirit of a good Minervois. There's also a Carignane-based **Indica Rosé** ($), plus a keg-based Carignane, alternately called—of course—Indo or Kush. See also Pinot Noir (page 189) and Chardonnay (page 197).

LOS PILARES: This label from Michael Christian and his partners hails from none other than San Diego—proof, along with Vesper Vineyards, of an unlikely spot providing a potentially brilliant approximation of arid Mediterranean-style terrain. After some bouts of home winemaking, and frustrated by their search for local table wines, they found grapes in eastern San Diego County—half Grenache from a 1,400-foot-elevation site in Ramona and half older-vine Carignane from a ranch in Pauma Valley—to craft a buoyant red fermented with whole berries and typically made without adding commercial yeasts or acid. The **Los Pilares Red** ($$) is aromatic and occasionally funky. Most important, they did this in a city whose wine industry is embryonic. "San Diego County, for me, is a blank slate," Christian says.

NEYERS VINEYARDS: Bruce Neyers certainly has a long history in Napa, having worked at Joseph

Phelps before moving to Kermit Lynch Wine Merchant. Neyers's first vintage was 1980. In its current incarnation the winery is based at his organically farmed ranch off Sage Canyon Road. Cabernet is the estate project, and there's also straightforward Chardonnay, plus the heady **Old Lakeville Road Syrah** ($$). But the truly interesting work from winemaker Tadeo Borchardt hails from old-vine parcels in Sonoma, Contra Costa, and Lodi. The **Evangelho Vineyard Carignan** ($$) is a top expression of those ancient Contra Costa vines, with a wood-ear mushroom savoriness, while the **Del Barba Zinfandel** ($$), from nearby, is a reminder of that grape's sleek power. The **Vista Luna Zinfandel** ($$), from Markus Bokisch's volcanic Lodi soils, is a tribute to the grape's fresh, plummier side, while the **Rossi Ranch Grenache** ($$), from a mass-selection planting in Sonoma Valley, brings out that grape's mineral nuance.

RIDGE VINEYARDS: Ridge's work with Zinfandel and its supporting cast has been so prominent for so long that it could just as easily be their calling card as their Monte Bello wines. Both the **Geyserville** ($$) and **Lytton Springs** ($$), from their respective parts of northern Sonoma, remain California paradigms for the grape. They have, if anything, gotten more focused and brighter in recent years as some replantings have matured.

Both these sites have a long lineage. Original winemaker Dave Bennion scouted Geyserville in 1966, and Draper selected nearby Lytton Springs in 1972. Three miles south of its namesake town, the Geyserville plantings host some California ancients, including 130-year-old vines in its Old Patch. The Geyserville uses not only Zinfandel (typically less than 75 percent), but also significant glugs of Carignane and Petite Sirah, plus Alicante Bouschet

and Mourvèdre. With an eight-day extraction and around 20 percent new American oak, this is the quintessence of do-less winemaking. Even with a new eco-friendly facility in Lytton Springs, the Geyserville is still aged in the old Monte Bello cellars.

As for Lytton Springs, its Dry Creek Valley location is only slightly younger than Geyserville (its oldest parcels are more than 110 years old), and it has a similar blend, although Petite Sirah plays a larger role here. Ridge finally acquired the land in the 1990s, reuniting the parcels once owned by William Litton in the 1870s. Lytton Springs is inevitably the fleshier of the two, again with about 20 percent new oak, and in certain years a modest tweak with acid or water (decisions now being openly discussed on Ridge's labels).

These compose just a fraction of Ridge's heritage-vine efforts. Lytton has given birth to a riper **Lytton Estate** ($$) bottle, and there are limited-release designate bottles from such vineyards as Alexander Valley's **Mazzoni Home Ranch** ($$), Fritz Maytag's **York Creek** ($$) property on Spring Mountain, and the old **Pagani Ranch** ($$) in Sonoma Valley, notable for its dose of inky Alicante Bouschet. From farther south comes the **Paso Robles Zinfandel** ($$), from the Benito Dusi Ranch, first planted in 1923 and a Ridge source since 1967; and the designate **Dusi Ranch** ($$). Finally, there is the **Three Valleys** blend ($$) from Sonoma—Ridge's table-wine candidate—as well as limited releases of Petite Sirah, Grenache, Syrah, and the **Buchignani Ranch Carignane** ($$). See also Chardonnay (page 203) and Cabernet (page 216).

SCHOLIUM PROJECT: Although Abe Schoener's white wines have gotten the most attention, his work with reds has become increasingly worthy, even if it is less radical. Schoener has an almost irrational fondness for Petite Sirah—could it be the grape's raw nature?—which is demonstrated in his **Bricco Babelico** ($$$) from Suisun Valley, the site of his winery, and his **Gardens of Babylon** blend ($$). Perhaps his most exquisite red is his **Arrows of Apollo** ($$$), a warm-spiced Zinfandel from Napa's Mead Ranch that is evocative of the grape's old-fashioned charms. Its spiritual twin is the **Sandlands** ($$), an occasional Carignane bottling from Tom Del Barba's century-old vines in Contra Costa. Scholium being Scholium, there's more esoterica: **Chuy Cabernet** ($$$$), from Sonoma; **Androkteinos** ($$) and **Golgotha** ($$$), Syrahs from Carneros's Hudson Vineyards; and the **Pergamos** ($$$$), an improbable Merlot from the Vanderkous Vineyard on north-facing slopes in the Contra Costa town of Martinez, south of the Carquinez Strait. See also The New Whites (page 248).

SKY VINEYARDS: Lore Olds once described his old cabin atop Mount Veeder—at the end of an axle-snapping dirt road—as "Napa's shittiest chateau." Architecture wags may quibble, but certainly Sky and its fourteen acres of vines, scattered along the fire road that marks the county line, represent Napa's preambition era. Raised in Berkeley, where his mother was a city councilwoman, Olds chose a solitary mountaintop existence, but fruit from his quince trees has been served at Chez Panisse, and his daughter Mayacamas is a respected viticulturist. The **Sky Zinfandel** ($$) is fresh and red-fruited, rarely topping 14 percent alcohol. It is often released after years of bottle aging, each vintage sporting a new piece of Lore's artwork.

Maps

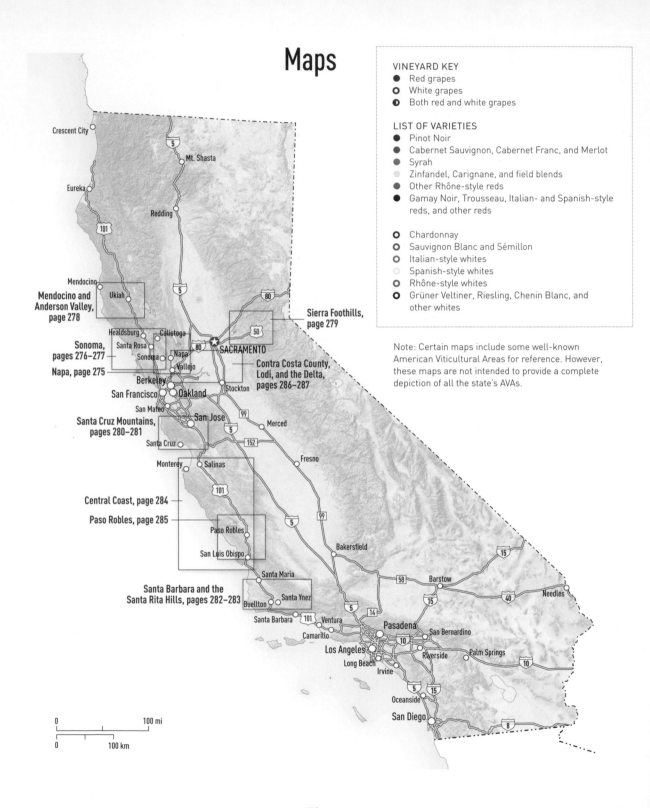

Mendocino and
Anderson Valley,
page 278

Sonoma,
pages 276–277

Napa, page 275

Santa Cruz Mountains,
pages 280–281

Central Coast, page 284

Paso Robles, page 285

Santa Barbara and the
Santa Rita Hills, pages 282–283

Sierra Foothills,
page 279

Contra Costa County,
Lodi, and the Delta,
pages 286–287

VINEYARD KEY
- ● Red grapes
- ○ White grapes
- ◑ Both red and white grapes

LIST OF VARIETIES
- ● Pinot Noir
- ● Cabernet Sauvignon, Cabernet Franc, and Merlot
- ● Syrah
- ● Zinfandel, Carignane, and field blends
- ● Other Rhône-style reds
- ● Gamay Noir, Trousseau, Italian- and Spanish-style reds, and other reds

- ○ Chardonnay
- ○ Sauvignon Blanc and Sémillon
- ○ Italian-style whites
- ○ Spanish-style whites
- ○ Rhône-style whites
- ◎ Grüner Veltliner, Riesling, Chenin Blanc, and other whites

Note: Certain maps include some well-known American Viticultural Areas for reference. However, these maps are not intended to provide a complete depiction of all the state's AVAs.

0   100 mi

0   100 km

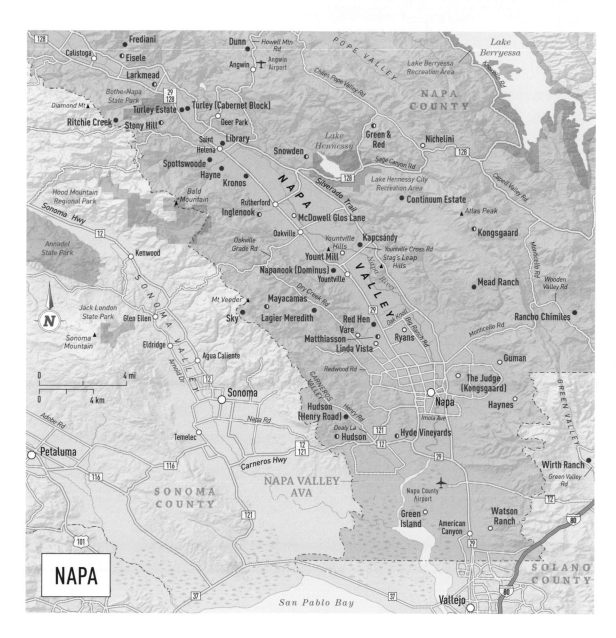

Continuum Estate ●
Dunn ●
Eisele ● ● ● ○
Frediani ●
Green & Red ● ○
Green Island ○
Guman ○
Hayne ● ●
Haynes ○

Hudson ○ ●
Hudson (Henry Road) ●
Hyde Vineyards ○ ● ●
Inglenook ●
The Judge
   (Kongsgaard) ○
Kapcsándy ●
Kongsgaard ● ○ ○
Kronos ●

Lagier Meredith ● ● ●
Larkmead ● ○ ○
Library ●
Linda Vista ○
Matthiasson ● ● ○
Mayacamas ● ○ ○
McDowell Glos Lane ○
Mead Ranch ●
Nichelini ○ ○

Napanook (Dominus) ●
Rancho Chimiles ●
Red Hen ●
Ritchie Creek ● ●
Ryans ○
Sky ●
Snowden ● ○
Spottswoode ● ●
Stony Hill ○ ○ ●

Turley
   (Cabernet Block) ●
Turley Estate ○
Vare ○
Watson Ranch ○
Wirth Ranch ●
Yount Mill ○

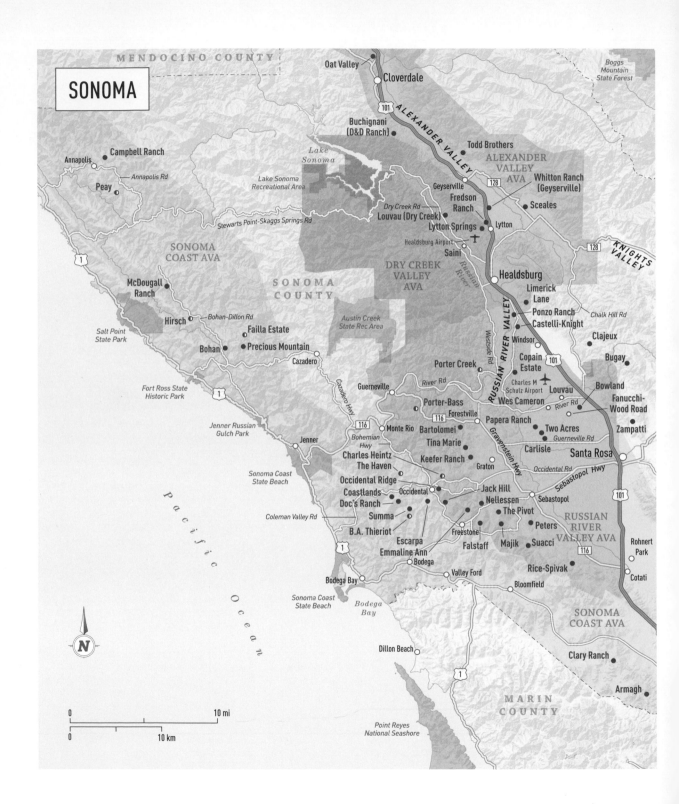

The New California Wine

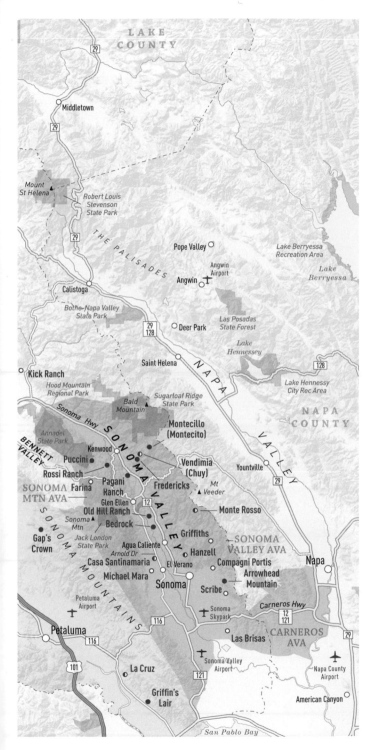

Armagh ●
Arrowhead Mountain ●
B.A. Thieriot ● ○
Bartolomei ● ●
Bedrock ● ● ●
Bohan ● ●
Bowland ○
Buchignani (D&D Ranch) ●
Bugay ●
Campbell Ranch ● ●
Carlisle ●
Casa Santinamaria ○ ○ ●
Castelli-Knight ●
Charles Heintz ○ ● ●
Clajeux ●
Clary Ranch ●
Coastlands ●
Compagni Portis ○
Copain Estate ●
Doc's Ranch ●
Emmaline Ann ●
Escarpa ●
Failla Estate ● ○ ●
Falstaff ●
Fanucchi-Wood Road ○
Farina ○
Fredericks ●
Fredson Ranch ●
Gap's Crown ● ●
Griffin's Lair ● ●
Griffiths ○
Hanzell ○ ●
The Haven ● ○
Hirsch ● ○
Jack Hill ●
Keefer Ranch ●
Kick Ranch ○
La Cruz ● ○

Las Brisas ○
Limerick Lane ●
Louvau ○
Louvau (Dry Creek) ●
Lytton Springs ●
Majik ●
McDougall Ranch ●
Michael Mara ○
Montecillo (Montecito) ● ●
Monte Rosso ● ● ○
Nellessen ●
Oat Valley ●
Occidental Ridge ●
Old Hill Ranch ●
Pagani Ranch ●
Papera Ranch ●
Peay ● ● ● ○
Peters ●
The Pivot ●
Ponzo Ranch ●
Porter-Bass ● ○
Porter Creek ● ○
Precious Mountain ●
Puccini ●
Rice-Spivak ●
Rossi Ranch ● ● ●
Saini ○
Sceales ●
Scribe ○
Suacci ●
Summa ●
Tina Marie ●
Todd Brothers ●
Two Acres ●
Vendimia (Chuy) ○ ●
Wes Cameron ○
Whitton Ranch ●
Zampatti ●

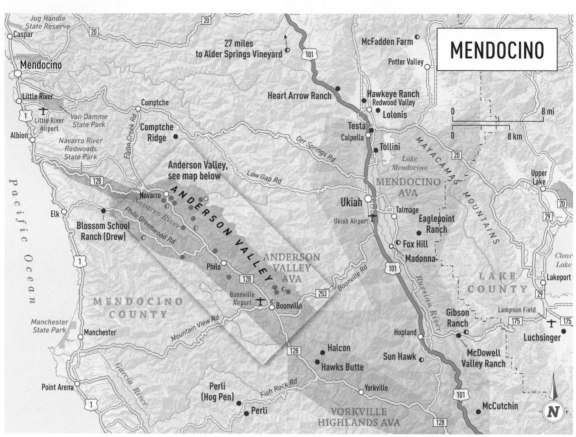

MENDOCINO

Jug Handle State Reserve
Caspar
20
Mendocino
Little River
Little River Airport
Van Damme State Park
Albion
Navarro River Redwoods State Park
1
128
Comptche
Flynn Creek Rd
Comptche Ridge
Navarro
Philo Greenwood Rd
Elk
Blossom School Ranch (Drew)
Philo
128
Boonville Airport
Boonville
Anderson Valley, see map below
Low Gap Rd
ANDERSON VALLEY
Navarro River
ANDERSON VALLEY AVA
253
Boonville Rd
MENDOCINO COUNTY
Manchester State Park
Manchester
Mountain View Rd
128
Point Arena
1
Garcia River
Perli (Hog Pen)
Perli
Fish Rock Rd
Halcon
Hawks Butte
Yorkville
YORKVILLE HIGHLANDS AVA
128
27 miles to Alder Springs Vineyard
101
20
McFadden Farm
Potter Valley
Heart Arrow Ranch
Hawkeye Ranch Redwood Valley
Lolonis
Orr Springs Rd
Testa
Calpella
Tollini
Lake Mendocino
MAYACAMAS MOUNTAINS
20
MENDOCINO AVA
Ukiah
Ukiah Airport
Talmage
Eaglepoint Ranch
Fox Hill
Madonna
101
Russian River
Hopland
Sun Hawk
Gibson Ranch
McDowell Valley Ranch
McCutchin
Upper Lake
29
Clear Lake
Lakeport
LAKE COUNTY
175
Lampson Field
Luchsinger
101
128
0   8 mi
0   8 km
N

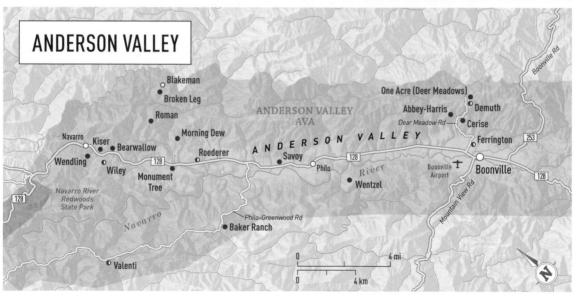

ANDERSON VALLEY

Blakeman
Broken Leg
Roman
Morning Dew
Navarro
Kiser
Bearwallow
Wendling
Wiley
Monument Tree
128
Navarro River Redwoods State Park
128
Navarro
Roederer
Savoy
Philo
Baker Ranch
Philo-Greenwood Rd
Valenti
ANDERSON VALLEY AVA
ANDERSON VALLEY
River
Wentzel
One Acre (Deer Meadows)
Abbey-Harris
Dear Meadow Rd
Cerise
Demuth
253
Ferrington
Boonville Airport
Mountain View Rd
Boonville
128
Boonville Rd
0   4 mi
0   4 km
N

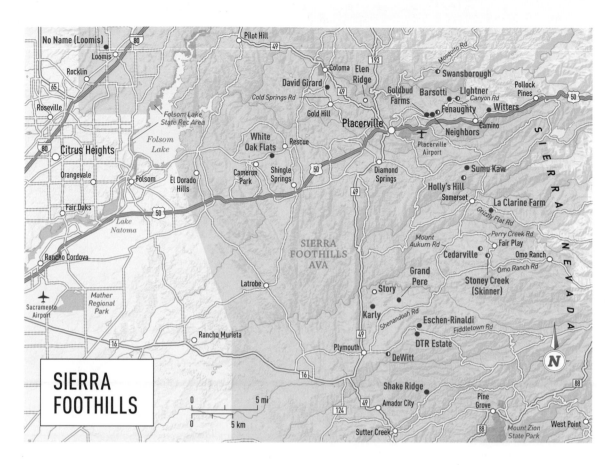

SIERRA FOOTHILLS

MENDOCINO

Alder Springs ● ● ● ● ○
Blossom School Ranch (Drew) ●
Comptche Ridge ●
Eaglepoint Ranch ● ●
Fox Hill ● ○
Gibson Ranch ○ ●
Halcon ●
Hawkeye Ranch ●
Hawks Butte ●
Heart Arrow Ranch ●
Lolonis ● ●
Luchsinger* ●
Madonna ○
McCutchin
McDowell Valley Ranch ● ●
○ ○

Located in Lake County

McFadden Farm ● ○
Perli ●
Perli (Hog Pen) ●
Sun Hawk ● ● ○
Testa ● ●
Tollini ●

ANDERSON VALLEY

Abbey-Harris ●
Baker Ranch ●
Bearwallow ●
Blakeman ○
Broken Leg ●
Cerise ●
Demuth ● ○
Ferrington ● ○ ○
Kiser ●
Monument Tree ●

Morning Dew ●
One Acre (Deer Meadows) ●
Roederer ● ●
Roman ●
Savoy ●
Valenti ● ● ●
Wendling ●
Wentzel ●
Wiley ● ○

SIERRA FOOTHILLS

Barsotti ●
Cedarville ● ○
David Girard ●
DeWitt ○ ●
DTR Estate ●
Elen Ridge ○
Eschen-Rinaldi ● ●

Fenaughty ● ● ○ ○
Goldbud Farms ●
Grand Pere ●
Holly's Hill ● ○
Karly ●
La Clarine Farm ● ● ●
Lightner ● ● ○
Neighbors ● ●
No Name (Loomis) ●
Shake Ridge ● ● ●
Stoney Creek (Skinner) ● ● ○
Story ○
Sumu Kaw ● ● ●
Swansborough ● ○ ○
White Oak Flats ● ● ●
Witters ●

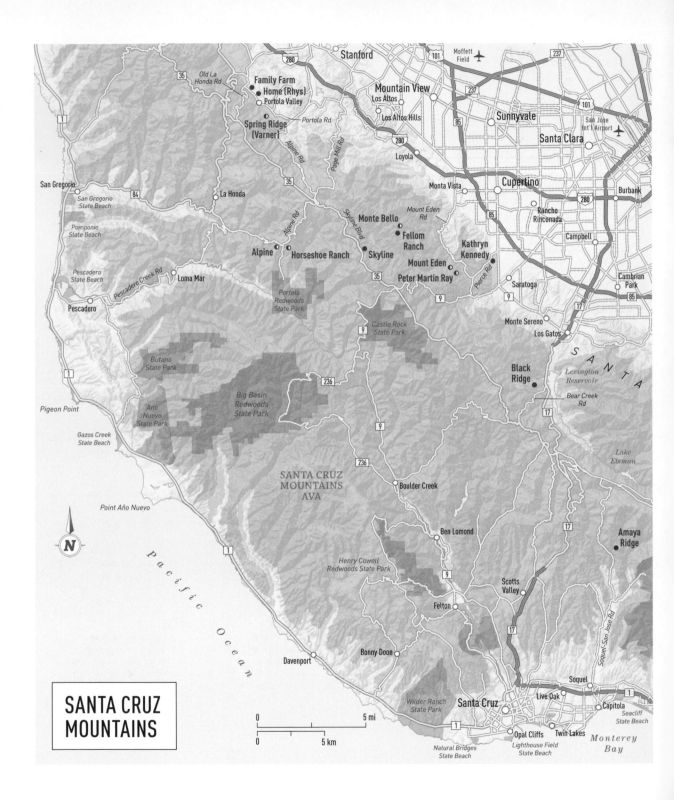

SANTA CRUZ MOUNTAINS

Pacific Ocean

Monterey Bay

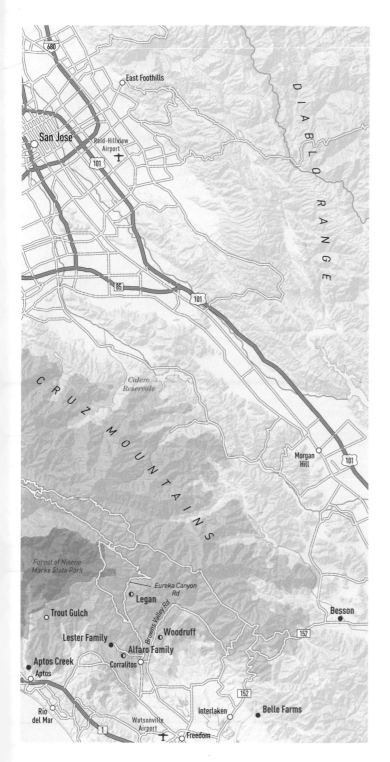

Alfaro Family ● ○ ○
Alpine ● ○
Amaya Ridge ●
Aptos Creek ●
Belle Farms ●
Besson ●
Black Ridge ●
Family Farm ●
Fellom Ranch ●
Home (Rhys) ●
Horseshoe Ranch ● ○ ●
Kathryn Kennedy ●
Legan ● ○
Lester Family ●
Monte Bello ● ○
Mount Eden ○ ● ●
Peter Martin Ray ● ○ ●
Skyline ● ●
Spring Ridge (Varner) ○ ●
Trout Gulch ○
Woodruff ● ○

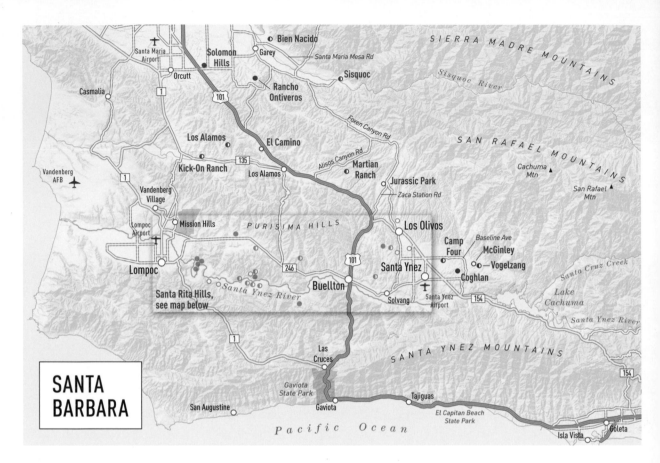

SANTA BARBARA

Santa Maria Airport • Bien Nacido • Garey • Solomon Hills • Santa Maria Mesa Rd • Sisquoc • SIERRA MADRE MOUNTAINS • Sisquoc River • Orcutt • Casmalia • 101 • Rancho Ontiveros • 1 • Los Alamos • El Camino • Foxen Canyon Rd • SAN RAFAEL MOUNTAINS • Vandenberg AFB • Kick-On Ranch • 135 • Los Alamos • Alisos Canyon Rd • Martian Ranch • Cachuma Mtn • Jurassic Park • Zaca Station Rd • San Rafael Mtn • Vandenberg Village • Lompoc Airport • Mission Hills • PURISIMA HILLS • Los Olivos • Camp Four • Baseline Ave • McGinley • Vogelzang • Santa Cruz Creek • Lompoc • 246 • 101 • Santa Ynez • Coghlan • Lake Cachuma • Santa Rita Hills, see map below • Santa Ynez River • Buellton • Solvang • Santa Ynez Airport • 154 • Santa Ynez River • 1 • SANTA YNEZ MOUNTAINS • 154 • Las Cruces • Gaviota State Park • San Augustine • Gaviota • Tajiguas • El Capitan Beach State Park • Isla Vista • Goleta • *Pacific Ocean*

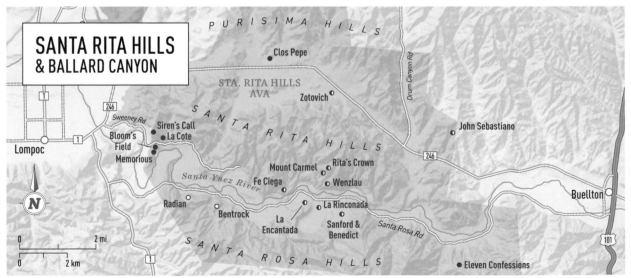

SANTA RITA HILLS & BALLARD CANYON

PURISIMA HILLS • Clos Pepe • STA. RITA HILLS AVA • Zotovich • Drum Canyon Rd • John Sebastiano • 1 • 246 • Sweeney Rd • SANTA RITA HILLS • Siren's Call • La Cote • Bloom's Field • Memorious • Lompoc • Santa Ynez River • Mount Carmel • Rita's Crown • 246 • Buellton • Fe Ciega • Wenzlau • Radian • Bentrock • La Rinconada • La Encantada • Sanford & Benedict • Santa Rosa Rd • 101 • N • SANTA ROSA HILLS • Eleven Confessions • 0 — 2 mi • 0 — 2 km • 1

The New California Wine

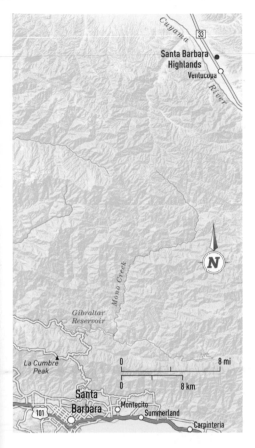

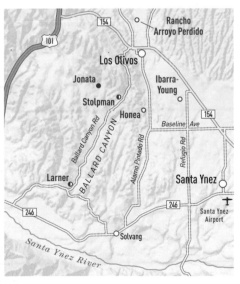

SANTA BARBARA
Bien Nacido ● ○ ●
Camp Four ● ○
Coghlan ●
El Camino ○
Jurassic Park ○
Kick-On Ranch ○ ●
Los Alamos ○ ●
Martian Ranch ● ● ○ ○ ●
McGinley ○
Rancho Ontiveros ●
Santa Barbara Highlands ● ●
Sisquoc ○ ●
Solomon Hills ●
Vogelzang ● ○ ●

SANTA RITA HILLS / BALLARD CANYON
Bentrock ○
Bloom's Field ●
Clos Pepe ●
Eleven Confessions ●
Fe Ciega ● ○
Honea ○
Ibarra-Young ○ ○
John Sebastiano ○ ● ○ ●
Jonata ● ● ●
La Cote ●
La Encantada ● ○
La Rinconada ● ○
Larner ○ ○ ● ●
Memorious ●
Mount Carmel ○ ●
Radian ○
Rancho Arroyo Perdido ○
Rita's Crown ○ ●
Sanford & Benedict ● ○
Siren's Call ●
Stolpman ● ● ○ ●
Wenzlau ● ○
Zotovich ○ ○ ●

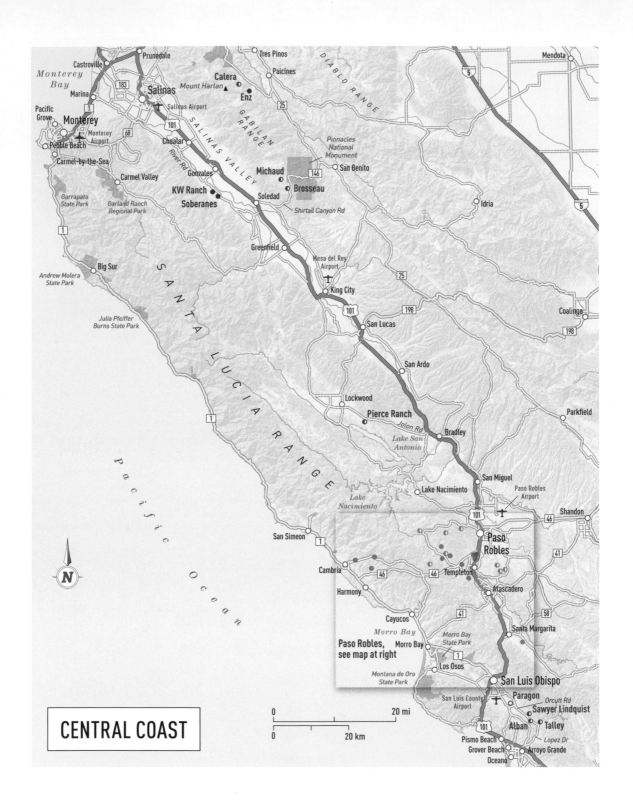

CENTRAL COAST

The New California Wine

PASO ROBLES

CENTRAL COAST
Alban ○ ● ●
Brosseau ● ○ ●
Calera ● ○ ○
Enz Vineyard ●
KW Ranch ●
Michaud ● ○ ○
Paragon ○ ●
Pierce Ranch ● ● ○
Sawyer Lindquist ● ○
Soberanes ● ●
Talley ● ○

PASO ROBLES
Adams Ranch ● ●
Alta Colina ○ ● ●
Ambyth ● ● ○
Bassetti ● ●
Benito Dusi Ranch ○
Black Seth ● ●
Boulder Ridge ● ●
Dante Dusi ○
Denner ● ● ○
James Berry ● ● ○ ○
Luna Matta ● ● ● ○ ○

Margarita ● ●
Martinelli ○
Pesenti ●
RBZ ● ○
Stolo ● ●
Tablas Creek ● ● ○
Terrizzi ○ ●
Ueberroth ○
Yount ● ● ○

Maps

285

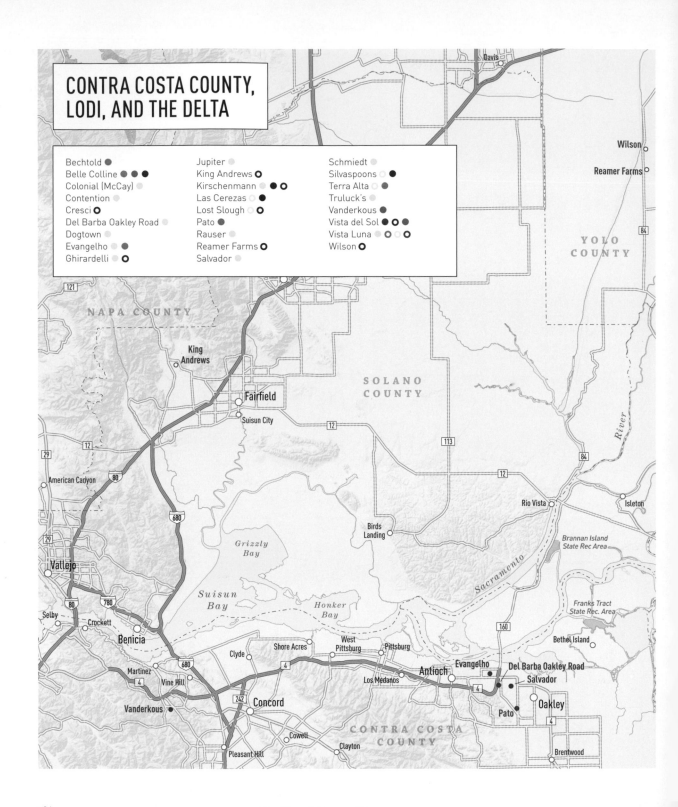

CONTRA COSTA COUNTY, LODI, AND THE DELTA

Bechtold ●
Belle Colline ● ● ●
Colonial (McCay) ○
Contention ●
Cresci ○
Del Barba Oakley Road ○
Dogtown ○
Evangelho ○ ●
Ghirardelli ○ ●

Jupiter ○
King Andrews ○
Kirschenmann ● ○ ●
Las Cerezas ●
Lost Slough ○ ●
Pato ●
Rauser ○
Reamer Farms ○
Salvador ○

Schmiedt ○
Silvaspoons ● ●
Terra Alta ○ ●
Truluck's ○
Vanderkous ●
Vista del Sol ● ○ ●
Vista Luna ○ ○ ○
Wilson ○

The New California Wine

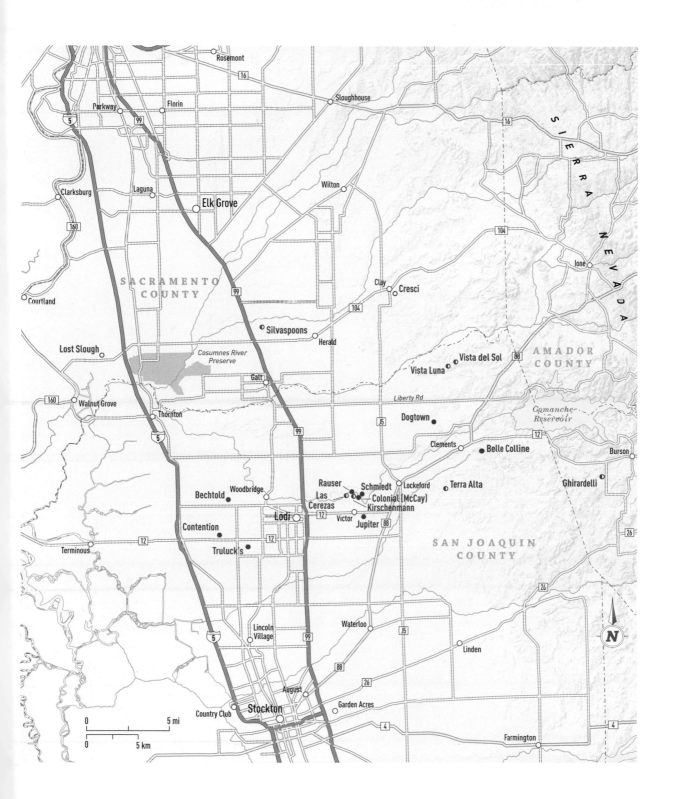

List of Producers

A Tribute to Grace
gracewinecompany.com
707-480-5343

Acha/Mark Herold Wines
markheroldwines.com
707-256-3111

Alfaro Family
www.alfarowine.com
831-728-5172

Anthill Farms
www.anthillfarms.com
707-385-9396

Araujo Estate
www.araujoestate.com
707-942-6061

Arbe Garbe
www.arbegarbewines.com
707-963-1043

Arnot-Roberts
arnotroberts.com
707-433-2400

Au Bon Climat
www.aubonclimat.com
805-963-7999

Bedrock Wine Co.
www.bedrockwineco.com
707-364-8763

Birichino
www.birichino.com
info@birichino.com

Blue Plate/Picnic Wine Co.
picnicwineco.com
707-287-6759

Bokisch Vineyards
www.bokischvineyards.com
209-334-4338

Brack Mountain
brackmountainwine.com
info@brackmountainwine.com

Brander
www.brander.com
805-688-2455

Broadside
www.broadsidewines.com
805-434-3075

Broc Cellars
www.broccellars.com
510-542-9463

Bucklin
www.buckzin.com
707-933-1726

Calera
www.calerawine.com
831-637-9170

Carlisle
www.carlislewinery.com
707-566-7700

Ceritas
ceritaswines.com
707-473-9482

Chanin
www.chaninwine.com
818-631-2007

Clos Saron
www.clossaron.com
530-692-1080

Cobb Wines
cobbwines.com
707-799-1073

Continuum Estate
www.continuumestate.com
707-944-8100

Copain
www.copainwines.com
707-836-8822

Corison
corison.com
707-963-0826

Dashe Cellars
www.dashecellars.com
510-452-1800

Denner Vineyards/Kinero
www.dennervineyards.com
805-239-4287

Domaine de la Côte
domainedelacote.com
805-736-9656

Dominus Estate
dominusestate.com
707-944-8954

Donkey & Goat
donkeyandgoat.com
510-868-9174

Dragonette Cellars
dragonettecellars.com
805-737-0200

Drew Family
www.drewwines.com
707-877-1771

Dunn Vineyards
www.dunnvineyards.com
707-965-3642

Edmunds St. John
www.edmundsstjohn.com
510-981-1510

Failla
www.faillawines.com
707-963-0530

Farmers Jane
www.farmersjanewine.com
707-812-1456

Favia
faviawine.com
info@faviawines.com

Field Recordings
fieldrecordingswine.com
805-503-9660

Folkway
folkwaywine.com
805-732-0991

Forlorn Hope
forlornhopewines.com
707-206-1112

Four Fields
www.fourfieldswines.com
info@fourfieldswines.com

Gamling & McDuck
www.gamlingandmcduck.com
gamlingandmcduck@gmail.com

Ghostwriter
www.hobowines.com
707-887-0833

Giornata
www.giornatawines.com
805-434-3075

Green & Red
www.greenandred.com
707-965-2346

Ground Effect
www.groundeffectwine.com
info@groundeffectwine.com

Habit
www.habitwine.com
habitwine@me.com

Hanzell
www.hanzell.com
707-996-3860

HdV
hdvwines.com
707-251-9121

Hirsch Vineyards
www.hirschvineyards.com
707-847-3600

Hobo/Folk Machine
www.hobowines.com
707-887-0833

Holly's Hill
www.hollyshill.com
530-344-0227

Horse & Plow
horseandplow.com
707-861-9586

Idlewild
idlewildwines.com
707-385-9410

Inglenook
www.inglenook.com
707-968-1161

Jolie-Laide
scott@jolielaidewines.com
707-501-7664

Kalin Cellars
www.kalincellars.com
415-883-3543

Kapcsándy Family
www.kapcsandywines.com
707-948-3100

Keplinger
keplingerwines.com
707-252-7477

Kesner
www.kesnerwines.com
707-975-6463

Kinero
notplonk.com
805-215-2442

Knez
www.knezwinery.com
707-895-3494

Kongsgaard
www.kongsgaardwine.com
707-226-2190

Kutch
kutchwines.com
917-270-8180

La Clarine Farm
laclarinefarm.com
530-306-3608

Lagier Meredith
www.lagiermeredith.com
707-253-0653

Larkmead
www.larkmead.com
707-942-0167

LaRue
laruewines.com
707-933-8355

Le P'tit Paysan
www.leptitpaysan.com
831-212-3660

Ledge
www.ledgevineyards.com
805-434-8663

Leo Steen
www.leosteenwines.com
707.433.2925

Leojami
www.leojamiwines.com
831-238-5187

Limerick Lane
www.limericklanewines.com
707-433-9211

Lioco
www.liocowine.com
707-595-2995
info@liocowine.com

Liquid Farm
www.liquidfarm.com
nikki@LiquidFarm.com

Littorai
www.littorai.com
707-823-9586

Longoria
www.longoriawine.com
805-688-0305

Los Pilares
www.lospilareswine.com
619-991-1918

Lost & Found
www.lostandfoundwine.com
info@lostandfoundwine.com

Marietta Cellars
www.mariettacellars.com
707-433-2747

Martian Ranch
www.martianvineyard.com
888-999-8406

Massican
www.massican.com
707-709-8400

Matthiasson
www.matthiasson.com
707-265-9349

Mayacamas Vineyards
www.mayacamas.com
707-224-4030

McCay Cellars
www.mccaycellars.com
209-368-9463

Mount Eden Vineyards
www.mounteden.com
408-867-5832

Native9 Vineyards
www.native9wine.com
805-830-1781

Neyers Vineyards
www.neyersvineyards.com
707-963-8840

The Ojai Vineyard
www.ojaivineyard.com
805-649-1674

Palmina
www.palminawines.com
805-735-2030

Parr Wines
www.parrwines.com
415-800-4751

Pax Wine Cellars
paxmahlewines.com
707-887-9100

Peay Vineyards
peayvineyards.com
707-894-8720

Porter Creek
www.portercreekvineyards.com
707-433-6321

Qupé
qupe.com
805-686-4200

Rhys Vineyards
www.rhysvineyards.com
650-419-2050

Ridge Vineyards
www.ridgewine.com
408-867-3233

Rivers-Marie
www.riversmarie.com
707-341-3127

Roark Wine Co.
roarkwinecompany.wordpress.com
805-736-8000

Ryme Cellars
rymecellars.com
707-431-8384

Salinia
www.salinia.com
707-527-7063

Sandhi
sandhiwines.com
805-688-1341

Sandlands
sandlandswine.com
info@sandlandswine.com

Scholium Project
www.scholiumwines.com
abe@scholiumwines.com

Scribe
www.scribewinery.com
707-939-1858

Skinner Vineyards
www.skinnervineyards.com
530-620-2220

Sky Vineyards
www.skyvineyards.com
707-935-1391

Snowden
www.snowdenvineyards.com
707-963-4292

Spottswoode
www.spottswoode.com
707-963-0134

Stony Hill
www.stonyhillvineyard.com
707-963-2636

Tablas Creek
www.tablascreek.com
805-237-1231

Tatomer
www.tatomerwines.com
805-570-8028

Turley Wine Cellars
www.turleywinecellars.com
805-434–1030

Two Shepherds
twoshepherdsvineyards.com
415-613-5731

Tyler
tylerwinery.com
805-769-4639

Varner/Foxglove (also Neely)
www.varnerwine.com
650- 321-4894

Vaughn Duffy
www.vaughnduffywines.com
707-696-3212

Verdad
www.verdadwine.com
805-686 4200

Vesper Vineyards
www.vespervineyards.com
760-749-1300

Waits-Mast
www.waitsmast.com
415-405-6686

Wind Gap
windgapwines.com
707-887-9100

Y. Rousseau
www.yrousseauwines.com
707-332-4524

Zepaltas
zepaltaswines.com
707-694-1813

Acknowledgments

Writing a very different sort of wine book required a thousand inspirations. But thanks go first to my dad, who instilled in me a love of wine from a surprisingly early age and started this whole thing.

I also owe deep thanks and gratitude to lots of other people for their hard work and support:

To Katherine Cowles, my literary agent and my dear friend, for her unwavering belief in a book that told a very different California story, and for making sure it got done right.

To the staff of Ten Speed Press: Aaron Wehner, for seeing the possibilities in an ambitious and complex project; Emily Timberlake, my editor, for her keen eye with the manuscript, for managing endless details, and for her enormous patience; Katy Brown, for bringing a unique visual sensibility to the often dull world of wine writing; and Kelly Snowden, for her innovative ideas on how to spread word about the book; along with Sharron Wood, Jasmine Star, and Ken Della Penta for diligent copyediting, proofing, and adding the final touches.

To Erik Castro, who from the start shared my zeal for finding a different tale to tell about California, and who spent months in the field to capture it with a remarkable eye.

To Mark Stroud, for his detailed cartographic work, and ability to capture an enormous amount of detail in maps that are vital to understanding the geography of the New California.

To my colleagues at the *San Francisco Chronicle*, especially in the Food & Wine department, who have always believed in my occasionally pointed approach to wine coverage, and whose support helped me to discover many of the people and places in this book.

To Betsy Andrews, James Oseland, and the team at *Saveur*, who inspired and published the article that shaped the original notion of the New California.

To the team at *Decanter* magazine, especially my former editor Guy Woodward, whose assignments helped me to ask crucial questions about California's current state.

To the many winemakers and farmers who believed in pursuing a different path for California wine long before this project took shape, who constantly let me taste their wines, and who were always generous with their time and information. Special thanks are due to Tegan Passalacqua and Steve Matthiasson, who answered a thousand pesky viticultural queries; as well as to Ted Lemon, Paul Draper and David Hirsch, who prodded me to ask vital questions about the meaning and tradition of winegrowing. Along those lines, an extra thanks to Robert Pincus, for reviewing my material on climate trends with a critical eye.

Most crucially, to Valerie, who has been my love and my intellectual foil through this whole process.

And finally, a particular thanks to my old advisor Ted Tayler, who long ago taught me the lesson of the cat, the pig, and the squiggle. That has made all the difference.

Index

The New California Wine

Porter-Bass Vineyard, 185, 194, 195, 202
Porter Creek, 119, 190
Portet, Bernard, 25
Pott, Aaron and Claire, 235
Poulsard, 262
Powell, Dave, 247
Precious Mountain, 49, 111
Prial, Frank, 208
Price, Bill, 79
Price categories, 172
Prohibition, effects of, 24–25

Q

Qupé, 224, 236

R

Radikon, Stanko, 242, 247
Radio-Coteau, 146
Ragan, John, 20
Rancho Santa Rosa, 189
Rankin, John, 20
Rauser, Jean, 137
Ray, Martin, 13, 25, 70, 127, 128, 129, 193, 198
Ray, Peter Martin, 127, 128
Raytek, John, 186, 189, 194–95, 197, 199
Red Car, 114
Renaissance des Appellations, 53
Renaissance Vineyard, 124, 233
Resnick, Stewart, 78
Respekt, 45
Reynaud, Emmanuel, 94
Rhône-style wines
    history of, 220–25
    producers of, 226–37
    three-bottle tour of, 225
Rhys Vineyards, 70, 130, 131, 146, 176, 180, 185–86, 236
Ribolla Gialla, 240, 242
Rice, Saron, 233
Ridge Vineyards, 2, 5, 25, 36–39, 70–71, 102, 129, 203, 210, 216–17, 272
Riesling, 238, 240
Ripeness, defining, 33
Ritchie Creek, 224, 232
Rivers-Marie, 190
Rixford, Emmet, 70, 129
Roark, Ryan, 253
Roark Wine Co., 253

Robert Mondavi Winery, 2, 25, 27, 28, 31–32, 88, 91, 140, 152, 204, 209, 210
Roberts, Nathan, 13–14, 128, 251, 262, 263
Robledo, Everardo, 111–12
Rochioli, Joe, Jr., 118, 119, 178
Rodriguez, Rafael, 59, 213
Roederer, Louis, 144
Roederer Estate, 250
Rolland, Michel, 30, 34, 53
Rorick, David, 244
Rorick, Matthew, 241, 244–45, 270
Rosenblum, Kent, 83–84, 107
Rotblatt, Richard, 83
Roth, Mike, 53, 229
Rothschild, Philippe de, 31, 207
Roulot, Jean-Marc, 93, 202
Roussanne, 224
Rousseau, Yannick, 240, 254–55
Rouzaud, Jean-Claude, 144
Rudd, Leslie, 209
Rulot, Guy, 14
Russian River Valley, 114, 115, 118–19
Ryan, Jim, 181
Ryme Cellars, 242, 247–48

S

Sadie, Eben, 105
Sagebrush Annie's, 167–68
Salinia, 236–37, 250
Salmina, Felix and John, 215
Salvador Vineyard, 106
Sandhi, 150, 155, 180, 190–91, 198–200
Sandlands, 268–69
Sanford, Richard, 151, 152, 153, 155, 176, 198
Sanford & Benedict, 152, 153, 155, 176, 191, 200, 201
San Francisco, winemaking in, 83, 84
Santa Barbara, 168, 282–83
Santa Cruz Mountains, 127–33, 280–81
Santa Cruz Mountain Vineyard, 177
Santa Rita Hills, 80, 148–55, 282–83

Sauvignon Blanc, 242–43
Savoy, Richard, 15
Saxum, 158, 160
Scharffenberger, John, 144
Schatzberg, Donnie and Linden, 111
Schindler, Emily and Stephan, 191
Schmiedt, 137
Schoener, Abe, 11, 15–16, 18–20, 107, 136, 242, 248–49, 273
Scholasch, Thibaut, 49
Scholium Project, 16, 18–19, 21, 91, 107, 136, 141, 248–49, 253, 273
Schoonmaker, Frank, 28, 206
Schramsberg, 250
Schultz, Scott, 252
Screaming Eagle, 29, 30, 31, 212, 214
Scribe, 253
Sea Smoke, 152, 153, 155, 177
Sebastiani, 78, 84
Selvaggio, Piero, 243
Selyem, Ed, 82, 113
Sémillon, 243
Seysses, Diana Snowden, 219
Shake Ridge, 123, 234, 268
Sherman, William Tecumseh, 74
Short, William, 216
Siduri, 177
Sierra Foothills, 120–25, 279
Sierra Vista Winery, 122
Sine Qua Non, 152, 223, 243
Skinner Vineyards, 123–24, 231
Skyline Vineyard, 70, 131, 186, 236
Sky Vineyards, 273
Sloan Estate, 78
Smart, Richard, 50
Smith, Andy, 215, 246
Smith, Clark, 34–35
Smith, Justin, 158, 160, 161, 235
Smith, Marcia, 212
Smith, Rod, 189
Snowden, Scott, 219
Solari, Larry, 215
Sonoma, 108–19, 276–77
Sonoma Coast, 114–15
Sonoma-Cutrer, 114, 193

Sorongon, Melissa, 148
South Coast, 104
Souverain, 64, 81, 260
Sparkling wines, 250
Sparks-Gillis, Brandon, 187
Spencer, Ben and Nadine, 236
Spenker, Joseph, 136
Spitzley, Susan and Jamie, 163
Spottswoode, 219, 243, 244, 253–54
Spring Ridge Vineyard, 92
Spurrier, Steven, 26
Stag's Leap Wine Cellars, 18, 25, 26, 56, 94, 206
Stamp, James, 71–72
Stanly Ranch Vineyard, 66, 81
Starr, Pam, 254
State Lane Vineyard, 207, 214
Steele, Jed, 35, 193
Stehly, Alysha, 237
Steiner, Rudolf, 42, 44, 45
Stewart, Lee, 81
Stolo, Don and Charlene, 162
Stolpman Vineyards, 155, 262
Stony Hill, 193, 203, 219
Story Vineyard, 80, 269
Sturgeon, Amanda Reade, 20
Suacci Vineyard, 191
Sullivan, Charles, 81, 129, 236
Summa, 113
Sumu Kaw Vineyard, 124, 235
Sunlight management, 50–53, 59
Sustainability, 58
Sutter Home, 5, 120, 140
Swan, Joseph, 68
Syrah, 220, 222–24, 225

T

Tablas Creek Vineyard, 122, 160, 222, 224, 237
Table wine, making, 86–99
Taittinger, 144
Talley Vineyard, 181, 228
Tancer, Forrest, 176
Tarlov, Mark, 182
Tatomer, Graham, 249
Tchelistcheff, André, 25, 27, 176, 179–80, 206, 238
Teller, Anne and Otto, 270
Tendu, 88
Terlato Wine Group, 152

The New California Wine

Copyright © 2013 by Jon Bonné
Photographs copyright © 2013 by Erik Castro

Published in the United States by Ten Speed Press, an imprint of the Crown Publishing
Group, a division of Random House LLC, New York, a Penguin Random House Company.
www.crownpublishing.com
www.tenspeed.com

Ten Speed Press and the Ten Speed Press colophon are registered trademarks
of Random House LLC.

Some material in this work includes quotes from or is based on pieces by Jon Bonné
originally published in the *San Francisco Chronicle*. Grateful acknowledgement is made for
the use of this material, as well as additional material from pieces originally published in
Decanter and *Saveur* magazines.

The photos on pages 15 and 35 appear courtesy of Ted Lemon

Library of Congress Cataloging-in-Publication Data
Bonné, Jon.
  The new California wine : a guide to the producers and wines behind a revolution
in taste / Jon Bonné.
    pages cm
1. Wine and wine making—California—Guidebooks. I. Title.
  TP557.B64 2013
  641.2'2—dc23
  2013017577

Hardcover ISBN: 978-1-60774-300-2
eBook ISBN: 978-1-60774-301-9

Printed in China

Design by Katy Brown
Cartography by Moon Street Cartography, Durango, Colorado

10 9 8 7 6 5 4 3 2 1

First Edition

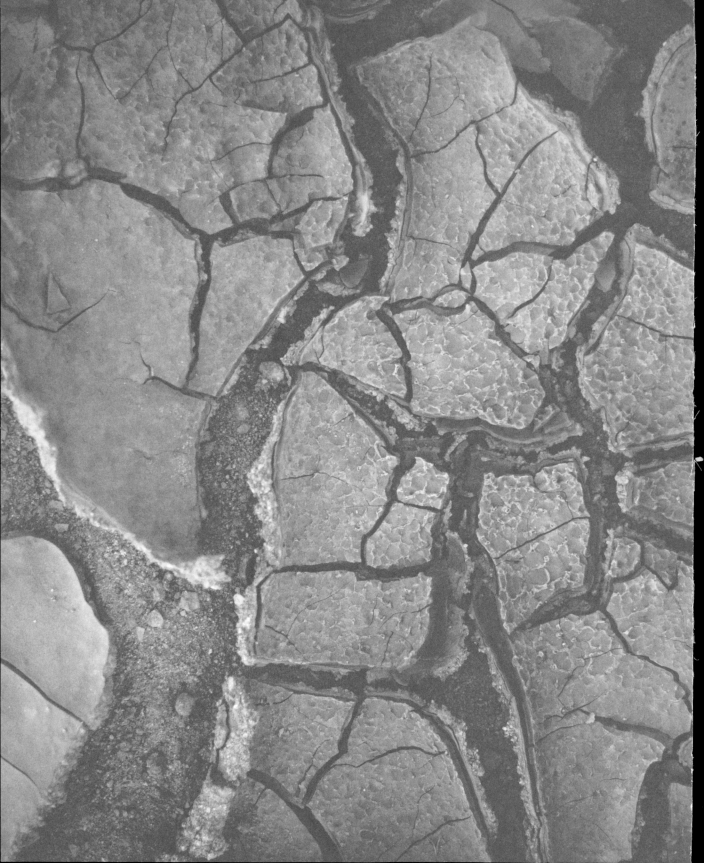